International Perspective on Indigenous Religious Rights

Studies in International Minority and Group Rights

Editors-in-Chief

Gudmundur Alfredsson and Kristin Henrard

VOLUME 17

The titles published in this series are listed at *brill.com/imgr*

International Perspective on Indigenous Religious Rights

Edited by

Claude Gélinas
Raphaël Mathieu Legault-Laberge
Sébastien Lebel-Grenier

BRILL | NIJHOFF

LEIDEN | BOSTON

This book is the result of a research project with funding (e.g. ERC, DFG, FWF, NWO). The funder and starting year are Social Sciences and Humanities Research Council (SSHRC) (2020).

Library of Congress Cataloging-in-Publication Data

Names: Gélinas, Claude, 1969- editor.| Legault-Laberge, Raphaël Mathieu, editor.| Lebel-Grenier, Sébastien, 1969- editor.
Title: International perspective on indigenous religious rights / edited by Claude Gélinas, Raphaël Mathieu Legault-Laberge, Sébastien Lebel-Grenier.
Description: Leiden ; Boston : Brill/Nijhoff, 2023. | Series: Studies in international minority and group rights, 2210-2132 ; 17 | Includes bibliographical references and index.
Identifiers: LCCN 2023045418 (print) | LCCN 2023045419 (ebook) | ISBN 9789004524323 (hardback) | ISBN 9789004524330 (ebook)
Subjects: LCSH: Indigenous peoples (International law) | Freedom of religion (International law)
Classification: LCC K3247 .I59 2023 (print) | LCC K3247 (ebook) | DDC 341.4/832—dc23/eng/20231002
LC record available at https://lccn.loc.gov/2023045418
LC ebook record available at https://lccn.loc.gov/2023045419

Typeface for the Latin, Greek, and Cyrillic scripts: "Brill". See and download: brill.com/brill-typeface.

ISSN 2210-2132
ISBN 978-90-04-52432-3 (hardback)
ISBN 978-90-04-52433-0 (e-book)
DOI 10.1163/9789004524330

This book is printed on acid-free paper and produced in a sustainable manner.

Contents

Foreword

The subject of religion is both exceedingly important and fraught with tensions. It is important because of the role religion plays in society and in the lives of many. It can provide a sense of identity, comfort, guiding values, community, and social cohesion. But at the same time religion divides humanity into diverse religious belief systems, and historically and still today religious divisions have brought conflicts, in many cases violent ones. As societies try to temper that division with secularization, what is secular seeks to divide itself from what is religious, and that division can also be conflictual.

Fully explaining the importance of Indigenous peoples' own religious traditions and practices is beyond what I'm able to do. But what can be readily observed is that Indigenous religious traditions are characteristically central to the identities of Indigenous peoples and pervade many, if not all aspects of life within Indigenous societies. Also characteristically, Indigenous religions are not hegemonic in the way Western religions are, or at least have been historically. Indigenous religions typically do not evangelize for converts. And the line between Indigenous religious life and secular life is usually blurred or even non-existent.

The tensions that relate to Indigenous religious traditions are not typically about competition with other religions or with secular life. Rather, the tensions lie more simply in how the religious beliefs and practices of Indigenous peoples are radically different from the religious and cultural patterns of the settler societies that have grown up around them. This difference often makes it difficult for the laws of the State and the majority society to make necessary accommodations for Indigenous religious practices. As a result, those practices are continually suppressed.

I want to tell you about a few stories from the United States to illustrate this suppression of Indigenous religions. I'll then discuss how the United Nations Declaration on the Rights of Indigenous Peoples (UNDRIP) calls for a *different model* for the treatment of Indigenous religious practices.

Jose Abeyta was a member of Isleta Pueblo, one of the several pueblo Indigenous tribes or nations in New Mexico, and he was part of the Katsina Society, a religious society that engages in traditional ceremonial practices rooted in the Pueblo religion. Jose killed a Golden Eagle to use the eagle parts in ceremonies, in keeping with religious tradition. The federal government criminally charged Jose for killing the eagle, alleging a violation of the federal Bald and Golden Eagle Protection Act. It just so happens that I was assigned to defend Jose against the criminal charges. At a hearing on our motion to dismiss the charges, we put forth expert testimony about the significance of eagle parts to Katsina religious practices and about the lack of an environmental justification for the restrictions on the taking of golden eagles. After the hearing, the federal district court dismissed the case based on the religious freedom provisions of the Treaty of Guadalupe Hidalgo and the U.S. Constitution. This was a rare judicial victory for an Indigenous religious practitioner and one that has not much been replicated. And even though he was successful in defending against criminal prosecution for taking an eagle, Jose Abeyta was forced to reveal and prove the religious significance of the use of eagle parts in a federal court. Shortly after the decision in Jose Abeyta's case, the U.S. Supreme Court, in another case, held that the Bald and Golden Eagle Protection Act abrogated Indian treaty rights to take eagles, including for religious purposes. Federal law and court decisions have since consistently restricted the taking of eagles and possession of eagle parts to the limited permit scheme imposed by the act.

A second story is about Alfred Leo Smith and Galen Black, who were members of the Klamath Nation and Indigenous religious practitioners who used peyote in religious ceremonies. Peyote is a small cactus that contains psychoactive alkaloids. It is used in religious ceremonies by Indigenous peoples in many parts of North America. Alfred and Galen were also drug and alcohol counselors for a private rehabilitation clinic. They were fired from their jobs because of their use of peyote, and the State of Oregon denied them unemployment benefits. Alfred and Galen challenged that denial based on the religious Free Exercise Clause of the U.S. Constitution, and their case made its way to the U.S. Supreme Court. The court held that the denial of employment benefits was valid because Oregon law prohibited the use of peyote including for sacramental purposes. The court found that the Free Exercise Clause of the Constitution does not protect against laws of general application, and the law prohibiting the use of peyote was such a general law. Later, Oregon law established an exception for the sacramental use of peyote, but the constitutional religious free exercise standard established by the Supreme Court has stood to continue to deny Indigenous religious practitioners protections against other laws and governmental actions that limit the practice of their religion.

A final story is about a mountainous area known as the San Francisco Peaks in northern Arizona. The San Francisco Peaks are sacred to the Navajo, Hopi, and several other Indigenous peoples in the area. These Indigenous people have long accessed the peaks for religious purposes and for the collection of medicinal plants. The peaks figure prominently in their spiritual and cultural narrative. The San Francisco Peaks and surrounding area are officially federal public land, and the area is administered by the U.S. Forest Service. In the 1970's, the Forest Service permitted the construction of expanded facilities for a ski resort called Snowbowl, despite opposition from the Indigenous peoples for whom the peaks are sacred. In 2005, the U.S. Forest Service permitted another expansion of the ski resort and, more controversially, for the use of reclaimed sewage water from the nearby city of Flagstaff to make artificial snow for the ski area. The Navajo Nation and other tribes sued in federal court, claiming that the use of sewage water for the making of snow on the mountain was a desecration, in violation of their rights under the federal Religious Freedom Restoration Act. That act requires the government to justify, with a compelling public interest, any "substantial burden" on the exercise of religion resulting from governmental actions. The case was ultimately decided by a federal court of appeals. The court held that the making of snow from wastewater did not substantially burden the religion of the tribes, because it did not coerce them into violating their religion. The court interpreted the concept of substantial burden restrictively to only include those burdens that coerce religious practitioners into actively violating their religion. Thus, according to the court, there was no violation of the federal Religious Freedom Restoration Act and the use of wastewater to make snow on the sacred mountain could proceed, as it did.

As these cases illustrate, domestic laws and practices are often inhospitable to Indigenous religious practices. The United States domestic legal order, like in many other countries, is built upon a Judeo-Christian religious tradition for which Indigenous religion is invisible, at best. Historically, European explorers and settlers regarded Indigenous peoples as heathens or barbarians, and their lack of Christianity served to justify efforts to conquer them and take their land. Even up to the middle of the last century, dominant governmental policies and social norms in many countries looked down on Indigenous religious traditions, and governmental agents and Christian churches worked actively to suppress Indigenous religious practices. Today what we see are structural barriers to the practice of Indigenous religions. These barriers arise from persistent lack of seeing Indigenous religious traditions as having value and being worthy of accommodation, if not protection, to the same degree that dominant religions are valued and deemed worthy of protection.

The UNDRIP calls for a different model. It was adopted in 2007 by the United Nations General Assembly of the United Nations, with an overwhelming majority of UN member states voting in favor. The few states that voted against adopting the Declaration – namely: Australia, Canada, New Zealand, and the United States of America – eventually reversed their positions and formally declared their support for it. The Declaration can now genuinely be seen as a consensus document that expresses a global policy on the rights of Indigenous peoples and a certain commitment to those rights. Significantly, the consensus around the Declaration is joined in not only by UN member states but also by Indigenous peoples from around the world who actively participated and even drove the discussions leading to the final document.

Another important aspect of the Declaration is that it does not create new rights. Rather, it builds upon long-time recognized international human rights, such as the rights to equality, self-determination, cultural integrity, and property, as well as the general human right to the free exercise of religion. The Declaration elaborates upon these rights in the specific context of Indigenous peoples and their communal bonds. In doing so, the Declaration affirms not just the individual rights of members of Indigenous nations or tribes, but also the collective rights of Indigenous peoples, as peoples. The logic of the Declaration is to understand that the human rights of Indigenous individuals, such as rights to language, traditional lands, and religion, are dependent on the collective rights of the Indigenous communities they are part of.

The Declaration includes 46 articles, 40 of them affirming specific rights and substantive norms. In each of these 40 articles, alongside the affirmation of a right is the requirement that states take positive measures to implement and protect the latter. In this way, the Declaration is consistent with international human rights law more generally, which requires that states not only respect human rights, that is, avoid active infringement of these rights, but also act affirmatively to protect and fulfill the rights.

Regarding religion, the Declaration states in the article 12:

> 1. Indigenous peoples have the right to manifest, practise, develop and teach their spiritual and religious traditions, customs and ceremonies; the right to maintain, protect, and have access in privacy to their religious and cultural sites; the right to the use and control of their ceremonial objects; and the right to the repatriation of their human remains.

In the second paragraph, Article 12 goes on to affirm:

> 2. States shall seek to enable the access and/or repatriation of ceremonial objects and human remains in their possession through fair, transparent and effective mechanisms developed in conjunction with indigenous peoples concerned.

Major human rights treaties that are binding on ratifying states, including the International Covenant on Civil and Political Rights and the American Convention on Human Rights, generally affirm the right to religion. As we can see, Article 12 of the Declaration interprets the general human right to religion in the specific context of Indigenous peoples and their realities. It makes specific mention of sacred sites and ceremonial objects, and it underscores that the right to religion is not just a right that pertains to Indigenous individuals but a right that is enjoyed *collectively* by Indigenous peoples, who in fact have collectively given rise to the Indigenous religious belief systems and practices.

Full appreciation of Article 12 requires the consideration of the Declaration's larger context. This document is essentially a remedial instrument. It exists because of the historical and ongoing patterns of oppression of Indigenous peoples and persistent denial of their human rights. Implicit in the Declaration is that, considering this history and the continuing situation of vulnerability of Indigenous peoples, states have a heightened duty to secure and protect their rights, including their right to religion. And in doing so, states must fully consider the particular aspects of Indigenous religions that are important, such as the access to sacred places and ceremonial objects.

Given the interconnectedness between religious practices and other aspects of life, other articles of the Declaration are also relevant to Indigenous peoples' right to religion. I'll just mention a few. First, Article 15 affirms that "Indigenous peoples have the right to the dignity and diversity of their cultures, traditions, histories and aspirations which shall be appropriately reflected in education and public information." Articles referring to rights over lands and territories are also relevant:

> Article 25
> Indigenous peoples have the right to maintain and strengthen their distinctive spiritual relationship with their traditionally owned or otherwise occupied and used lands, territories, waters and coastal seas and other resources and to uphold their responsibilities to future generations in this regard.
>
> Article 26
> 1. Indigenous peoples have the right to the lands, territories and resources which they have traditionally owned, occupied or otherwise used or acquired.

The sacred places of Indigenous peoples are characteristically included within lands of this description. And under Articles 27 and 28, states have an obligation to establish fair procedures to "recognize and adjudicate the rights of indigenous peoples pertaining to their lands, territories and resources [...] which have been confiscated, taken, occupied, used or damaged without their free, prior and informed consent."

Also important regarding Indigenous religions is Article 19, which establishes a safeguard for all the rights affirmed in the Declaration. It requires that states "consult and cooperate in good faith with the indigenous peoples [...] in order to obtain their free, prior informed consent before adopting and implementing legislative or administrative measures that may affect them." This requirement of consultation with the objective of consent applies to administrative measures – such as the U.S. government's approval of the expansion of the Snowbowl ski area and the use of wastewater to make snow on the sacred San Francisco peaks. In that case, the government engaged only in minimal consultations, and certainly made no effort to gain the consent of the affected Indigenous peoples.

So, with all this, we can see that the Declaration advances robust protections for Indigenous religious practices. Further, the Declaration articulates a heightened standard that the government must meet as a condition for taking any actions that might limit Indigenous religious practices. Let's briefly examine that standard by which a government might legitimately limit the exercise of Indigenous religions.

Generally, under international humain rights law, the government can limit rights, with few exceptions. The rights not to be tortured or subjected to genocide, for example, are absolute rights that cannot be limited. The right to religion and most other rights, though, are subject to limitation under specific conditions. The Declaration itself has a limitation clause that is consistent with the limitation clauses in the major international human rights treaties, including in connection with the right to religion. Article 46 states that "the exercise of the rights set forth in this Declaration shall be subject only to such limitations as are determined by law and in accordance with international human rights obligations. Any such limitations shall be non-discriminatory and strictly necessary solely for the purpose of securing due recognition and respect for the rights and freedoms of others and for meeting the just and most compelling requirements of a democratic society."

This provision establishes a standard of proportionality of governmental actions limiting rights that can be met only in pursuit of one of the stated objectives. For example, governments cannot simply limit Indigenous peoples' access to sacred places or objects for *any* reason, but only for a nondiscriminatory, valid public purpose related to the human rights of others or the most compelling requirements of a democratic society. And the limitations must be only as necessary to achieve such a legitimate objective. This is a much more exacting standard than that applied by U.S. Courts to assess the validity of governmental actions affecting religious practices. First of all, under the Declaration and international human rights law more generally, *any* limitation on Indigenous religions is subject to scrutiny, not just those limitations or burdens that coerce Indigenous peoples to act contrary to their religious beliefs. And the limitations must be *strictly necessary* for one of the stated valid purposes, which do not include a commercial or recreational purpose. The development of a ski area is not a valid purpose.

Moreover, in assessing the validity of any governmental limitation of Indigenous religions, the overall objectives of the Declaration must be considered. And those objectives include, as I stated earlier, remedying the historical and ongoing patterns of oppression of Indigenous peoples and denial of their fundamental rights. The Declaration envisions a future in which Indigenous peoples, and their religious traditions, can thrive. And the state has an affirmative obligation to allow the space and conditions for that to happen. Any limitation on Indigenous religions cannot ultimately undercut that obligation. Now of course what I've just laid out in my remarks raises several questions that I have left unanswered. Perhaps foremost among these is how the protections for Indigenous religions advanced by the UNDRIP can be practically implemented by states throughout the world.

S. James Anaya

Introduction

Claude Gélinas, Raphaël Mathieu Legault-Laberge and Sébastien Lebel-Grenier

This book is the result of an international and interdisciplinary symposium organized by the Centre de recherche Société, Droit et Religions de l'Université de Sherbrooke (SoDRUS), in collaboration with the Équipe de recherche sur les cosmopolitiques autochtones (ERCA). It was held in Longueuil (Quebec, Canada) from May 12 to 14, 2022. The event, entitled "International Perspective on Indigenous Religious Rights," brought together specialists from various disciplines with unique expertise in the field of Indigenous religious rights in different national and international contexts. The aim of the symposium was to take stock of the state of this law in the world, to identify the main advances and problems that characterize it, and to explore ways in which states can adequately recognize and protect the religious rights of Indigenous peoples, in a manner consistent with the provisions of the United Nations Declaration on the Rights of Indigenous Peoples (UNDRIP) regarding to the practice, promotion, transmission, protection, and access to spiritual heritage. As James Anaya notes in the foreword, it remains the main challenge throughout the world.

The same objectives guide this book, which brings together some of the papers presented at the symposium and other texts solicited in parallel. Without claiming to be exhaustive, the case studies presented here provide an illuminating account of the main formal features of the law regarding Indigenous religions, by illustrating the diversity of normative protections already in force at the international and national levels. From a formal perspective, there is a wide range of policy and legal provisions in this area, beginning with international instruments and extending to constitutional rights, legal protections for religious freedom and equality, collective and sui generis rights, and provisions in ordinary statutes, political agreements, and treaties at the state level. In addition, there may be a heightened sensitivity on the part of the courts to the cultural and religious specificities of Indigenous peoples when adjudicating their rights. Finally, some kind of informal normativity may prevail, in the form of symbolic recognition of Indigenous religions in ceremonial contexts or through institutional policies related, for example, to the repatriation of religious objects. All this in a context in which, in several countries, a popular interest in a better understanding and recognition of the cultural and spiritual specificities of Indigenous peoples is noticeable.

 | DOI:10.1163/9789004524330_002

However, the configuration and application of these normativities vary considerably from one national context to another, which makes the field of Indigenous religious rights particularly complex and eclectic, although certain underlying and transversal trends prevail. In order to better circumscribe the latter, a large-scale comparative approach has been favoured here, which is in itself unique, since studies drawing parallels between different state normative contexts regarding Indigenous religious rights have so far been rare and based on limited samples (Collins 2003; Bryan 2017; Årsheim 2018; McDermond 2019; Gélinas 2021a). Such an approach is instructive in that it identifies some fundamental issues that Indigenous peoples consistently face in defending and protecting their religious rights, regardless of national contexts. In the following chapters, three issues emerge prominently: the representation of Indigenous religions and spiritualities, the effective respect of formally recognized rights, and the autonomy granted to Indigenous peoples in the exercise of their religious life.

1 Issues of Representation

The term "religion" is used in this book with the understanding that it is not necessarily the most appropriate to describe or account for the cosmological or ontological dimension of Indigenous peoples. In Indigenous' spiritual systems, the relationship to the supernatural is not an isolable category of beliefs and practices, as it transcends the various dimensions of their way of life. The normativity or custom itself has a spiritual charge, since the ethics that govern relationships among human beings and with the environment are inherited from the Creator or an equivalent supernatural entity (Guéno 2020; Féral, this volume). In the course of Indigenous-settler relations and under the influence of Christianization, Islamization, and other campaigns, Indigenous peoples have been led to categorize some of their beliefs and practices as belonging to a specifically "religious" sphere, but this categorization does not necessarily reflect the fullness and complexity of their belief systems. In addition, components of their religiosity that are still often described as "traditional" have persisted under the guise of exogenous religious traits or behaviors that appear to be secular in nature.

However, this process of categorization, and the resulting inadequate terminology, is reflected at both the international and national levels in the difficulty of properly recognizing and defining the legal object constituted by Indigenous religious beliefs and practices. Indigenous religiosity that is to be recognized and protected is generally defined as such by policy makers under the influence of their own cultural conceptions. Moreover, not only is there a wide variety of representations of Indigenous religions (Årsheim, this volume), but Indigenous peoples may be forced to mobilize and promote features that are more strategic than culturally based in their claims and assertions (Hall, this volume). Such a context is conducive to questioning the authenticity or value of religious beliefs and practices and, more generally, to justifying state policies that range from denial to valorization. In some cases, such as in New Caledonia (Féral, this volume), historical conversion to a dominant religion is the state's excuse for simply ignoring the Indigenous religious question, since nothing would remain of its precolonial specificity (Claridge 2018). Elsewhere, state or official religions have been established or privileged, ignoring Indigenous religions or placing them in an unequal relationship (Buana, Oladiti, Xaxa, this volume). In other national contexts, Indigenous' belief systems or parts of them are still considered less valuable, less credible, leading to forms of devaluation and even condemnation of certain claims (Xaxa, this volume; Gélinas 2021b). This can also lead to Indigenous people not displaying or declaring their religious identity, which in turn contributes to a sense of marginality. Elsewhere, Indigenous religious particularities are largely ignored or misunderstood by state law (see for example Maddox 1999; Willheim 2008; Carroll 2020).

Furthermore, current Indigenous rights at both the international and national levels tend to subsume the Indigenous religious dimension – which is otherwise defined more in terms of its observable features rather than intangible components (Niezen 2011) – under broader notions of cultural and collective rights. Among other consequences, this tends to discount the potential utility of the right to religious freedom as a defense or claim strategy for Indigenous peoples (McNally 2017; Årsheim, this volume). At the same time, majoritarian cultural prisms can take hold at the judicial level when it comes to the use of operative terms such as "religion" or "spirituality" (Berger 2008; McNally 2015), and thus prove detrimental to a proper understanding and appreciation of Indigenous claims (Dussias, Årsheim, this volume). In response, the Indigenous strategy may be to push religious claims under the umbrella of other, often less ideologically charged, subsidiary rights, such as cultural rights (Kimura, this volume), environmental law (Cloud, this volume), intellectual property (Blakenay 2013), or even under the umbrella of another politically, legally, and socially advantaged religion (Buana, Kimura, this volume). Although such strategies sometimes lead to success, they also reflect a deficit in recognizing Indigenous religions for what they are.

On a practical level, any effort to conceptualize Indigenous belief systems has its pitfalls, beginning with essentialism (Hall, this volume). Usually presented as a unified and intrinsic component of a so-called traditional culture, the relationship to religion in Indigenous contexts is more often eclectic and subject to debates about identity. For example, some Indigenous populations have a primarily Christian or Muslim profile, while maintaining traditional beliefs and practices in a syncretic or hybrid form and on a more or less individual basis (Årsheim, Simon, Féral, this volume). Others remain closer to such a traditional system of religious beliefs, while incorporating exogenous religious influences. In fact, many Indigenous communities exhibit religious pluralism, which may be complemented by the promotion of identity-based spiritualities, such as Pan-Indianism, more or less rooted in local cultures. Hence, the possibility that formal religious rights may be claimed or recognized on the basis of characteristics that only partially represent the needs of the populations concerned or prove to be a source of conflict among them (Xaxa, this volume), while maintaining inaccurate public representations of Indigenous religious beliefs and practices.

Consequently, there is a clear need to bring the Indigenous perspective to the fore front in order to develop national legal frameworks that provide adequate recognition and protection of Indigenous religious rights (Carpenter 2020). Just as self-identification is now considered a criterion for the recognition of Indigenousness, a principle of self-definition should prevail in determining what constitute Indigenous religious beliefs and practices, and the definitions thus proposed should benefit from legal protections already established. Still, from a decolonial perspective, and in order to strengthen the legitimacy of such recognition and legal protection, political authorities would benefit from assuming a duty of education in order to make Indigenous religions and the aggressions to which they have historically been subjected better known (Tomaselli and Xanthaki, 2021). Again, these initiatives should be carried out in collaboration with Indigenous peoples and their legitimate representatives.

2 Problems in the Application of the Law

Most of the chapters in this book recall the history of territorial dispossession, policies of assimilation and conversion, and the destruction or usurpation of cultural heritage that have affected the relationship of Indigenous peoples to their religious traditions. While there is now a basic trend at the international and national levels to achieve forms of reparation, restitution, and reappraisal regarding Indigenous religious patrimony, it should also be noted that progress in the recognition and protection of Indigenous religions is often limited to the symbolic level. In several countries, Indigenous ritual practices are now welcomed in the public sphere, especially in ceremonial contexts or in the wake of political events (Legault-Laberge, this volume). Indigenous religious practices can be integrated into legal processes and spiritually safe environments provided in public services. Indigenous religions can also be taught in schools (Gélinas, this volume). When it comes to the formal and legal recognition of rights, however, overall progress has been more modest, often driven by courts rather than policymakers (Buana, this volume), and still subject to state normative frameworks. Rights now recognized by international political bodies are implemented at the national level with variable geometry, ranging from voluntary ignorance of international law to implementation initiatives (Simon, this volume). For example, interpretations of international legal provisions may vary from one country to another; Japan, as a signatory of the UNDRIP, recognizes only the cultural dimension of Indigenous peoples' rights, not the freedom to engage in religious practices (Kimura, this volume). Moreover, in all cases, the existing mechanisms for the recognition and protection of Indigenous religions have limitations with respect to the key issues of access to and protection of territory and tangible and intangible heritage.

The fundamental connection between Indigenous peoples and their lands is now widely recognized and has even been legally recognized by state courts (Willheim, this volume). Nevertheless, much remains to be done to ensure access to the territory and to protect and preserve the sacred sites and resources that they contain (Bucumi, Oladiti, Dussias, this volume). In addition to issues related to economic development (Willheim, this volume), factors such as pollution can affect access to resources of spiritual value (Kimura, this volume), as well as climate change on a broader scale (Thomas 2018). As the case of the Ainu also illustrates, precarious living conditions can lead Indigenous peoples to cede territories which are considered as sacred spaces (Kimura, this volume). Again, the UNDRIP contains provisions that speak about the link between religious beliefs and practices and territory, but their application at the state level is likely to encounter structural barriers and processes of "vernacularization" (Anaya, this volume). In some countries, territories of spiritual interest to Indigenous peoples have been granted protected status, whether in the form of national parks or natural reserves, which more or less shields them from developmental activities (Årsheim, this volume). Heritage laws may also provide protection for Indigenous sites of religious interest, but their scope is limited, either because the sites to be protected must be of national, not just Indigenous interest, or because the criteria for evaluation are not necessarily in line with the cultural and religious interests of Indigenous peoples (Årsheim, this volume).

Indigenous peoples have also been given the opportunity to be consulted or involved in discussions about developmental projects in different ways and at different times, based on the principle of free and informed consent. In Canada, jurisprudence has imposed on the Crown a duty of consultation when developmental projects affect lands to which Indigenous peoples have a claim, but the country's Supreme Court justices have cautioned that this is not a veto right (Gélinas, this volume). Thus, in contexts where the state must arbitrate between economic interests and the cultural and spiritual needs of Indigenous peoples, the former still generally prevails. While some success has been achieved through such consultation processes, the ultimate decision-making power usually rests with the dominant political authorities, who in some cases go so far as to devaluate Indigenous cultures in order to justify developmental policies and projects (Bucumi, this volume). Therefore, frameworks for consultation and implementation need to be designed to take a better account and respond to Indigenous positions, which is not necessarily the case in practice (Dussias, this volume). To date, significant advances in the recognition of Indigenous territorial rights have come from the courts. For example, the Australian High Court rejected the *terra nullius* doctrine and held that Australian common law recognizes a form of native title that reflects the right of the country's Aboriginal inhabitants to their traditional lands, in accordance with their laws and customs (Wilheim, this volume). In Africa, courts have proven to be a useful avenue for Indigenous peoples in territorial disputes with the state (Bucumi, this volume), as well as in Indonesia where the Constitutional Court has distinguished between state-owned forests and those traditionally owned by Indigenous peoples, who can now dispose of them in accordance with their customs (Buana, this volume).

Another important issue for Indigenous peoples is access to and protection of components of their material religious heritage, such as ritual objects, human remains, and funerary objects. The UNDRIP also contains provisions in this regard (arts. 11 and 12), but their implementation at the national level also varies considerably from country to country. Some have specific policies and regulations regarding access to, management, protection, preservation, or repatriation of human remains and objects associated with Indigenous peoples (Law Library of Congress 2019), while others still have at best only a partial body of law in this area. In addition, existing provisions may contain limitations on their scope with respect to private domain, state jurisdiction, or the age or characteristics of the heritage to be protected. Above all, existing laws tend to conceive and treat this type of heritage from a property rights perspective rather than a religious rights perspective (Seidemann 2020).

Most of the legal provisions already in force are still largely inadequate to ensure the protection of the religious rights of Indigenous peoples, either because their parameters do not necessarily allow for the consideration of Indigenous cultural specificities, or because, on the contrary, they allow for their ignorance. In some countries, a framework of secularism can provide legitimacy to a government that is unwilling to legislate on religion for the benefit of Indigenous peoples (Kimura, this volume). The emphasis on belief in the assessment of religion not only tends to obscure the importance of its practical aspect in the Indigenous context but can also give the impression that general legal provisions on freedom of religion and equality are de facto sufficient to protect the religious rights of Indigenous peoples (Årsheim, this volume). Policymakers' lack of understanding of Indigenous cultural realities can also result in well-intentioned legal provisions that undermine Indigenous religious freedom at other levels (Simon, this volume). This is particularly the case when a legal framework requires Indigenous people to publicly disclose the secrecy of their beliefs or the location of sacred sites, the very objects they seek to protect, in order to obtain protection (Cloud, Willheim, this volume). Elsewhere, environmental and species protection laws may contribute to the restriction of Indigenous religious practices (Anaya, Dussias, this volume). Finally, in some cases, laws are directly detrimental to Indigenous religions, such as in Nigeria, where the secret dimension is prohibited (Oladiti, this volume), or in other African countries, where the criminalization of witchcraft, which may be considered desirable in view of the harm it can cause, especially to children, may also prove to be a pretext for revenge initiatives (Bucumi, this volume).

In response to such normative contexts, Indigenous peoples may be led to hide the religious components of their claims, whether in political discourse or in court (Cloud, Kimura, this volume), and to defend their religious rights under the disguise of other religious traditions that enjoy greater political recognition (Buana, Simon, this volume), or to present their claims as falling within the broader realm of cultural rights, as noted above. In all cases, the result is a form of invisibilization of Indigenous religious realities; yet, as Simon (this volume) correctly states, "[f]ull religious rights are possible only when all variants of religion are made visible and recognized as central in the lifeworlds of sovereign Indigenous peoples." Currently, the scope of laws and the interpretation of their provisions are ultimately decided by dominant majorities based on their knowledge and representations of Indigenous peoples and their own interests. Not only does it make the outcome of Indigenous religious rights claims unpredictable (Dussias, this volume), but it also gives the impression, from the perspective of Indigenous peoples, of incoherence and inconsistency in normative frameworks, especially when prevailing legal principles are readjusted, ignored or circumvented according to circumstances (Willheim, this volume).

3 The Stakes of Autonomy

With a few notable exceptions, such as Bolivia (Legault-Laberge, this volume), the law of Indigenous religions falls within the parameters of a common law determined by non-Indigenous majorities, which at best tends to delegate powers to Indigenous communities rather than to integrate their customary rights, values, and worldviews into the national normative framework. Not only do states primarily determine who are the subjects of the law, those entitled to Indigenous status, but they also establish the broad ideological, moral, political, economic, and legal guidelines through which the legal object of the law, i.e. Indigenous religions, are viewed.

State policies governing relations with Indigenous peoples, which can be placed on a spectrum ranging from denial of existence to self-determination, and which can be oriented toward the goals of subjugation, reconciliation, or reparation, primarily influence respect for religious rights. While some countries refuse to recognize the presence of Indigenous peoples on their territory by officially denying their existence, others achieve the same effect of invisibilization by reducing these populations to the status of ethnic minorities (Årsheim, this volume), or by recognizing their members only as citizens, which allows them to evade international conventions (Bucumi, this volume) or to deny Indigenous' collective rights (Féral, this volume). Elsewhere, without denying the existence of Indigenous peoples, states avoid granting them constitutional recognition (Willheim, this volume) or attributing special rights to them, for example, because they are spread over several national territories (Bucumi, this volume). On the other hand, some countries have given constitutional guarantees to the rights of Indigenous peoples and have adopted legal measures granting them a certain degree of autonomy, but such seemingly more favorable frameworks do not necessarily guarantee the full recognition and protection of religious rights (Simon, Gélinas, this volume). Not to mention that such state policies are subject to change, sometimes as quickly as the governments that promote them (Willheim, this volume).

The treatment of Indigenous religious rights is also influenced by state policies for managing cultural and religious diversity. Republican-inspired regimes are generally less inclined to value cultural diversity and to recognize collective rights to Indigenous peoples (Féral, this volume). Conversely, multiculturalist policies are a priori less reluctant to recognize, promote, and protect cultural and religious differences, but within a framework of coexistence that is nonetheless largely shaped by the moral and normative concerns of the majority (Povinelli 2002; Ashcroft and Bevir 2019). Meanwhile, secular regimes produce different effects on Indigenous religious rights, depending on the interpretation of their underlying constituent principles. The principle of neutrality can serve both as a guarantee of protection for Indigenous peoples' religious freedom and as a pretext for inaction in the face of inequalities (Kimura, this volume). The definition and scope of the principle of religious freedom vary from one state to another, especially where Indigenous' belief systems do not enjoy the same status as other religions.

Thus, despite significant advances, the law of Indigenous religions remains firmly subordinated to broader political and legal frameworks. This fact explains why, notwithstanding the existence of many formal legal protections for religious freedom, Indigenous peoples around the world are forced to claim and defend their rights in this area within a broader context of struggle to regain political self-determination (Legault-Laberge, this volume). This struggle may involve a direct and formal assertion of sovereignty (Simon, this volume), or it may be organized around the establishment of political bodies to counterbalance the dominant institutions, as in the case of the Norwegian Sámi Parliament (Årsheim, this volume), or in the wake of broader political movements that may also use the spiritual dimension as a unifying symbol (Hall, Buana, Legault-Laberge, this volume). Other groups, such as the Arctic Shaman Circle, are formed to revive, defend, and promote their cultural and religious heritages (Arsheim, this volume).

As Anaya points out in the foreword of this volume, since the spiritual dimension is integral to Indigenous identity and way of life, to belittle spirituality is to belittle identity and culture. The treatment of religion reflects the treatment of Aboriginal people. Likewise, since the religious aspect is likely to transcend all the components of the Indigenous way of life, the recognition of religious rights presupposes the full recognition of all rights related to social life (Féral, this volume). It is therefore important to envisage Indigenous religious rights that go beyond the merely symbolic forms of recognition that currently prevail at best, in order to be fully inscribed within the existing normative frameworks of the state, in a manner that is compatible with the normative and cultural perspectives of Indigenous peoples (Wright 2007; Johnson 2020; Féral, this volume). Such integration would be all the more fundamental with respect to Indigenous religious rights, as custom has an intrinsic religious component (Kelly 2014), particularly in relation to territory (Willheim, this volume).

States still struggle to acknowledge the specific and inherent nature of Indigenous peoples' rights (Borrows 2008; Lindberg 2018), even in countries where customary law is legally recognized; in practice, it is expected to be compatible with state law and public policy (Bucumi, this volume). In large part, this is because the recognition of collective rights, which is well grounded in the provisions of the UNDRIP, remains fundamentally at odds with the liberal principles of many states or the interests of dominant groups. Accordingly, it requires a reconceptualization and reconciliation of the notions of individual and collective rights (Otis 2007; Neihart 2013; McNally 2020). At the same time, such a commitment to internormativity would require not only a co-construction approach that welcomes and translates Indigenous peoples' expectations into shared normative frameworks, but also the possibility of recourse to third-party forums to avoid the state continuing to act as judge and jury in the event of conflict (Shrubsole 2019; McNally 2020), and to ensure that Indigenous autonomy, and the respect for religious rights that it entails, does not prevail only insofar as it satisfies the interests of the dominant groups in society (Atiemo 2014; Coertzen 2014). This is what a genuine process of decolonization should be all about.

References

Årsheim, Helge. "Including and Excluding Indigenous Religion through Law." *Numen* 65, no. 5–6 (2018): 531–561.

Ashcroft, Richard T., and Mark Bevir. *Multiculturalism in the British Commonwealth. Comparative Perspectives on Theory and Practice*. Oakland: University of California Press, 2019.

Atiemo, Abamfo. "Fighting for the Rights of the Gods: Tradition, Religious Human Rights, and the Modern Nation-State in Africa – A Ghanaian Case Study." In *Trajectories of Religion in Africa*, edited by C.N. Omenyo and E.B. Anum, 233–247. Amsterdan: Rodopi, 2014.

Berger, Benjamin. "Law's Religion: Rendering Culture." In *Law and Religious Pluralism in Canada*, edited by R. Moon, 264–296. Vancouver: University of British-Columbia Press, 2008.

Blakenay, Michael. "Protecting the Spiritual Beliefs of Indigenous Peoples – Australian Case Studies." *Pacific Rim Law & Policy Journal* 22, no. 2 (2013): 391–427.

Borrows, John. "Living Law on a Living Earth: Aboriginal Religion, Law, and the Constitution." In *Law and Religious Pluralism in Canada*, edited by R. Moon, 161–191. Vancouver: University of British-Columbia Press, 2008.

Bryan, Michelle. "Valuing Sacred Tribal Waters within Prior Appropriation." *Natural Resources Journal* 57, no. 1 (2017): 139–182.

Carpenter, Kristen A. "Religious Freedoms, Sacred Sites and Human Rights in the United States." In *UNDRIP Implementation. Comparative Approaches, Indigenous Voices from* CANZUS, Special Report, Centre for International Governance Innovation, 57–65, 2020.

Carroll, Michael P. "What Evicting Grizzly Bear Spirit Does (and Doesn't) Tell Us about Indigenous 'Religion' and Indigenous Rights." *Studies in Religion/Sciences religieuses* 49, no. 1 (2020): 32–49.

Claridge, Lucy. "Litigation as a Tool for Community Empowerment: The Case of Kenya's Ogiek." *Erasmus Law Review* 11, no. 1 (2018): 57–66.

Collins, Richard B. "Sacred Sites and Religious Freedom on Government Land." *Journal of Constitutional Law* 5, no. 2 (2003): 241–270.

Coertzen, Pieter. "Constitution, Charter and Religions in South Africa." *African Human Rights Law Journal* 14 (2014): 126–141.

Gélinas, Claude. "Les tribunaux et la configuration des identités spirituelles autochtones. Une comparaison des contextes canadien et australien." *Anthropologie et Sociétés* 45, no. 3 (2021a): 87–105.

Gélinas, Claude. "Droits ancestraux et réconciliation: quelques incompatibilités à la lumière de la décision *Hamilton Health Sciences Corp. v. D.H.*" *Recherches amérindiennes au Québec* 50, no. 3 (2021b): 55–65.

Guéno, Michael P. "On Lifeways and Litigation: Rethinking Native American Religious Freedom." *Berkley Forum*, October 21, 2020, https://berkleycenter.georgetown.edu/responses/on-lifeways-and-litigation-rethinking-native-american-religious-freedom, November 24, 2022.

Johnson, Greg. "Religious Freedom, Direct Action, and Rethinking Foundations." *Berkley Forum*, October 21, 2020, https://berkleycenter.georgetown.edu/responses/on-lifeways-and-litigation-rethinking-native-american-religious-freedom, November 24, 2022.

Kelly, Danial T. "The Legal and Religious Nature of Aboriginal Customary Law: Focus on Madayin." *University of Notre Dame Australia Law Review* 16 (2014): 50–73.

Law Library of Congress. *Protection of Indigenous Heritage in Selected Jurisdictions*. Global Legal Research Directorate, File No. 2019-017187, LRA-D-PUB-002429, 2019.

Lindberg, Darcy. "Miyo Nehiyawiwin (Beautiful Creeness): Ceremonial Aesthetics and Nehiyaw Legal Pedagogy." *Indigenous Law Journal* (*University of Toronto*) 16 (2018): 51–66.

Maddox, Marion. *Indigenous Religion in Secular Australia*. Research Paper 11, 1999–2000, Parliamentary Library, Parliament of Australia, 2000.

McDermond, Malcolm. "Standing for Standing Rock: Vindicating Native American Religious and Land Rights by Adapting New Zealand's Te Awa Tupua Act to American Soil." *Dickinson Law Review* 123, no. 3 (2019): 785–814.

McNally, Michael D. "From Substantial Burden on Religion to Diminished Spiritual Fullfillment: The San Francisco Peaks Case and the Misunderstanding of Native American Religion." *Journal of Law and Religion* 30, no. 1 (2015): 36–64.

McNally, Michael D. "Religion as Peoplehood: Native American Religious Traditions and the Discourse of Indigenous Rights." In *Handbook of Indigenous Religion(s)*, edited by G. Johnson and S.E. Kraft, 52–79. Leiden: Brill, 2017.

McNally, Michael D. *Defend the Sacred. Native American Religious Freedom Beyond the First Amendment*. Princeton: Princeton University Press, 2020.

Neihar, Bryan. "Awas Tingni v. Nicaragua Reconsidered: Grounding Indigenous Peoples' Land Rights in Religious Freedom." *Denver Journal of International Law & Policy* 42, no. 1 (2013): 77–99.

Niezen, Ronald. "Indigenous Religion and Human Rights." In *Religion and Human Rights. An Introduction*, edited by J. Witte et M.C. Green, 119–134. Oxford: Oxford University Press, 2011.

Otis, Ghislain. "Revendications foncières, 'autochtonité' et liberté de religion au Canada." In *Les systèmes religieux amérindiens et inuit*, edited by C. Gélinas and G. Teasdale, 169–189. Québec and Paris: In Situ and L'Harmattan, 2007.

Povinelli, Elizabeth A. *The Cunning of Recognition: Indigenous Alterities and the Making of Australian Multiculturalism*. Durham: Duke University Press, 2002.

Seidemann, Ryan M. "'Colonizing' the Dead: Former Colonial Nations' Treatment of Indigenous Peoples' Human Remains." *Baylor Law Review* 72, no. 2 (2020): 271–293.

Shrubsole, Nicolas. *What Has No Place, Remains. The Challenges for Indigenous Religious Freedom in Canada Today*. Toronto: University of Toronto Press, 2019.

Tomaselli, Alexandra, and Alexandra Xanthaki. "The Struggle of Indigenous Peoples to Maintain Their Spirituality in Latin America: Freedom of and from Religion(s), and Other Threats." *Religions* 12, no. 10 (2021): 869–885.

Thomas, Elizabeth. "Protecting Cultural Rights in the South Pacific Islands: Using UNESCO and Marine Protected Areas to Plan for Climate Change." *Fordham Environmental Law Review* 29, no. 3 (2018): 413–483.

Willheim, Ernst. "Australian Legal Procedures and the Protection of Secret Aboriginal Spiritual Beliefs: A Fundamental Conflict." In *Law and Religion in Theoretical and Historical Context*, edited by P. Cane et al., 214–245. Cambridge: Cambridge University Pres, 2008.

Wright, Fiona. "Law, Religion and Tikanga Maori." *New Zealand Journal of Public and International Law* 5, no. 2 (2007): 261–299.

Wiessner, Sigfried. "Re-enchanting the World: Indigenous Peolples' Rights as Essential Parts of Holistic Human Rights Regime." *UCLA Journal of International Law and Foreign Affairs* 15, no. 1 (2020): 239–288.

The Pachamama, the Trojan Horse of an Indigenous Ontological Diplomacy at the Convention of Biological Diversity?

Ingrid Hall

At the 15th Conference of the parties (COP15) of the Convention on Biodiversity (CBD), in December 2022, Mother Earth made her entry into one of the official texts, the Global Biodiversity Framework (GBF) that establishes the outlines of a master plan aiming to conserve worldwide biodiversity up to 2030. Section A of the document reads as follows:

> Biodiversity is fundamental to human well-being and a healthy planet, and economic prosperity for all people, including for living well in balance and in harmony with **Mother Earth**, we depend on it for food, medicine, energy, clean air and water, security from natural disasters as well as recreation and cultural inspiration, and it supports all systems of life on earth.

The text gave rise to intense debates throughout COP15, so much so that it was feared, up until the last moment, that no agreement might be reached. Certain points, such as the percentage of marine and terrestrial surface areas to be protected, and the status of Indigenous protected areas, were particularly sensitive. Yet this passage was accepted without any discussion. It is not a binding text, however this reference, as well as the reference to Living Well (*Buen vivir, Sumaq kawsay*), represent significant steps forward symbolically because they set a precedent. This results from an arduous struggle over many years by Indigenous peoples and certain non-Indigenous allies. In this text, I propose to set out the issues involved in this struggle since the 1990s, focusing particularly on the period 2018 to 2022.

My hypothesis is that the mention of Mother Earth in the Global Biodiversity Framework marks a significant step in challenging the modern, neoliberal nature regime (Escobar 1999) that prevails in global governance of natural resources, particularly in the CBD (Aubertin, Pinton, and Boisvert 2007; Büscher et al. 2012; Thomas and Boisvert 2015). Since its ratification in 1992, the CBD has established milestones concerning the recognition of the rights of Indigenous peoples over their natural resources, with Article 8j recognizing the importance of their knowledge.[1] In continuity with this, representatives of

1 The text is available at https://www.cbd.int/doc/legal/cbd-en.pdf, consulted on 04/24/2023.

 | DOI:10.1163/9789004524330_003

Indigenous peoples – grouped under the banner of Indigenous People and Local Communities (IPLCs) in the framework of the CBD – have taken advantage of this opening by foregrounding the importance of their culture, with the help of non-Indigenous actors. In doing so, they have deployed cultural politics (Escobar 1999; Hale 2006; Povinelli 1995), embodied particularly in the authorities of global environmental governance (Dove 2006; Sousa Santos (de), Arriscado Nunes, and Meneses 2007; Tsing 2007; Ulloa 2010). Ulloa (2010: 216–217) even proposes that IPLCs have claimed an "ecological identity," and case studies attest the validity of this proposition (Canessa 2006; Escobar 1998).

The reference to Mother Earth has appeared at the same time as this emergence of cultural politics, but has also laid the ground for a new phase, namely the entry into politics of Earth-Beings, to use the term proposed by Cadena (2010; 2015), which marks a cosmopolitical turning point (Cadena 2010; Latour 2007; Stengers 2005) within the CBD. Far from simply being a kindly spiritual figure who is acknowledged for her cultural relevance, this figure potentially has the power to challenge the opposition between nature and culture that is at the foundation of the naturalist, neoliberal nature regime (a concept proposed by Escobar, 1999). Mobilizing this figure helps to open the door to organic nature regimes, which do not separate nature and culture. In this sense, Mother Earth can be understood as an "ontological diplomat" who works for the recognition of hybrid communities, made up of both humans and non-humans, thus disrupting modern collectivities and allowing the development of a new "common world" (which is evolving and constantly negotiated) (Latour 2004: 209–215). Thus I propose to analyze how Mother Earth brings a challenge to the ontological status of nature or, to put this another way, a Trojan Horse in the politics of nature (Escobar 1999; Povinelli 1995; 2015).

This work is based on analysis of various sources, including a significant number of documents drawn up by the CBD, but also observations and interviews carried out at various meetings held by this institution, particularly in 2019 and 2022. It is important to note that these observations have been crucial in order to contextualize the analysis of documents and the way actors position themselves. I focus, for the purpose of this chapter, on the second part of COP15 (December 7 to 12, 2022) as well as preparatory meetings, particularly the 11th meeting of the Working Group on Article 8j (WG8j, November 20–22, 2019), which took place in Montreal. At these meetings, I concentrated on the discussions involving the IPLCs and during which the concepts of nature, culture, and the links between the two were invoked. In fact, various debates took place on "links between nature and culture," and various Nature-Culture declarations were made in 2018 and 2022, during COP14[2] and

---

2 https://www.cbd.int/doc/c/8b76/d85e/c62f920c5fd8c4743e5193e1/cop-14-inf-46-en.pdf, consulted on 17/02/2023.

COP15[3] respectively. I take inspiration from research already carried out on the CBD by social science researchers.[4] My approach, however, is different from previous work in its combination of several choices: first, I take into account meetings that prepare the COP and not only the COP itself; second, I take an ethnographic approach that combines the analysis of documents, speeches, interviews, and ethnographic observations; third, I concentrate on the links between nature and culture. In doing so, the work of Anna Tsing (2005) has been a source of inspiration, with her methodological reflections on "Ethnographic patches" and the concept of "frictions" that helps us to grasp the way different actors negotiate the signification of a particular idea through their interactions.

In this text I first briefly present the CBD and the conditions of participation for IPLCs to take part in its debates. Secondly, I detail how Mother Earth has become a cultural icon over the course of the 1990s and 2000s. The third section aims to show how she is on the way to becoming a Trojan Horse of nature politics.

1 The Convention on Biological Diversity and the Participation of Indigenous People and Local Communities

To make clear my intention in this text, it is important to understand what the CBD is, how it works, and how IPLCs take part in it. The CBD is a Framework Convention of the United Nations, the mission of which is to produce various kinds of texts to formalize principles and mechanisms concerning a range of biodiversity-related topics.[5] Promulgated in 1992 following the Earth Summit in Rio de Janeiro,[6] it was signed by 195 countries (state parties). Its creation results from the convergence of concerns that are difficult to reconcile: on the one hand the need to organize "biodiversity markets,"[7] and on the other hand to

3 https://iifb-indigenous.org/2022/12/19/the-yunnan-tiohtiake-nature-culture-summit-declarationtowards-flourishing-diversity/, consulted on 17/02/2023.

4 Parks 2018; Parks & Schröder 2018; Aubertin & Filoche 2011; Boisvert & Caron 2002; Campbell et al. 2014; Escobar 1997; Foyer 2015; Reimerson 2013; Suiseeya 2014.

5 For an explanation of the workings of the CBD more generally see Le Prestre (2017).

6 See for example: Aubertin, Pinton, and Boisvert 2007; Boisvert and Vivien 2012; Hermitte 1992; Le Prestre 2017; Thomas and Boisvert 2015.

7 These markets, based on bioprospection, were thought to be very promising at the time (Aubertin, Pinton, and Boisvert 2007; Thomas and Boisvert 2015). The countries of the North, rich in technology but poor in biodiversity, wished to take advantage of countries with great genetic wealth but without the technology necessary to give it monetary value. The latter countries include megadiverse countries, including many Central and Latin American countries, such as Peru.

protect the rights of Indigenous peoples.[8] The state parties, who are generally the same as the countries who signed the Convention, constantly negotiate the texts resulting from previous meetings with a view to their validation at the COP, which are the most essential political moments in the life of an international convention.

During the COPs and most of the related meetings, only the state parties are allowed to negotiate and vote. IPLCs are observers, which means that they cannot vote and they can only express themselves in a highly constrained manner: in two minutes, at the end of the negotiations on a specific text, together with all the other observers including NGOs, women, youth, academics, and representatives of the private sector.[9] Nevertheless, the CBD is recognized as having one of the most advantageous participation mechanism for Indigenous peoples among the Framework Conventions of the United Nations (Friis 2020; Kurasawa 2004; Sousa Santos (de), Arriscado Nunes, and Meneses 2007; Ulloa 2010). In certain meetings there are improved participation mechanisms that allows IPLCs to express themselves, to defend their positions, and potentially to vote. To understand how IPLCs take part in debates, it is important to not restrict ourselves to the COPs but also to take into account the other meetings that take place beforehand, during which they have been able to express themselves at greater length. This entails considering "negotiations" in a broad sense, i.e. beyond the formal negotiations on texts during plenary sessions, which often involve only the state parties. Furthermore, careful attention must be paid to the specific rules in place concerning the participation of IPLCs (Campbell et al. 2014: 6) to understand the stances they take.

The various meetings of the CBD are very different in terms of objectives, duration, attendance, but also in terms of IPLC participation. While the Thematic dialogue is almost only for IPLCs, the WG8j is a much bigger event. At the WG8j, IPLCs can still express themselves, whereas they are highly constrained during the COPs. Besides the formal negotiation in plenary sessions, there are several spaces in which IPLCs can express themselves during the meetings and that contribute to a broader and more diffuse kind of negotiation. For my purposes I identified the opening ceremonies of events, the formal presentations in plenary, the Side-events and the Nature-Culture Summits. Each meeting combines these spaces in a specific way as shown in Table 1.

8 The IPLCs hold the knowledge relevant to many of the biological resources that are the object of these biodiversity markets (Hermitte 2009; Michon 2002; Suiseeya 2014; Terán 2016). Moreover, they actively contribute to the conservation of these resources (Bolam et al. 2020).

9 Refer to Hall (2022b) to see how IPLCs use this format to negotiate.

TABLE 1 The various types of spaces in which IPLCs can express themselves according to meetings

Meetings	Thematic dialogue	WG8j	COP
Date of the event	November 17–18, 2019, Montreal	November 20–22, 2019, Montreal	December 7–19, 2022, Montreal
Number of participants	60 people, mostly IPLCs	Approx. 500 people, less than 100 IPLCs	17 000 people, maybe around 200 IPLCs
Participation of IPLCs to the governance of the meeting	IIFB co-organizes the event with the Secretariat	IIFB co-organizes the event IPLCs are considered as a Party IPLCs form a caucus group	IPLCs are observers IPLCs form a caucus group
Participation in the formal negotiations in plenary	Not relevant as there are no formal negotiations, the report of the event will inform the further negotiations	IPLCs can express themselves and vote during the formal negotiations	IPLCs cannot express themselves or vote during the formal negotiations

Spaces available for IPLCs for more informal negotiation	IPLCs can express themselves freely during the meeting	IPLCs can express:
		– In plenary
		  – during the opening (often)
		  – during the negotiations as a caucus group
		  – considered as a Party, can express and vote
		  – in formal presentations (often)
		– In Side-events (numerous)
			IPLCs can express:
			– In plenary
			  – during the opening (possibly)
			  – during the negotiations as a caucus group
			  – after the formal negotiations, in a two minutes format like other observers (possibly)
			  – in formal presentations (possibly)
			– In Side-events (numerous, but a lot of them are on other subjects)
			– Nature-Culture Summit
			– IPLC day

1.1 *Opening Ceremonies at the Events*

Prior to both the WG8j in 2019 and the COP15 in 2022, ceremonies held by a Mohawk elder were carried out at the opening of the meetings. This illustrates a practice, now common in North America, of acknowledging the Indigenous territory where an event takes place. As the meetings were held in Montreal, a city established on Mohawk territory, this Nation was called upon for the ceremonies. Since the CBD Secretariat is based in Montreal, the Mohawks became the First Nation of reference for the CBD; certain texts even use Mohawk terminology (CDB 2018; 2019). This emphasis on Indigenous peoples might not be so important in other meetings held in countries that do not count with or do not recognize Indigenous peoples. Ceremonies of this kind may also mobilize other Indigenous peoples, as it occurred during IPLC Day and the Nature-Culture Summit during COP15 in Montreal, for example, as we will see later.

1.2 *Participation in Plenaries*

Depending on the meeting, IPLCs may be called upon to make presentations before negotiations in plenary sessions. In this case, the speaker addresses the whole audience (hundreds or thousands of people) in 10 minutes. This depends, in large part, upon the participation mechanisms that are in place. During the WG8j meetings, the IPLCs are co-chairs with the CBD Secretariat, which gives them a greater say in the choice of speakers and leads to positions being taken that are more favorable to IPLCs or their allies (especially the United Nations Educational, Scientific and Cultural Organization – UNESCO –, the International Union for the Conservation of Nature – IUCN – or the Intergovernmental Science-Policy Platform on Biodiversity and Ecosystem Services – IPBES). During the COP, as IPLCs are not co-chair, the choice of speakers is driven by a different logic and the interests of IPLCs are sidelined, which is reflected in the choice of the speakers.

To ensure this participation of the IPLCs, a specific structure has been put in place by the CBD: the International Indigenous Forum on Biodiversity (IIFB). This forum was created in 1996 to facilitate the participation of IPLCs in the meetings of the CBD. It provides support in coordinating the participation of IPLCs, in agreeing on strategies to further the recognition and respect of Indigenous rights, and in influencing debates at international or national levels. Choosing the persons who will represent IPLCs in IIFB is a complex exercise: the candidates must be put forward by an Indigenous organization or recognized by the CBD Secretariat, and also must have a certain knowledge of CBD mechanisms.[10] IIFB structures IPLCs as a caucus group, following the

10 For more information, see https://iifb-indigenous.org/, or Friis (2020: 41).

model of regional groups (like the European Union or Latin America). It gathers representatives from Indigenous organizations, Indigenous non-governmental organizations, and Indigenous scholars and activists. For at least the last ten years, there has been strong leadership from the Latin American delegation in the IIFB, which influences the IPLCs caucus group more broadly.[11]

These presentations allow IPLCs to be present in the debate even though they might not have a voice or a vote – as during the COP. IPLCs receive more or less visibility depending on how they participate, but in any event these presentations represent a space in which IPLCs can express their viewpoint, either directly or through the intermediary of the IIFB. Allies may also be mobilized to highlight the importance of IPLCs in biodiversity conservation or to bring the interests of IPLCs to the forefront.

1.3 *Side-Events*

Another kind of space is opened up to IPLCs during the WG8j, and even more so during the COPs: Side-events. This terminology highlights the fact that this kind of event is parallel to the actual legal negotiations. Various stakeholders including IPLCs, researchers, NGOs, international institutions, or the private sector can propose to hold a Side-event on a topic of their choice. The Secretariat selects and schedules them during lunch break or after the plenary sessions. There are many Side-events every day, for all interests. The aims of these Side-events are to shed light on the various issues related to the questions debated in plenaries, to inform participants about research and other initiatives, and to facilitate networking. These events allow many observers not directly participating in plenary debates to express their opinions and to enlarge their networks.

The IPLCs take part in a significant number of these events. Often, they present the results of projects financed by an institution such as the Global Environment Facility (GEF) or NGOs. The CBD Secretariat may co-organize such events, with partners like the IUCN, or international institutions such as UNESCO who may also propose activities on their own. The IIFB is often called upon in such an interinstitutional context and in such cases, as we will see, the Latin American and Andean perspectives are foregrounded. This kind of space is very important for IPLCs, since it gives them the opportunity to express their viewpoints in a more flexible way, with the support of various kinds of allies.

11 M. Francisco Ramiro Batzín Chojoj was co-chair for the IIFB during WG8j in 2019 and COP15, for example, and other Latin American representatives, such as Ms. Maria Yolanda Terán Maigua (Kichwa, Ecuador) or Ms. Florina Lopez Miro (Kuna people, Panama), were also present.

1.4 *The Nature-Culture Summits*

We must consider one last kind of event held at the COPs, the Nature-Culture Summits. In 2022 the fourth edition of a Global Forum on Biocultural Diversity, also called the Nature-Culture Summit, was held.[12] This type of event results from a collaboration between the IIFB, the CBD Secretariat, UNESCO, and the IUCN. The IPLCs are heavily involved and the objective of the events is to foreground their role and the importance of their knowledge – particularly the cultural component of their knowledge. Thus, the importance of culture is underscored. Organizing this kind of event may give rise to a nature-culture Declaration, as was the case during COP14 in 2018 or COP15 in 2022. This kind of document has no legal value, but it enables a statement to be made, loud and clear, on the importance of taking culture into account.

If the IPLCs have trouble positioning themselves in official negotiations, particularly at the COPs, they have access to various other spaces that allow them to express their viewpoints, to take part in debates, and to further certain ideas and demands.

2 Mother Earth and Pachamama, American Idols of a Cultural Politics

The mentions of Mother Earth, Mother Nature, and Pachamama in the context of the CBD should be understood in a larger historical context. North American Indigenous movements involved in environmental causes since the 1960s and 1970s have foregrounded the figure of Mother Earth. Gill (1991), who has retraced its emergence, shows that it was not familiar to all Indigenous peoples from North America, and that it was through dialogue between First Nations and academics that it gradually became established in the 1960s, then becoming indispensable in the 1970s and afterwards. The rise of Mother Earth has gone together with the rise of environmental struggles that mobilized the image of American First Nations: the figure of the "ecological Indian" (Krech 1999) also called "ecological native" (Ulloa 2010).[13] Yet it is not only a North American image. Since the 1960s there has been an internationalization of Indigenous and environmental struggles. Links have been built with people from other parts of the world, especially with Latin America. Mother Earth, nevertheless, remained a central figure.

12 https://www.cbd.int/article/cop15-nature-culture-summit.

13 On this topic also see Fabricant & Postero 2018, Hall 2022b, Igoe 2010, and Ramos 1994.

In the 1980s, and even more so in the 1990s, environmental issues were tightly linked to social and cultural demands, especially for IPLCs (Tsing 2007), and in Latin America in particular as Escobar (1999), Ulloa (2010, 31 and subsequent pages), and Ramos (1994) have shown. These demands were framed in the context of the wide-scale adhesion of Latin American countries to Convention no. 169 of the International Labor Organization (ILO 1989) and the ratification of multicultural constitutions at the beginning of the 1990s. From this moment on, especially in Latin America, social demands have been articulated around cultural differences (Escobar 1997; 1998; Ulloa 2010: 31 and subsequent pages). This allowed for the rise of "cultural politics" (Escobar 1997; Hale 2006; Povinelli 1995), which largely relied on Mother Earth. In this context, biodiversity became a field of power struggles (Sousa Santos (de) et al. 2007) and the CBD became a very important arena at an international level for IPLCs (Aubertin 2005; Boisvert and Caron 2002; Escobar 1997; 1999; Sousa Santos (de), Arriscado Nunes, and Meneses 2007; Ulloa 2010).

In the first decade of the 21st century, the demands of IPLCs were framed in terms of worldviews or cosmovisions, concepts that were recognized by the CBD during COP10. In 2010, a joint program between the Secretariat of the CBD and the UNESCO recognized "the convergence between biological and cultural diversity," and the fact that "[e]nsembles of biodiversity are developed, maintained and managed by cultural groups. Diversity of cultural practices depends upon specific elements of biodiversity for their existence and expression."[14] The growing attention paid to culture has translated into emphasis on the concept of bioculturality, which seeks to place the biological and cultural components of biodiversity on the same level. This concept has been debated by academics since the 1990s (Maffi 2001; Posey & Dutfield 1988; Posey 1997). Posey, especially, together with other scholars and activists, brought these ideas to the CBD. It was inscribed in the Nature-Culture declaration during COP10 in 2010, and a definition was proposed in 2017 by the WG8j: "Within the context of the Convention, [...] [b]iocultural diversity is considered as biological diversity and cultural diversity and the links between them."[15] Latin American Indigenous peoples and the academics that supported them were very important in this process.

Meanwhile, Mother Earth established herself as a reference point in institutions involved in the worldwide governance of genetic resources (Escobar 1999; Ulloa 2010). This central figure turned into an "icon" (Ulloa 2010: 200)

14 https://www.cbd.int/lbcd/, consulted 04/19/2023.

15 https://www.cbd.int/doc/guidelines/cbd-8j-GlossaryArticle-en.pdf, consulted 2023/03/28. On biocultural rights see Girard et al. 2022b.

that brought together IPLCs claims and represented them in cultural terms, but more precisely in religious ones. During this period, references to the sacred were powerful arguments to defend IPLCs rights, since the IUCN had succeeded in imposing the category of sacred sites amongst the categories of spaces to protect (Verschuuren 2010). Another development, in 2008 and 2009, increased the importance of the Mother Earth figure. Bolivia and Ecuador recognized the Andean figure of Mother Earth, the Pachamama, in their new constitutions. The influence of these countries within the CBD was to grow, while that of the North American countries was to fade away as the USA did not sign the CBD (Graddy-Lovelace 2022) and although Canada did, it did not sign the Nagoya Protocol in 2010. By contrast, the CBD remains an authority of great importance for the Latin American countries that are both signatories of the CBD and the Nagoya Protocol, and also hold great biodiversity to protect within their borders.

In 2019 and 2022, the interventions following the opening ceremonies of the WG8j and COP15 highlighted how important it is to value the knowledge held by IPLCs and to reconsider the links between nature and culture. Such interventions were made by Ms. Elizabeth Maruma Mrema, Executive Secretary of the Convention on Biological Diversity, Mr. Xing Qu, Deputy Director-General of UNESCO, Ms. Sonia Peña Moreno, Director of the International Policy Centre of the IUCN, and Ms. Lucy Mulenkei, Co-chair of the International Indigenous Forum on Biodiversity (IIFB). These speakers all emphasized worldviews, cosmologies, or other cultural dimensions to biodiversity. Their interventions also made use of the figures of Mother Earth or Mother Nature. In their interventions, a significant number of IPLCs also mentioned the feminine figure Mother Earth, Mother Nature, or Pachamama. Pachamama was mentioned by the Andean representatives either in the presentations before the plenary conferences or at Side-events, especially when IIFB was called upon to represent IPLCs. The figure of Pachamama was brought up mostly by Bolivian or Ecuadorian representatives. The way that this figure is presented, even by the Andean representatives, ignores the complexity and ambivalent aspect of Pachamama in the Andean context (Allen 2019; Harris 2000). Mother Earth thus becomes nebulous, or more precisely she is deprived of cultural context (Ulloa 2010: 200). Yet this figure allows IPLCs to display a collective identity, to join forces under the same flag, and to make themselves identifiable. In a context where they are an overwhelming minority, performing[16] Mother Earth/Pachamama allows IPLCs

16 Campbell et al. (2014: 6) invoke the concept of "politics of performance."

to gain some recognition.[17] Moreover, it allows them to take advantage of the spell-binding power this figure has over non-Indigenous populations (Ulloa 2010; on the same topic see also Fabricant & Postero 2018; Hall 2022b; Igoe 2010; Ramos 1994; Harris 2000). Nevertheless, this strategy has its limits.

The dominant discourse tends to crystalize around the figure of the "ecological native," an idealized image that has its value but also tends to maintain the subaltern position of Indigenous populations and contribute to the reproduction of a colonial heritage (Ulloa 2010: 201). Moreover, this cultural politics built upon the figure of Mother Earth leaves little space for cultural and religious diversity and creates tensions. Not all the IPLCs have a figure equivalent to Mother Earth and certain members of IPLCS, whether they are Indigenous or from local communities, feel that it has nothing to do with them. Several representatives from Sri Lanka, the Philippines, and Caribbean communities, for instance, spoke to me of their discomfort in the face of this argument, judged to be "too cultural" – let's say too ethnocentric – to take into account their specific viewpoint. This situation also appeared at the opening ceremonies for the meetings in Montreal (2019 and 2022), when the Mohawk ceremony-holder first mentioned the Creator, before elaborating at greater length on the importance of Mother Earth in a discourse aligned with the stances set out by the Latin American IPLC representatives. Within this politics of culture, therefore, it is quite difficult to deal with cultural diversity.

The figure of Mother Earth/Pachamama has thus been mobilized to emphasize the importance of culture for biodiversity conservation at a global level. It has become the icon of a "cultural politics." Although it was North American actors who first brought this figure to the stage, the Latin American, then Andean, representatives took over from them subsequently. This strategy has been a unifying force for the IPLCs, and it helped to establish alliances.

3 Engaging with a Politics of Nature

The cultural politics deployed in the 2010s, has evolved somewhat. To understand what is at stake, it is important to come back to the Bolivian and Ecuadorian constitutions. The acknowledgement given to Pachamama and to Living Well in the constitutions of these two countries allows the development of a strategy that goes beyond the framework of cultural politics.

17 In the sense of Povinelli (1997: 20), i.e. to be given a specific status in relation to other actors.

At a first glance, Pachamama is proposed as an equivalent of nature in these constitutions. But the recognition of Pachamama is linked to Living Well, the latter being also mentioned in the GBF in 2022. The way Living Well is conceptualized in both constitutions combines Indigenous concepts[18] and concepts from other actors, including academics such as anthropologists or sociologists engaged with IPLCs causes and potentially in politics.[19] This concept implies the need for a reciprocal and harmonious relationship between humans and Pachamama, or more broadly, between humans and nature. The references to Living Well thus raise issues regarding the ontological status of Earth beings like Pachamama. According to Cadena (2010), Pachamama becomes cosmopolitical. The constitution of Ecuador, especially, raises issues concerning the legal recognition of non-human entities (like rivers), and more broadly the emergence of rights of nature. This is significant because it means that a shift from an anthropocentric conception of nature to an ecocentric one is at stake (Hermitte 2011; Larrère 2006; 2012). These propositions, then, go beyond the recognition of Pachamama as a cultural icon and raise the issue of recognizing different ontological regimes. This happens in a context in which multiculturalism receives increasing criticism for its neoliberal aspects (Gros 2006; Viveiros de Castro 2014), especially since it assumes a naturalist nature-regime, which Viveiros de Castro calls mono-naturalism.

In the CBD, this idea is making headway. In the second edition of the Local biodiversity outlook (Forest people programme, 2020),[20] we read that "[w]orldview that separate nature and culture are an underlying cause of biodiversity loss, as cultures condition behaviours and frame people's relationships with other people and with the natural world."[21] The opposition between nature and culture is identified as one of the causes of biodiversity loss, in fact it is even the first "key message" identified in this document. The debate is no longer framed so much in cultural terms; instead, the relevance of the opposition between nature and culture is questioned (even if the cultural framework remains in the background). We may note that in this excerpt

18 Allen (2019), Arnold (1999) and Harris (2000) put forward an interesting reflection on this subject. Harris (2000) discusses the specific influences of the Catholicism and the urban mestizos in the way Pachamama became essential in the Bolivian context.

19 These constitutions were debated in constituent assemblies (*asambleas constituyentes*) made up of all sectors of the population (Landivar and Ramillien 2015). A large literature exists on the topic (Bretón Solo de Zaldívar 2013; González & Vázquez 2015; Hidalgo-Capitán & Cubillo-Guevara 2017 for example). In one of his texts, Escobar (2010) gives a detailed comparison of the process in the different Andean countries.

20 In the Local biodiversity outlook, IPLCs make some recommendations based on the Global biodiversity outlook (Bolam et al. 2020).

21 https://www.cbd.int/gbo/gbo5/publication/lbo-2-summary-en.pdf.

the term worldview is not only used to describe the conceptualizations held by the IPLCs, but also those of scientists and other non-Indigenous populations, putting into practice a "symmetrization" of the concept in the sense of Latour. We move, therefore, from the valorization of cultures to a challenging of nature-culture dualism, marking a significant evolution compared to the previous decades.

In this shift, one can also see the strong influence of the Latin-American leaders. The report of the First Global Thematic Dialogue held in 2019 in Montreal (CBD 2019)[22] shows this clearly. The Latin American delegation explicitly defended an approach that challenges the dominant nature regime in demanding "respect and recogni[tion for] the sacred and holistic approach that indigenous peoples have to nature and biodiversity." The other IPLC representatives did not seem to want to follow the Latin American delegation onto this terrain, and the rest of the document is much more technical and informed by legal issues.

Some non-Indigenous agents also support this shift. A certain number of state parties also supports it, with Bolivia and Ecuador at the forefront, and more recently Colombia and Mexico. As state parties, they can raise these issues during the proper negotiations of the texts, backing IPLC actors during WG8j or at other meetings like the COPs, as it occurred during COP15. Other institutional actors also support this shift, one of the most important of these being the Secretariat of the CBD itself and more specifically the "people and biodiversity" unit that coordinates the WG8j (Friis 2020: 13). The Secretariat has a prominent role as it helps to defend this position, creating spaces for IPLCs to express themselves at various meetings: the WG8j, of course, but also Side-events or Nature-Culture summits. Others institutional actors are concerned, such as the UNESCO, the IUCN or the IPBES (a scientific advisor body of the CBD, the equivalent of the Intergovernmental Panel on Climate Change for the climate).[23] As a result, building upon a dynamic that has been in place since 2010, a Nature-Culture alliance has been reinforced over the last few years between these institutions. Thus, complex interinstitutional synergies are built and the creation of specific spaces for the expression of viewpoints is in itself a way to further reflection on the nature regimes that should be criticized or valorized within the CBD. It is important to point out the difficulty, for such institutions, in fully challenging the naturalist nature regime that was predominant at their establishment and that characterized their founding texts. Yet

22 https://www.cbd.int/doc/c/245c/aee3/33cabfb2c1daa9c539b3c5ed/post2020-ws-2019-12-02-en.pdf.

23 On this subject, see Dunbar 2019.

they do play a key role alongside IPLCs. Other international instruments are also relevant, such as the International Treaty on Plant Genetic Resources for Food and Agriculture which recognized the importance of Mother Earth. This figure is also mentioned in the United Nations Declaration on the Rights of Peasants and Other People Working in Rural Areas adopted in 2018.[24]

In this sense the Nature and Culture Summit that took place at COP15 in 2022 was emblematic. This event was organized with help from the CBD Secretariat, UNESCO, and the IUCN. The IIFB was a co-organizer and the event was moderated by Mr. Q'apaj Conde, who is an Aymara from Bolivia. At this event, much space was given over to IPLCs, and since the event was taking place in Canada, there was a strong presence of Indigenous groups from this country.[25] During this summit, Dario Mejia from Colombia, Chair of the United Nations Permanent Forum on Indigenous Issues,[26] expressed his opinion clearly: "The distinction between culture and nature is the creation of a specific way of understanding the world, developed by Western, or mainstream, society. But for most Indigenous Peoples, this distinction between culture and nature does not exist."[27] He continued by saying that "Mother Earth is the bearer of our basic rights and fundamental values that shape the life of beings, including humans [...] This is what scholars may call 'culture.' But for us, as Indigenous Peoples, nature sets the rules of life." Dario Mejia is referring to Mother Earth, insisting that she is important, but he challenges the cultural representation of this figure to stress its cosmopolitical dimension.[28]

As the various speakers over the two days of the Summit made clear, their aim was to push for the integration of IPLC demands into the post-2020 GBF. There was less participation in this event from state parties, although certain countries more committed to their IPLCs, such as Colombia and Bolivia, were present. Nonetheless, the event helped to apply pressure to the negotiations while also refining strategy and strengthening alliances between IPLCs and other actors (state actors or other ones), including various initiatives brought to the table by NGOs.

This challenging of the opposition between nature and culture reveals itself to be the new unifying argument. In fact, an important number of interventions

---

24 https://www.geneva-academy.ch/joomlatools-files/docman-files/UN%20Declaration%20on%20the%20rights%20of%20peasants.pdf, consulted on 16/09/2023.

25 These were mainly English-speaking, although the event was in Quebec.

26 https://www.un.org/development/desa/indigenouspeoples/about-us/permanent-forum-on-indigenous-issues.html, consulted on 05/03/2023.

27 https://www.un.org/development/desa/indigenouspeoples/news/2022/12/unpfii-en-cop15/, consulted on 04/03/2023.

28 This shows that the United Nations Permanent Forum on Indigenous Issues reciprocally builds upon the CBD, even if the fact that local communities are also involved in this arena might be seen as problematic.

from IPLCs overlapped on this key point: it does not make sense to oppose nature and culture and to consider nature from the neoliberal and naturalist perspective. This leaves more room for cultural and religious diversity. Thus, during the inaugural session of WG8j in 2019, Josefa Isabela Tauli, an Indigenous representative from the Philippines[29] (for the Global Youth Biodiversity Network) highlighted the importance of the concept of *ili* for the Kankanaey, which shows in an exemplary way that nature and culture are intimately linked (see Adonis & Couch 2018, who elaborate on this concept). There was no need for her to refer to Mother Earth. In the same vein, during COP15, especially during IPLC day, a diversity of viewpoints appeared clearly. A representative from each region of the world proposed a significant gesture to open the event, and only the Ecuadorian representative referred to Pachamama. Each representative was able to make their own contribution, and the representative for African communities, for example, read a verse from the Koran.

At COP15, many North American leaders were present, given geographical proximity and due to mobilization by the Canadian government and civil society. They contributed to these reflections with a singular voice, foregrounding the concepts of respect and rationality, as did Ben Sherman, member of the Oglala Lakota people from the USA. This framing is informed by debates that took place in another context, the United Nations Permanent Forum on Indigenous Issues, in which the Indigenous peoples of North America participate actively (Morin 2012). Moreover, the previously mentioned Dario Mejia represented precisely this other Framework Convention of the United Nations. These principles of respect and relationality are central in the United Nations Declaration on the Rights of Indigenous Peoples (UNDRIP).[30] In this text, the concepts of respect and relationality are applied to humans only, but in the context of the CBD, during COP15, they were applied to humans and nonhumans to characterize the relation between them. They helped to underline the importance of respecting nature, animals, plants, and the importance of establishing respectful relationships with them. This synergy with the UNDRIP, and the concepts brought to the table by the North American IPLCs, seem to hold promise for an innovative approach.

The arguments have thus gradually evolved and the culprit now in the dock is the nature-culture division that prevails in the dominant nature-regime of the CBD. The new framing promotes what Escobar calls an organic nature regime, in which "the natural world is integral to the social world" (1999: 7–8;

29 Philippines are also historical actors in IPLC issues in the CBD and more broadly in the UN.

30 https://www.un.org/development/dsa/indigenouspeoples/wp-content/uploads/sites/19/2018/11/UNDRIP_E_web.pdf, consulted 04/18/2023.

see also Viveiros De Castro 2014). If we look closely enough at "links between nature and culture," it should appear that they are so strong that it would be pointless to distinguish the two. The concept of nature itself then becomes irrelevant. This is a sign that IPLCs have made a move from cultural politics to a "politics of nature" (Escobar 1999; Povinelli 2015).

4 Conclusion

Mentioning Mother Earth in a text such as the Global Biodiversity Framework might come across as a gesture of openness towards Indigenous cultures and religiosities. In a globalized context, where this image resembles a motherly, kindly nature-woman, almost virginal, and overall very cliché, this mention seems somewhat condescending but mostly inoffensive. Yet a deeper analysis of the issues underlying the conservation of natural resources within the CBD and the consideration of Indigenous peoples shows a quite different panorama and reveals the subversive potential of this reference to Mother Earth.

Since the 1990s, biodiversity conservation has been an issue of prime importance for Indigenous peoples, and especially the CBD. However constrained though it may be, in this forum IPLCs can express their viewpoints, advocate for their rights and gain recognition. In this context, foregrounding Mother Earth in the 1990s helped to reach these goals, putting a spotlight on cultural specificities, often understood in terms of spirituality and sacredness. This framing was consistent with a broader context of recognizing Indigenous rights internationally, especially in Latin America. The cultural dimension of knowledge related to natural resources was highlighted and the concept of biocultural diversity, an indicator of this evolution, appeared on the scene.

Gradually, on the sidelines of the valorization of culture, a different line of argumentation emerged, questioning the hegemonic neoliberal and naturalist nature regime. Over the 2000s decade, in a context marked by the debates taking place in Bolivia and Ecuador in 2007 and 2008, the opposition between nature and culture was identified as problematic. In the new constitutions of these countries, Living Well appeared as a potential alternative model. The recognition of Pachamama in these constitutions, which fits in with the overall cultural logic analyzed above, allows for a link to be made between two lines of argumentation. From cultural icon, Pachamama turned into a cosmopolitical icon, an ontological diplomat. She harbors an alternative nature regime – an organic one, to use Escobar's term (1999) – that calls into question the opposition between nature and culture, and even the relevance of these two categories.

Given the way that Indigenous peoples participate in the institutions of the CBD, the IPLCs must play on both their resemblances and also be able to take account of their differences, which is quite a challenge. As we have seen, cultural politics entails a generalization, while a politics of nature seems better suited to account for cultural diversity since the main arguments concern nature regimes. The work of ontological diplomacy rests, of course, upon the IPLCs, but it is carried out in collaboration with other institutional actors, state parties or others such as the CBD Secretariat, the IUCN, UNESCO, and IPBES.

What is gradually coming to light is the need to review the nature regime, to carry out a "transformative change." On this point the section of the GBF dedicated to the "theory of change" is quite disappointing. It rests on an economic and environmental logic, and does not extend to ontological considerations. Yet these ontological considerations are highlighted in the IPBES publications concerning the conceptual framework for thinking about links between nature and culture (Diaz et al. 2015) or rethinking the values associated with nature (IPBES 2022). These somehow make their way into the CBD.

Let us be careful: cultural politics has not been abandoned, since it still is far too useful in the context of formal negotiations where a politics of nature would make no sense. The neoliberal and naturalist nature regime still constitutes the basis for the global governance of natural resources. If one has two minutes to speak in the name of IPLCs in order to position oneself as a caucus on a given topic, one is better off expressing oneself in a way that will be easily understood and focusing on the most technical aspects of negotiation. Cultural politics, therefore, is still very useful. A politics of nature is deployed in more open contexts than formal negotiations: presentations before the negotiations, Side-events, and Nature-culture summits. In these spaces, Mother Earth is the figure around which a strong line of argumentation has crystallized, and who has burst into the GBF, the master plan for protecting biodiversity up until the horizon of 2030. Writing Mother Earth into this document is the beginning of a more radical strategy, a politics of nature.

Of Indigenous North American inspiration, this figure was developed by various actors in the 1960s and 1970s. She then became "Latinized" at the turn of the century, before finally being "Andeanized." She has become a globalized figure. The Andean Pachamama herself has been stripped of her ambivalent and plural character. This framing has the advantage, on the one hand, of allowing actors to "speak with one voice," as one interlocutor told me, and also of rallying non-Indigenous actors. Thus IPLCs and their allies resort to an archetypal image. The effectiveness of the strategy has a price, the essentialization of Indigenous peoples, which may be partly strategic, as I have observed in fieldwork in the Andes (Hall 2022a). This is not a problem in itself, but it tends to frame local discourses in naturalist ways, leaving no place for the plural and dynamic conceptions people have (Cepek 2016). Are we not stuffing the egg into the chicken by letting the figure of Mother Earth be imposed on all Indigenous people, due to inadequate participation mechanisms? If a non-Indigenous audience is uncomfortable with a male creator figure because it is associated with patriarchy and colonialism, should this be an issue for Indigenous people?

The references to the figure of Mother Earth, and its Andean avatar Pachamama, is central in this long-running history of negotiation at an international level. The Mother Earth figure foregrounded at the CBD is thus globalized and deterritorialized, but she is also powerful and seems able to explode the concept of nature![31] It allows this "transformational shift" from a politics of culture to a politics of nature, and helps discussions to go beyond the recognition of culture towards embracing a different relationship to nature (Bavikatte 2014: 6; Hermitte 2009; Parks 2018). At stake is the possibility of taking account of a diversity of worldviews – that some call the "pluriverse" (Cadena & Blaser 2018; Latour 2007; Mignolo 2013) – and the potential remaking of a "common world" (Latour 2007; Stengers 2005). Yet this is a weapon to wield with care, given its essentializing impacts. Would the concepts of respect and relationality, applied to the context of the CBD, be better suited to controlling this tendency and allowing a less essentializing politics of nature?[32] This would be wonderful, but the road is still long and lain with pitfalls: writing Mother Earth and Living Well into the GBF is a small step in this direction …

References

Adonis, Digna L., and Jen Couch. "Ili-Based Community Organising: An Igorot Indigenous Peoples' Concept for Grassroots Collaboration." *Journal of Social Inclusion* 9, no. 1 (2018): 58–70. https://doi.org/10.36251/josi.131.

Allen, Catherine J. "Righting Imbalence: Striving for Well-Being in the Andes." *Science, Religion and Culture* 6, no. 1 (2019): 6–14. https://doi.org/10.17582/journal.src/2019.6.1.6.14.

Arnold, Denise Y. "The Mythological Figure of the Earth Mother." In *To Make the Earth Bear Fruits. Ethnographic Essays on Fertility, Work and Gender in Highland Bolivia*, edited by Olivia Harris, 201–219. London: University of London, 1999.

31 To refer to an expression from Descola https://www.letemps.ch/societe/sciences-humaines/philippe-descola-lanthropologue-dynamite-lopposition-entre-nature-culture, consulted on 04/24/2023.

32 This echoes what Escobar (1999) calls an antiessentialist political ecology.

Aubertin, Catherine. *Représenter La Nature? ONG et Biodiversité*. Paris: IRD éditions, 2005.

Aubertin, Catherine, and Geoffroy Filoche. "The Nagoya Protocol on the Use of Genetic Resources: One Embodiment of an Endless Discussion." *Sustentabilidade Em Debate* 2, no. 1 (2011): 51–63. https://doi.org/10.18472/SustDeb.v2n1.2011.3906.

Aubertin, Catherine, Florence Pinton, and Valérie Boisvert. *Les marchés de la biodiversité*. Paris: Institut de recherche pour le développement, 2007.

Bavikatte, K.S. *Stewarding the Earth: Rethinking Property and the Emergence of Biocultural Rights*. Oxford: University Press, 2014.

Boisvert, Valérie, and Armelle Caron. "The Convention on Biological Diversity: An Institutionalist Perspective of the Debates." *Journal of Economic Issues* 36, no. 1 (2002): 151–166. https://doi.org/10.1080/00213624.2002.11506447.

Boisvert, Valérie, Armelle Caron, and Franck-Dominique Vivien. "Towards a Political Economy Approach to the Convention on Biological Diversity." *Cambridge Journal of Economics* 36, no. 5 (2012): 1163–1179.

Bolam, Anne, Kate Branthomme, Eduardo S. Brondizio, and Neil Burgess. *Global Biodiversity Outlook 5*. Montréal: Convention sur la Diversité Biologique, 2020.

Bretón Solo de Zaldívar, Víctor. "Etnicidad, Desarrollo y 'Buen Vivir': Reflexiones Críticas en Perspectiva Histórica." *European Review of Latin American and Caribbean Studies* 95, (2013): 71–95.

Büscher, Bram, Sian Sullivan, Katja Neves, Jim Igoe, and Dan Brockington. "Towards a Synthesized Critique of Neoliberal Biodiversity Conservation." *Capitalism Nature Socialism* 23, no. 2 (2012): 4–30. https://doi.org/10.1080/10455752.2012.674149.

Cadena, Marisol de la. "Indigenous Cosmopolitics in the Andes: Conceptual Reflections Beyond 'Politics.'" *Cultural Anthropology* 25, no. 2 (2010): 334–370. https://doi.org/10.14506/.

Cadena, Marisol de la. *Earth Beings: Ecologies of Practice across Andean Worlds*. Durham: Duke University Press, 2015.

Cadena, Marisol de la, and Mario Blaser, eds. *A World of Many Words*. Durham: Duke University Press, 2018.

Campbell, Lisa M., Catherine Corson, Noella J. Gray, Kenneth I. MacDonald, and J. Peter Brosius. "Studying Global Environmental Meetings to Understand Global Environmental Governance: Collaborative Event Ethnography at the Tenth Conference of the Parties to the Convention on Biological Diversity." *Global Environmental Politics* 14, no. 3 (2014): 1–20.

Canessa, Andrew D.M. "Todos Somos Indígenas: Towards a New Language of National Political Identity." *Bulletin of Latin American Research* 25, no. 2 (2006): 241–263.

Convention on Biological Diversity. Report of the Global Thematic Dialogue for Indigenous Peoples and Local Communities on the Post-2020 Global Biodiversity Framework. Montreal: Convention on Biological Diversity, 2019.

Convention on Biological Diversity. *The Rutzolijirisaxik Voluntary Guidelines for the Repatriation of Traditional Knowledge of Indigenous Peoples and Local Communities Relevant for the Conservation and Sustainable Use of Biological Diversity*. Montreal: Convention on Biological Diversity, 2018.

Convention on Biological Diversity. *Mo' Otz Kuxtal Voluntary Guidelines*. Montreal: Convention on Biological Diversity, 2019. https://www.cbd.int/doc/publications/8j-cbd-mootz-kuxtal-en.pdf.

Cepek, Michael L. "There Might Be Blood: Oil, Humility, and the Cosmopolitics of a Cofán Petro-Being." *American Ethnologist* 43, no. 4 (2016): 623–635. https://doi.org/10.1111/amet.12379.

Diaz, Sandra, S. Demissew, J. Carabias, C. Joly, M. Lonsdale, N. Ash, A. Larigauderie, and al. "The IPBES Conceptual Frramework – Connecting Nature and People." *Current Opinion in Environmental Sustainability* 14, (2015): 1–16.

Dove, Michael R. "Indigenous People and Environmental Politics." *Annual Review of Anthropology*, no. 35, (2006): 191–208.

Dunbar, William. "From Biocultural Diversity to a Nature-Culture Alliance." The Nature of Cities (blog), 17 mars 2019. https://www.thenatureofcities.com/2019/03/17/biocultural-diversity-nature-culture-alliance/.

Escobar, Arturo. "Cultural Politics and Biological Diversity: State, Capital, and Social Movements in the Pacific Coast of Colombia." In *The Politics of Culture in the Shadow of Capital*, edited by Lisa Lowe, David Lloyd, Stanley Fish, and Fredric Jameson, 201–226. New-York: Duke University Press, 1997. https://www.degruyter.com/document/doi/10.1515/9780822382317-008/html.

Escobar, Arturo. "Whose Knowledge, Whose Nature? Biodiversity, Conservation, and the Political Ecology of Social Movements." *Journal of Political Ecology* 5, no. 1 (1998): 53–82.

Escobar, Arturo. "After Nature: Steps to an Antiessentialist Political Ecology." *Current Anthropology* 40, no. 1 (1999): 1–30. https://doi.org/10.1086/515799.

Escobar, Arturo. "Latin America at a Crossroads." *Cultural Studies* 24, no. 1 (2010): 1–65. https://doi.org/10.1080/09502380903424208.

Fabricant, Nicole, Nancy Postero. "Performing Indigeneity in Bolivia: The Struggle Over the TIPNIS/Executando Indigeneidade Na Bolivia: A Luta Pelo TIPNIS. (Report)." *Anthropological Quarterly* 91, no. 3 (2018): 905–36. https://doi.org/10.1353/anq.2018.0044.

Foyer, Jean, ed. *Regards croisés sur Rio+20: la modernisation écologique à l'épreuve*. Paris: Centre National de la Recherche Scientifique, 2015.

Friis, Justine. "La participation des peuples autochtones et communautés locales dans les instances internationales: le cas de la Convention sur la diversité biologique." Internship Report, Master's degree in environment and sustainable development, Université de Montréal, 2020.

Gill, Sam D. *Mother Earth: An American Story*. Chicago: University of Chicago Press, 1991.

Girard, Fabien, Ingrid Hall, and Christine Frison, eds. *Biocultural Rights, Indigenous Peoples and Local Communities*. London: Routledge, 2022.

González, Pablo Alonso, and Alfredo Macías Vázquez. "An Ontological Turn in the Debate on Buen Vivir – Sumak Kawsay in Ecuador: Ideology, Knowledge, and the Common." *Latin American and Caribbean Ethnic Studies* 10, no. 3 (2015): 315–334. https://doi.org/10.1080/17442222.2015.1056070.

Graddy-Lovelace, Garrett. "From Obstruction to Decolonization?: Contested Sovereignty, the Seed Treaty, and Biocultural Rights in the U.S./Turtle Island and Beyond." In *Biocultural Rights, Indigenous Peoples and Local Communities*, edited by Fabien Girard, Ingrid Hall, and Christine Frison, 141–164. London: Routledge, 2022.

Gros, Christian. "Nationaliser l'Indien, ethniciser la nation. L'Amérique latine face au multiculturalisme." In *Être indien dans les Amériques: spoliations et résistance: mobilisations ethniques et politiques du multiculturalisme*, edited by Christian Gros, and Marie-Claude Feltes-Strigler, 263–272. Paris: Éditions de l'Institut des hautes études de l'Amérique latine, 2006.

Hale, Charles R. "Cultural Politics of Identity in Latin America." *Annual Review of Anthropology* 35, (2006): 191–208.

Hall, Ingrid. "Sumaq Kawsay (Good Living) and Indigenous Potatoes: On the Delicate Exercise of Ontological Diplomacy." In *Biocultural Rights, Indigenous Peoples and Local Communities*, edited by Fabien Girard, Ingrid Hall, and Christine Frison, 90–111. London: Routledge, 2022.

Hall, Ingrid. "Unmaking the Nature/Culture Divide: The Ontological Diplomacy of Indigenous Peoples and Local Communities at the CBD." In *Biocultural Rights, Indigenous Peoples and Local Communities*, edited by Fabien Girard, Ingrid Hall, and Christine Frison, 112–140. Durham & London: Routledge, 2022.

Harris, Olivia. "The Mythological Figure of the Earth Mother." In *To Make the Earth Bear Fruit: Ethnographic Essays on Fertility, Work and Gender in Highland Bolivia*, 201–219. London: Institute of Latin American Studies, 2000.

Hermitte, Marie-Angèle. "La Convention sur la diversité biologique." *Annuaire français de droit international* 38, no. 1 (1992): 844–870. https://doi.org/10.3406/afdi.1992.3098.

Hermitte, Marie-Angèle. "Souveraineté, peuples autochtones: le partage équitable des ressources et des connaissances." In *La Bioéquité. Batailles autour du partage du vivant*, edited by Florence Bellivier, and Christine Noiville, 115–135. Paris: Autrement, 2009. http://www.cairn.info/article.php?ID_ARTICLE=AUTRE_BELLI_2009_01_0115.

Hermitte, Marie-Angèle. "La nature, sujet de droit?" *Annales. Histoire, Sciences Sociales* 66, no. 1 (2011): 173–212.

Hidalgo-Capitán, Antonio Luis, and Ana Patricia Cubillo-Guevara. "Deconstruction and Genealogy of Latin American Good Living (Buen Vivir). The (Triune) Good Living and Its Diverse Intellectual Wellsprings." *International Development Policy* 9, no. 9 (2017): 23–50. https://doi.org/10.4000/poldev.2351.

Igoe, Jim. "The Spectacle of Nature in the Global Economy of Appearances: Anthropological Engagements with the Spectacular Mediations of Transnational Conservation." *Critique of Anthropology* 30, no. 4 (2010): 375–97. https://doi.org/10.1177/0308275X10372468.

IPBES. 2022. "Summary for Policymakers of the Methodological Assessment of the Diverse Values and Valuation of Nature of the Intergovernmental Science-Policy Platform on Biodiversity and Ecosystem Services (IPBES) | Zenodo." IPBES Secretariat. https://zenodo.org/record/6522393#.ZEazOPaZNPa.

Krech, Shepard. *The Ecological Indian: Myth and History*. New York: W.W. Norton & Co., 1999.

Kurasawa, Fuyuki. "A Cosmopolitanism from Below: Alternative Globalization and the Creation of a Solidarity without Bounds." *European Journal of Sociology* 45, no. 2 (2004): 233–255. https://doi.org/10.1017/S0003975604001444.

Landivar, Diego, and Emilie Ramillien. "Reconfigurations ontologiques dans les nouvelles constitutions politiques andines." *Tsantsa, revue de la Société suisse d'ethnologie* 20, (2015): 29–40.

Larrère, Catherine. "Éthiques de l'environnement." *Multitudes* 24, no. 1 (2006): 75–84.

Larrère, Catherine. "Les éthiques environnementales." *Natures Sciences Sociétés* 18, no. 4 (2012): 405–413.

Latour, Bruno. *Politiques de la nature: comment faire entrer les sciences en démocratie*. Paris: La Découverte, 2004.

Latour, Bruno. "Quel cosmos? Quelles cosmopolitiques?" In *L'émergence des cosmopolitiques*, edited by Jacques Lolive, and Olivier Souberyran, 69–84. Paris: La Découverte, 2007. https://www.cairn.info/article.php?ID_ARTICLE=DEC_LOLIV_2007_01_0069.

Le Prestre, Philippe G. *Governing Global Biodiversity the Evolution and Implementation of the Convention on Biological Diversity*. London/New York: Routledge, 2017.

Maffi, Luisa. *On Biocultural Diversity: Linking Language, Knowledge, and the Environment*. Washington, DC: Smithsonian Insitute Press, 2001.

Michon, Geneviève, Catherine Aubertin, Hubert de Foresta, and Patrice Levang. "Du discours global aux pratiques locales, ou comment les conventions sur l'environnement affectent la gestion de la forêt tropicale." In *Développement durable? Doctrines, pratiques, évaluations*, edited by Jean-Yves Martin, and Guillaume Leroy, 183–203. Paris: IRD, 2002. http://www.documentation.ird.fr/hor/fdi:010029275.

Mignolo, Walter. "On Pluriversality," 20 octobre 2013. http://waltermignolo.com/on-pluriversality/.

Morin, Françoise. *La déclaration des Nations Unies sur les droits des peuples autochtones à l'épreuve du temps (2007–2012)*. Montréal: DIALOG et INRS, 2012.

Parks, Louisa. "Spaces for Local Voices? A Discourse Analysis of the Decisions of the Convention on Biological Diversity." *Journal of Human Rights and the Environment* 9, no. 2 (2018): 141–170. http://dx.doi.org/10.4337/jhre.2018.02.02.

Parks, Louisa, and Mika Schröder. *What We Talk about When We Talk about 'Local' Participation in International Biodiversity Law. The Changing Scope of Indigenous Peoples and Local Communities Participation under the Convention on Biological Diversity.* Lecce: University of Salento, 2018. https://doi.org/10.1285/I20356609V11I3P743.

Posey, Darrell A., *Cultural and Spiritual Values of Biodiversity: A Complementary Contribution to the Global Biodiversity Assessment.* Nairobi: PNUD/Intermediate technology publications, 1997.

Posey, Darrell A., and Graham Dutfield. « Déclaration de Belem », 1988. http://www.ethnobiology.net/wp-content/uploads/Decl-of-Belem-in-French.pdf.

Povinelli, Elizabeth A. "Do Rocks Listen? The Cultural Politics of Apprehending Australian Aboriginal Labor." *American Anthropologist* 97, no. 3 (1995): 505–518.

Povinelli, Elizabeth A. "Reading Ruptures, Rupturing Readings: Mabo and the Cultural Politics of Activism." *Social Analysis: The International Journal of Social and Cultural Practice* 41, no. 2 (1997): 20–28.

Povinelli, Elizabeth A. "The Rhetorics of Recognition in Geontopower." *Philosophy & Rhetoric* 48, no. 4 (2015): 428–442.

Ramos, Alcida. "The Hyperreal Indian." *Critique of Anthropology* 14, no. 2 (1994): 153–171. https://doi.org/10.1177/0308275X9401400203.

Reimerson, Elsa. "Between Nature and Culture: Exploring Space for Indigenous Agency in the Convention on Biological Diversity." *Environmental Politics* 22, no. 6 (2013): 992–1009. https://doi.org/10.1080/09644016.2012.737255.

Sousa Santos (de), Boaventurade, Joao Arriscado Nunes, and Maria Paula Meneses. "Opening up the Canon of Knowledge and Recognition of Diference." In *Another Knowledge Is Possible: Beyond Northern Epistemologies*, edited by Boaventura Sousa Santos (de), XIX–LXII. London: Verso, 2007. http://www.boaventuradesousasantos.pt/media/Introduction(3).pdf.

Stengers, Isabelle. "The Cosmopolitical Proposal." In *Making Things Public*, edited by Bruno Latour, and Peter Weibel, 994–1003. Cambridge: MIT Press, 2005. http://mnissen.psy.ku.dk/Undervisning/Stengers05.pdf.

Suiseeya, Kimberly R. Marion. "Negotiating the Nagoya Protocol: Indigenous Demands for Justice." *Global Environmental Politics* 14, no. 3 (2014): 102–124.

Terán, Maria Yolanda. "The Nagoya Protocol and Indigenous Peoples." *International Indigenous Policy Journal* 7 (April 2016). https://doi.org/10.18584/iipj.2016.7.2.6.

Thomas, Frédéric, and Valérie Boisvert, eds. *Le pouvoir de la biodiversité: néolibéralisation de la nature dans les pays émergents*. Marseille and Versailles: IRD éditions and Éditions Quae, 2015.

Tsing, Anna Lowenhaupt. *Friction: An Ethnography of Global Connection*. Princeton, NJ: Princeton University Press, 2005.

Tsing, Anna Lowenhaupt. "Indigenous Voice." In *Indigenous Experience Today*, edited by Marisol de la Cadena, and Orin Starn, 33–68. Oxford and New York: Berg, 2007.

Ulloa, Astrid. *The Ecological Native. Indigenous Peoples' Movements and Eco-Governmentality in Colombia*. New York and London: Routledge, 2010.

Verschuuren, Bas, ed. *Sacred Natural Sites: Conserving Nature and Culture*. London: Washington, D.C.: Earthscan, 2010.

Viveiros de Castro, Eduardo. *Cannibal Metaphysics*. Translated by Peter Skafish. Online resource (230 pages). Univocal Publishing. Minneapolis: University of Minnesota Press, 2014. http://site.ebrary.com/id/11152875.

Spiritual, Religious or Cultural? Religion and Sámi Human Rights in the Nordic Countries

Helge Årsheim

The religious freedom of Indigenous peoples is a neglected topic in the Nordic countries.[1] While all the countries in the region support and commit to European and International human rights regimes – including strong support for the movement for the rights of Indigenous peoples – the role of Indigenous religious beliefs and practices and the rights claims these may generate has been largely overlooked by human rights activists, politicians, and scholars. The reasons for this negligence are complex and vary between the Nordic countries. Nevertheless, some general, key characteristics and features of the Indigenous peoples, their religious histories and present outlooks, and the different roles they play in the political orders of the Nordic countries may provide at least a partial explanation.

First, Indigenous religiosity was explicitly seen as something to be eradicated by the early modern nation states in the region, all of which were strongly confessionally tied to Evangelical Lutheranism, with the Eastern regions also featuring considerable influence from Orthodox Christianity. Largely unaffected by the movements towards greater religious toleration that followed in continental Europe in the wake of the Reformation in the 16th century and the "Westphalian moment" in modern statecraft, the Nordic states tended towards confessional absolutism from the 17th century onwards, with draconian laws to preserve and maintain Lutheran orthodoxy at all social, political, and legal levels. The intolerance of the early modern Nordic countries was clearly articulated in the concerted efforts to eliminate and repress the traditional beliefs and religious practices among the Sámi. Throughout the region, albeit with varying intensity, overlapping intentions and occasional competition, the Sámi were subjected

1 While there is no official definition of "Nordic" countries, the term is conventionally used to refer to Norway, Sweden, Denmark, Finland, and Iceland. For the purposes of this chapter, the "Nordic" epithet will be used to denote Norway, Finland, and Sweden, unless otherwise specified, mainly because of their shared and overlapping responsibility to protect the rights of the Sámi, which is a heterogenous family of Indigenous peoples that live in and across the borders of these states. Another option would have been to use the internationally well-established term "Scandinavia," but this term refers to Norway, Sweden, and Denmark, and is based on their shared proximity to the South Swedish landscape historically referred to as "Scandia," which is roughly equivalent to the present-day region of Skåne.

 | DOI:10.1163/9789004524330_004

to missionary expeditions and initiatives that were driven by the combined purpose to eradicate traditional beliefs and religious practices and to replace them with Christianity, as a part of what was perceived to be a "civilizing mission."[2] As a result, the worldviews and practices of pre-Christian Sámi religion are poorly understood, and do not represent a major aspect of contemporary Sámi self-understanding.[3]

Second, throughout the 20th century, the Sámi rights struggle has been dominated by efforts to challenge the main pillars of assimilation policies across the Nordic region: language, culture, land ownership, and land use. From official apologies for forced schooling in the majority language and the taxed mountains case in Sweden in the 1980s, to the Alta controversy over hydroelectric dam construction in Norway (1978–1980), the rise of Indigenous rights concerns in the region in the post-War era and the gradual dismantling of assimilationist policies can largely be attributed to battles fought over language use and land rights. Across these instances, which have been instrumental to the creation and galvanization of the Sámi rights movement, religious beliefs and practices have been virtually non-existent among the concerns raised.

Third, Indigenous rights activism in the Nordic countries has always been strongly connected to the international movement for Indigenous peoples' rights, holding the same deep concerns about self-determination and cultural integrity that have been instrumental to this movement. Although spiritual and religious concerns featured already in the landmark study of Indigenous rights issues conducted by the UN-appointed special rapporteur José Martínez Cobo in 1982, their influence on the formation and institutionalization of the Indigenous rights movement has until recently been negligible. In the major international legal frameworks for Indigenous rights – International Labour Organization (ILO) Convention no. 169 (1989) and the UN Declaration on the Rights of Indigenous Peoples (UNDRIP, 2007) – religious beliefs and practices are primarily protected as a subset of the relationship between Indigenous peoples and their ownership and use of land, although the latter instrument may open the door for more comprehensive formulations of Indigenous religious freedom (see below).

Despite the near eradication of Sámi religious beliefs during Christianization and the lack of emphasis on religion in both the national, regional, and

2 While there is reliable evidence that the Sámi had encountered Christianity from at least the 11th century and onwards, concerted efforts towards conversion were not started until the 17th century. By this time, several Sámi groups were already Christianized, often with substantial intermingling between Christian and traditional beliefs and practices.

3 This is a generalization – see below for a more nuanced depiction of the situation.

international movements for Indigenous rights, there are signs that this situation may be gradually changing. Interest in and knowledge of pre-Christian Sámi religious beliefs and practices is growing, both among scholars and among Sámi communities; the conservation and protection of sacred landscapes and artefacts is becoming more important to Sámi rights activists, and the role of Indigenous worldviews and practices are becoming increasingly important to environmental and cultural heritage protection initiatives, respectively.

This chapter sets out to map and discuss these changes – how they have come about, and what their consequences for the future of Indigenous religious rights in the Nordic region may be. The argument is developed in five steps: first, a brief presentation of the Sámi; second, an outline of the Sámi rights struggle and its intertwinement with the international movement for Indigenous rights; third, a discussion of contemporary notions of pre- and post-Christian Sámi religious beliefs and practices; fourth, a mapping of existing standards for the protection of human rights in the Nordic countries, with a particular emphasis on the legal framework on religion; and fifth, a discussion of the potential influence of the protections for religion in the UNDRIP in the Nordic countries, including a set of case studies where Sámi religious beliefs and practices have been evoked to strengthen their rights claims.

1 The Sámi

The Sámi live in the Northwesternmost reaches of the Eurasian continent, in Norway, Sweden, Finland, and Russia. There is no official registry or roster of the Sámi, and estimations of their population vary from 50 000 to 100 000, with the majority living in the border areas between the Norwegian county Finnmark and the Finnish county Lapland, both of which have been named after earlier names for the Sámi.[4] The Sámi can be subdivided in numerous subgroups according to geography, cultural practices, and language. Despite

4 The term "lapp" has been used in all languages spoken by neighboring peoples to the Sámi. While the etymology is uncertain, it may be derived from a tool used in trade with the Sámi, and the first known written source using the term dates to the 11th century CE. "Finn," whose precise etymology is also uncertain, dates to at least the 1st century CE through the writings of Tacitus, enters the vocabulary used to categorize the Sámi in the 13th century, and has been more widespread in the Western areas, while "lapp" has been dominant in the Eastern area. Neither term has any relation to the self-designations used in any of the Sámi languages and can as such be seen as a category imposed from the outside. Because of the increasingly racist policies against the Sámi in the early modern area, the terms have become associated with these policies and were rejected by the early Sámi rights movement. (cf. Berg-Nordlie 2021a; Berg-Nordlie 2021b).

the internal diversity among the Sámi, the concerns of the Sámi community tend to be conflated with those of the Northern Sámi, whose language and cultural practices have the widest and most recognized distribution.[5]

The area in which the Sámi have traditionally resided is collectively known as Sápmi (see Figure 1). It stretches from Trondheim in the middle of Norway, via Norrland in Sweden and to the Kola peninsula in Russia. Although there are no formal boundaries to this area, it is widely recognized as the Sámi "heartland" in the Nordic countries, and in Russia, where the Sámi are a recognized ethnic minority – although not an Indigenous people. Unlike Indigenous peoples in settler societies, the Sámi have always interacted to a greater or lesser degree with other peoples in their vicinity, including the majority populations further south. Their distinctiveness from these other populations have been a major topic of contention in Nordic historiography, but there appears to be a consensus today about the fact that differences between a proto-Sámi population group and a proto-Germanic population group developed over the course of the first millennium AD (Hansen and Olsen 2022). These differences occurred partly because of interactions with neighboring societies – the Northern groups interacting Eastwards towards Siberia, the Southern groups interacting Southwards towards continental Europe, and partly because of socio-economic changes along the coastal areas of Sápmi (Hansen and Olsen 2022: 41). Despite gradually evolving differences, there is undisputed evidence that interactions have been continuous and comprehensive between these groups, cultural and linguistic differences notwithstanding. The written sources that have come down to us from the Norse cultures interacting with the Sámi in the early centuries after 1000 AD bear evidence of a respectful distance, in which the Sámi are valued trade partners, while also being perceived as powerful sorcerers, magicians, and truth tellers with hidden powers (Hansen and Olsen 2022: 62).

Through the combined forces of increased economic integration with lands further south, increased settlements of non-Sámi settlers in Sápmi, and the Christianization of the Norse cultures, the relative stability of medieval Sámi-Norse interactions gradually changed and became more strained (Hansen and Olsen 2022: 139). From the 1200s and onwards, the Sámi were increasingly beset with overlapping regimes of taxation, economically and politically motivated settlements in the coastal areas to exploit the increasingly important fisheries, and confessionally oriented states that established new parishes and churches

5 This chapter also adopts this tendency – Sámi placenames and other Sámi terms will be rendered in Northern Sámi. The cultural practices that are discussed most extensively are also those of Northern Sámi, because they are the ones that had the largest impact on the legal and political recognition of Sámi rights as an Indigenous people.

FIGURE 1 Sápmi
WIKIMEDIA COMMONS

throughout the region. As the embryonic Nordic nation states formed in the 16th century, the interests in regulating and taxing trade in Sápmi grew, complemented by increasingly expansionist national churches and their missionaries, who took an interest in Christianizing the Sámi population, which still mostly adhered to their own religious beliefs and practices.

These converging pressure points, combined with the rising ideology of nationalism that presumed nation states to be ethnically and linguistically homogeneous, gave rise to the 19th century policies aiming toward the assimilation of the Sámi. This process was most strongly pronounced in Norway and Sweden, where educational policies towards the Sámi were based on the eradication of the Sámi language and their forced introduction into formal citizenship status. These processes continued throughout the first half of the 20th century but were gradually dismantled in the decades following World War II, in the wake of the incipient international Indigenous rights movement.

2 Sámi Human Rights Struggles

Throughout the post-War period, Sámi rights activism grew, partly inspired by international movements, partly in resistance to assimilation attempts by the Nordic nation states, and partly in opposition to gradual encroachments on land in Sápmi. A high-water mark in this process was the establishment of the Sámi Council in 1956, an international non-governmental organization working to promote the rights of the Sámi in Norway, Sweden, Finland, and Russia.[6] The Sámi Council has been instrumental to the consolidation of cross-border issues that concern the Sámi people as a whole. Among the Nordic states, Finland was the first to establish a "State Committees on Sámi Affairs" (in 1949–1951 and 1971–1973), resulting in the establishment, in 1972, of a democratically elected advisory body to the Parliament, the Sámi Delegation (Müller-Wille 1979).

Court cases have been key to the evolving Sámi rights movement. In Sweden, the taxed mountains case (1981) and in Norway the Alta hydroelectric dam case (1982) were both determined in disfavour of Sámi interests and rights relating to reindeer herding and land ownership. Nevertheless, the cases helped highlight unresolved tensions between Sámi rights perceptions and the rights of developers and the State to expropriate and use land in Sápmi. They led to the establishment of law commissions that were given the task of drafting a more comprehensive legal framework for the interactions between the Nordic states and the Sámi. The Norwegian commission delivered its report in 1984, proposing a wholesale legal reform that included constitutional recognition of the cultural, linguistic, and social rights of the Sámi (adopted in 1988), and the establishment of a Sámi Parliament (inaugurated in 1989). The Swedish commission delivered its report in 1989, echoing many of the proposals of the Norwegian commission and resulting in the creation of a Swedish Sámi Parliament (inaugurated in 1993), but stopping short of granting constitutional recognition of the rights of the Sámi. In Finland, the advisory capacity of the Sámi Delegation went through comprehensive reforms from 1990 onwards, resulting in the establishment of a Sámi Parliament (inaugurated in 1996) modelled on the Norwegian and Swedish institutions. Following the establishment of these institutions, and the increasing influence of international law on the human rights framework in each of the Nordic countries, "Sámi law" has emerged as a "distinctive as well as autonomous" legal discipline (Allard and Skogvang 2015: 4) that cuts through several established legal disciplines.[7]

6 The original name of the organization was the Nordic Sami Council. At the 15th Sami conference in Helsinki in 1992, the Council admitted its first Russian member organization, and removed "Nordic" from its name, becoming for the first time a truly pan-Sámi organization (Berg-Nordlie 2021c).

7 Because of the holistic nature of Sámi rights claims, Sámi law brings together perspectives from most areas of Norwegian law, including, but not limited to: international law, customary

Although the emergence of Sámi law and the expansion of mechanisms through which the Sámi can gain recognition of their rights represent an important development in the interactions between the Sámi and the Nordic nation states, several cases remain unresolved. This is particularly in relation to land use and land ownership, where several high-profile court cases have been heard in the Nordic court systems over the course of the last years.[8] A key concern throughout these cases has been the scope and range of the term "culture" under the International Covenant on Civil and Political Rights (ICCPR) Article 27, which has become the most frequently used provision in international human rights law in matters concerning the rights of Indigenous peoples.[9] Crucially, while the article protects "ethnic, religious or linguistic minorities," it is the right of such minorities to "enjoy their own culture," and not the complementary right to "profess and practice their own religion," that has been most closely associated with the plight of Indigenous peoples, both internationally and in the Nordic countries. More recent international law instruments on the rights of Indigenous peoples – the UNDRIP in particular – provide protections for the spiritual and religious rights of Indigenous peoples but have so far failed to gain significant traction in the legal systems of the Nordic countries (see below).

3 Sámi Religion

In the centuries of writing on Sámi beliefs and behaviours, the term "religion" is used only sparingly, as their worldviews and ritual practices have been more commonly designated pejoratively as sorcery, paganism, heathenism, superstition, witchcraft, magic, or, crucially, "shamanism," due to perceived structural similarities between the role of the Sámi religious specialist – the *noaidi* – and

law, property law, law on child protection, torts law, penal law, laws on area management, hunting, animal welfare, fisheries, language, education, cultural heritage, and nature conservation (Skogvang 2022).

8 Among the most high-profile cases are the Nordmaling case (NJA 2011, s. 109), the Rönnbäcken case (Swedish Supreme Administrative Court, 443-11), the Girjas case (T 853-18), the Selbu case (Rt. 2001 p. 769), the Svartskogen case (2001 p. 1229), the Stjernøya case (HR-2016-2030-A), the Nesseby case (HR-2018-456-P), the Saarivuoma case (HR-2021-1429-A) and the Fosen case (HR-2021-1975-S) (cf. Ravna 2021; Mörkenstam 2019).

9 Despite the gradually evolving range of instruments that offer specific protections for Indigenous peoples, the ICCPR Article 27 remains the single most important legal instrument for Indigenous peoples, partly because of its early emergence in 1966, and partly because of its inscription into the ICCPR and attendant monitoring by the UN Human Rights Committee, by far the most authoritative of the UN human rights "treaty bodies."

the "shamans" of other peoples in the circumpolar North (Kaikkonen 2020). These designations have been instrumental to persistent efforts to marginalize and repress Sámi beliefs and practices in exchange for Catholic, Orthodox, and Lutheran forms of Christianity.

The written sources that are available to us that detail the contents and practices of Sámi religion were created from the 16th century onwards, several hundred years after the Sámi encountered various forms of Christianity for the first time. Hence, the religion depicted by missionaries had already been interacting and interchanging with Christian beliefs and practices for centuries, and we have no way of indicating what a truly "pre-Christian" Sámi worldview would have consisted of. Today, "Sámi religion" can be used in (at least) four different ways. First, to designate folk beliefs and practices that are predominant among the Sámi but have merged with elements from Christianity. This is by far the most fuzzy and non-specific form of Sámi religion, but it is also likely to be the most widespread, as most of the Sámi are – at least nominally and habitually – Evangelical Lutherans. This form of Sámi religion is constituted not through the establishment of canons, formal institutions or prescribed rituals, but through everyday practices, or "ways of life" (Pollan 2005: 414). Second, Sámi religion can designate distinctive cultural and spiritual practices, particularly related to land use and ritualized offerings at designated offering places (*sieidi*s). These practices are inseparable from the local contexts and configurations of which they are part, and they vary considerably among the different parts of Sápmi. Third, Sámi religion can be used to designate a variety of new religious movements. Most of these movements characterize their worldviews and practices as shamanistic or neo-shamanistic and merge aspects from international trends, such as the "Mother Earth" movement, with local practices, from drum sessions to sweat lodges and a range of other ritualized practices. Fourth, Sámi religion can be used to designate the worldviews and practices that are described in the written accounts of missionaries working in Sápmi from the 16th century and onwards, and that can be inferred from the still growing archaeological evidence of ritualized activities in Sápmi. This way of depicting Sámi religion is by far the most prevalent in textbooks and introductory texts on religion in the Nordic countries and the circumpolar areas, and for all means and purposes it represents the most deeply engrained and embedded notion of Sámi religion in the Nordic societies today (Andreassen and Olsen 2020; Berglund 2013). This list is neither exhaustive, nor are the items exclusive – multiple other meanings can be attributed to the term "Sámi religion," and the boundaries between each of the four different meanings listed above are fluid and subject to continuous contestation and negotiation.

Although the complexity of determining the boundaries of any "religion" is more or less universally recognized within the field of religious studies, the colonialist and assimilationist legacy further exacerbates this task in the case of Sámi religion. As alluded to in the introduction of this chapter, these difficulties are among the likely explanations for the lack of religion and spirituality in the Sámi human rights struggle: without the defining characteristics of religiosity presupposed by international human rights law, the formulation of rights claims related to religion have not been seen as a relevant addition to the cause for increased recognition of the rights of the Sámi.

4 Legal Protections for Religion in the Nordic Countries

The Nordic nation states that emerged from the gradual development from absolutism to constitutional monarchies – and, in the case of Finland, republic – adopted an altogether different view of religious toleration from their predecessor states. Legal guarantees for religious freedom were adopted in Finland (1923), Sweden (1951) and Norway (1964),[10] and have since been gradually adjusted to keep in line with developments in international human rights law, notably the Universal Declaration of Human Rights (1948), the European Convention on Human Rights (ECHR, 1950), and the ICCPR (1966), all of which have been turned into binding legal provisions in each of the Nordic countries. Despite a long-standing tradition of established churches in the region, today, all churches are formally disestablished, but they retain a "special relationship" with the State that includes substantial economic contributions to their operations. To safeguard the rights of other religious communities, all religious organizations are eligible for some economic support, albeit with some technical differences, and subject to continuous revisions, as the management of eligible religious communities has become a battleground issue in debates about multiculturalism and integration, particularly in Norway, where the legal framework was recently substantially revised (Årsheim 2021). In addition to protections for the freedom of religion or belief and for religious organizations, all the Nordic countries have adopted extensive legal protections against indirect and direct religious discrimination, in private and public matters, in the workplace and in housing.

10 Whereas Sweden and Finland have separate religious freedom laws, Norway has a constitutional provision on religious freedom. For an overview of the different legal frameworks, see EUREL – Sociological and legal data on religions in Europe and beyond, https://www.eurel.info/?lang=en.

The boundaries of "religion" for legal matters are maintained and negotiated through a fine-grained web of legal provisions that, together and over time, have amalgamated into a distinctive legal subfield, or "religion law" – not unlike the gradual development of Sámi law discussed above.[11] These regulations govern the role of religion in refugee protection, burial, marriage, taxation, conscription, incarceration, education, animal welfare, kindergartens, zoning, data protection, health service provision and much else. Although the majority of these regulations simply paraphrase international legal materials on the duty of the State to provide for and accommodate the freedom of religion or belief in a variety of different settings, contextual factors tend to significantly influence these considerations, effectively adding new and specific interpretative layers to the otherwise bare words of international law materials.[12] Significantly, the sum total of such regulations can be decisive to the very taxonomy and repertoire, not only of law and the legal process, but of social movements, rights movements, and ultimately also the self-identification of individuals, through the process of "legal framing" (Årsheim and Slotte 2017).

The gradual development of religion law in the Nordic countries has happened in close interaction with similar developments internationally, and in particular through the growing influence of the case-law of the European Court of Human Rights (ECtHR), which oversees the implementation of the ECHR. Several landmark decisions from the court have been decisive to the management of religion in the Nordic countries, from the *Folgerø v. Norway* (case no. 15472/02, 2007) decision that found the religious education in Norwegian primary schools to be in violation of the convention and its optional protocol, to the *S.A.S. v. France* (case no. 43835/11, 2014) decision, which found the French ban on the niqab to be acceptable, opening up the possibility of similar bans in the Nordic countries.

The development of Nordic religion law has had little to no effect on Sámi law, as the prevalent forms of Sámi religion (see above) have failed to register with available legal forms. In Nordic religion law, as in international human rights law more generally, beliefs that attain "a certain level of cogency, seriousness, cohesion and importance" are front and centre of any legal discussion that relates to religion or spirituality.[13] While the proper methodology for identification, standard of evidence, and relative weight of such beliefs tend to vary

11 For a theoretical discussion of "religion law," see Sandberg 2011.

12 For an appreciation of contextual factors in different domains, see Årsheim and Slotte 2017; Årsheim 2021.

13 This standard was established by the predecessor to the ECtHR, the European Commission on Human Rights, in the case *Campbell and Cosans v. United Kingdom* (1982) and has since been affirmed by the court on numerous occasions. No similar standard has been

considerably between different cases, the necessity of some form of belief for communities and individuals that wish to gain access to the rights associated with religion under international human rights law remains.[14]

Additional to the presupposition that belief is the primary criterion for the legal conception of religion is the requirement that any external "manifestation" of religion – in worship, prayer, dress, observance, teaching, or any other dimension – must be linked to belief to be eligible for legal protection. This requirement, that there should be a "nexus" between the "inner" and "outer" dimensions of religion, has been crucial to the exclusion of Indigenous religion from the ambit of international legal protections for religion. Unlike the more widely recognized "world religions," Indigenous religious forms tend to lend themselves less readily to the belief-manifestation nexus expected by international law. While generalizing about Indigenous religions in themselves represents a host of definitional problems (Kaikkonen 2020; Hartney and Tower 2017; Tafjord 2012), the narrowness with which the international legal protection for religion has been constructed is well-documented and affects not only Indigenous peoples, but a broad range of minorities whose convictions and practices do not fit the template offered by international and domestic human rights law (Bielefeldt, Ghanea and Wiener 2016: 437).

5 Religionizing Indigenous Rights

Over the course of the last decades, the international movement for the recognition of Indigenous peoples' rights has increasingly coalesced and become enmeshed with parallel rights movements that have formed to promote cultural heritage, environmental sustainability, and to fight climate change and biodiversity loss. Across these efforts, Indigenous peoples have emerged as key collaborators and force multipliers, acting with the coming generations in mind, as the embodiment and continuation of a bygone era of sustainable custodianship and more gentle land use. The role of Indigenous peoples in these parallel rights movements has been highlighted in several political and legal instruments, from the Convention on Biological Diversity (CBD, 1992) and the operational guidelines of the World Heritage Convention (1972), to the

developed by the UN Human Rights Committee, which oversees the implementation of the ICCPR.

14 The pre-eminence of belief in the understanding of religion in international law is attested by the technical adjustment of the designation of religious communities, which have been characterized as "religion or belief communities."

UN Framework Convention on Climate Change (1994), the development of the UN Agenda 2030, and the Sustainable Development Goals (2015).

Across these instruments, Indigenous peoples are given key roles as purveyors of sustainable practices that can be instructive to form a more holistic world order, but they are also portrayed as important victims of the combined ecological and climatic crises that face humanity. This view of Indigenous peoples echoes the much-derided Enlightenment stereotype of the "noble savage," but with an ecological twist. Indigenous peoples are seen to have "knowledge, innovation and practices [that embody] traditional lifestyles relevant for the conservation and sustainable use of biological diversity,"[15] their agricultural practices "can contribute to overcoming the combined challenges of climate change, food security, biodiversity conservation, and combating desertification and land degradation,"[16] while their land management practices and "traditional and Indigenous knowledge" can contribute to the conservation of World Heritage properties.[17]

Arguably, these ideas about the role of Indigenous peoples as custodians of nature is hardwired into the notion of indigeneity itself. Growing out of the early post-War rights movement, the movement for Indigenous rights has always been based on a conception of indigeneity that presupposes a separate status defined by historical continuity, local knowledge, and considerate and sustainable land use and land possession. The emphasis on these qualities in the post-War era is not coincidental but aligns closely with growing criticism towards earlier views of development, modernization, and assimilation in the pursuit of ethnically and culturally homogenous nation states, elements that have come to be associated with repressive political regimes and cultural, social, and environmental destruction.

Despite long-standing critiques from anthropological researchers sceptical of the accuracy of the portrayal of Indigenous peoples as specialists of conservation, ecological land use, and sustainability (cf. Nadasdy 2005; Raymond 2007), the image of the "ecological noble savage" persists, and has been put to use also in the Nordic countries, where Sámi lifeways have increasingly come to represent a more wholesome, holistic, and environmentally friendly management of natural resources than those of the rest of society. Amalgamating with claims towards repatriation, reconciliation, and restoring former injustices, the argument that Sámi lifeways are inherently sustainable has become central

15 CBD, Article 8(j).

16 Intergovernmental Panel on Climate Change, 2019, https://lcipp.unfccc.int/homepage.

17 UNESCO. World Heritage and Indigenous peoples. https://whc.unesco.org/en/activities/496/.

to the rights claims of the Sámi. From reindeer herding[18] to duck hunting,[19] Sámi practices have been portrayed as ecologically sustainable, adding on to their crucial role as carriers of cultural cohesion and belonging.

The depiction of Indigenous peoples as custodians of nature and carriers of knowledge and practices that are crucial to the wellbeing of the planet finds one of its most potent expressions in the international legal provisions that stress and safeguard the spiritual relationship they cultivate with their land. The ILO Convention no. 169, Article 7, and the UNDRIP, Article 25 both stress the spiritual relationship between Indigenous peoples and the lands that they have traditionally occupied. These articles require states parties to create efficient mechanisms that can assess and minimize whatever damages may be done to this relationship through development and changes in land use. All the Nordic countries have ratified the UNDRIP but have yet to adopt specific legislation that would make its provisions binding. While Norway is alone in also ratifying the ILO convention, both Sweden and Finland have pledged to do so.

The provisions of the UNDRIP have created a new and hitherto little used line of reasoning to Sámi rights activists, by offering an opportunity to expand the importance of Sámi custodianship of nature to the point where it converges and complements their spiritual relationship with their traditional lands. Crucially, Article 12(1) of the UNDRIP establishes a conceptual bridge between the religion of Indigenous peoples and the freedom of religion or belief more generally:

> Indigenous peoples have the right to manifest, practise, develop and teach their spiritual and religious traditions, customs and ceremonies; the right to maintain, protect, and have access in privacy to their religious and cultural sites; the right to the use and control of their ceremonial objects; and the right to the repatriation of their human remains.

Read in conjunction with the traditionally more belief-centred protections offered by the ECtHR and the ICCPR, this article involves a significant expansion of what kinds of religion may be eligible for protective measures under

18 See Benjaminsen et al., 2016.

19 See the decision in the Norwegian High Court case LH-2020-149654, where a duck hunter had been acquitted for hunting out of season by the lower court because of the centrality of spring duck hunting to Sámi culture, but was convicted by the High Court, which found the prohibition of hunting out of season to be more in line with sustainability as portrayed by statutory law. The Sámi Parliament was consulted in the case and argued for the sustainability of the hunting practice.

international – and by inference domestic – human rights law.[20] Under this definition, "belief" has no place. It is replaced by a set of actions that circle around the maintenance, protection, and access to specific sites. Read in conjunction with Article 25, which safeguards the right of Indigenous peoples to "maintain and strengthen their distinctive spiritual relationship with their traditionally owned or otherwise occupied and used lands," Article 12 and its implementation in domestic law implies and requires a wholesale reorientation of what "religion" is and should be for legal purposes.

6 The Difference That the UNDRIP Can Make

The adoption of the UNDRIP in 2007 and its gradual implementation around the world represents a significant milestone in the Indigenous rights movement. It has the potential to spark instances of what Kristen Carpenter and Angela Riley has characterized as a "jurisgenerative moment" for Indigenous rights,

> a moment when human rights have the potential to become more capacious, embracing norms of equality and self-determination, and multiple means of implementation, to reflect the ways that individuals and peoples around the globe live, and want to live, today (Carpenter and Riley 2014: 234).

Recent court cases and controversies surrounding wind power development and mineral extractions in Sápmi have featured increasing concerns about the extent to which Sámi spirituality, and Sámi sacred sites in particular, may be destroyed, compromised or disturbed through such initiatives. These concerns have been voiced by individuals, by reindeer herding communities, by rights promoting groups, by neo-shamanism groups, by Sámi parliaments, and by members of the Norwegian Parliament. Across such concerns, actors draw in different measures on the repertoire of Sámi religion discussed above, staking their claims by references to the spiritual relationship with the land that the UNDRIP requires and emphasizes.

Cultural heritage legislation is a vital element in bridging the division between the conventional understanding of religion in international human rights law and the more expansive notion of a spiritual relationship with the land among Indigenous peoples. Across the Nordic region, the Finnish *Antiquities*

20 For an analysis of a Norwegian Supreme Court decision that could have drawn on this expanded notion of "religion," see Årsheim 2018.

Act (1963), the Swedish *Historic Environment Act* (1988), and the Norwegian *Cultural Heritage Act* (CHA, 1978) all offer protections for traces and remnants of human activities, including "places associated with historical events, beliefs and traditions."[21] Such "places" tend to be more readily available for heritage protections if they can be conclusively connected to prior usage in terms of material objects, remnants of buildings, burial grounds, cairns or the like. Without the presence of such tangible items, places cannot be legally recognized. This challenge is illustrated by the fact that in *Askeladden*, the database of the Norwegian Directorate for Cultural Heritage, only one Sámi sacred mountain has been found to be eligible for protection under the Act, despite persistent claims among different Sámi communities stating that the real number of sacred sites is considerably higher (see below).

Over the course of the last five years, as energy developments and mineral extraction proposals have increased considerably in the Norwegian part of Sápmi, the discussion about which conceptions of "sacredness" should be eligible for legal protection has intensified considerably. The uncertainty about the documentary evidence required to designate an area as sacred came to the forefront in 2013, in the review of a proposal to build a hydroelectric dam in Stikkelvika (Hattfjelldal), a municipality in the southern part of Norwegian Sápmi. Following a hearing process where the Sámi Parliament and a local reindeer herding community (*siida*) with herds in the area both opposed the development because of its detrimental effects on reindeer herding, the Ministry of Petroleum and Energy (MPE) approved the project in 2018, issuing a license to start the construction. Soon after, a religious community was formed under the name of Arctic Shaman Circle (ASC). According to its bylaws, the main purpose of the organization is to "help all Sami and other indigenous people in the north get back and develop their spiritual cultural heritage, according to U.N.'s human rights." Its first annual report, published in 2019, cited the development at Stikkelvika as a "pilot case" for such efforts (Kraft 2020: 341–342).

A report documenting the sacred nature of the surrounding area was submitted to the MPE, authored by Hege Dalen, board member of the ASC. According to the report, the mountain area Aakansnjurhttjie, close to Stikkelvika, has always been sacred and significant for the Sámi, as indicated by its name, its distinctive profile and visibility from the surrounding area, its position within the siida, findings of offering places in the vicinity, ways in which reindeer traverse the area, and, crucially, the "special respect attributed to the mountain, its power and the calm that it instils." Most of the report details personal

21 *CHA*, Section 2. See https://lovdata.no/dokument/NLE/lov/1978-06-09-50.

experiences with and feelings for the mountain among locals.[22] In this way, the ASC blended and brought together a variety of different aspects of Sámi religion (see above) to give authority to their claims. Following several protests and reactions from the local community against the development, the Sámi Parliament issued a statement where it reiterated its concerns with the consequences for the reindeer herders in the area. Simultaneously, however, it dismissed claims about the sacredness of the area, citing lacking evidence from archival source materials and pointing to ambivalence in the interpretation of the name of the mountain.[23] The MPE finally approved the construction of the power plant, which is currently underway.

Parallel to the development proposal in Stikkelvika, the Norwegian Energy Regulatory Authority (NVE) launched, in 2019, a government-commissioned national plan for land-based wind power, reviewing the potential for future wind power farms in all the Norwegian mainland and singling out 13 areas as particularly well suited for such projects.[24] During the development of the plan, the Sámi Parliament stressed that wind power farms should not "violate Sámi sacred places, burial grounds or other places with significant cultural heritage," and underlined that "Sámi traditional knowledge" should be equally important to scientific knowledge in the identification of eligible areas for development.[25] Concerns for Sámi sacred places were also voiced by the Directorate for Cultural Heritage.[26] During the public hearing, the plan was roundly criticized for its potential effects on wildlife, nature, the environment, and reindeer herding.

Complementing the concerns voiced by the Sámi Parliament about the impact of these projects on Sámi cultural heritage, the siida Leavvajoga ja Rastigaissa (LRS) also submitted a comprehensive complaint against the development. Unlike submissions from other siidas, LRS focused exclusively on the detrimental effects of wind power development on a landscape the Sámi held to be sacred. Unlike the ASC, LRS explicitly linked the sacrality of the area around Leavvajohka to Sámi "manifestation of faith," and backed up their claim by

22 ASC. Aahkansnjurhtjie/Kjerringtinden og Stikkelvika Kraftverk Sijti Jarnge 22.11.2018 Hege Dalen RAPPORT. On file with MPE.

23 Sametinget. *Vedrørende utbyggingen av Stikkelvika kraftverk, Hattfjelldal kommune*, Sak 18/4909, 03.02.2020.

24 NVE. Nasjonal ramme for vindkraft, https://www.nve.no/energi/energisystem/vindkraft/nasjonal-ramme-for-vindkraft/.

25 Nasjonal ramme for vindkraft på land – Sametingets innspill til metodebeskrivelse, 09.06.2017.

26 Nasjonal ramme for vindkraft på land – Riksantikvarens innspill til eksklusjonsrunde 3. Tema: Kulturminner og kulturmiljøer.

reference to the writings of Jakob Fellman (1795–1875), who worked as a priest in the area in the early 19th century, combined with archaeological findings that together proved the existence of Sámi siidas in the area "probably several millennia BC." Referring to the closing of Uluru in Australia, LRS stressed the commitments of the Norwegian State towards its Indigenous population, the Sámi people.[27] Following the many critical responses, the Norwegian national plan for land-based wind power was eventually scrapped.

The discrepancy between officially recognized sacred sites and the growing perception of a higher number or such sites among the Sámi was noted by the Norwegian Green Party Member of Parliament, Per Espen Stoknes. In 2020, he fronted a proposal to map the presence of mountains held to be sacred by the Sámi and to initiate protective measures to ensure their conservation. Also referring to Uluru and other sacred sites around the world, Stoknes pointed to the preference for material remains in cultural heritage policy, stressing the dangers and risks associated with increased wind power and mineral extraction developments. The proposal was dismissed by Parliament, as the government observed that the listing of one sacred mountain in the registry of officially protected sites was evidence that the requisite measures for protection were already in place.[28]

Following up on the initiative from the ASC, Saemien Sitje, a South Sámi museum and cultural centre in Snåsa (Norway), initiated a documentation project in 2019, intended to map sacred areas in the Southern part of Sápmi. Drawing on a combination of historical source materials and interpretations of existing placenames, the report, published in 2021, found more than 50 localities that were likely held to be sacred among the Sámi in earlier times.[29] The report highlights the lack of protections offered by both Norwegian and Swedish cultural heritage legislation, and also criticizes natural conservation efforts in the area, both because they fail to recognize the distinctive spiritual significance of the area and because they sometimes pose an obstacle to Sámi traditional land use. Also in 2021, a report prepared by the Sámi Parliament on cultural heritage management in Sápmi acknowledged the difficulties involved in settling the status of sacred places. Observing that any such process would have to involve "empirical data [such as] oral traditions, written sources, placenames and archaeological evidence," the report especially highlighted the fact that the lack of a unified methodology in registering sacred places constituted

27 Letter from LRS to NVE, 04.03.2019.

28 Stortingstidende. Referat fra møter i Stortinget Nr. 61 · 23. mars Sesjonen 2020–2021, 4039–4042.

29 Saemien Sitje. Prosjektrapport Bissegh – Samiske hellige fjell og offerplasser, 2021, at 15.

an obstacle to their protection.[30] Pledging to develop such a methodology, the report also stressed the need to involve traditional knowledge-bearers in this process to ensure legitimacy, while also highlighting the need to subject any claim to sacredness to rigorous source criticism.

In the summer of 2021, an application was filed for exploratory drilling for minerals in the Northern part of Norwegian Sápmi, in the municipality of Lebesby. However, unlike previous developments, the recognition of the mountain in question – Vadasbakti – as a sacred area was highlighted not only by the Sámi Parliament, but also by the developer, Metamorphic. Crucially for this particular project, a section of the mountain is officially registered in the database of the Directorate for Cultural Heritage, due to several written sources and findings of numerous reindeer antlers, signifying historical ritual importance to the Sámi.[31] Recognizing the potential challenges this status may entail for the project, Metamorphic submitted an assessment of the ramifications of exploratory drilling, dismissing the potential to disturb or destroy any material artefacts. On the other hand, they also explicitly recognized the possibility that drilling in itself may be considered detrimental.[32] In a written submission, the Sámi Parliament referred to the registration of the sacredness of the mountain in the heritage database, and concluded that three of the four drilling localities would be detrimental to the area.[33] In early 2022, Metamorphic decided to drop the drilling project, informing the respondent ministry that the exploratory drilling was "no longer relevant."

Although discussions about the role of wind power and mineral extraction in Sápmi have also intensified in Sweden and Finland (Koivurova, Masloboev, and Petre 2015; Lawrence 2014; Nysten-Haarala, Joona, and Hovila 2021), there are so far few signs in open and available sources that these initiatives are felt to endanger areas and places held to be sacred by the Sámi, at least not at the level seen in Norway. Part of the explanation of those observed differences between the Nordic countries may be found in the status of the Norwegian Sámi Parliament, which is the national overseer of Sámi cultural heritage issues, granting the Sámi a voice in any developmental project that may affect their cultural heritage in a way not available to the parliaments in Sweden and

30 Sametinget. Sametingsmelding om samisk kulturminnevern, 2021, at 33.

31 The presence of reindeer antlers is a well-established sign of Sámi ritual activity, confirmed both by historical, written sources, and by multiple archaeological findings across Sápmi (Äikäs 2015: 21).

32 Metamorphic. Undersøkelsesarbeider – Finnmark. Søknad om særskilt tillatelse til undersøkelser på statens mineraler i Finnmark (§ 17 mineralloven), 22.06.2021.

33 Sametinget. Uttalelse vedrørende søknad om særskilt tillatelse til undersøkelsesarbeider i Váđasbákti, Gbnr 18/1, Lebesby kommune. 06.08.2021.

Finland. Additionally, large sections of the Finnish and Swedish parts of Sápmi already enjoy protected status as national parks or natural reserves, preventing proposals for wind power and mineral extraction developments,[34] obviating the need for further protections.

7 Conclusion

Viewed from the perspective of the many centuries of interactions between the Sámi and neighboring peoples, the period during which Sámi religion has been virtually extinct – if it ever really vanished – is fairly brief. Likewise, the Sámi rights struggle, which is still very much underway, is a recent phenomenon that is only now finding its form through gradually evolving legislative frameworks, institutional structures, and individual and collective rights activism directed towards restitution and reconciliation with the difficult period of assimilation and repression of Sámi culture, language, land ownership, and lifeways. As part and parcel of this struggle, a continuous reinterpretation of the spiritual relationship between people and the lands they possess and use appears to be taking shape, in close interaction with the similarly evolving international regulatory framework for Indigenous peoples' rights, first and foremost the UNDRIP. However, parallel to this emancipatory process, existing legal, administrative, and political structures in the Nordic states continue to present obstacles to a complete restoration of Sámi cultural heritage, outlooks, and ways of life, also posing threat to the process of reconciliation. Arguably, these obstacles are hardwired into the legal framework of modern nation states, whose existence is based on an individual and universalist rights framework, that has only recently started expanding to the point where it can accommodate the rights of Indigenous peoples. In this process, the legal regulation of religion stands out as a particularly complicated challenge, as the notions of religion that dominate modern, state-driven law are in marked contrast to those cultivated by Indigenous peoples around the world. While a "jurisgenerative moment" may be emerging through the role of sacred places in the growing resistance towards wind power and mineral extraction in Norwegian Sápmi, it remains to be seen how successful this resistance will be in the long run. Throughout the 2020s decade, all the Nordic countries will receive comprehensive reports from truth and reconciliation commissions established

34 This protection is not uncontroversial, as it is designated to protect the "untouched" and "wild" aspects of the areas in question, sometimes colliding with Sámi reindeer herding interests. See Kleppe and Mulk 2007.

to document the impact of assimilation targeting both the Sámi and other minorities. In the aftermath of the works of these commissions, the Nordic states will likely have to take concrete legal steps to implement the UNDRIP in their domestic legal frameworks, forcing forward a debate about what a merger between Sámi law and religion law may entail.

References

Äikäs, Tiina. *From Boulders to Fells: Sacred Places in the Sámi Ritual Landscape*. Translated by Sarianna Silvonen. Helsinki: Monographs of the Archaeological Society of Finland 5, 2005.

Allard, Christina, and Susann Funderud Skogvang. *Indigenous Rights in Scandinavia: Autonomous Sami Law*. London and New York: Routledge, 2015.

Andreassen, Bengt-Ove, and Torjer A. Olsen. "'Sami Religion' in Sámi Curricula in RE in the Norwegian School System: An Analysis of the Importance of Terms." *Religions* 11, no. 9 (2020): 448.

Årsheim, Helge. "Including and Excluding Indigenous Religion through Law." *Numen* 65, no. 5–6 (2018): 531–561. https://doi.org/10.1163/15685276-12341511.

Årsheim, Helge. "Fra rett og moral til trusler og rettigheter. En beretning om folkeviljens makt og vilkårene for økonomisk støtte til trossamfunn i Norge." In *Populisme og kristendom*, edited by Sven Thore Kloster, and Sturla Johan Stålsett, 102–117. Oslo: Cappelen Damm Akademisk, 2021.

Årsheim, Helge, and Pamela Slotte. *The Juridification of Religion?* Leiden: Brill, 2017. https://doi.org/10.1163/9789004359864.

Benjaminsen, Tor Arve, Eira Inger Marie Gaup, and Sara Mikkel Nils. *Samisk reindrift: norske myter*. Bergen: Fagbokforl, 2016. https://urn.nb.no/URN:NBN:no-nb_digibok_2020081207137.

Berglund, Jenny. "Swedish Religion Education: Objective but Marinated in Lutheran Protestantism?" *Temenos – Nordic Journal of Comparative Religion* 49, no. 2 (2013): 165–184.

Bielefeldt, Heiner, Nazila Ghanea, and Michael Wiener. *Freedom of Religion or Belief. An International Law Commentary*. Oxford: Oxford University Press, 2016.

Carpenter, Kristen A., and Angela R. Riley. "Indigenous Peoples and the Jurisgenerative Moment in Human Rights." *California Law Review* 102, no. 1 (2014): 173–234.

Hansen, Lars Ivar, and Bjørnar Olsen. *Samenes historie fram til 1750*. Oslo: Cappelen Akademisk Forlag, 2022.

Hartney, Christopher, and Daniel Tower. "Indigenous Religion: Its Validity and Problematics." In *Religious Categories and the Construction of the Indigenous*, 1–7. Leiden: Brill, 2017. https://brill.com/view/book/edcoll/9789004328983/B9789004328983-s002.xml.

Kaikkonen, Konsta. "Sámi Indigenous(?) Religion(s)(?) – Some Observations and Suggestions Concerning Term Use." *Religions* 11, no. 9 (2020): 432.

Kleppe, Else Johansen, and Inga-Maria Mulk. "Religion Embedded in the Landscape." *UBAS Nordisk* 3, no. 1 (2007): 14.

Koivurova, Timo, Vladimir Masloboev, and Anna Petre. "Legal Protection of Sami Traditional Livelihoods from the Adverse Impacts of Mining: A Comparison of the Level of Protection Enjoyed by Sami in Their Four Home States." *Arctic Review on Law and Politics* 6, no. 1 (2015): 11–51.

Kraft, Siv Ellen. "Spiritual Activism. Saving Mother Earth in Sápmi." *Religions* 11, no. 7 (2020): 342.

Lawrence, Rebecca. "Internal Colonisation and Indigenous Resource Sovereignty: Wind Power Developments on Traditional Saami Lands." *Environment and Planning D: Society and Space* 32, no. 6 (2014): 1036–1053.

Müller-Wille, Ludger. "The Sami Parliament in Finland: A Model for Ethnic Minority Management?" *Études/Inuit/Studies* 3, no. 2 (1979): 63–72.

Mörkenstam, Ulf. "Organised Hypocrisy? The Implementation of the International Indigenous Rights Regime in Sweden." *International Journal of Human Rights* 23, no. 10 (2019): 1718–1741. https://doi.org/10.1080/13642987.2019.1629907.

Nadasdy, Paul. "Transcending the Debate over the Ecologically Noble Indian: Indigenous Peoples and Environmentalism." *Ethnohistory* 52, no. 2 (2005): 291–331.

Nysten-Haarala, Soili, Tanja Joona, and Ilari Hovila. "Wind Energy Projects and Reindeer Herders' Rights in Finnish Lapland." *Elementa: Science of the Anthropocene* 9, no. 1 (2021): 37.

Pollan, Brita. "Samisk religioni Norge." In *Norges religionshistorie*, edited by Arne Bugge Amundsen, 414–456. Oslo: Universitetsforlaget, 2005.

Ravna, Øyvind. "Norwegian Courts and Sámi Law." *Arctic Review* 12 (2021): 179–185. https://doi.org/10.23865/arctic.v12.3417.

Raymond, Hames. "The Ecologically Noble Savage Debate." *Annual Review of Anthropology* 36, no. 1 (2007): 177–190.

Sandberg, Russell. *Law and Religion*. Cambridge: Cambridge University Press, 2011.

Skogvang, Susann Funderud. *Samerett. 3. utgave*. Oslo: Universitetsforlaget, 2022.

Store norske leksikon. "Finner (samer)." Accessed December 19, 2022. https://snl.no/finner_-_samer.

Store norske leksikon. "Lapper." Accessed December 19, 2022. https://snl.no/lapper.

Store norske leksikon. "Samerådet." Accessed December 19, 2022. https://snl.no/Samer%C3%A5det.

Tafjord, Bjørn Ola. "Indigenous Religion (s) as an Analytical Category." *Method & Theory in the Study of Religion* 25, no. 3 (2012): 221–243.

Indigenous Religious Rights in India

Virginius Xaxa

According to the 2011 census, India was home to more than 104 million members of so-called tribal communities, representing 8.6 percent of the country's total population. Such individuals live throughout the country, speaking a variety of languages that mainly belong to the Indo-Aryan, Dravidian, Austro-Asiatic, and Tibeto-Burman language families. As for the Anthropological Survey of India conducted as part of the People of India Project, it identified 461 different tribal communities in the country (Khubchandani 1992: 2; Singh 1993: 17).

But despite their diversity, India's tribal communities share certain aspects of social organization that differentiate them from the numerically, economically, and politically dominant segments of the Indian population. For their part, the different groups making up mainstream Indian society are aligned with a limited number of religious traditions: Hinduism (the largest), Buddhism, Jainism, Islam, Sikhism, and Christianity. Accordingly, colonial administrators tended to divide the country's population along religious rather than ethnic lines. In the case of tribal communities, attention was also paid to habitat (hills, forests, etc.) and patterns of livelihood. Moreover, British administrative and ethnographic accounts emphasize the supposedly savage or uncivilized nature of these communities, as well as their geographical and social isolation, as defining characteristics. Nevertheless, religion ultimately emerged as the primary marker of their differentiation from other segments of Indian society – a fact clearly evident by the 1901 census.

Although the anthropological literature broadly describes the religious traditions of tribal communities in terms of animism or naturism, each community originally had a distinct system of beliefs and practices to which all its members adhered. The advent of British rule and the subsequent establishment of Christian missions led to conversions and intra-community divisions. However, Christian beliefs and practices also came to serve as a basis for inter-community solidarity. Later, Hindu social and religious organizations followed the example of Christian missionaries by seeking to assimilate Indigenous peoples through political, socio-cultural, and educational initiatives. These groups constitute the strongest religious influence on Indigenous peoples in India today.

Such is the backdrop against which this chapter discusses the religious rights of Indigenous peoples in India. The first of three sections looks at the political relationship between tribal communities and the state, including

 | DOI:10.1163/9789004524330_005

the nature of Indigenous political demands. The second section explores the intersection between Indigenous religion and the law. Finally, the third section takes a deeper look at some of the key issues raised earlier in the chapter.

1 An Overview of Indigenous-State Political Relations

1.1 *Definition and Recognition of Indigenous Status*

Since independence, Indian authorities have consistently referred to Indigenous peoples as "tribes," a term that has retained its colonial-era associations with savagery and primitiveness. Indeed, efforts by anthropologists to reconceptualize the notion of tribe have not had much impact outside the discipline. In post-colonial India, both state practices and the popular imagination have been largely shaped by discourses that blame poverty and other related issues faced by tribal communities and the supposed social, cultural, and economic backwardness of the communities themselves. As a result, issues associated with international Indigenous rights discourse – such as the impact of colonialism and the appropriation of Indigenous lands, forests, and other resources – have been consistently overlooked.

Since the 1920s, the presence of Indigenous peoples in India has been acknowledged through the use of an equivalent term: "Adivasi." By the eve of independence, this expression had become embedded in the collective consciousness of tribal communities living in present-day Jharkhand and adjacent regions of bordering states. At the Constituent Assembly established in 1946, prominent Adivasi leader Jaipal Singh strongly argued for adopting the term as part of the constitutional nomenclature of an independent India. Instead, those groups that have been referred to simply as tribes under British rule came to be known as Scheduled Tribes. Nevertheless, members of Scheduled Tribes have consistently described themselves as Adivasis, especially in peninsular India. Furthermore, other social groups sometimes refer to them as such. In fact, the Adivasi identity transcends individual communities, groups, languages, and dialects. Nor is it restricted to those Scheduled Tribes recognized under the constitution. Rather than an administrative category, it reflects a claim to being the India's original inhabitants.

By contrast, Article 366(25) of the Indian constitution specifically refers to "such tribes or tribal communities or parts of or groups within such tribes or tribal communities as are deemed under Article 342 to be Scheduled Tribes for the purposes of the Constitution." For its part, Article 342(1) describes the president's power to "specify the tribes or tribal communities or parts of or groups within tribes or tribal communities" that constitute Scheduled Tribes by means of public notification (Govt. of India 2015: 217). In short, although all Scheduled Tribes are tribes in an anthropological sense, not all tribes are Scheduled Tribes in a legal sense. However, the order establishing an initial list of Scheduled Tribes, which was based on the census of 1931, proved far from exhaustive. Various excluded groups and communities immediately began demanding constitutional recognition. In the absence of clear criteria, the Indian government established the Lokur Committee (named for its chairman) to study the issue. It decided that Scheduled Tribes should be defined in terms of primitive traits, distinct cultures, geographical isolation, economic backwardness, and aversion to contact with the outside world (Govt. of India 1965: 7).

Through its participation in the activities of the United Nations Sub-Commission on the Promotion and Protection of Human Rights (previously the Sub-Commission on Prevention of Discrimination and Protection of Minorities), the United Nations Working Group on Indigenous Populations, and other international forums, the Indian government has consistently argued that the country's Scheduled Tribes, as well as any other groups that might claim Indigenous status, do not constitute Indigenous peoples. Basically, it claims that because "tribal" and "Indigenous" are not synonymous, they cannot be equated. Meanwhile, Adivasi activists and organizations have emphasized the extent to which the two expressions describe the same phenomenon. But looking beyond narrow questions of terminology, these debates revolve around two criteria used to define Indigenous peoples, namely: (1) to be a descent from the populations which inhabited the country, or geographical region to which the country belongs, at the time of conquest or colonization, and (2) the retention of some or all of their own social, economic, cultural, and political institutions, irrespective of their legal status (Xaxa 2000: 30).

Citing various experts – from anthropologists and social reformers to census commissioners – the Indian government has specifically argued that the tribal communities established in the country lack distinct social, economic, political, and cultural identities. For instance, officials have frequently cited G.S. Ghurye's observation that religious, occupational, and racial characteristics have proven highly inadequate for distinguishing between the country's tribal and non-tribal populations (Prasad 1992). They have also referred to the various forms of continuity with broader Indian society identified by sociologist André Beteille, who has discussed the difficulty of defining tribal communities in India (Prasad 1992). At the same time, the government has conveniently overlooked Beteille's argument that "groups which correspond closely to the anthropologists' conception of the tribe have lived in long association with communities of an entirely different type," not to mention Ghurye's view that the Adivasis do, in fact, represent the original inhabitants of India.

Furthermore, the Indian government has sought to convince international forums that tribal communities generally and Scheduled Tribes specifically constitute administrative categories rather than historical ones. They serve to support the implementation of social welfare measures, not to recognize Indigenous peoples in any way. Once again, this provides a basis for rejecting any automatic connection between "tribal" and "Indigenous" (Prasad 1992). Such arguments stand in the way of any real assessment of the historical presence of Indigenous peoples in the country. Indeed, because the notion of Indigenous peoples is closely associated with the effects of European conquest and colonization, there is a tendency in India to define indigeneity solely in reference to British colonial rule. From this perspective, the country's entire population could be considered Indigenous, making formal recognition redundant. By contrast, the Adivasis point to a much longer history of subjugation and colonization, dating to the arrival in India of a different group of outsider: the Aryans.

Despite its refusal to recognize tribal communities as Indigenous, India has been a party and signatory to various international agreements on Indigenous peoples. For instance, Indian negotiators made no objection to the use of the term in the International Labour Organization's Indigenous and Tribal Populations Convention of 1957 (ILO Convention No. 107), a treaty the country later ratified. However, it is important to note how this document emphasizes the need to integrate the Indigenous and tribal peoples within mainstream social and political systems (ILO 1957). By 1989, when the ILO adopted its Indigenous and Tribal Peoples Convention (no. 169), the focus had shifted to questions of rights and empowerment (ILO 1989). This prompted a change of heart, and India has yet to ratify the more recent convention. Nevertheless, the country is a signatory of the United Nations Declaration on the Rights of Indigenous Peoples (UNDRIP) and has accepted development funding earmarked for Indigenous peoples from agencies such as the World Bank, the International Fund for Agricultural Development, the United Nations Development Programme, and UNESCO.

1.2 *State Governance and Ideological Orientations*

Where Scheduled Tribes are concerned, constitutional provisions are key to understanding the nature of state governance. Beyond the rights enjoyed by all citizens, the Indian constitution addresses the governance of what it describes as tribal communities in various explicit ways.

Like other citizens, members of Scheduled Tribes have the right to equality before the law and they enjoy protection from discrimination on the basis of religion, race, caste, sex, or place of birth. They are also guaranteed equality of opportunity in the context of state employment, the abolition of the caste system, etc. Likewise, members of Scheduled Tribes are covered by constitutional provisions regarding freedom of speech, expression, and peaceful assembly, as well as the right to form associations, move freely throughout the country, reside or settle in any part of India, and practice any profession (subject to reasonable restrictions designed to safeguard national sovereignty, public order, or morality). Finally, all Indian citizens enjoy the right against exploitation, freedom of religion, cultural and educational rights, and the right to constitutional remedies.

The Indian constitution also includes general provisions for the protection and promotion of tribal communities, alongside certain other groups. To begin with, reservation, a form of affirmative action, ensures access to state employment, public institutions of higher education, and political institutions such as the national parliament and state legislatures. Article 14(4) deals with reservation in general and Article 16(4) addresses its use in favor of Scheduled Tribes (Govt. of India 2015: 6–7). However, Article 335 makes access to state employment contingent on the maintenance of efficiency through educational requirements and other qualifications (Govt. of India 2015: 210). These provisions also reflect a broader mandate to address the widespread oppression, exploitation, and discrimination historically experienced by Scheduled Tribes and Scheduled Castes (i.e., Dalits, formerly known as "untouchables") by seeking to ensure their active and equal participation in public life (Oommen 2014: 98). As one of the Directive Principles of State Policy, Article 46 requires government to promote "the educational and economic interests of the weaker sections of the people," while making direct reference to Scheduled Tribes (Govt. of India 2015: 23). Articles 330 and 332 reserve seats for Scheduled Tribes in both the national parliament (Article 330) and state legislatures (Article 332) (Govt. of India 2015: 206–209). And although Article 19(1)(e) states that every citizen has the right "to reside and settle in any part of the territory of India," Article 19(5) allows reasonable restrictions on this right to protect the interests of the general public or those of any Scheduled Tribe. In addition, Article 29 protects the right of any citizen to conserve their "distinct language, script or culture" (Govt. of India 2015: 9–10).

Articles 244 and 244A refer to highly significant measures specific to tribal communities in what are commonly referred to as scheduled areas (Govt. of India 2015: 156–157; Chakraborty 2011). The Fifth Schedule of the Indian constitution provides for the separate administration of tribal areas in ten states located in mainland and peninsular India, where members of Scheduled Tribes make up the majority of the population: Andhra Pradesh, Chhattisgarh, Gujarat, Himachal Pradesh, Jharkhand, Madhya Pradesh, Maharashtra, Orissa, Rajasthan, and Telangana. In these areas, a Tribes Advisory Council must be established to advise the state governor on matters related to the "welfare and advancement" of Scheduled Tribes. An arguably more important provision allows governors to refrain from applying any act of the national parliament or a state legislature within a scheduled area, or to apply such legislation with exceptions and modifications designed to protect the interests and welfare of Scheduled Tribes. Governors of states covered by the Fifth Schedule can also "make regulations for the peace and good government" of any scheduled area – including measures related to the transfer of land, the allotment of land, and money lending – while amending or repealing existing laws as required. However, any such actions must be taken in consultation with the Tribes Advisory Council and be submitted to the Indian president for assent (Govt. of India 2015: 293–296).

The powers assigned to state governors under the Fifth Schedule are rooted in those exercised by colonial administrators during British rule (Misra 2012). However, since independence, they have rarely been used to protect the interests and welfare of tribal communities. This inaction inspired a movement for self-governance, leading to the passage of the *Provisions of Panchayats (Extension to Scheduled Areas) Act* (PESA) in 1996. Similar to other legislation providing for the extension of local self-governance in rural India, it focuses on restoring traditional tribal systems of governance (Choubey 2016).

As for the Sixth Schedule of the Indian constitution, it provides for the establishement of autonomous district councils (ADCs) and autonomous regional councils (ARCs) in the tribal areas of Northeast India. In 1971, calls for greater autonomy led to the creation of four tribal states alongside the four ADCs established in 1950. Decades later, two additional ADCs were created in response to demands for a separate state by different tribal communities in Tripura and by the Bodo in Assam. Altogether, the Sixth Schedule applies to six of Assam's twenty-one districts, although each ADC enjoys slightly different powers; to the whole of Meghalaya, except for the Shillong Cantonment; to three districts in Mizoram; and to the Tripura Tribal Area, which spans over five hill ranges in four districts and covers about 68 percent of the state's territory (Xaxa 2022: 400–405).

ADCs established under the Sixth Schedule can exercise legislative, executive, and judicial powers in a number of areas, including the regulation of land to protect and promote the interest of inhabitants, the regulation of traditional or customary practices, and the management of non-reserved forests. ADCs are also involved in the administration of justice, as well as the establishment and management of schools, dispensaries, markets, transportation infrastructure, etc. Furthermore, the Sixth Schedule specifies that no act of the national parliament or a state legislature can be applied to an autonomous district (except for those in Meghalaya) without the consent of the relevant ADC (Govt. of India 2015: 297–320).

All things considered, the various constitutional provisions concerning the governance of India's tribal communities reflect an ideology of integration. On the one hand, they provide for the participation of Scheduled Tribes (and other historically excluded groups) in the national parliament and state legislatures, as well as in the public service. The desire to build a more inclusive society is also reflected in education, health, and economic initiatives launched by the state, including transportation and communication infrastructure projects. But approaches to managing the relationship between tribal communities and mainstream Indian society vary from one region to another, based on historical developments. In Northeast India, a measure of autonomy and self-governance has been achieved through the ADCs established under the Sixth Schedule. Elsewhere, a more paternalistic approach has persisted since colonial times, with responsibility for ensuring the interests and welfare of tribal communities being vested in regional administrators. The general failure of post-independence governors to fulfill this responsibility has been a major source of concern for Adivasi leaders and activists. And although the passage of the PESA by the national parliament in 1996 provided for a degree of village-level self-governance, amendments adopted by state legislatures (local governance falls under state jurisdiction) have left the act watered down and often without a framework for implementation. As a result, those Scheduled Tribes not covered by the provisions of either the Fifth Schedule or the Sixth Schedule have largely remained in what might be described as a state of benign neglect.

1.3 *Indigenous Political Demands*

The Adivasis have put forward a variety of political demands. In fact, several autonomy movements date to the eve of independence. For instance, in Northeast India, Naga insurgents carried on a prolonged armed conflict with the country's armed forces. In 1963, Indian authorities sought to contain the movement by creating the separate state of Nagaland, which enjoys special constitutional status under Article 371A.[1] In subsequent decades, similar movements based elsewhere in the region also abandoned a peaceful and democratic approach in favor of armed revolt. Once again, the favored solution was to establish separate states where the majority of the population belongs to a Scheduled Tribe: Mizoram, Meghalaya, and Arunachal Pradesh.[2] Furthermore, in areas where members of Scheduled Tribes are in the minority, ADCs have been created under the Sixth Schedule. There have also been two autonomy movements worthy of note outside Northeast India. In Gondwana, demands for an independent state largely failed to inspire concrete or sustained action (Xaxa 2008: 56). In Jharkhand, the movement experienced a series of ups and

1 https://egyankosh.ac.in/bitstream/123456789/78972/1/Unit-8.pdf.
2 https://egyankosh.ac.in/bitstream/123456789/78972/1/Unit-8.pdf.

downs. And by the time a separate state was created in 2001, the arrival of large numbers of outsiders drawn in by the region's industrial development had reduced the proportion of Adivasi to 26.3 percent of the population.

Given that Scheduled Tribes enjoy well-defined constitutional rights and privileges, various unlisted tribal communities have focused their political energies on the fight for recognition. Although some have been successful, others are still waiting for a response. Some of the oldest outstanding claims relate to groups that were uprooted from their ancestral lands in Eastern India and Central India to work as indentured laborers on tea plantations in Assam, in Northeast India between the mid-nineteenth century and the second decade of the twentieth century. Alongside lobbying and petitioning efforts, communities seeking recognition as Scheduled Tribes regularly organize meetings, marches, and rallies (Ananthanarayanan 2010: 290–303).

A second set of political demands has involved calls to implement constitutional and statutory provisions for ensuring the interests and well-being of Scheduled Tribes. The general failure of governors to enforce relevant measures has inspired campaigns for village-level self-governance. In response, the national parliament adopted the PESA, which sought to restore the village's traditional role as a focus of decision-making and administration for tribal communities. In 2006, sustained pressure from Adivasi and civil organizations led to the passage of the *Scheduled Tribes and Other Forest Dwellers Act*, designed to address the historical injustices faced by tribal communities and to restore their rights over their traditional lands and forests. However, demands for these two pieces of legislation to be implemented have been met with both indifference and resistance from state administrations reluctant to relinquish authority to village-based institutions (Choubey 2016).

Since the early decades of India's independence, Adivasi communities in various parts of the country have often been less focused on political demands than on efforts to resist being dispossessed of their lands and displaced from their traditional territories. Today as in the past, this has meant opposing state-sponsored infrastructure developments in the form of road and railway construction, the building of dams and irrigation systems, mining and industrial projects, and even the establishment of wildlife sanctuaries and national parks.

2 Indigenous Religions and the Law

Before considering the question of Indigenous religion, it is important to remember the ambiguity surrounding the term "Indigenous" in the Indian context. Whereas countries in the Americas and Europe commonly and explicitly refer to the original inhabitants of their territories as Indigenous, India's Scheduled Tribes are not officially recognized as such. As discussed above, the Indian state prefers to portray the entire Indian population as Indigenous in the context of British colonialism and its legacy. The term is also commonly used to contrast foreign or modern influences with homegrown science, technology, philosophy, medicine, religion, knowledge, etc. It is neither exclusively nor primarily used to designate those tribal communities that claim to be the original inhabitants of India.

The Adivasis have a rich religious heritage. Although British colonial administrators broadly described it in terms of animism and naturism – as have some anthropologists – such abstract categorizations obscure the vast diversity of religious beliefs and practices. Indeed, it could be argued that there are as many religions as there are tribal communities in India. Furthermore, it can be difficult to determine the precise names originally used to designate these various religious traditions. In many cases, the terms currently in use reflect recent processes of formalization or institutionalization that are based on the names of major deities, like those of the Tani people in Arunachal Pradesh, or places of worship, such as the sacred groves used by many tribal communities in Jharkhand (Chaudhuri 2013: 259–277; Oraon 2021: 102–129).

Nearly two centuries of colonial rule brought many changes to India's tribal communities, with the disruption of traditional religions being among the most significant. In the course of consolidating their power over the Adivasis, British administrators called on Christian missionaries to civilize tribes that were viewed as savage. Alongside the introduction of new forms of education and health care, various Christian denominations and sects gained a foothold in tribal communities, whose populations often came to be divided between Christians and those whose religious practices predated contact with Christian missionaries – practices referred to in this chapter as traditional religions, and that align with the notion of Indigenous religions.

2.1 *Legal Provisions*

None of the religious provisions in the Indian constitution apply specifically to Scheduled Tribes. Nevertheless, Article 25(1) guarantees, "[s]ubject to public order, morality and health […] freedom of conscience and the right freely to profess, practice and propagate religion." Article 26 gives every religious denomination or sect the right "to establish and maintain institutions for religious and charitable purposes," "to manage its own affairs in matters of religion," "to own and acquire movable and immovable property," and "to administer such property in accordance with the law." Article 27 exempts religions and denominations from paying taxes on expenses incurred for their promotion or maintenance. Article 28 prohibits religious instruction "in any educational institution wholly maintained out of state funds." In addition to protecting distinct languages and cultures, Section 29 also prohibits state-run and state-funded educational institutions from denying admission solely on the grounds of religion, race, caste, and/or language. Finally, Section 30 grants all religious or language minorities "the right to establish and administer educational institutions of their choice." Accordingly, in addition to the constitutional right to freedom of religion, members of Adivasi communities who practice a traditional religion are also covered by constitutional provisions that apply to religious minorities (Govt. of India 2015: 13–14).

As for Christian Adivasis, their religious activities have been the target of state-level anti-conversion laws. The first examples were passed in Orissa (1967) and Madhya Pradesh (1968). Arunachal Pradesh (1978), Tamil Nādu (2002), Gujarat (2003), Rajasthan (2006), Himachal Pradesh (2006) and Jharkhand (2017) later followed suit. Except for Tamil Nādu and Arunachal Pradesh, all these states are covered by the Fifth Schedule of the Indian constitution, which provides for the separate administration of tribal areas (although this has been the case for Jharkhand only since 2017). This fact highlights the extent to which such legislation is specifically designed to prevent Christian missionaries from converting members of tribal communities (Xaxa 2017: 6–9). Indeed, the Adivasis make up a significant portion of each state's population, except in the case of Tamil Nādu. The latter's anti-conversion act was repealed in 2004, after the party responsible for introducing it had a poor showing in the national elections. This setback was attributed partly to a loss of support among religious minorities that had opposed the legislation.[3] Meanwhile, Arunachal has been slow to develop an implementation framework for its anti-conversion law, most likely out of fear that moving forward would be interpreted as an attack on a group that forms 68 percent of the state's population, according to the 2011 census.

By 2021, ten of India's twenty-eight states had laws in place designed to prevent conversion by fraud, allurement, coercion, etc. (US Department of State 2022). Any anticipated conversions must be reported to state authorities well in advance, and violators can face fines and imprisonment. In some states with significant Adivasi populations, such as Madhya Pradesh and Gujarat, amendments made in response to inquiries and objections from the courts have strengthened the acts by placing the onus of proof on the accused, by making it more difficult to obtain bail, and by increasing fines and prison sentences (US Department of State 2022).

3 https://www.csw.org.uk/2004/05/20/press/334/article.htm.

2.2 *Issues of Religious Recognition*

Traditional Adivasi religions lack official recognition in present-day India, often despite having enjoyed it prior to independence. As a result, their followers are commonly categorized as Hindus and assigned a Hindu identity. Meanwhile, mainstream religions followed by Adivasis – most often Christianity – are formally recognized under the law. But when it comes to applying constitutional and statutory provisions, such as the right to affirmative action in state employment, officials often refuse to recognize Christians as having Scheduled Tribe status by conflating belonging to a tribal community with continuing to practice a traditional religion, often treated as a part of Hinduism.

The push for the denial of Scheduled Tribe status to Christian Adivasis can be traced to a 1963 election in the Lohardaga Parliamentary Constituency, a seat being reserved for candidates belonging to a Scheduled Tribe. The results were challenged by the runner-up on various grounds, including the fact that the winning candidate was a Christian. It was argued that Christians were not eligible to benefit from constitutional provisions designed to protect and promote members of Scheduled Tribes. A suit was filed and the case was heard by the Election Tribunal, which upheld the election results on the grounds that Christian Oraons remain Oraons despite their conversion and are equally entitled to any rights or privileges enjoyed by members of this Scheduled Tribe under the Indian constitution. The decision noted how the winning candidate and other Christian converts maintained a tribal way of life, used the name of their tribe as their surname, observed tribal festivals that do not directly conflict with Christianity, were called Christian Oraons and not Indian Christians, etc. It also pointed out that even Tana Bhagats, who practice a reformed version of the traditional religion, were still considered Oraons despite refraining from animal sacrifices at the Puja – which was once considered a fundamental aspect of religious practice. The Patna High Court subsequently upheld the judgment of the Election Tribunal.[4]

But such court decisions have done little to discourage efforts to de-schedule Christian Adivasis. In fact, de-scheduling has become a key strategy for right-wing Hindu nationalist organizations, such as the Rashtriya Swaymsewak Sangh (RSS) and its various partners: the Vishwa Hindu Parishad (VHP), the Bajrang Dal, Bhartiya Janta Party (BJP), and the Akhil Bhartiya Vidyarthi Parishad (the BJP's student wing). They emphasize Christianity's non-Indic roots, portraying it as an alien religion whose followers should be suspected of disloyalty to India. Furthermore, Christian Adivasis have tended to be particularly successful when it comes to asserting their constitutional rights and

4 https://indiankanoon.org/doc/204475/.

benefiting from affirmative action programs. Non-Christian Adivasis active in groups like the ones mentioned above regularly appeal to a general right-wing aversion to assertions of minority rights to drum up support for de-scheduling. For while they accept the recognition of Scheduled Tribes, the RSS and its affiliates see them as exclusively belonging to a broader Hindu community. This notion of a common Hindu religious identity is actively promoted through the activities of educational, social, and cultural institutions run by the Vanvasi Kalyan Ashram and other social welfare organizations affiliated with the BJP.

The spread of Christianity within India's tribal communities and the distinction between Christian Adivasis and those who practice traditional religions can be traced to the advent of British rule. Colonial administrators sought help with integrating supposedly uncivilized populations into mainstream Indian society from Christian missionaries who focused their efforts on evangelization, education, and health. Today, the proportion of Adivasis who practices Christianity varies depending on the region and the specific tribal community. It tends to be the largest in Northeast India, where many states have a Christian majority. However, in other parts of the region Christians only account for a small fraction of the population. Historically, Hinduism has also had a presence in Northeast India, due to the expansion of the Hindu kingdoms into tribal areas. However, modern nationalist organizations like the RSS and Hindu Mahasabha have made a more concerted effort to draw Adivasi communities into Hindu political, social, and cultural movements. As a result, Hinduism has become an important presence in almost all tribal regions of India – including remote areas where it was largely absent until very recent decades. This has served to further accentuate religious divisions within tribal communities, where traditional religions, Christianity and Hinduism now predominate.

Given the wide diversity of traditional Adivasi beliefs and practices, they cannot be treated as a single faith, as in the case of Hinduism and Christianity. Rather, the notion of a tribal religion (singular) tends to be based on very general characteristics, especially the features of a natural (as opposed to founded) religion and the absence of sacred texts. And just as major founded, text-based religions often claim greater legitimacy than their tribal counterparts, the post-independence Indian state has adopted a similar view of what defines an authentic religion. This bias in favor of founded religions with sacred texts is perhaps most evident in how followers of Adivasi religions have stopped being separately enumerated in the census.

The census has long been an important tool of statecraft in India, and colonial administrators used it to track followers of traditional religions with a view to implementing special measures to protect tribal communities. However, since independence, although the census has continued to track membership in tribal communities, it has stopped tacking the practice of traditional religions within those communities. This is in spite of the fact that traditional religions are, as a whole, more widespread than some of the six remaining choices: Hindu, Muslim, Christian, Sikh, Buddhist, and Jain. Until 1951, followers of Adivasi religions were considered animists or nature worshipers and recorded under "Other Religions." But for reasons unknown, this subgroup was removed from the 1961 census. Since that time, members of tribal communities have increasingly been enumerated as Hindus (Oraon 2021: 35–61). In other words, the census has come to exclusively define religious affiliation in terms of founded religions and/or religions based on sacred texts, to the complete exclusion of others. And Hinduism has come to be treated as the default category for anyone who does not follow Christianity, Islam, Buddhism, Sikhism, or Jainism.

Faced with the modern state's apparent denial of very legitimacy of natural religions that lack sacred texts, Adivasi communities have increasingly called for the reintroduction of a census category for followers of traditional religions. In many parts of India, Adivasi leaders even called for a boycott of the 2001 census, in addition to lobbying and petitioning the Census Commissioner to include a separate code for followers of traditional religions in the Census Household Schedule of 2011. Meanwhile, Adivasi communities have made efforts to institutionalize and formalize their traditional religious practices. Regular prayer assemblies have been held, belief systems have been documented, and theological concepts have been elaborated, with some groups even building temple or church-type structures. Some of the most striking examples involve followers of the Donyi-Polo religion in Arunachal Pradesh, the Seng-Khasi movement in Meghalaya, and the Sarna Dharma belief system in Jharkhand (Chaudhuri 2013; Oraon 2021). The individuals involved are motivated by two main desires: curtailing the conversion of fellow community members to other religions (especially Christianity) and securing official recognition of their distinct religious practices. And insofar as their work represents a bulwark against the spread of Christianity, they have received both tacit and open support from the RSS and its affiliates. However, such Hindu nationalist organizations have no real desire to have traditional Adivasi religions officially recognized, preferring to see the followers of such religions treated as Hindus. By contrast, calls for recognition have found open support among Christians members.

Most members of tribal communities in India prefer to call themselves Adivasis, which literally means first inhabitants. The term is also widely used in public discourse on Indigenous issues, whether at meetings and academic conferences, or in the press and scholarly literature. However, Indian governments (central and state) continue to insist on referring to Scheduled Tribes (or simply "tribes"). Meanwhile, the RSS and the larger Sangh Parivar movement speak in terms of the Vanvasi (which means forest dwellers), a choice that reflects an ideological commitment to Hindutva (political Hinduism as the foundational principle of the Indian state). By refusing to use a term that associates tribal communities with India's first inhabitants, Hindu nationalists seek to bolster their own claim that the Aryans, who brought Vedic civilization to the country, are the original inhabitants of the land.

The Sangh Parivar has set up a plethora of organizations that are active in tribal communities. Prominent examples include Vanvasi Kalyan Ashram, Ekal Vidyalaya, Sewa Bharati, Vivekananda Kendra, Bharat Kalyan Pratishthan, and Friends of Tribal Society. There are also many allied NGOs working to promote tribal welfare through initiatives in fields like education. These various groups use a range of strategies to draw tribal communities into mainstream Hindu society. But above all, they seek to impose a Hindu identity on Adivasis by associating and indoctrinating them into Hindu religious ideas and practices, as well as by promoting animosity and hatred against members of other religions, especially Christianity and Islam, regardless of whether the targeted individuals belong to a tribal community. Finally, as part of a program called Ghar Wapasi (homecoming), these organizations strive to convince individuals who have embraced Christianity or Islam to return to the Hindu fold (Xaxa 2000: 23–36).[5]

3 Discussion

Alongside Dalits, tribal communities were the most marginalized segment of the Indian population on the eve of independence. Their marginalization has persisted, despite various constitutional and statutory provisions designed to protect and promote them. This is not to deny the positive impact of affirmative action in state employment and higher education, guaranteed representation in the national parliament and state legislatures, or the creation of local institutions of self-government. As in the case of modern educational initiatives pursued by the state and NGOs, these measures generally reflect a desire to integrate Adivasi communities into mainstream Indian society through participation in state institutions. However, notwithstanding some significant development in Northeast India, authorities have largely failed to implement

5 See also: https://www.outlookindia.com/website/story/adivasi-vs-vanvasi-the-hinduization-of-tribals-in-india/217974.

the various constitutional and statutory provisions intended to protect the lands, territories, languages, and religions of tribal communities. Instead, priority has been given to development and nation building; state governments have resisted efforts to grant local autonomy; and alien languages, histories, cultures, religious beliefs, practices, and values have been imposed through the education system and social welfare measures.

Especially in peninsular India, constitutional and statutory protections seem to have been just for show, having done little to preserve the social identity of Adivasi communities. This is perhaps most evident with respect to language and religious practice. The influence of non-traditional religions has created internal divisions. Followers of traditional religions, Christians, and Hindus now form three distinct religious identities within Adivasi communities, with Hinduism having become a dominant force.

Alongside Christians, followers of traditional religions have been reduced to minority status. Both these groups have found themselves targeted, albeit in different ways, by the RSS and affiliated groups, including the VHP, Bajrang Dal, and the different wings of the BJP. On the one hand, there has been a growing refusal to recognize the distinctiveness of religious traditions rooted in tribal communities, a distinctiveness that had nevertheless been recognized during the colonial period. Instead, followers of traditional religions have come to be treated as Hindus in post-independence India. As early as the 1940s, Govind Sadashiv Ghurye, a well-known sociologist and Indologist, was referring to them as "backward Hindus." And far from being a simple administrative decision, the removal of a separate census category for followers of traditional religions was the result of a sustained effort by Hindu nationalist organizations such as the Hindu Mahasabha to consolidate the Hindu vote. Since the change, census enumerators (primarily drawn from the country's dominant religious community) have tended to automatically enumerate non-Christian members of Adivasi communities as Hindus. In the decades following independence, low levels of education and social mobilization prevented the development of a collective consciousness that would have led followers of traditional religions to insist on being enumerated separately, an option that remained available to a number of other groups. Such a consciousness began to emerge around 2001, prompting clearly articulated demands for official recognition of Adivasi religions, demands supported by formal submissions to the relevant authorities. But although meetings, marches, and rallies have been organized in many locations – including New Delhi and different state capitals – the movement remains confined to certain regions of the country and specific tribal communities.

For Adivasis who follow traditional religions, being categorized as Hindus also means facing significant cultural pressure to abandon their beliefs and practices, considered inferior by mainstream Hindus, in favor of Hindu gods and goddesses, along with forms of prayer and worship prescribed by Hindu religious texts and customs. A lack of respect for traditional religions in mainstream Indian society is also clearly reflected in the seizure and destruction of Adivasi lands and forests for infrastructure projects (industry, mining, transportation, dams and irrigation, etc.) without any consideration of the sacred and historical significance of such sites.

As for Adivasi Christians, they have faced restrictions on their ability to assert their constitutional and legal rights as members of Scheduled Tribes. In particular, Hindu nationalists have targeted provisions designed to protect lands, forests, and other resources in tribal areas. The fact that Christians often bear the brunt of such attacks can be explained in terms of RSS ideology. It is rooted in the view that India is the nation of the Hindus, who consider the country to be their motherland (matrbhumi), the land of their ancestors (pitrbhumi), and their holy land (punya bhumi). And whereas faiths like Sikhism, Buddhism, and Jainism align with Hinduism on these points, the holiest sites of Christianity and Islam lies outside the borders of India. As a result, Hindu nationalists see Muslims and Christians as having divided loyalties that pose a threat to the nation so long as these groups refuse to embrace Hinduism (Savera 2015: 6–12; Tharoor 2018).

Since the initial decades of the post-independence era, Christian members of tribal communities have also faced opposition to their conversion efforts and privileged access to the job market. One legacy of the strong presence of Christian missionaries in the country has been improvements to education, health, and social infrastructure in tribal communities. As a result, Adivasi Christians have been especially well positioned to benefit from affirmative action in state employment and other related measures. Attacks on Christians, especially those who are engaged in defending Indigenous rights or who engage in proselytization, has taken various forms – including harassment, discrimination, and violence. Places of worship have been vandalized and desecrated. Furthermore, anti-Christian sentiment has inspired ongoing efforts to undermine constitutional and statutory protections for minorities by withdrawing recognition from certain Scheduled Tribes or de-scheduling specific individuals.

The growing presence of groups like the RSS and its affiliates has made the tribal areas of India important sites of religious division, tension, and conflict. As part of their mission to build a Hindu nation, these organizations seek to impose a Hindu identity on the Adivasis while rejecting expressions of non-Hindu culture, assertions of minority rights, and demands for local autonomy. Accordingly, Hindu nationalists virtually never oppose state infrastructure projects involving the seizure or destruction of lands, forests, and other resources claimed by the Adivasis. In fact, the RSS and its affiliates invariably dismiss protests against such projects as Maoist or anti-national. The sole objective of these organizations remains the assimilation of tribal communities into mainstream Hindu society and the erasure of their social and cultural distinctiveness.

Ultimately, the Indian constitution's guarantees of "freedom of conscience and the right freely to profess, practice and propagate religion" stand in stark contrast to the situation on the ground. This paradox arises from dynamics at both the national and the state level, where mainstream politics invariably run contrary to the economic, educational, linguistic, and religious interests of Adivasi communities. And since they represent only a small segment of the country's total population, these communities are largely powerless to reshape the larger political landscape. At the same time, mainstream groups actively play on divisions within Adivasi society, the most significant of which are based on religion. As a result, the Adivasis have increasingly lost control over their lands, forests, and other resources. Amid disproportionately high rates of poverty and low levels of education and health, they face the steady erosion of their languages along with significant constraints on the exercise of their religious rights.

References

Ananthanarayanan, Sriram. "Scheduled Tribe Status for Adivasis in Assam." *South Asia: Journal of South Asia Studies* 33, no. 2 (2010): 290–303.

Chaudhuri, Sarit Kumar. "The Institutionalization of Tribal Religion Recasting the Donyi-Polo Movement in Arunachal Pradesh." *Asian Ethnology* 72, no. 2 (2013): 259–277.

Choubey, Kamal Nayan. "The State Tribals and Law: The Politics Behind the Enactment of PESA and FRA." *Social Change* 46, no. 3 (2016): 355–370.

Chakraborty, P. *Fifth & Sixth Scheduled to the Constitution of India* (*Updated and Annotated*). Delhi: Capital Law House, 2011.

Government of India, Department of Social Security. *Report of the Advisory Committee on the Revision of the Lists of Scheduled Castes and Scheduled Tribes*. New Delhi: Government of India, 1965.

Government of India, Ministry of Law and Justice. *The Constitution of India*. New Delhi: Government of India, 2015.

International Labour Organization. *Indigenous and Tribal Populations Convention* (C107). Geneva: International Labour Organization, 1957.

International Labour Organization. *Indigenous and Tribal Peoples Convention (C169)*. Geneva: International Labour Organization, 1989.

Khubchandani, Lachman Mulchand. *Tribal Identity. A Language and Communication Perspective*. Shimla: IIAS, 1992.

Misra, Baniprasanna. "Keynote Address. National Seminar on Governance, Socio-Economic Disparity and Unrest in the 'Scheduled Areas' of India." Tata Institute of Social Sciences, Guwahati, November 22–24, 2012.

Office of International Religious Freedom. *2021 Report on International Religious Freedom: India*. US Department of State, 2022. https://www.state.gov/reports/2021-report-on-international-religious-freedom/india/.

Oommen, Tharaileth Koshy. *Social Inclusion in Independent India: Dimensions and Approaches*. New Delhi: Orient Blackswan, 2014.

Oraon, P.K. "Religious Mobilisation and Sarna Identity: The Predicament and Assertion of Tribals in Jharkhand." PhD diss. submitted to the Centre for the Study of Social Exclusion and Inclusive Policy. New Delhi: Jamia Millia Islamia, 2021.

Prasad, Jayant. "Statement made on behalf of the Delegation of India in the Working Group on the Indigenous population at Geneva." Samata, 1992.

Savera. "The RSS Goal of Hindu Rashtra, The National Movements and its Continuing Communalism." CPI(M) publications, 2015.

Singh, Kumar Suresh. "Marginalised Tribes." *Seminar* 412 (1993): 1–7.

Stuligross, David. "Autonomous Councils in Northeast India: Theory and Practice." *Alternatives* 24, no. 4 (1999): 497–526.

Tharoor, Shashi. "Veer Savarkar: The man credited with creating Hindutva didn't want it restricted to Hindus." *The Print*, February 26, 2018. https://theprint.in/pageturner/excerpt/veer-savarkar-hindutva-india/38073/.

Xaxa, Virginius. "Tribes, Conversion and Sangh." *Jnanadeepa: Pune Journal of Religious Studies* 3, no. 1 (2000): 23–36.

Xaxa, Virginius. *State, Society, and Tribes. Issues in Post-Colonial India*. New Delhi: Pearson Education India, 2008.

Xaxa, Virginius. "Voiceless in Jharkhand, Freedom of Religion Act." *Economic and Political Weekly* 52, no. 40 (2017): 23–26.

Xaxa, Virginius. "Sixth Schedule." In *The Routledge Companion to Northeast India*, edited by Jelle J.P. Wouters and Tanka B. Subba, 400–405. London: Routledge India, 2022.

Australia Has Failed to Protect the Religious Rights of Its Indigenous People

Ernst Willheim

> … myself, my family, our elders and our ancestors are in mourning at the desecration of our sacred site. This is part of our land that we are deeply connected to and which was an important feature of our future. Healing is slow and painful and will not come easily. Our trust in the system and our partners has been broken completely. I hope that some good can come out of our pain as we all work to build a new future for ourselves and future generations.[1]

•••

> It has been 862 days since the establishment of the Djab Wurrung heritage protection embassy to protect sacred women's country from the Victorian government's Western Highway duplication project in the state's western district.
>
> Country is who we are, country is what guides us and what grounds us in all that we do as First Nations people. This particular 12km stretch, where the expansion of a road between Melbourne and Adelaide is planned, holds a deep intimate connection for Djab Wurrung women, with birthing trees that are more than 800 years old. Thousands of generations of Djab Wurrung babies have been born in this country.
>
> Over the last two years Djab Wurrung people have risen to protect these trees. Our determination to rise has been fuelled by the deep power our country holds. That power is one that guards our spirit and our soul when coming up against the coloniser.[2]

1 Puutu Kunti Kurrama and Pinikura (PKKP) traditional Owner, Burchell Hayes, after the 24 May 2020 Juukan Gorge disaster.

2 Sissy Eileen Austin following the destruction of a sacred tree on Djab Wurrung country, October 27, 2020.

 | DOI:10.1163/9789004524330_006

1 Preliminary

On May 24, 2020 a multinational mining company, Rio Tinto, destroyed a 46,000-year-old sacred site at Juukan Gorge in the northwest of Australia, overriding objections by the Puutu Kunti Kurrama and Pinikura (PKKP) people. This wanton act led to national and international outrage. Senior Rio Tinto executives, including the Chief Executive Officer, resigned. Australian governments, Commonwealth (i.e. the federal government) and state, had failed to protect this important site. Numerous other Aboriginal sacred sites in Australia are currently threatened, some by mining companies, others by road and other developments. Australia governments, Commonwealth and state, Australian courts, companies, and businesses have failed, and continue to fail, to protect the religious values of its Indigenous peoples. Destruction of Aboriginal sacred sites diminishes Australia's heritage.

2 Indigenous/State Political Relations

Australia does not recognize its Indigenous peoples in its constitution.[3] Europeans invaded/settled[4] Australia in the late 18th century.[5] Many of the first Australians were massacred,[6] many died of introduced diseases, settler policies have been described as genocide (AHRC 1997), no treaties have been signed with Australia's Indigenous peoples[7] and Australia's Aboriginal people have never ceded sovereignty. It was not until the High Court's decision in *Mabo v Queensland (No 2)*[8] that the Australian High Court rejected the doctrine that Australia was *terra nullius* (land belonging to no-one) at the time of

3 The new Labor government, elected on June 21, 2022 is committed to a referendum to amend the Australian Constitution-see *postscript*.

4 Traditional Australian history refers to "discovery" of Australia and European settlement. Aboriginal activists are increasingly referring to invasion. Australia's national day, commemorating European settlement, is also referred to as "invasion day."

5 There are no accurate estimates of the Australian population prior to European settlement in 1788. According to the Australian Bureau of Statistics estimates range from a minimum of 315,000 to over 1 million people (ABS 2008: 196).

6 Academic historians have recently published an interactive map showing details of colonial massacres: https://c21ch.newcastle.edu.au/colonialmassacres/map.php. For a detailed account of shocking massacres of Yolŋu people including mass shooting of women and children and gifts of poisoned meat, see Trudgen (2013: 12–28).

7 The new Labor government, elected on June 21, 2022 is committed to a *Makaratta*, or treaty, with Aboriginal Australians.

8 (1992) 175 CLR 1.

European settlement and held that the common law of Australia recognized a form of native title that reflected the entitlement of the Indigenous inhabitants of Australia, in accordance with their laws and customs, to their traditional lands.

After extensive consultations with Aboriginal and Torres Strait Islander people, including a Referendum Council which travelled widely throughout Australia and 13 regional dialogues, on May 26, 2017 the First Nations Constitutional Convention adopted the Uluru Statement from the Heart calling for a "First Nations Voice" in the Australian Constitution and a Makarrata[9] Commission to supervise a process of "agreement-making" and truth-telling between the Australian government and Aboriginal and Torres Strait Islander peoples. On October 26, 2017, the Australian government rejected the statement, saying: "The government does not believe such a radical change to our Constitution's representative institutions has any realistic prospect of being supported by a majority of Australians in a majority of states." The newly elected Australian Labor Party government[10] is committed to the Uluru Statement, including a constitutional referendum.

Australia is a federation. The Commonwealth (federal) Parliament has the constitutional competence to legislate in relation to Indigenous religious rights (curiously, the source of the power is the "race" power, Constitution, s. 51(xxvi)). Key legislation includes the *Native Title Act 1993* and the *Aboriginal and Torres Strait Islander Heritage Protection Act 1984*, which, as will be seen, has had limited success. The Australian states and territories are also competent to protect Indigenous religious rights, but state and territory legislation and state and territory administrations have also proved ineffective against the competing pressures of mining and other interests.

3 The Nature of Aboriginal Religious Beliefs

There is no single Aboriginal religion. Before the European invasion/settlement of Australia there were many hundreds of distinct Aboriginal communities, sometimes referred to as tribes or nations, some 300 languages[11] and considerable religious diversity. Notwithstanding this diversity, there were common threads. A particular common thread, now identified as "the Dreaming,"

9 A treaty or Makarrata is much more than just a synonym for treaty. It is a complex Yolngu word describing a process of conflict resolution, peacemaking, and justice.

10 Australia has a two-party system. The Australian Labor Party was successful in elections held on June 21, 2022, see postscript.

11 The Australian Institute of Aboriginal and Torres Strait Islander Studies has published a map of Indigenous languages: https://aiatsis.gov.au/explore/map-indigenous-australia.

consists of stories about ancestors and spirits. The special feature of Aboriginal religious beliefs is that these ancestors and spirits have relationships with people, with places (commonly referred to as sacred sites) and objects. Religious rituals and religious ceremonies are associated with sacred sites and sacred objects. Spiritual powers play a major part in Aboriginal life. Living people, Aboriginal elders, are connected mystically to places, to sacred sites. Power, or energy, and the right to use it, may be associated with sacred sites and with sacred objects. Aboriginal people venerate the places where power or force is believed to be concentrated. Only the right person, ordinarily a senior elder, with the right ritual, can release the mystical power from a sacred site or from a sacred object.

Secrecy is an essential element of Aboriginal religious belief. Knowledge about a particular sacred site or sacred object may be restricted to a particular elder or elders. Elders "own" stories, songs and dances. Only the elder or elders who own the knowledge have the authority to speak about it. It is the duty of the elder or elders to guard that knowledge and to pass it on selectively, at the appropriate time, to the next generation. Many beliefs, rituals and ceremonies are gender related. Men may have general awareness of women's rituals and women of men's rituals, but they will not have specific knowledge of the sacred sites important in the ceremonies of the other sex and they are not able to speak about them. Men will not disclose such information to women and women will not disclose information to men. For example, women have beliefs, rituals, and ceremonies, particularly relating to puberty and childbirth, in which men do not share (although men will be aware that they are not to enter a particular site because it is a women's site). Men have sites associated with male initiation rites, these involve induction of young men by stages into the fellowship of the most senior men who understand the religious mysteries, some only in part, a very few the whole. The ultimate purpose is to ensure the passage to and the retention by the rightful persons of the knowledge necessary for the continuance of life itself.

These beliefs, ceremonies, and rituals are the core of the religious life of the community. They govern social relations and customs at all stages of life, including birth, initiation, and burial. Access to religious knowledge is a basis for power in the community. Conversely, restrictions on disclosure are part of "The Law." Disclosure contrary to "The Law" is thought to have adverse consequences for the community as a whole. Improper disclosure may be "dangerous." "Sickness" may result. The traditional authority of the elders and the social stability of the community may be undermined.

After European settlement/invasion, early Christian missionaries sought to prohibit Aboriginal religious practices and to eradicate Aboriginal culture. Aboriginal children in Christian mission schools were even prohibited from speaking in their own Aboriginal languages. Loss of language inevitably led to loss of culture and to loss of religious beliefs and religious practices. More recently, some Christian institutions are now at the forefront of seeking reconciliation.[12]

3.1 *Aboriginal Connection to Land is Spiritual and Religious*

The Australian Parliament and Australian courts have recognized the spiritual nature of Aboriginal connection to land. As long ago as 1976, Section 3 of the *Aboriginal Land Rights (Northern Territory) Act 1976* defined 'traditional Aboriginal owners' in relation to land to mean:

> a local descent group of Aboriginals who –
> (a) Have common spiritual affiliation to a site on the land, being affiliations that place the group under a primary spiritual responsibility for that site and for the land.

In a series of cases Australian courts have recognized that Aboriginal connection to land is intrinsically different from traditional common law concepts of ownership. In *Milirrpum v Nabalco Pty Ltd*, Blackburn J said that:

> the fundamental truth about the aboriginals' relationship to the land is that whatever else it is, it is a religious relationship [...] There is an unquestioned scheme of things in which the spirit ancestors, the people of the clan, particular land and everything that exists on and in it, are organic parts of one indissoluble whole.[13]

Some years later in *R.v Toohey; Ex parte Meneling Station Pty Ltd*, in the High Court of Australia, Brennan J wrote: "Aboriginal ownership is primarily a spiritual affair ...,"[14] a statement specifically adopted in the joint High Court judgment of Gleeson CJ, Gaudron, Kirby and Hayne JJ in *Yanner v Eaton.*[15] Many years later, in *Western Australia v Ward*, Gleeson CJ, Gaudron, Gummow and Hayne JJ confirmed that:

> As it is now well recognized, the connection which Aboriginal peoples have with "country" is essentially spiritual. [...] It is a relationship which

12 For example, the Australian Centre for Christianity and Culture states that "indigenous reconciliation is a 'core business of the Centre.' The Centre is 'engaged' in understanding the depths and wellspring of indigenous spirituality."

13 (1971) 17 FLR 141 at 167.

14 (1982) 158 CLR 327, 358.

15 (1999) 201 CLR 351.

> sometimes is spoken of as having to care for, and being able to "speak for," country. [...] The difficulty of expressing a relationship between a community or group of Aboriginal people and the land in terms of rights and interests is evident. Yet that is required by the NTA [*Native Title Act*]. The spiritual or religious is translated into the legal.[16]

In a recent landmark decision,[17] involving a claim for compensation in respect of construction of a series of public works which extinguished or impaired native title rights, the Australian High Court has held that native title rights include, in addition to physical and material aspects, cultural and spiritual aspects. It followed that the compensation payable to native title holders for extinguishment of their native title included, in addition to conventional compensation for economic loss, very substantial compensation (in this case $A1.3m) for cultural loss, essentially the spiritual and metaphysical relationship which the Ngaliwurru and Nungali Peoples (the claim group) had with their country. This type of loss had previously been articulated as "non-economic loss" or "solatium," language which the High Court saw as distracting from the deeper purpose of the *Native Title Act*. The Court's task was to determine the essentially spiritual relationship which the claimant group had with their country and to translate the spiritual hurt from the compensable acts, in this case the public works, into compensation. Significantly, the compensation for cultural loss substantially exceeded the compensation for economic loss ($A1.3m as against $A320,250). The Court in its judgment referred extensively to rituals and ceremonies inextricably bound to the relevant lands, four Dreaming sites, various works damaged or threatened to damage sites of Dreaming or other spiritual significance and referred to the claim group's deep spiritual connection to land. The Court had to translate the spiritual hurt caused by the compensable acts into compensation (para 216).[18] The decision may have far reaching implications.

In earlier proceedings in the same case, an order had been made suppressing publication and disclosure of evidence:

> the restricted transcripts and reports relate to matters that are restricted in their transmission or communication to ritually qualified men according to customary Aboriginal practices. Such matters (gender restricted knowledge, which includes performance, song, narrative and objects)

16 (2002) 213 CLR 1, at 14.

17 *Northern Territory v Mr A. Griffiths (deceased) and Lorraine Jones on behalf of the Ngaliwurru and Nungali Peoples* [2019] HCA 7.

18 Ibid., especially at paras 23, 41–44, 53,54, 155, 161, 167, 180, 187 and 199.

> are a fundamental component of Aboriginal religious belief and practice. The integrity of their restricted domain is sustained through a structured system where knowledge is controlled by some and allocated to others according to customary rules for its dissemination. Failure to comply with those rules is believed to result in exposure to harmful and potentially fatal spirituality. Those who break the rules for transmission may be subjected to social opprobrium and spiritual reprisals that may be deadly. The men who gave the restricted men's evidence [...] would not have been prepared to give evidence had they known that it might later be read in transcript by a woman. If that were to occur the men concerned would be vulnerable to the social opprobrium, spiritual reprisals and other deeply held fears of the kind mentioned.[19]

4 Protection of Aboriginal Religious Beliefs: A Mixed Story

The story of protection of Australian Aboriginal religious beliefs is long and mixed. Aboriginal sacred sites have been threatened, sometimes destroyed, by mining and other developments. Sometimes governments have stepped in to block developments, other times governments have failed to act. Courts have at times overturned government decisions, preferencing common law principles over Aboriginal values. On the other hand, courts have recognized the spiritual nature of Aboriginal connection to land.

4.1 *A Major Step: The Commonwealth Government Stopped Mining on Coronation Hill* (Guratba)

Coronation Hill was the site of a valuable mineral deposit, with reserves of gold, palladium, and platinum. It was also an important Aboriginal sacred site. The mining industry argued that allowing the mine to go ahead would create jobs and increase export earnings. It was argued that stopping the mine would have a negative impact on investor confidence and heighten international perception of sovereign risk, to Australia's national economic detriment.[20]

19 Ibid., para 3.

20 I have been involved, as a government lawyer, with other negotiations with a multinational mining company where the company has consistently argued that if the government demanded too much for Aboriginal people the company would leave Australia and mine in Canada. (First Nations leaders in Canada have informed me the same company argues the reverse in Canada – if requirements for protection of First Nations interests in Canada are too tough, they will go to Australia).

For the Jawoyn Aboriginal people the hill, which they called Guratba, was the site of a spiritual being, Bulla. The area was "sickness country." Disturbing the site would give rise to physical disasters and other adverse consequences for Aboriginal people.

The issue generated bitter national debate and political division, including in the cabinet. One prominent Minister described the area as "clapped out buffalo country." Another Minister referred derogatorily to the Jawoyn people and their spirit, Bulla, as "Bulla-shit." Labor Prime Minister Hawke headed an able cabinet and cabinet debate was extensive. I was not present at the five-hour cabinet meeting, on June 19, 1991, but I understand the final count was 12 in favor of allowing the mine, 8 against. When the Prime Minister summarized the debate, that there would be no mining, no member of the cabinet objected. The Prime Minister was respected, and all understood his deep personal commitment to the Aboriginal people. I was called in to the Prime Minister's office late that evening. The atmosphere there was tense. Around midnight the Prime Minister instructed me to have a bill (to prohibit mining) on his desk by 8 a.m. the next morning. Some six months later, there was a successful leadership challenge and Hawke ceased to be Prime Minister. In an interview shortly before his death, he attributed his loss of the leadership to the Coronation Hill decision. He emphasized his commitment to the Jawoyn people. He was sickened by the sneers of some of his colleagues, people who accepted virgin birth, holy trinity, and resurrection but rejected the religious beliefs of the Jawoyn people.

Coronation Hill is important because it is the only significant Australian mining project that has been stopped to protect Aboriginal religious beliefs. And the Australian Prime Minister who drove that protection lost his job.

5 Aboriginal Religious and Spiritual Beliefs and the Courts

I have referred to some judicial decisions favorable to Aboriginal people. The outcome of litigation relating to protection of Aboriginal sacred sites and beliefs has been mixed. Protection declarations made by the Commonwealth Government, aimed at protecting Aboriginal sacred sites, have been successfully challenged in the courts. Common law principles of open justice and procedural fairness have prevailed over the secret nature of Aboriginal religious and spiritual beliefs. In contrast, in native title cases, the courts have given weight and recognition to Aboriginal religious, spiritual, and cultural beliefs, sometimes in the face of contrary submissions by Commonwealth, state and territory governments.

5.1 *A Court Prohibits Sale and Distribution of a Book with Gender Specific Sensitive Information*

The first judicial decision protecting the secret nature of Aboriginal religious beliefs was an injunction prohibiting the sale and distribution, in the Northern Territory of Australia, of a book, *Nomads of the Australian Desert*, by an amateur ethnographer, C.P. Mountford (*Foster and Others v Mountford and Rigby*).[21] This book was a classic study of the traditional lives of Australian Aborigines in central Australia, with many black and white photographs. The plaintiffs were members of an unincorporated association, the Pitjanjara Council, representing the Pitjanjara people. The application sought to protect gender specific confidential information of the Pitjanjara people published in *Nomads* that the applicants claimed was provided to Mountford in confidence more than 35 years earlier.

5.2 *Government Submissions Reject Aboriginal Spiritual Beliefs*

I refer next to two court cases involving Aboriginal claims relating to sacred sites where governments, in one case a state government and in the other case the Commonwealth (federal) Government, have strongly opposed those claims. It is proper that I disclose that I was counsel in each case.[22]

Gender related issues in Aboriginal heritage protection cases arose in *Western Australia v Minister for Aboriginal and Torres Strait Islander Affairs*,[23] the first case in which the Federal Court made an order effectively preventing a member of the legal profession having access to evidence related to gender on grounds of cultural sensitivity. The state of Western Australia challenged the validity of declarations made by the Commonwealth Minister for Aboriginal and Torres Strait Islander Affairs under the *Aboriginal and Torres Strait Islander Heritage Protection Act 1984*. The Minister's declarations related to a site claimed by the Yawuru people to be a traditional Aboriginal area associated with male initiation ceremonies. The site was threatened by a proposal to extend a crocodile farm.

In the course of giving discovery, the Minister disclosed a number of anthropological reports (referred to in the proceedings as the Sullivan Report) and affidavits provided to the Minister on condition that they not be reproduced or be seen by women or by uninitiated Aboriginal men. Late on Wednesday, July 27, 1994, the state of Western Australia made application to the Federal

21 14 ALR 76 (1971).

22 In the first case, I was counsel for the Commonwealth Minister, in the second case I was an *amicus curiae* applicant, opposing the Commonwealth's submissions.

23 (1994) 54 FCR 144.

Court for orders requiring the production of the Sullivan Report to its counsel and solicitor (who were both women). I was briefed on July 28 to appear for the Commonwealth Minister to oppose that application and flew from Canberra to Perth that evening (Perth is on the west coast of Australia, almost 4000 km west of Canberra, in a different time zone). The matter was heard the next day, July 29, 1994. Submissions by senior counsel for Western Australia were very aggressive, including highly derogatory comments about Aboriginal beliefs. Amongst other things she asserted that an affidavit by an Aboriginal man explaining the reasons for secrecy, referring to a Dreaming story, was illogical and should be rejected. This was an important and very serious submission: an Aboriginal Dreaming story, claims relating to Aboriginal spiritual and religious beliefs, should be rejected because they lacked logic. This was not an ill prepared submission by a junior lawyer. Counsel for the state was an experienced senior counsel (not much later, she was appointed to be a Justice of the Supreme Court). It is inconceivable that such a direct attack on Aboriginal spirituality was made without clear instructions. I also think it inconceivable that she would have been unaware how offensive that submission was to Aboriginal people, how derogatory it was of the spiritual beliefs of the world's oldest living culture.

Unfortunately, this is a typical example of the attitudes of a conservative state government to Aboriginal spiritual beliefs. Frankly I was shocked. Here was a state government openly contending, in the Federal Court, that claims relating to Aboriginal spiritual and religious beliefs should be rejected because they lacked logic. As if logic was a necessary ingredient of spiritual and religious beliefs. I was counsel for the Commonwealth Minister. As counsel, I had to put to the Court the Minister's views, not my own. Fortunately, the Minister's chief of staff was in court with my instructing solicitor. Over the lunch break, I was able to obtain instructions from the Minister to submit, in reply, that aspects of mainstream religious beliefs such as a virgin birth, resurrection, and reincarnation could also be seen by some as lacking logic. Religious beliefs depended on faith, not logic, and should be respected. My submissions opposing disclosure drew also on Section 27 of the Act, the prejudice to the Aboriginal applicants, together with a substantial argument based on public interest immunity; the information concerning secret initiation ceremonies was inherently confidential, public interest immunity extended to Aboriginal secrets or a fresh category of public interest immunity covering secret and sacred Aboriginal information and beliefs should be recognized.

In an *ex tempore* judgement Carr J ordered that the Sullivan Report be produced for inspection by the state's counsel and solicitors save that only one of such persons should be female. In his reasons, he explained that the interests of justice required that at least one of the state's counsel and solicitor have access to the report. By excluding one of them, there should be no real prejudice to the applicant's case and the interests of the Yawuru people were protected to the fullest extent possible.[24]

Wurridjal v The Commonwealth[25] was a constitutional challenge, in the High Court of Australia, brought by Reggie Wurridjal and Joy Garlbin, senior members of the Dhukurrdji clan, to provisions of Australian legislation establishing what had become known as the Northern Territory Intervention. This controversial legislation was a response to reports of child sexual abuse of Aboriginal children, graphically described in a report to the Northern Territory Government entitled *Ampe Akelyernemane Meke Mekarle – Little Children are Sacred* (2007). The conservative Howard government introduced so-called emergency legislation, relying on the "territories power" (Australian Constitution, s 122) and the "race power" (Australian Constitution, s 51(xxvi)), to provide for five-year leases in favor of the Commonwealth on Aboriginal land. The alleged purpose of these statutory leases was to enable the Commonwealth to repair houses and infrastructure. The Aboriginal plaintiffs, traditional owners of Maningrida land, in a constitutional challenge in the High Court of Australia,[26] claimed that provisions of the legislation amounted to an unlawful acquisition, without payment of "just terms,"[27] of their traditional rights, including their right to participate in ceremony including on identified sacred sites.

The Commonwealth Government changed; it now fell to the newly elected Labor government to defend the constitutional challenge. The government lodged two demurrers,[28] one asserted that the alleged right to participate in ceremony on identified Aboriginal sites did not constitute property for the purposes of Section 51(xxvi) of the Constitution. I was incensed at the apparent denigration of Aboriginal religious/spiritual beliefs and with Professor Kim Rubenstein[29] made an *amicus curiae* application to the High Court to put to the Court extensive international authorities supporting the rights of Indigenous people to practice their religion and culture which, so we submitted, would assist the Court in determining whether the rights claimed by the plaintiffs,

24 See Willheim 1994.

25 (2008) 237 CLR 309; [2009] HCA 2.

26 The High Court of Australia, Australia's highest court, has original jurisdiction in constitutional matters.

27 Section 51(xxxi) enables the Commonwealth Parliament to legislate for the acquisition of property "on just terms."

28 A demurrer is a technical legal procedure by which a party contends that even if the facts alleged are established, the claims are not good in law.

29 Head of the Centre for Public and International Law, ANU College of Law.

the right to participate in ceremony on identified Aboriginal sacred sites, were property for the purposes of Section 51(xxvi).[30]

The underlying proposition, the very idea that a spiritual belief may have legal status, may surprise some. A claim to access land to conduct a religious ceremony may not constitute a claim to a property right under traditional common law principles. Why should a claim by Indigenous people to access a sacred site to conduct ceremony be viewed differently. The answer requires an understanding that, while native title is recognized by the common law, native title owes its origins and derives its content from Indigenous traditions and customs. It is to those traditions and customs that one must turn to understand the nature and content of native title rights.[31] The claims asserted by the plaintiffs were undoubtedly different from conventional property rights commonly recognized by traditional Australian property law. That was no reason to reject those rights as property rights. The purpose of the Northern Territory's land rights legislation (*Aboriginal Land Rights* (*Northern Territory*) *Act 1976*) and the subsequent recognition by the High Court of Australia of native title under the common law (*Mabo v Queensland* (*No 2*)) were to give recognition, in the Australian legal system, to a system of traditional ownership not previously recognized. Native title was different from traditional common law property and included the spiritual elements of Indigenous traditions, including a right to conduct ceremonies on land.[32] Such rights are not components of conventional common law title. The content of a system of native title is inherently different from the content of conventional common law title. It is necessary to look to Aboriginal custom and traditions to determine the content and character of a native title right. An analysis that seeks to assess native title rights by reference to traditional common law principles is therefore fundamentally flawed. Aboriginal spiritual beliefs involve close Aboriginal connection with traditional land including, according to Aboriginal custom and tradition, rights and obligations to conduct ceremony on sacred sites. For Aboriginal Australians, ceremony is an attribute of spiritual connection with their land. Indeed, there is a two-way relationship between ceremony and ownership, reflecting the spiritual bond between people and land. The conduct of ceremony is an assertion of ownership. It is also one of the obligations of ownership.

30 The Australian High Court takes a very narrow view in relation to *amicus curiae* applications. An *amicus* applicant must show to the Court that submissions sought to be made cover relevant issues not being raised by the parties. That is why our *amicus* submissions were confined to international law principles and authorities.

31 This was made clear in *Mabo v Queensland* (*No 2*) (1992) 175 CLR 1, [64].

32 *Fejo v Northern Territory* (1998) 195 CLR 6, [47].

I put together extensive written submissions, drawing on a wide range of international legal materials, international conventions, UN General Assembly resolutions, and decisions of a range of international tribunals which in our submission established that the rights of Indigenous peoples to practice their religion and culture were legally significant. It followed, so we submitted, that the Commonwealth's demurrer should be overruled.

Our *amicus* application was refused, by majority, Kirby and Crennan J dissenting. Kirby J, in his dissenting judgment, cited extensively the international materials which we had put before the Court, noting that, although the *amicus* application itself had been refused, these materials were all publicly available. Much of my extensive research is therefore now on the public record in a (dissenting) judgment of the High Court. Many Aboriginal organizations subsequently contacted me expressing appreciation of this material which they believed would be influential in the future.[33] I add that I met the Attorney-General at a legal conference a short time after the case was argued and asked him why, having regard to the Labor government's professed support for Aboriginal interests including land rights, the Government had submitted that the rights Wurridjal asserted did not constitute property. The Attorney-General responded that he had simply approved the recommendation of the Department. In my view this response (assuming it is accurate) reflects poorly on both the Attorney-General's interest in and understanding of the issues and the understanding on the part of departmental officers of underlying government policies.

Wurridjal is not an isolated example. The issue arises again and again, for example, in relation to a proposed nuclear waste dump at Manuwangku or Muckaty in the Northern Territory, land described by a Government Minister as "in the middle of nowhere" (Crispin 2013: 6). One writer has poignantly observed: "It can be difficult for non-indigenous people to understand the Aboriginal spiritual connection with landscape, or to comprehend the deep suffering of those who are unable to defend their traditional country from the ravages of industry." (Crispin 2013: 2) In this example, it seems the Government Minister failed even to address the customs and beliefs of the Aboriginal people. To ignore the traditional roles of Aboriginal people as custodians of their land and to ignore their spiritual connection to their land is to ignore

33 I subsequently gave conference papers and published articles on the High Court's approach to *amicus* issues, drawing attention to deficiencies in the principles the Court applied and the Court's procedures and suggesting better approaches and better procedures (Willheim 2010). I also wrote to the Chief Justice drawing attention to procedural deficiencies. Some of those problems have subsequently been rectified.

the reality of their rights and interests in land. Those rights and interests are clearly valuable to them and demanding of proper legal recognition.

An issue not raised in the *Wurridjal* proceedings, and apparently also not raised in the Manuwangku or Muckaty dispute, is whether laws impeding access to sacred sites for the performance of traditional ceremony would be contrary to the provisions of s 116 of the Australian Constitution, preventing the Commonwealth from making any law "for prohibiting the free exercise of any religion." Authority on the scope of the Section 116 prohibition is limited, but it may be noted, first, that in the *Scientology case*[34] Murphy J would have extended Section 116 to Indigenous religions.[35] Secondly, the prohibition does not extend to executive or administrative action.[36] Thirdly, it seems that in light of *Kruger v The Commonwealth*, where the High Court rejected the claim that the removal of Aboriginal children from their parents breached their right to the free exercise of their religion, Section 116 does not invalidate laws that have only an indirect effect on the free exercise of religion.

5.3 *Common Law Principles Defeat Claims for Protection of Sacred Sites*

It is somewhat ironic that core values of the common law system can defeat the religious values of Australia's Aboriginal people. How can this be? I have explained the secret nature of certain Aboriginal beliefs. Core values of the common law system as it operates in Australia include openness and transparency in both the judicial process and public administration together with the core principles of natural justice and procedural fairness. When Aboriginal people seek protection of sacred sites, these core values and principles of the dominant legal system govern the administrative and legal processes pursuant to which protection is sought. Briefly put, to pursue protection, Aboriginal people may be required publicly to disclose the secret nature of their beliefs, the very things they are trying to protect. This fundamental conflict between the principles of the common law legal system and the religious or spiritual values of Aboriginal Australians, the dilemma Aboriginal people face when seeking to protect those values, are best illustrated by reference to one of the leading cases, *Tickner v Chapman*[37] commonly referred to as *the Hindmarsh Bridge case*.

34 *Church of the New Faith v Commissioner of Pay-Roll Tax (Vic)* (1983) 154 CLR 120.

35 Ibid, 151.

36 *Kruger v Commonwealth* (1997) 190 CLR 1, 86, 131.

37 (1995) 57 FCR 451. It is proper that I disclose that I appeared as counsel for the appellant, Robert Tickner, Minister, for Aboriginal and Torres Strait islander Affairs, in the Federal Court appeal. I did not argue the matter at first instance.

The *Hindmarsh Bridge case* involved an application for protection of an area of spiritual significance to Aboriginal women made to the Australian Minister for Aboriginal and Torres Strait Islander Affairs under Section 10 of the *Aboriginal and Torres Strait Islander Heritage Protection Act 1984*. The protection application was made by the Aboriginal Legal Rights Movement, concerned about a proposal to build a bridge over the mouth of the Murray River to improve access to Hindmarsh Island in connection with a proposed marina and real estate development. The Ngarrindjeri women believed construction of the proposed bridge would have devastating spiritual consequences.

The Act establishes a process for protection of areas and objects of particular significance to Aboriginal people. Somewhat unusually for Australian legislation at that time, the Act includes a purpose clause: "The purposes of this Act are the preservation and protection [...] of areas and objects [...] that are of particular significance to Aboriginals" (s 4). The protection process is initiated by an application, made to the Minister, by an Aborigine or a group of Aborigines. An application may be made orally or in writing, an innovative provision as legal processes usually depend on much greater formality. Recognizing that threats to Aboriginal heritage may require urgent responses, the Act makes provision for the making of an emergency declaration (s 9), for a limited period, and for a permanent declaration (s 10). A declaration may make provision for protection of an area from injury or desecration. Before making a "permanent" (s 10) declaration, the Minister must appoint a person to prepare a report. The reporter must give public notice of the purpose of the application for protection, invite interested persons to make representations and report to the Minister. The Minister must then consider the report and the representations. The Minister, Robert Tickner, appointed a reporter, eminent Professor of Constitutional Law, Cheryl Saunders. She gave public notice, presented her report to the Minister and the Minister made a Section 10 declaration. Professor Saunder's report and Minister Tickner's declaration were both successfully challenged. The Court applied all the technicalities of the common law.

I briefly mention the ground for quashing Professor Saunder's report. The notice published by Professor Saunders referred to "significant Aboriginal areas in the vicinity of Goolwa and Hindmarsh (Kumarangk) island." Applying authorities developed in the context of notices relating to proposed local government developments, which required a great degree of particularity, the Court held the notice Professor Saunders published did not provide sufficient particularity. Since the notice was defective, it followed that the whole Section 10 process was fundamentally flawed.

Was this inevitable? Submissions drawing on the beneficial purpose of the legislation, that detailed public notification of the area might lead to further injury or violation of traditional beliefs, that because applications may be made orally great formality should not be required, that, because one of the matters to be dealt with in the report was the area to be protected, it could not have been intended that the public notice must closely define the area, submissions that Professor Saunders received over 400 representations, submissions that everyone knew the purpose of the protection application, were all of no avail. The Court focused on formal compliance.

One can understand the need for particularity in a local government context. Lack of particularity may indeed disadvantage people potentially affected. But in this case, there was no finding that any of the objectors were disadvantaged by any lack of detail in the published notice. The Court did not even find it necessary to consider whether any of the objectors were disadvantaged. The judgments focused on formality. I add that, in relation to protection of Aboriginal sacred sites, the court's approach may create real difficulty. Sometimes Aboriginal people are uncomfortable about disclosing the exact location of a sacred site, for example a birthing site or a male initiation site. From an Aboriginal perspective, it should be open to the Section 10 reporter to publish a notice and for the Minister to make a declaration preventing a development that would interfere with a sacred site without the need for disclosure of the precise location of the site itself.

The Court also quashed Minister Tickner's Section 10 declaration on the ground that he had failed to "consider" the representations attached to the report. Professor Saunders' report included an anthropological report relating to the significance of the area sought to be protected and referred to "secret oral tradition" and "secret women's knowledge." This material was placed in sealed envelopes marked "to be read by women only." This material was later referred to, derogatively, in the public debate, as "secret women's business." Professor Saunders in her report concluded: "Hindmarsh and Mundoo Islands and the waters surrounding them have a supreme spiritual and cultural significance for the Ngarrindjeri people, within the knowledge of Ngarrindjeri women, which concerns the lifeforce itself. If destroyed, the Ngarrindjeri people believe they will be destroyed [...] Dr Fergie's report describes the area [...] as 'crucial for the reproduction of the Ngarrindjeri people and of the cosmos which supports their existence. The adequate functioning of this area is vital to Ngarrindjeri existence.'" (Saunders 1994)

It was not in dispute that Minister Tickner, a man, had not personally read the material in the sealed envelopes, marked "to be read by women only." The evidence was that this material had been read by his female adviser, Ms Kee, the Minister had discussed the material with Ms Kee and she had advised him that the material was consistent with the body of the Saunders report. Submissions on behalf of the Minister that this in substance satisfied the consideration requirement were rejected. Again, the Court focused on its technical interpretation of "consider." There was no finding that the outcome might have been different had the Minister read the material in the sealed envelopes. The Court did not even address whether the fact the Minister did not read the material may have affected the outcome. Bearing in mind that the material was clearly marked "to be read by women only," it is somewhat ironic that the Court found legal error when the Minister did not read material the applicants so clearly did not want him to read. Ordinarily, it would have been open to the Court to refer the matter back to the Minister for re-consideration but as the notice given by Professor Saunders was defective the process was fundamentally flawed.

The saga continued. A new Section 10 application was made. Following a request from the applicants and a recommendation from Minister Tickner, the Prime Minister appointed a female Minister, Senator Rosemary Crowley, to act on behalf of Minister Tickner. Minister Crowley appointed a highly regarded Federal Court Judge, Jane Matthews, to prepare the Section 10 report. In the meantime, the Full Federal Court in another challenge to a Section 10 declaration (the *Broome Crocodile Farm* case), a declaration relating to a male initiation site, held that natural justice/procedural fairness principles applied to the Section 10 reporting process.[38] A federal election intervened. The Labor government was replaced by a conservative coalition government. The new Minister, Senator John Herron, was not sympathetic towards the Ngarrindjeri women. He refused requests that he arrange for a female Minister. The developers of the proposed marina now sought access to all the material the applicant women had submitted. When the new Section 10 reporter, Matthews J, advised the Ngarrindjeri women that, considering the decision in the *Broome Crocodile Farm* case, she was obliged to make their representations available to the objectors, who were male, and that Senator John Herron, a male, would receive her report, the Ngarrindjeri women withdrew the substance of their application. It followed that there was insufficient evidence to support a declaration.

This is where common law principles and Aboriginal cultural, religious, and spiritual values come into conflict. The making of a declaration may have

38 *Minister for Aboriginal and Torres Strait Islander Affairs v State of Western Australia* (1996) 66 FCR 40.

serious adverse consequences for non-aboriginal interests; for example, a declaration may prevent construction of a mine or a dam or other developments. In the *Hindmarsh Bridge case*, the declaration if effective would have prevented the construction of a bridge. The Federal Court has grafted common law procedural fairness and natural justice principles onto the simple procedural steps the *Aboriginal and Torres Strait Islander Heritage Protection Act 1984* establishes for the reporting process. It follows, so the Federal Court has determined, that those who would be adversely affected by the making of a declaration are entitled to access to the application for protection, including the submissions in support of protection. Arguably, this is a routine outcome of an administrative process. It follows from the common law principles of natural justice and procedural fairness that one is normally entitled to access to the opposing case and the opportunity to counter opposing submissions.

The difficulty in the context of Aboriginal heritage protection is that secrecy may be an inherent quality of an Aboriginal religious, sacred, site. The location of the site itself and the reasons it is sacred may be secret. The purpose of a protection application may be to protect that secrecy. Yet applying common law principles, natural justice, and procedural fairness to the procedures for protection of the site may require disclosure of the location of the site and the reasons for its significance. That disclosure may destroy the value of the site. Aboriginal people face a dilemma. They must disclose that which they seek to protect. They must break their religious rules or forego the protection of the law. Because the Federal Court has grafted common law principles of natural justice and procedural fairness onto the procedures established by the legislation, the Australian legal system is unable to accommodate the secret nature of Aboriginal religious beliefs. The system the Parliament has established to protect Aboriginal sacred sites is fundamentally flawed. Only the Parliament can correct this problem. A different process, an Aboriginal process for initial investigation of a protection application, must be established.

The Hindmarsh Bridge saga continued. The constitutional validity of the appointment of Matthews J to prepare the Section 10 report was successfully challenged, on the ground that the Section 10 reporting role was incompatible with her judicial office.[39] Her report was therefore a nullity. In any event, a fresh Section 10 application was made. The new application clearly triggered an obligation on the part of Minister Herron to commission a new Section 10 report. Minister Herron refused.[40] Instead, the government introduced new

39 *Wilson v Minister for Aboriginal and Torres Strait Islander Affairs* (1996) 189 CLR 1.

40 I carefully explained to Minister Herron that, upon receipt of the Section 10 application, the legislation required him to appoint a Section 10 reporter. The Minister bluntly refused:

legislation to prevent the making of a declaration in relation to the Hindmarsh Island area (*Hindmarsh Island Bridge Act 1997*). The Ngarrindjeri women challenged the constitutional validity of the legislation, contending that the relevant constitutional power enabled only beneficial legislation, but the challenge failed.[41]

That was the end of the protection application process. But there was further litigation on another front. Those who had opposed Minister Tickner's Section 10 declaration now brought proceedings against Minister Tickner, Professor Saunders and others seeking damages for losses incurred because of the Section 10 declaration. Von Doussa J made a series of findings favorable to the Ngarrindjeri women, including that the spiritual importance of the Islands (Hindmarsh Island and Mundoo Island) and surrounding waters will be injured or desecrated if Hindmarsh Island is linked to the mainland.[42] The Ngarrindjeri women were vindicated. But the bridge was built.

6 The Destruction of Juukan Gorge

On May 24, 2020 Rio Tinto, one of the world's largest multinational mining companies, conducted a blast as part of its extension of the Brockman 4 iron ore mine in northwest Australia. The blast devastated Aboriginal heritage sites at Juukan Gorge, including two rock shelters of great cultural, ethnographic, and archaeological significance. One of these shelters had provided evidence of continuous occupation going back some 46,000 years, making it a site of national and international significance. For the Puutu Kunti Kurrama and Pinikura (PKKP) peoples, it was something even worse – the theft of a vital part of their living culture. The Joint Standing Committee on Northern Australia of the Australian Parliament inquiry described their grief at the loss, which the Committee witnessed at first-hand on visiting the site, as indescribable (JSCNA 2020).

Mr Burchell Hayes, a proud descendant of Juukan (his grandfather), told the Joint Committee inquiring into this destruction:

> Juukan Gorge is an anchor of our culture, with a number of individual cultural sites that makes it unique, an important place. […]

"If you don't provide me with the legal advice I want, I will obtain it from the private sector."

41 *Kartinyeri v Commonwealth of Australia* (1998) 195 CLR 337.

42 *Chapman v Luminis Pty Ltd (no 2)* (2000) FCR 229, [343].

> Juukan Gorge also includes the distinctive and sacred rock pool that used to hold water long after the rain had fallen. The shape of a snake's head entering the ground forms the shape of what used to be a permanent water source. This rock pool is a very spiritual place, which is still visited by the spirits of our people. The Juukan Gorge is known to be a place where the spirits of our relatives who have passed away, even recently, have come to rest. It is a place that the very, very old people still occupy. Purlykuti has been specifically referred to by the old people as a place of pardu, which refers to the special language only spoken during ceremonies in the Pilbara. Our elders state that it is certain that the spirits are very disturbed, and their living relatives are also upset at this. This is why Juukan Gorge is important. It is in the ancient blood of our people and contains their DNA. It houses history and the spirits of ancestors and it anchors the people to this country. (JSCNA 2020: para 1.2)

Mr Hayes emphasised that the loss of the Juukan caves was not just a loss for his people:

> The loss of Juukan Gorge rock shelters is also a loss to all First Nations people and the community within Australia and internationally – communities who have lived to continuously endure the destruction of their physical, cultural and spiritual land with little to no reprieve through legislation or the courts. It is yet another example of the low importance attached to Aboriginal people and Aboriginal culture.
>
> There are other groups, including our Kurrupa neighbours, who have a direct connection with this place through their own knowledge and songlines and through the creation stories and through families. They have told us that they also feel powerless and angry at this having happened. We have an obligation to look after country in accordance with traditional law and customs. It is our obligation to the old people, who also looked after it. It was on loan to us to pass on to our future generations, our Puutu Kunti Kurrama and Pinikura children, and the future generations yet to come. The disaster has now left a gaping hole in our ability to pass on our heritage to our children and grandchildren. (JSCNA 2020: para 1.3).

6.1 *Could This Have Been Prevented?*

The state of Western Australia and the Commonwealth both had legislation directed at Aboriginal heritage protection but for different reasons both pieces of legislation proved ineffective. Rio Tinto had the necessary approvals under

Section 18 of the Western Australian *Aboriginal Heritage Act 1972*, approval obtained back in 2013 without Aboriginal input. The Joint Committee of the Australian Parliament reported that the Act did not provide for any meaningful involvement of Aboriginal people in the decisions made over their heritage (JSCNA 2020: para 1.22). The PKKP were not even contacted by state government officials for their views on the application for the Section 18 consent. That legislation had been recognized as deficient and was already under review when the Juukan Gorge was destroyed. In its final Report, the Joint Committee concluded the Act had not protected Aboriginal heritage and, in some instances had even facilitated the destruction of sites (JSCNA 2021: para 4.29). The focus of the administrative regime was on authorization of destruction rather than protecting cultural heritage. Ministers regularly allowed applications to destroy sites (JSCNA 2021: para 4.37). Rio Tinto had been able to use approval under Section 18 of the Act to destroy Juukan Gorge (JSCNA 2021: para 4.40). Traditional owners had no procedural rights, no right to be heard, no right to initiate any enforcement processing, no right to seek review of decisions (JSCNA 2021: para 4.36, 4.40).

Commonwealth legislation, the *Aboriginal and Torres Strait Islander Heritage Protection Act 1984*, already considered above in relation to Hindmarsh Bridge, would have enabled the Commonwealth Minister to make an emergency declaration and a permanent declaration preventing the destruction. For several reasons that legislative mechanism was not activated. Applications were initially made to the wrong minister. Curiously, the legislation was administered by the Environment Minister, not the Aboriginal Affairs Minister. It seems the PKKP and their legal advisers were not well informed. Commonwealth authorities had done little to familiarize Aboriginal communities with the available protection mechanisms. Telephone calls made to the office of the correct Commonwealth Minister, on May 20, 2020 were not returned. Had they been returned, a protection application could have been made orally and an emergency declaration could have been made. A further impediment was that the PKKP was bound by confidentiality clauses in its Agreements with Rio Tinto, Agreements which confer financial benefits on the PKKP in exchange for confidentiality undertakings. The Joint Committee also noted criticisms of the Agreements between the PKKP and Rio Tinto, including their complexity and confidentiality or gag clauses that prevented the PKKP from discussing the terms of the Agreements and from seeking heritage protection, without first advising Rio Tinto. Other traditional owners reported similar gag clauses that only served to protect the interests of the resources company (JSCNA 2021: para 3.66). The Joint Committee described Rio Tinto's conduct as reflecting "a corporate culture which prioritized commercial gain over the kind of meaningful engagement with Traditional Owners that should form a critical part of their social license to operate." (JSCNA 2020: para 1.18)

The consequences for Rio Tinto were in some respects staggering, in other respects negligible. Rio Tinto suffered enormous reputational damage. Rio Tinto's actions were described in the Australian Parliament as "inexcusable and an affront not only to the PKKP peoples but to all Australians." (CA 2021: 9434) Language used in the parliamentary debate was strong:

> What the committee uncovered was the historical abuse of power by the mining industry in Western Australia, enabled by Western Australian law, to effectively corral, ignore and override the rights and interests of traditional owners, to use every legal trick to do this and to do so without recrimination or penalties or the need to properly compensate Aboriginal people in Western Australia for the exploitation of their traditional lands and the destruction of their heritage. (CA 2021: 9435)

Destruction has been described as "disgraceful, negligent and wilful" (JSCNA 2021: 211), and a leading Australian newspaper, the Australian Financial Review, reported the destruction as "an egregious story of corporate blindness" (JSCNA 2021: 211). The company's chairman, chief executive and at least three other senior executives resigned, consequences unprecedented in the corporate world, but left with "golden handshakes" reportedly worth tens of millions of dollars each (JSCNA 2021: 212). No financial penalties or regulatory sanctions were imposed on the company. Rio Tinto had not broken any laws.

On November 16, 2021 the Western Australian (State) Government introduced new Aboriginal heritage protection legislation. The state premier's department said the bill would focus on reaching agreement with Aboriginal groups and on obtaining full, prior and informed consent for development. The government insisted the bill had been the subject of extensive consultation and would ensure the principles of free, prior and informed consent would be embedded in negotiations between land users and traditional owners. The new bill would require proponents to consult with Traditional Owners and agree together on cultural management plans where the former wants to develop near heritage sites. But that is only part of the picture. Where agreements cannot be reached, the final say will go to the Aboriginal Affairs Minister. This is the critical issue. Notwithstanding government rhetoric about consultation, agreement, and informed consent, the *Aboriginal Cultural Heritage Act 2021* does not give Aboriginal people any right to withhold consent in relation to destruction of their sacred sites. There is no right of Aboriginal veto. The final decision is to be taken by the Minister. And Aboriginal people have no right to appeal against the Minister's decision.

Aboriginal reaction has been strong and swift. The Aboriginal Heritage Alliance said the State government had refused to share drafts of the bill with any Indigenous groups: Aboriginal groups were only shown the final legislation the day it was publicly released. They say they have not been adequately consulted. The government has ignored their concerns by retaining the ultimate decision-making power on the destruction of cultural heritage sites. "It's a devastating day for Aboriginal heritage," said Tyronne Garstone, chief executive of the Kimberley Land Council. The Bill would create a "cultural catastrophe." "Fundamentally, this bill will not protect Aboriginal cultural heritage and will continue a pattern of systematic structural racial discrimination against Aboriginal people [...] The state government has proved it is too close to industry and too dependent on royalties to be objective and transparent when it comes to matters concerning Aboriginal heritage." (Ramsey 2021; Reuters 2021)

Gundjitmara Djabwurrung man and National Native Title Council chief executive Jamie Lowe said the legislation ignored the recommendations of the Joint Committee. "Essentially the new bill seems like a convoluted version of the old act, with the ultimate decision-making power still up to the minister and still no real right to appeal for Aboriginal people," "What we have been delivered is [...] the Minister making unchallenged decisions on whether cultural heritage may be destroyed." (NNTC 2020) Tony Bevan, acting chief executive of the Wintawari Guruma Aboriginal Corp, said the bill also put a lot of extra bureaucratic requirements on poorly resourced and financed Aboriginal groups. In contrast, "The Chamber of Minerals and Energy, which represents miners including Rio, BHP Group and Fortescue Metals Group, noted 'extensive consultation' with government ministers, and said it could work with the new laws." (Reuters 2021) Here is the issue. The miners say they were consulted. Aboriginal people say they were not adequately consulted. Critically, who should have the final say? Should Aboriginal people have the right to withhold consent to destruction of their sacred sites? If the Minister is to have the final say, should there be a right of appeal. After three years of review of the old act, the bill was listed as "urgent" and enacted. The Bill has now been passed, unchanged.

The Hindmarsh Bridge and Juukan Gorge cases illustrate fundamental problems with the Commonwealth's *Aboriginal and Torres Strait Islander Heritage Protection Act*. Hindmarsh Bridge showed how the Act is unable to protect secret Aboriginal beliefs. Juukan Gorge exposed fundamental defects in Commonwealth administration. Above all, the Act establishes a non Aboriginal process that fails to give effect to core principles of the UN Declaration on the Rights of Indigenous peoples such as the right of Indigenous people to give prior and informed consent to, for example, destruction of sacred sites. After three years of review of the Western Australian legislation, the new Act suffers similar defects.

Destruction of the Juukan Gorge attracted national and international attention. The Joint Committee found the destruction of cultural heritage sites was an alarmingly common occurrence (JSCNA 2021: para 3.89). It expressed concern over the power held by the mining industry over negotiations and agreement making (JSCNA 2021: para 3.90), and found a shocking power disparity between Aboriginal and Torres Strait Islander people and large mining companies (JSCNA 2021: para 3.7). The Joint Committee also noted evidence from one member of Parliament "with being threatened, having their reports modified by mining corporations, and being dismissed for refusing to amend reports in favour of the proponent's desires" (JSCNA 2020: para 3.3), while expressing its dismay that some companies continue to endanger critical heritage sites (JSCNA 2021: para 3.92).

6.2 *Juukung Gorge Is Not an Isolated Example*

Sadly, destruction of Juukan Gorge was not a one-off. I mention some shocking examples of site destruction, drawn from the Joint Committee's Report:

> Located on Guruma country is Marandoo [...] an important cultural area for the Eastern Guruma people for a range of cultural, spiritual, historical and familial reasons. Marandoo is on the southern flanks and lowlands of Punurunha-Mount Bruce, the mountain from which Law stems and all songs are stored. Punurunha is one of a collection of several prominent hills and mountains that form a complex of sacred sites, with each hill an embodiment of different aspects of Law and spiritual practice. The Law that flows from Maradoo is sacred to the Guruma people, and neighbouring Aboriginal groups. It is considered to be the place where Creation was started, and where all of Creation is regenerated. (JSCNA 2021: para 3.20)

It transpired that cultural material excavated from a 18,000 year old rock shelter had accidently been taken to the Darwin tip (JSCNA 2021: para 3.28). The Eastern Guruma believe that the dumping of material related to at least 20 sites. For some of these sites the material was the only remaining proof of the sites' existence. The Eastern Guruma were not made aware of this loss at the time and only became aware in 2021. What happened to Marandoo was devastating for the Eastern Guruma people, the losses of cultural sites on an unprecedented scale and their treatment at the time made them feel powerless. Their discovery that their cultural materials had been lost was deeply distressing. They were angry that this information had been kept from them. To this day, the Eastern Guruma do not have proper access to Marandoo sacred sites (JSCNA 2021: para 3.32, 3.33).

The Joint Committee cited the Eastern Guruma people's description of the importance of sites affected by mine expansion: "12 sites were identified by Eastern Guruma people to be of great cultural importance, being sites where customary law originated, birthing places, rockshelters dating back to earlier than 40,000 years ago, ceremonial sites, sites for storing sacred objects and rock art sites." (JSCNA 2021: para 3.55) It also noted submissions that there was no role for Traditional Owners in mining approval processes (JSCNA 2021: para 3.54), the Minister did not take up offers from traditional owners to meet but mining companies seemed to meet with the Minister at will (JSCNA 2021: para 3.56), and there were accusations that bureaucrats arbitrarily amended the sacred sites register to make way for mining applications (JSCNA 2021: para 3.60). One group, The Yindjibarndi, were dissatisfied that over 3,000 sites from the Pilbara were removed from the Register, including 172 that belonged to the Yindjibarndi. They have never received an explanation for the removal, but they suspect that the removal was due to mining (JSCNA 2021: para 3.61).

Many thought the national and international outcry over the destruction of Juukan Gorge would lead to dramatic improvements. Sadly, this appears not to be the case. More recently the Northern Territory Government has approved expansion of the McArthur River mine, the largest lead and zinc mine in the world, owned by multinational giant Glencore, against the advice of its own Aboriginal Areas Protection Authority (AAPA) which had warned about potential damage to sacred sites. AAPA chairman Bobby Nunggamajbarr expressed concern the NT Government had not listened to traditional owners.[43] One of the biggest impacts of the mine's transition from an underground mine to an open-cut mine was the diversion of the McArthur River, which "destroyed the back of the Rainbow Serpent" (JSCNA 2021: 5.126). AAPA's chief executive Benedict Scambary told a parliamentary inquiry the expansion would approach an Indigenous sacred site, Barramundi Dreaming.[44] Others claim 22 sacred sites the Gurdanji, Yantuwa, and Garrawa people have been fighting to protect are under threat (Getup! 2021).

In April 2021, the Kimberly Land Council (KLC), which acts for the Malarngowen traditional owners, expressed outrage that Kimberly Granite Holdings damaged two sacred sites. Douglas D'Antoine, deputy chief executive of the

43 www.abc.net.au/news/2020-11-19/nt-government-approves-mcarthur-river-mine-exp.
44 www.australianmining.comau/news.

KLC, said the damage to the site was like "the destruction of a church […] this particular dreaming is a serpent dreaming, a snake dreaming, and it's manifested by granite and it undulates on the surface of the ground […] That dreaming, the granite […] has been cut up into blocks, […] put on the back of a truck, and taken via Wyndham to China […] that's the source of much distress." (Wahlquist 2021)

Other threats of damage to sacred sites continue. Sometimes governments react. Sometimes they don't. Sometimes economic considerations override Aboriginal heritage protection. Gomeroi lands were under threat of an open-cut mining project in the Liverpool Plains in New South Wales. The project belonged to Shenha Watermark, a Chinese company. Threatened heritage included a mortuary trail, burial sites, grinding grooves and a place of post-colonial massacre. The Gomeroi made an application for protection under the *Aboriginal and Torres Strait Islander Heritage Protection Act 1984*. The Minister agreed the mine would destroy sacred places and cause spiritual devastation but chose not to make a declaration on the grounds that the "expected social and economic benefits of the mine […] outweighed the destruction of these areas of immeasurable cultural values." (JSCNA 2020: para 6.17)

At the time this paper was being finalized, construction of the Barton Highway, just outside Canberra, Australia's capital city, was paused after the Onerwal Aboriginal Land Council expressed concern about damage to spiritual trees (Vue 2021). Almost exactly a year earlier, the Djab Wurrung heritage protection embassy was unable to protect sacred women's country from the Victorian government's Western Highway duplication project. The area held a deep intimate connection for Djab Wurrung women, with birthing trees that are more than 800 years old, where thousands of generations of Djab Wurrung babies had been born. The Aboriginal women explained their determination had been fuelled by the deep power their country holds; "That power guards our spirit and our soul when coming up against the colonizer." (Austin 2020) Ms Sissy Austin, Djab Wurrung Traditional Owner, in evidence to the Joint Committee, said "its traumatic being Djab Wurrung women, in having to try to convince a very male dominated legal system of the significance and importance of women's country to us, as Djab Wurrung women." (JSCNA 2021: 231)

7 Conclusions

There have been some very limited successes. Some sites have been saved. Courts have suppressed publication of secret Aboriginal religious beliefs. Compensation has been awarded for loss of spiritual relationship with country. These are isolated examples. Overall, Australia has failed, and continues to fail, to protect the religious rights of its Indigenous people. The legislative framework is inadequate. Mining companies and developers have ruthlessly pursued profits regardless of Aboriginal values. Courts have relied on common law principles developed to protect private property to defeat heritage protection. Government administration has failed. While destruction of Juukan Gorge has enhanced community awareness of the importance of Aboriginal heritage protection, no Commonwealth legislation has been changed, changes to Western Australian legislation fall short of Aboriginal aspirations, identified defects in public administration have not been rectified, and there is still no Aboriginal process for heritage protection. It remains to be seen whether governments, mining companies, developers and the courts will change.

8 Postscript

On May 21, 2022 Australia's conservative (centre-right) coalition government was defeated. The new Labor (centre-left) government is committed to implementing the Uluru Statement from the Heart, including a constitutional referendum to incorporate a First Nations Voice to Parliament (an Indigenous advisory assembly) into the Australian Constitution. The new Labor Government includes two Indigenous ministers, The Honorable Linda Burney is Minister for Indigenous Australians and a member of the cabinet and Senator The Honourable Malarndirri McCarthy is Assistant Minister for Indigenous Australians and Assistant Minister for Indigenous Health. On July 30, 2022 Prime Minister Anthony Albanese attended the Garma Festival, a major Indigenous festival in the remote Northern territory of Australia, and announced that his Government would be seeking an amendment to the Australian Constitution to insert the following three sentences into the Constitution:

1. There shall be a body, to be called the Aboriginal and Torres Strait Islander Voice.
2. The Aboriginal and Torres Strait Islander Voice may make representations to Parliament and the Executive Government on matters relating to Aboriginal and Torres Strait Islander Peoples.
3. The Parliament shall, subject to this Constitution, have power to make laws with respect to the composition, functions, powers and procedures of the Aboriginal and Torres Strait Islander Voice.

Constitutional amendment in Australia is a complex and difficult process. If the proposed constitutional amendment is successful, the proposed Aboriginal and Torres Strait Islander Voice will be able to make representations to the Parliament and the Executive Government in relation to, for example, protection of sacred sites.

References

AHRC (Australian Human Rights Commission). *Bringing Them Home, Report of the National Inquiry into the Separation of Aboriginal and Torres Strait Islander Children from Their Families*. Commonwealth of Australia, 1997.

ABS (Australian Bureau of Statistics). *2008 Year Book Australia*. No. 90. Canberra. ABS Catalogue no. 1301.0, 2008.

Ampe Akelyernemane Meke Mekarle – Little Children are Sacred. Report of the Northern Territory Board of Inquiry into the Protection of Aboriginal Children from Sexual Abuse. Northern Territory Government, 2007.

Austin, Sissy Eileen. "The destruction of a sacred tree on Djab Wurrung country has broken our hearts." *The Guardian*, October 27, 2020.

CA (Commonwealth of Australia). *Parliamentary Debates, House of Representatives Official Hansard, Monday, 18 October 2021, Forty-Sixth Parliament, First Session – Eight Period*, 2021.

Crispin, Judith. *Manuwangku, Under the Nuclear Cloud*. Manning Clark House, 2013.

Getup! Circular, June 25, 2021 (getup.org.au).

JSCNA (Joint Standing Committee on Northern Australia). *Never Again. Inquiry into the destruction of 46,000 year old caves at the Juukan Gorge in the Pilbara region of Western Australia – Interim Report*. Canberra: Commonwealth of Australia, Parliament of the Commonwealth of Australia, 2020.

JSCNA (Joint Standing Committee on Northern Australia). *A Way Forward. Final Report into the destruction of Indigenous Heritage Sites at Juukan Gorge*. Canberra: Commonwealth of Australia, Parliament of the Commonwealth of Australia, 2021.

NNTC (National Native Title Council). "Call for urgent UN intervention on Aboriginal Cultural Heritage Bill (WA)." 2020. https://nntc.com.au/media_releases/call-for-urgent-un-intervention-on-aboriginal-cultural-heritage-bill-wa/.

Ramsey, Michael. "WA heritage revamp 'cultural catastrophe.'" *The Canberra Times*, November 17, 2021. https://www.canberratimes.com.au/story/7514400/wa-heritage-revamp-cultural-catastrophe/.

Reuters. "Aboriginal groups criticize Australian state's heritage bill." *Mining[dot]Com*, November 16, 2021. https://www.mining.com/web/western-australia-state-to-consider-aboriginal-heritage-protection-bill/.

Saunders, Cheryl. *Report to the Minister for Aboriginal and Torres Strait Islander Affairs on the Significant Aboriginal Area in the vicinity of Goolwa and Hindmarsh (Kumarangk) Island, Pursuant to Section 10(4) of the Aboriginal and Torres Strait Islander Heritage Protection Act 1984*. Melbourne: Centre for Comparative Constitutional Studies, University of Melbourne, 1994.

Trudgen, Richard Ian. *Why Warriors Lie Down & Die: Towards an Understanding of Why the Aboriginal People of Arnhem Land Face the Greatest Crisis in Health and*

Education Since European Contact: Djambatj Mala. Nhulumbuy: Northern Territory Why Warriors Pty Ltd, 2013.

Vue, Toby. "Barton Highway upgrades pause as NSW Transport holds more consultations about culturally significant sites." *Canberra Times*, October 24, 2021, p. 8.

Wahlquist, Calla. "'Cutting our culture up': outrage after WA decides not to prosecute over alleged destruction of sacred site." *The Guardian*, April 16, 2021.

Willheim, Ernst. "Western Australia and Others v Minister for Aboriginal and Torres Strait Islander Affairs." *Aboriginal Law Bulletin* 3, no. 69 (1994): 17–18.

Willheim, Ernst. "Amici Curiae and Access to Constitutional Justice in the High Court of Australia." *Bond Law Review* 22, no. 3 (2010): 126–147.

Kanak Custom and Ancestral Culture in Colonial Context

François Féral

A South Pacific archipelago lying east of Australia, New Caledonia has been under French colonial occupation since the mid-nineteenth century. Notwithstanding official denials of this reality, colonialism has deeply traumatized the Indigenous Kanak people, who today account for only 45 percent of the total population. Meanwhile, social indicators point to the failure of assimilationist policies. As a result, the ongoing presence of an Indigenous society alongside a settler population remains the territory's central political issue.

Following a major crisis in 1984 and under international pressure from the United Nations, France introduced a complex legal and institutional arrangement designed to decolonize New Caledonia in a manner consistent with the territory's political culture. Accordingly, the state recognized Kanak custom (*la coutume*) through the introduction of a so-called personal (or customary) civil status.[1] However, the French Republic's attachment to a unitary model of citizenship has prevented any real recognition of the collective and Indigenous dimensions of Kanak interests, as recognized in the 2007 United Nations Declaration on the Rights of Indigenous Peoples (UNDRIP). As a result, there has so far been no formal acknowledgement of community identity, ancestral rights, or the harms of colonization.

In this way, the principles of republican secularism and equality of citizenship have had an insidious impact on what is not so much a Kanak religion but the Kanak way of life and collective identity. The resulting posture of denial has served to fuel and magnify an ongoing social crisis that has undermined the cultural foundations of this small South Pacific society as it simultaneously struggles with the destabilizing effects of globalization.

This chapter delves into New Caledonia's history and sociodemographic characteristics with the aim of contextualizing and explaining post-colonial Kanak reality. In the first half, I discuss how, despite being rooted in the Enlightenment, the French political and legal tradition has shaped the unconsciously ethnocidal

1 *Loi n° 99–210 du 19 mars 1999 relative à la Nouvelle-Calédonie*, https://www.legifrance.gouv.fr/loda/id/JORFTEXT000000576057. "Adopted on 19 March 1999, *Institutional Act No. 99–210* granted New Caledonia special status, a key aspect of which was the recognition of customary civil status in the field of private law" (Siffrein-Blanc 2011).

 | DOI:10.1163/9789004524330_007

tendencies of the colonial state. The second half of the chapter cites challenges to the legitimacy of customary authorities as evidence of how the autonomist institutions established in 1999 and the ongoing, externally imposed decolonization process have failed to safeguard either Kanak indigenous rights or Kanak identity.

1 A Colonial History of Ethnocide against the Kanak People

Imperial France "took possession" of New Caledonia in the mid-19th century. Previously encountered by the British, the archipelago's inhabitants had already been subject to the proselytizing efforts of Catholic and Protestant missionaries for several decades. Annexation reflected the colonial ambitions of Napoleon III, who sought to extend the French empire into the Pacific as a way of countering nearby British territorial gains, including Australia and New Zealand. More broadly, the period was marked by colonial rivalries between European powers engaged in a scramble to control territories in the tropics. In practice, Christian missionaries, explorers, adventurers, and scientists established a bridgehead that facilitated military conquest and gunboat diplomacy.

1.1 *French Colonial Ambitions and the Kanak People: From Evangelization to Military Violence*

The insidious ideological violence perpetrated by civilizational superiority laid the groundwork for Western colonization through military conquest. It served as a vehicle for the spread of Christian religious values and rites, as well as the mythology and bureaucratic apparatus of the modern state. In the nineteenth century, evangelizing "lesser peoples" and subjecting them to the authority of European governments served as a pretext for taking control of Indigenous lands and resources. New Caledonia's Kanak population would bear the brunt of this twofold process of control, whereby French colonialism manifested itself through militarized missionary activity and a policy of settlement through dispossession.

1.2 *Evangelization of the Kanaks as a Civilizing Mission in the Mid-19th Century*

Although traditionally portrayed as having missionary aims, efforts to convert the Kanaks to Christianity could not have taken hold, let alone triumphed, without support from the colonial military machine. Consider the conditions under which the first conversions took place. Accounts of the Christianization process normally begin around 1840 with the efforts of the London Missionary

Society. In 1842, two Samoan missionaries were massacred on the Isle of Pines. That same year, other Protestant missionaries were forced to flee Grande Terre, although they had succeeded in gaining their first converts a year earlier, in the Loyalty Islands (Maré and Lifou). For their part, Catholic missionaries landed at Balade in late 1843. In 1847, they founded an evangelical mission at Pouébo, where a missionary was massacred.[2]

Evangelization was pursued against the backdrop of open competition between Protestant and Catholic missionaries, as well as between England and France. In this context, the 1847 assassination of a Catholic missionary mentioned above provided the pretext for France to intervene in a context where ensuring "the protection of the Catholic missions" meant taking possession of New Caledonia. Clearly, Catholicism could only flourish under French military protection.

Annexation was immediately followed by the founding of a Catholic mission on the Isle of Pines. Then, in 1848, the Marist Fathers reestablished themselves in the northeastern region of Grande Terre, which they had previously been forced to flee. In this way, French sovereignty secured a monopoly for Catholic institutions in the face of the British Protestant threat, while providing military protection to missions established amid hostile populations. For Indigenous New Caledonians and especially the inhabitants of Grande Terre, Catholicism meant French Catholicism, given that most of them converted under the aegis of the Second French Empire's dominant religion. As a proponent of ultramontanism, Spanish-born Empress Eugenie de Montijo was no stranger to the intense efforts to promote the Church of Rome in the Antipodes. Ultimately, any attempt to distinguish between Christian proselytism and colonial expansion (including its more violent manifestations) in the Pacific proves disingenuous.

1.3 *Toward a Minority Indigenous Population: Dispossession, Displacement, and Disempowerment*

Contrary to the overseas colonial tradition France had followed since the 16th century, New Caledonia (like Algeria) was treated as a colony of settlement. Military conquest and control immediately opened the door to the establishment

2 Akhila, "Religion catholique en Nouvelle-Calédonie," *Gloire à Dieu*, accessed December 13, 2022, https://www.gloireadieu.com/actualite-religion/religion-catholique-en-nouvelle-caledonie.html; Jean-François Zorn, "Les débuts de l'évangélisation en Nouvelle-Calédonie," *Amicale des pasteurs à la retraite*, accessed 13 December 2022, https://amicale-pasteurs.com/les-debuts-de-levangelisation-en-nouvelle-caledonie. Neither the Catholic nor the Protestant version of events mentions the Indigenous Kanak religion. Both present missionary activity by either church as evidence of progress, despite the clear competition between them.

of a penal colony that housed some 27,000 convicts between 1864 and 1924. On the one hand, the 700-strong prison staff was supported by a "native" police force. On the other hand, European prisoners were mobilized to put down Kanak revolts and work on farms belonging to free settlers. Meanwhile, the development of New Caledonia attracted a second wave of settlers who came from not only metropolitan France, but also French colonies in Indochina and the Maghreb (de Deckker 1994: 88).

During the first seventy years of French occupation, health issues caused a sharp decline in the Kanak population. In fact, by the end of the First World War, European colonists were hoping for nothing less than its complete disappearance.[3] And although the situation began to slowly improve after 1945, the Indigenous population never returned to pre-colonial levels, meaning that the Kanaks would remain a minority on their own lands.

On Grande Terre, settlement efforts were accompanied by a policy of dispossession that saw the Kanak people placed on reserves, a form of apartheid previously unheard of in the French colonial tradition. Furthermore, in terms of individual rights, the so-called Native Code (*régime de l'indigénat*) placed the Kanak population on a lower footing than its settler counterpart. As a result, Kanaks were forcibly resettled on remote "native lands," within whose boundaries customary law and special security measures were applied alongside ordinary French colonial law.

Amid the theft of lands along the western coast of Grande Terre, applying these policies of isolation also involved the displacement of entire communities, especially to the eastern coast of the main island. Upsetting a tradition of relatively free inter-clan movement, these deportations fueled tensions in the newly established customary areas, causing increased division within an already fractured Kanak world.

All told, the Kanaks endured more than a century of overtly racist and discriminatory French policy. A thirty-year war of conquest was followed by more than a half-century (1887–1946) under the Native Code, whose measures included an 8 p.m. curfew and a head tax. "The governor had at his disposal special powers, allowing him to punish the native population through measures that would have had no legal standing in France: administrative detention, sequestration, collective fines. Natives could be punished under special

3 The Paris Colonial Exposition of 1931 put a group of 111 Kanaks on display at the Bois de Vincennes Zoological Park, billing them as "The last cannibals of the distant and fragrant South Pacific Islands" in the April 1, 1931 edition of the *Excelsior* newspaper. At the time, the Kanak people were seen as occupying "the lowest rung of the evolutionary ladder," based on the conclusions of anthropologists and other European scholars (Chataigner 2019).

regulations [...] [relating to] styles of dress, conspicuous signs of respect for the colonial authorities, compliance with conscription and forced labor directives, payment of the head tax, travel restrictions" (Kurtovitch 1997: 125).

Given this history, it is essential that the continued presence of a large Indigenous population be acknowledged as the key issue to be addressed as part of New Caledonia's decolonization process. Previous decolonization efforts have largely failed to meet the needs and expectations of this dispossessed, marginalized, and tightly controlled community that represents nearly 45 percent of the territory's total population. Meanwhile, most Kanaks associate the return of pre-colonial assets with issues of ethnic and even racial discrimination.

Furthermore, as the process moves forward and alongside efforts to address New Caledonia's shameful history of racism and dispossession, the myth of republican citizenship needs to be recognized as a tool of assimilation. Although rooted in the principles of state neutrality and equal rights for all individuals, the French notion of citizenship nevertheless tends to dismiss the injustices of colonialism as historical aberrations. Despite its passion for commemoration, France has shown little concern for the rights of the colonized peoples it continues to govern. Granted, Kanak individuals now enjoy formal rights equivalent to those of all French citizens. However, their ancestral rights, especially their claims to Grande Terre and marine areas, have never been recognized and French authorities have no plans for a restitution process. And any decolonization process that fails to ensure the restoration and reconstruction of the Indigenous population's ancestral rights will leave an enduring sense of injustice and failure.

2 The Status of the Kanak People after More Than a Century of French Colonization

The French republican myths of secularism and egalitarianism have fueled the denial of Kanak suffering, indigeneity, and ancestral rights. This refusal to acknowledge political and colonial realities incited the insurrectionary movements of the 1980s, which hardened divisions between New Caledonia's Indigenous and settler populations.

2.1 *The Clash between the Traditional Kanak Worldview and Republican Secularism*

If religion were to be defined solely in terms of an individual's attachment to a church or sect, any discussion of a present-day Kanak religion would be wholly irrelevant. As for French secularism, its roots lie in eighteenth-century efforts to counter Catholic obscurantism. It began as a reaction to the horrors of the Wars of Religion; as a republican response to the persecution of Jews and Protestants by the Catholic Church and a condemnation of the latter's blind support for the monarchy in political affairs. Accordingly, secularism can be understood in terms of the state's responsibility to protect individuals from religious authority by treating religion exclusively as a matter of freedom of conscience and worship.

Following the French conquest of New Caledonia, the question of a Kanak religion never really arose, insofar as it was settled by the wholesale conversion of the Indigenous population to Christianity. By all appearances, nothing remains of the pre-colonial Kanak religion since virtually all Kanaks belong to either a Protestant or Catholic church. And yet, social and historical evidence points to the vestiges of a Kanak religion in twenty-first-century New Caledonia. Since time immemorial, religion has gone hand in hand with politics; the two promote a shared set of values that govern society. Deities, religious stories, and worship have shaped not only family, village, and community life but also entire societies, including state societies.

It therefore becomes possible to seek out traces of a supposedly lost Kanak religion in Kanak customary law and, more broadly, in Kanak social codes. As Hamid Mokaddem has explained, "*La coutume* is a generic term used by Western observers to describe the normative framework of practices, transactions, and rituals that structure indigenous social relations. Leenhardt's (1985) thoughts on personhood and myth have informed legal constructs of customary personhood based on the recognition of indigenous ways of understanding an individual's role in transactions and connection to the land" (Mokaddem 2016: 107). Although it also raises certain issues, this viewpoint has a twofold significance for the situation in New Caledonia:

- A legal significance for the colonial republic since Kanak custom has been officially recognized through a special private law status applicable to "Natives."
- A societal significance for anthropologists since, among the Kanaks of New Caledonia, a customary system rooted in a pre-colonial religion continues to govern various aspects of clan and family life.

The Kanak people face a paradoxical situation that lays bare the extent to which republican ideals are circumscribed by colonial legacies. Specifically, the so-called Kanak question raises a pair of issues regarding the republican and secular principles that provided the basis for the French constitution of 1958:

- The denial of a Kanak people and nation, one that could form part of a larger French people but that would maintain a distinct identity and retain specific rights in recognition of the colonial legacy.

– The denial of a pre-colonial Kanak civilization that requires recognition to be protected and recovered.

In the French context, "people" and "nation" are exclusive notions; French law recognizes only one French nation and a single French people. Furthermore, the dominant political discourse promotes the view that all Kanaks became Christians (either Catholic or Protestant) from the moment France took control of New Caledonia. From this point of view, present-day Kanaks have no connection to a pre-colonial religion. This constitutes an adulteration of the principles of secularism, which also guarantee freedom of religion and the ability of religions to co-exist on French territory.

Because secularism treats religion as a purely personal affair, the collective, spiritual, and cultural dimensions of religion cannot be subject to any type of legal consideration. Even proselytizing is forbidden, especially in the public sphere. On the surface of things, the Kanak population appears wholly unconcerned by issues of secularism since it is not considered a religious community. Nor are the Kanaks considered an Indigenous community; French republican principles and the French constitution provide no basis whatsoever for recognizing their collective or communal existence, whether as a people or as a nation.

2.2 *Decolonization Amid Entanglement: Insurgency and Cultural Duality*

As mentioned above, due to the settler population's resistance to any reforms proposed in metropolitan France, the repulsive provisions of the Native Code remained in force until 1946. In a country that proclaimed freedom, equality, and justice as its defining values, the Kanaks were not even recognized as citizens until a year after the end of the Second World War. They would have to wait another eleven years for the right to vote. As Louis-José Barbaçon has argued, "[y]ounger New Caledonians know nothing of real colonization – of burned huts, land dispossession, forced labor, and displacement. They have only ever been presented with the civilizing aspects of colonization: hygiene, health, education, technology. [...] Even today, whether out of ignorance or pride, the distinguished term 'pioneers' is used to describe the first European settlers in New Caledonia, without mentioning that most of them were forced migrants" (1992: 15).

The wave of decolonization and independence that swept through Africa and Madagascar in the 1960s failed to reach the South Pacific. In fact, France proceeded to tighten its colonial grip on Polynesia once the region became vital to the country's nuclear ambitions, after Algerian independence prevented continued weapons testing in the Sahara. Under pressure from the settler population, authorities in Gaullist France refused to decolonize New Caledonia, based on a formal understanding of rights. To this day, and despite all the evidence to the contrary, the official line remains the same: New Caledonia is not a colony. This helps explain Kanak participation in the Pacific independence movement of the 1970s, which led to the emergence of multiple island microstates in Oceania. At the time, most of the Indigenous population threw its support behind the FI, a pro-independence political faction that later spawned the FLNKS.[4] However, widespread support for the Gaullist and later Giscardian right within the wider New Caledonian electorate prompted authorities in metropolitan France to simply ignore the independence movement. In fact, it was this wholesale denial of Kanak aspirations for autonomy that fueled a strong desire within the settler population for a political crackdown. On the ground, a militia-like atmosphere sometimes prevailed as measures were taken to protect settler-owned properties against the "savages."

The brewing crisis eventually triggered an insurgency that lasted from 1984 to 1988, culminating in the dramatic Ouvéa Cave hostage taking of May 1988. Six police officers and nineteen Kanak hostage takers were killed between the two rounds of the French presidential election. This gruesome event marked a key milestone insofar as it shocked many into political awareness. In subsequent years, the trauma associated with more than three decades of confrontation came to be addressed through a long-term peace process. The French state brokered two major agreements between those demanding independence and those committed to having New Caledonia remain part of France. Whereas the Matignon Accord of 1988 brought an end to the latent civil war, the Nouméa Accord of 1998 formally recognized New Caledonian autonomy while providing for up to three independence referendums. Adopted in 1999, the *Institutional Act Concerning New Caledonia* reorganized the territory's political and administrative institutions in a way that provided a legal framework for implementing the provisions of the Nouméa Accord.[5] This set the stage for the independence referendums of 2018, 2020 and 2021, with a majority in every polls voting to remain part of France. Nevertheless, the process served to reinforce the concept of a colony with two distinct populations.[6]

4 The Front de libération nationale kanak et socialiste is a political alliance founded in 1984, immediately upon the dissolution of the Front indépendantiste, which had been established in 1979.

5 For instance, the act divided New Caledonia into three provinces, two of which have a Kanak majority. It also established an all-party administration, a congress with some legislative power, and a customary senate with advisory powers. The latter is composed of representatives of the traditional Kanak chiefdoms.

6 The results in all referendums highlighted the existence of "two voting blocs." And although the pro-independence side was defeated, it rallied a significant minority whose size increased

New Caledonia's political problems can still be traced to the disastrous consequences of colonization, now manifested in the divide between two opposing communities. To begin with, the issue is rooted in ethnic differences highlighted by physical traits: there is clearly a divide between "Whites and Blacks," between descendants of Europeans or migrant laborers and Indigenous Melanesians. Unlike in French Polynesia, ethnically mixed couples and children are rare in New Caledonia. For Kanaks, this cultural duality has been reinforced by decades of living on reservations and having a different legal status. As a result, two ways of life, two sets of traditions, two ways of relating to institutions have developed side-by-side, yet largely cut off from each other. Socioeconomic disparities only accentuate the divide, with Kanaks accounting for most of the poor, the delinquent, and the unemployed. This is true not only in those regions of New Caledonia with a strong Kanak majority but also in certain urban neighborhoods of Nouméa where the Kanak population is clearly marginalized. All things considered, New Caledonia is clearly home to two distinct societies, contrary to the political rhetoric of French politicians and republican legal principles based on the abstract ideal of individual citizens maintaining a direct relationship with the state, each enjoying equal rights regardless of origin or identity.

And yet, France has adopted and signed the 2007 UNDRIP (albeit while expressing some reservations). This places the French state in a hypocritical and contradictory position. On the one hand, it has recognized the presence of Indigenous peoples in various parts of the world and affirmed the need to establish and respect their rights. On the other hand, it continues to reject the idea that there are any Indigenous peoples or communities within France and to deny the existence of any remaining French colonies.

2.3 *The Significance of Kanak Civilization for the New Caledonian Decolonization Process*

Longstanding anti-Kanak discrimination, starting with the military conquest of New Caledonia and continuing through the creation of reserves and the seizure of Indigenous lands, has produced a dual legal system. Recent decolonization efforts, belatedly undertaken in response to an insurrection, aim to "accommodate the Kanaks within the Republic" by adopting certain specific

in the second referendum. By making the presence of two distinct populations more obvious than ever, the referendum results placed New Caledonia's large ethnic minority in an even more difficult position. In spite of the Kanaks' opposition because the Covid 19 disease, the third referendum was organized by the French government in December 2021. The Kanak community boycotted the consultation. As a result of this boycott, the opposition to independence obtained an overwhelming majority with very low turnout. The gap between the two communities has only deepened.

measures while insisting on republican principles. This drawn-out and pragmatic legal process was forged in the crucible of a racialized history defined by the denial of the colonized group's humanity.[7]

A series of developments have shaped the Indigenous population's new legal status. Initial resistance to the military occupation of Kanak lands explains why colonial authorities placed the Kanak population on reserves. In turn, this policy of segregation justified imposing an inferior legal status until the end of the Second World War. Finally, the first tentative steps toward decolonization have perpetuated marginalization through the introduction of a special customary civil status. This new status has become a major political issue that has fueled debates on modernity, liberalism, and development.

2.4 *The Politicization of Kanak Custom and "Indigenous Lifeways"*

Beyond demands for independence, Kanak custom itself has become a politically sensitive topic amid debates on the decolonization of New Caledonia. As the basis for a personal civil status, it has been recognized under the *Institutional Act Concerning New Caledonia* as an alternative to ordinary family law and, in the case of certain Kanak assets, property law. However, it has also been criticized from a "liberal" perspective for undermining human rights and economic development.

2.5 *Recognition of Kanak Custom Exclusively in Relation to an Individual's Choice of Civil Status*

As mentioned above, Article 7 of the act holds significant importance for the status of New Caledonia's Indigenous population: "persons whose personal status […] is the Kanak customary civil status […] shall be governed in matters of civil law according to their customs."[8] It is important to note that the recognition of a special Kanak civil status applies to "persons," not to the group they may collectively constitute. Indeed, carefully limiting the scope of these reforms to civil matters reflects a commitment to the principles of secularism and unitary citizenship discussed earlier in the chapter. As a result, Kanak custom has come to be treated as a personal matter, not a matter of community or religious affiliation.

7 Recent in-depth academic work on this legal process includes Anne-Lise Madinier's doctoral thesis in public law (2018). For details on all stages of the process, see Mapou 2020. The book is based on Mapou's doctoral thesis in public law (2018).

8 This is not an entirely new development. In New Caledonia, the existence of a legally recognized Kanak personal status dates to the 1920s and 1930s, when it was applied in administrative matters and in case law (see Lafargue 2010).

How is the institutionalization of Kanak customary law significant? Its legal recognition was one outcome of the negotiations undertaken by the Kanak leader Jean-Marie Tjibaou in 1988. He saw Kanak custom as the essence of a collective Indigenous identity, an identity whose preservation was a key objective of those who supported independence. But although the act recognized Kanak custom as a component of New Caledonian civil law, this concession was made in exchange for the surrender of the Kanak people's ancestral sovereignty. Hence the political and symbolic importance of Kanak custom as a vestige of Indigenous memory and civilization.

However, the focus on individual status stands in the way of any collective recognition of the minority Indigenous population as a civilization in its own right. In addition, the act explicitly limits recognition to "matters of civil law," going on to specify in Section 19 that "only ordinary civil courts have jurisdiction over matters and petitions involving customary civil status or customary lands [...]." Furthermore, a local statute adopted on January 15, 2007 defined customary acts overseen by customary authorities as contractual arrangements, thereby suggesting that they constitute little more than voluntary agreements between the parties involved.[9] For its part, the *Institutional Act Concerning New Caledonia* provides no details on the nature, role, jurisdiction, or powers of the "customary authorities" mentioned in the second paragraph of Article 16. Ultimately, the recognition of Kanak custom appears to grant a right devoid of any associated mechanisms, institutions, procedural rules, or legal capacity. Furthermore, two years before the Nouméa Accord, the Court of Cassation ruled that there is "no text recognizing the power of any customary authorities to impose and apply penalties as punishment, even on persons with customary civil status."[10] This decision effectively barred customary authorities from directly imposing customary punishments or coercive measures on persons with customary status. "Civil" in nature, involving "contractual relationships," unenforceable by customary authorities ... Clearly, Kanak customary law has been subjugated to a Roman legal tradition that prevents it from operating in a coherent manner. Under these conditions, the establishment of a customary legal order remains impossible: "If distinct French and Kanak legal systems share jurisdiction over civil affairs, how is it possible that those

9 *Loi du pays n° 2006–15 du 15 janvier 2007 relative aux actes coutumiers*, https://juridoc.gouv.nc/juridoc/jdtextes.nsf/bf6beb54c697d8974b2574c200019ae8/8b3fb09dbbc6ff514b2574ce00780055/$FILE/Loi-du-pays_2006-15_du_15-01-2007_ChG.pdf.

10 *Cass. crim., 10 octobre 2000, pourvoi n° 00-81.959*, https://www.legifrance.gouv.fr/juri/id/JURITEXT000007611327/. Granted, the words "no text" (*aucun texte*) implicitly suggest that such a one could exist and that the Institutional Act of 1999 would serve to give it judicial status.

guilty of transgressions can only be punished according to the mechanisms of French law?" (Leca 2017).

Ultimately, the belated and minimal legal progress achieved through the 1998 Nouméa Accord fails to resolve the Kanak question and does nothing to bridge the societal gap that separates New Caledonia's two populations. Instead, a range of issues – poverty, delayed access to education and health, a lack of infrastructure and public services on customary lands, racism and prejudice, delinquent youth – have made the Kanaks outcasts on their own lands: "One lasting effect of this pattern of colonization has been the persistence, even today, of ethnicity as a major determinant of socioeconomic disparity and health inequality" (Hamelin, Salomon and Lert 2010: 9). Underlying this sad state of affairs is the fact that "[…] the problem of colonialism in New Caledonia has nothing, or at least very little, to do with the situations associated with underdevelopment in other parts of the world: famines, high mortality, etc. Rather, the Kanak people have been dispossessed of their history" (Vienne 1985: 1602).

As a result, alongside its non-collective legal dimension, Kanak custom has become a trap: it simultaneously functions as the crucible of Kanak identity and the symbol of its marginality. Many Kanaks find themselves torn by this contradiction. On the one hand, they refrain from criticizing Kanak custom lest they undermine their own identity. On the other hand, they recognize that accepting and perpetuating the legal status quo means continuing to accept an inferior status based on their origins.

2.6 *Convergent Liberal Attacks on Kanak Custom*

Various external voices have begun to call on Kanaks to abandon an identity rooted in customary law. A chorus of anthropologists has highlighted how the current situation fails to reflect traditional practice insofar as the underlying clan networks and tribal structures have been distorted by colonialism. In this way, Kanak custom is disparaged for being both a product of colonization (!) and an infringement of individual rights. While building their careers on the study of Kanak life, teams of researchers based in metropolitan France see fit to condemn Kanak chiefs, deriding the "desire currently expressed by the Customary Senate and a certain number of metropolitan jurists for Kanak custom to be reestablished, including the recognition of chiefs […], often justified with reference to the 'good old days' associated with 'traditional life,' but which primarily reflects memories of the prewar period, when the colonial order and the Native Code held sway" (Merle and Muckle, cited in Confravreux 2019).

Likewise, scholars have strongly criticized infringements of individual rights associated with Kanak custom, citing the status of women and youth, patriarchal practices, and clan rules. However, such expressions of disapproval fail to consider either the twisted civilizational roots of Kanak custom (Chataigner 2019; Hamelin, Salomon and Lert 2020) or the remarkable developments of recent years that belie any notion of stagnant cultural practices and values.[11] Of course, these authors represent the same "scientific community" that placed the Kanak people at the "lowest rung of the evolutionary ladder" during the Paris Colonial Exhibition of 1931 (Chataigner 2019).

These attacks by social scientists also give legitimacy to the work of liberal economists who see Kanak custom as a "managerial millstone" around the neck of the Indigenous population. From this perspective, collective and inalienable ownership of customary lands as well as the clan-based decision-making process stand in the way of development (Doumenge 2010; Leblic 2007; Le Meur 2008). Customary practices are portrayed "as hampering the implementation of good governance, with local traditions deemed a particularly serious obstacle to 'reform' [...]. This critique focuses on traditional land tenure. It blames collective land ownership for reducing agricultural productivity and hindering export development" (Babadzan 2007).[12] Such arguments trace all the ills of Kanak society back to its attachment to traditions rooted in chiefly authority and customary law, traditions that have been distorted by colonialism. Produced by a curious mix of left-wing anthropologists and liberal economists, this literature seeks to delegitimize Indigenous peoples' demands for autonomy, under the guise of protecting individual rights.

2.7 *The* Charter of the Kanak People *as an Act of Indigenous Resistance*

In response to such attacks and to fend off the erasure of Kanak identity, an Indigenous movement encompassing all the Kanak chiefdoms has issued a constitutional declaration. Through a discussion of memory, values, and social norms, the document sets out the principles of Kanak community life. Sadly, efforts to promote this vital contribution to the decolonization process have been thwarted by divisions within Kanak society and dismissive colonial attitudes that persist in New Caledonia and among elites in metropolitan France.

2.8 *Asserting Kanak Indigeneity through a Charter of Values and Customary Law*

Amid attacks launched by liberals and anthropologists alike, voices supportive of Indigenous memory have also made themselves heard: "[...] I regularly hear people argue that Kanak custom hampers development [...]. If they mean

11 On the issue of whether Kanak custom is inconsistent with individual rights, see Féral 2017 and Madinier 2016.

12 See also Babadzan 2007 for an overview of the vast literature on Indigenous customs, much of which has been produced in Australia.

to say that it stands as an impediment to capitalism and the operation of a market economy, then I would say 'Yes, that's correct' [...]. The reserves have provided a space for resisting attacks on customary law [...]. The construction of a Kanak identity has involved not only drawing on traditions but also constantly adapting those traditions in response to socioeconomic change" (Leblic 2007: 126). By embracing this perspective and in response to attacks on the Indigenous civilizations of the Pacific, Kanak chiefs have produced a document of considerable legal and societal significance. The *Charter of the Kanak People: Foundational Values and Fundamental Principles of Kanak Civilization* was released on April 26, 2014, after a year of deliberations and discussions organized by New Caledonia's Customary Senate.[13]

The charter could be described as the "Gospel of Kanaky," insofar as it reaffirms the origins and values of Kanak society while describing the latter's structure, its public and private institutions, and the principles of community life. A careful examination of the document reveals a set of social norms largely inspired by the pre-colonial Kanak religion. It begins by tracing the "memory" of the Kanak people, describing the stages through which the territory of the archipelago was organized over the course of four millennia, as well as the impact of the colonial war and subsequent occupation, events that not only dispossessed the Indigenous inhabitants but also severed their ties to other Melanesian populations. The charter's preamble also emphasizes the role of customary authorities in representing the Kanaks, contrasting the chiefs' legitimacy to that of Western democratic institutions: "In Kanak history and tradition, the chiefdoms constitute the fundamental components of indigenous sovereignty" (Article 29).

Parallels could certainly be drawn with an organized religion structured according to a priesthood, lineages, and distinct hierarchies. In any case, the document clearly expresses a religiosity rooted in morality and spirituality. Consider the first chapter, which contains eighteen paragraphs listing the "values of Kanak society." It describes how individuals are socialized and interpersonal hierarchies are forged in the crucible of ancestral and earthly origin stories. In addition to fostering virtue, in the form of respectful and courageous

13 *Charte du Peuple kanak. Socle commun des valeurs et principes fondamentaux de la civilisation kanak*. A total of some 2000 people participated in the development of the charter by attending at least one of the four estates general (Koé-Touho, Nouville, St Paul-Wetr, and Centre Tjibaou), four seminars (Canala, Ouvéa, Koné and Bourail), ten workshops, and more than twenty presentations organized following a set of introductory meetings. Three hundred individuals closely followed all the various working sessions held during 2013. For details on the content of the charter, its development, and its adoption, visit https://www.senat-coutumier.nc. Regarding its proclamation and scope, see Féral 2014a.

behavior, these processes establish ritualized social obligations that promote peace and harmony. In response to liberal doubts, the text insists on the compatibility of such personal virtues – a sense of right and wrong, of integrity – with not only Christian and republican values but even the principles of the United Nations Charter. This "Kanak morality" is at the heart of the Indigenous movement's concept of civilization insofar as it structures Kanak ways of life, economic relations, and human relationships.

The following chapter essentially addresses the application of these Kanak values: "The general principles of Kanak civilization" are based on "the word of the elders," who act as memory keepers and set the path. In other words, they define a Kanak "social structure," especially where clans and families are concerned: "Individuals define themselves in relation to their respective paternal and maternal clans" (Article 30).[14] In addition to a detailed discussion of "the social structure and chiefdoms" (Articles 38 to 55), this chapter also includes a long section on "the cycle of life and the individual" (Articles 56 to 72), with a focus on interpersonal, family, clan, and inter-clan relations. Finally, it sets out the principles of Kanak community life with reference to land and resource access, intangible heritage, and education (Articles 73 to 93).

Although, as a matter of principle, Kanak custom is "articulated at the clan level" and the word "codification" (the antithesis of "custom") never appears, the normative and practical significance of this content extends to all Kanak chiefdoms. And although the charter "does not articulate Kanak custom" (only customary authorities have the power to do so), it does outline the principles that govern customary decision-making. It can therefore serve as a legal matrix for customary authorities. It also has pedagogical value for those in metropolitan France or New Caledonia itself whose understanding of Kanaky (the Kanak name for New Caledonia) is shaped solely by colonial prejudices or folkloric anthropology. The charter's remaining articles (94 to 115) and closing provisions, which constitute the chiefs as an "Assembly of the Kanak people" responsible for preserving Indigenous sovereignty and demand a new social contract with the French Republic, reveal the document's eminently political aims, spirit of dissension, and constitutional importance.

2.9 *Political Obstacles to Implementing the Charter's Vision of Kanak Identity*

Government institutions have refused to recognize this remarkable work of introspection, which has faced even stronger opposition from social scientists

14 Interestingly, this echoes Émile Durkheim's idea that one does not choose one's language or religion.

critical of indigeneity. In New Caledonia and metropolitan France alike, the document has been willfully ignored by the entire political class, including the Kanak pro-independence party (which generally opposes official recognition of chiefly authority).[15] Nevertheless, the charter stands as the only serious attempt at coming to terms with the nebulous notion of a "shared future" enshrined in the 1998 Nouméa Accord, insofar as it explores the values, collective memory, and lifeways of the Indigenous population – a primary stakeholder in that shared future.

The institutional and political contempt shown for the charter betrays an insidious anti-Indigenous bias. Supported by a group of experts, lawyers, and researchers based in metropolitan France, the colonial state finds itself incapable of perceiving the Kanak people as able to independently undertake a constitutional process or articulate principles of community life in legal and political terms. This explains why the charter's detractors often accuse Western experts of being behind its development, thereby implying that the Kanaks themselves are incapable of independent constitutional and political thought. While claiming to support progress and integration, such discourses reflect an implicit racial bias.[16]

In fact, the *Institutional Act Concerning New Caledonia* devotes only marginal attention to Kanak identity, in a symbolic concession made in exchange for the withdrawal of demands for Kanak sovereignty and ancestral Indigenous rights. As discussed above, the notion of "personal civil status" reduces Indigenous identity to an individual choice, while precluding any collective recognition of the Indigenous group. There has been no official recognition of a Kanak people, a Kanak nation, or even a Kanak community. Far from constituting a recognized legal and political entity, the Kanaks are considered nothing more than a collection of individuals subject to a specific family and property law regime, based on an incomplete set of traditional practices articulated by authorities who lack any power to enforce customary law. Moreover, a ridiculous local statute[17] considers the decisions of Kanak chiefs, not to mention their deliberations, to be "contractual," even though these customary authorities have day-to-day responsibility for resolving thousands of issues and disputes at the clan and tribal level.[18]

15 For an illustration of the rift between Kanak elected officials and customary chiefs, see Trépied 2009.

16 In particular, see Doumenge 2010 and Le Meur 2008.

17 On the legal force of the decisions made by customary authorities, see Féral 2014b. On the charter's judicial status, see El Kaïm and Féral 2015.

18 On the difficulty of enforcing customary decisions and the inflexibility of French law in relation to its Indigenous counterpart, see Féral and Madinier 2021.

3 Conclusion

The Kanak people's decolonization journey is far from complete. Although symbolic steps were taken following the insurgency of the 1980s, administrative practices have hardly changed. Nor have economic and social conditions or the level of discrimination faced by Kanaks. Granted, a Kanak political class has become invested in the territory's new republican political institutions, adopting the official jargon while benefitting from honors and patronage. However, the emergence of such a path to success within the framework of the colonial state has only further undermined the ancestral values of this small, long-suffering population. Three decades into the decolonization process, divisions within Kanak society have only deepened amid debates on development, modernity, and progress. Meanwhile, there is a pressing need to re-envision an independence movement that, in its current form, appears unlikely to succeed in bridging the societal and racial divide that has plagued New Caledonia since colonization began.

References

Babadzan, Alain. "Le crépuscule de la Coutume: culture et politique à l'heure du tournant néolibéral dans le Pacifique Sud." *Critique internationale* 37, no. 4 (2007): 71–92. https://doi.org/10.3917/crii.037.0071.

Barbançon, Louis-José. *Le pays du Non-Dit. Regards sur la Nouvelle-Calédonie*. Nouméa: Éditions Humanis, 1992.

Bouquet El Kaïm, Jérôme, and François Féral. "Note sur la juridicisation de la Charte du peuple kanak et reconnaissance de la coutume dans l'ordre juridique néo-calédonien." *Actes de l'Atelier Juridique du sénat coutumier « Charte du peuple kanak et pluralisme juridique en Nouvelle-Calédonie »*, Paris, November 24–25, 2014. Nouméa: Éditions de la Maison de la Nouvelle-Calédonie, 2015.

Chataigner, Margaux. "Les Kanaks exhibés en marge de l'Exposition coloniale en 1931: le mythe du « sauvage cannibale »." *CASOAR*, June 19, 2019. https://casoar.org/2019/06/19/les-kanak-exhibes-en-marge-de-lexposition-coloniale-en-1931-le-mythe-du-sauvage-cannibale/.

Confravreux, Joseph. "En Nouvelle-Calédonie, l'héritage de l'indigénat." *Médiapart*, October 9, 2019. https://www.mediapart.fr/journal/culture-idees/091019/en-nouvelle-caledonie-l-heritage-de-l-indigenat.

de Deckker, Paul. *Le peuple du Pacifique et de la Nouvelle-Calédonie au XIXe siècle. Condamnés, colons, convias, coolies, chân Dang*. Paris: L'Harmattan, 1994.

Doumenge, Jean-Pierre. "Le Pacifique insulaire en 2010, un monde éclaté en grande mutation, tiraillé entre traditions « autochtonistes » et valeurs de « métissage »." *Cahiers d'Outre-Mer*, no. 252 (2010): 499–524. https://doi.org/10.4000/com.6107.

Féral, François. "L'adoption de la Charte du peuple kanak de Nouvelle-Calédonie. Les prémices d'un pluralisme juridique: origine, fondements et perspectives des droits autochtones du peuple kanak." *Academia*, 2014. https://www.academia.edu/6921583/.

Féral, François. "Note relative à la réforme des actes coutumiers des autorités coutumières kanakes." *Academia*, 2014. https://www.academia.edu/8332143/.

Féral, François. "Le droit républicain à l'épreuve de l'autochtonie kanake." In *Pluralisme juridique et Droits fondamentaux*, edited by Fabrice Hourquebie, 161–180. Bayonne: Institut Universitaire Varenne, 2017.

Féral, François, and Anne-Lise Madinier. "Le règlement des conflits kanaks en Nouvelle-Calédonie." *Les cahiers de la Justice* 1, no. 1 (2021): 51–66.

Hamelin, Christine, Christine Salomon, and France Lert. "Les violences sexuelles dans l'enfance chez les femmes kanakes de Nouvelle-Calédonie: vers un abaissement du seuil des violences tolérées." *Sciences sociales et santé* 28, no. 4 (2010): 5–31. https://doi.org/10.3917/sss.284.0005.

Kurtovitch, Ismet. "Sortir de l'indigénat: cinquantième anniversaire de l'abolition de l'indigénat en Nouvelle-Calédonie." *Journal de la Société des Océanistes* 105, (1997): 117–139. https://doi.org/10.3917/gen.091.0028.

Lafargue, Régis. *La Coutume face à son destin. Réflexions sur la coutume judiciaire en Nouvelle-Calédonie et la résilience des ordres juridiques infra-étatiques*. Paris: LDGJ Éditions, 2010.

Leblic, Isabelle. "Café, développement et autochtonie en Nouvelle-Calédonie." *Études Rurales*, no. 180 (2007): 117–130. https://doi.org/10.4000/etudesrurales.8533.

Leca, Antoine. "Le droit pénal est-il vraiment régalien? ou les limites du monisme pénal à la française." Communication présentée aux *Actes du colloque sur la question pénale du Sénat coutumier*, Nouméa, 24 février 2017.

Le Meur, Pierre-Yves. "Réflexions sur un oxymore. Le débat du « cadastre coutumier » en Nouvelle-Calédonie." In *La Nouvelle-Calédonie vers un destin commun?* edited by Elsa Faugère and Isabelle Merle, 101–126. Paris: Éditions Karthala, 2008.

Madinier, Anne-Lise. "La remise en cause de l'essentialisme ou la reconnaissance d'un droit autochtone kanak." In *Peuples autochtones: regards Pacifique*, edited by Laurent Sermet, 77–87. Nouméa: Presses électroniques de la Maison de la Mélanésie Paul de Deckker, 2016.

Madinier, Anne-Lise. "L'État-nation face à la revendication autochtone: Essai sur les institutions juridiques kanakes en Nouvelle-Calédonie." PhD diss., University of Ottawa, 2018. http://dx.doi.org/10.20381/ruor-21889.

Mapou, Raphaël. "Analyse dialectique des transformations du droit en Nouvelle-Calédonie: l'état colonial républicain face aux institutions juridiques Kanakes." PhD diss., Université de Perpignan, 2018. https://tel.archives-ouvertes.fr/tel-02117111/document.

Mapou, Raphaël. *Analyse dialectique des transformations du droit en Nouvelle-Calédonie. La civilisation kanake face à l'impérialisme juridique de la France*. Paris: L'Harmattan, 2020.

Merle, Isabelle, and Adrian Muckle. *L'Indigénat. Genèses dans l'Empire français*. Paris: CNRS Éditions, 2019.

Mokaddem, Hamid. "Le moment critique de l'anthropologie en Nouvelle-Calédonie." *cArgo, Revue internationale d'anthropologie culturelle et sociale*, (2016): 107–115. http://www.cargo.canthel.fr/wp-content/uploads/2016/06/CargoHSAffergan-Mokaddem.pdf.

Siffrein-Blanc, Caroline. "Dissolution du mariage et droit coutumier kanak: absence de contrôle à l'ordre public." *Dalloz actualité*, January 4, 2011. https://www.dalloz-actualite.fr/breve/dissolution-du-mariage-et-droit-coutumier-kanak-absence-de-controle-l-ordre-public/.

Trépied, Benoît. "Coutumiers kanak contre élus FLNKS. La bataille de l'eau à Koné (Nouvelle-Calédonie, 2004)." In *Luttes autochtones, trajectoires postcoloniales (Amériques, Pacifique)*, edited by Bastien Bosa and Éric Wittersheim, 27–56. Paris: Karthala, 2009.

Vienne, Bernard. "Nouvelle-Calédonie 1985: La fin du colonialisme?" *Les temps modernes*, no. 464 (1985): 1602–1611.

The Ainu Struggle for Sovereignty and Religious Freedom

Takeshi Kimura

Although religious freedom is considered a universal and inalienable human right in contemporary democratic societies, the ways in which it is understood and implemented vary considerably from one country to the next. For instance, the ambivalence toward religion that prevails in Japan produces very different attitudes toward religious freedom from those found in Western countries. But regardless of how the concept is treated in a given society, Indigenous peoples can face persistent social and legal barriers that prevent them from freely practicing their religious traditions. This chapter explores the situation of the Ainu people in Japan.

The Ainu mainly live on Hokkaido, Japan's northernmost island. However, there is also a significant Ainu population in large urban centers elsewhere in the country, such as Tokyo. Under the terms of the United Nations Declaration on the Rights of Indigenous Peoples (UNDRIP, 2007), both the upper and lower houses of the Diet (the Japanese parliament) now officially recognize the Ainu as Indigenous. However, UNDRIP provisions related to self-government and the control of ancestral lands remain largely unimplemented. On the one hand, given the long history of discrimination and assimilation they have faced at the hands of the Japanese government, some members of the Ainu community have been reluctant to raise issues of sovereignty. On the other hand, although the Japanese constitution requires the separation of religion and the state while guaranteeing religious freedom, various social and legal factors prevent the Ainu from freely and fully practicing their religious traditions. Nevertheless, within the context of a larger historical struggle to assert their human rights, the Ainu have undertaken some notable recent efforts to challenge such constraints.

In the pages that follow, I examine several barriers to religious freedom affecting the Ainu in contemporary Japan. However, it is important to note that my perspective is that of a non-Ainu Japanese whose views do not necessarily reflect those of the Ainu themselves.[1] Accordingly, the chapter is based solely on an academic analysis of available sources. The first section discusses the

1 On the issue of mainstream Japanese scholars studying the Ainu and the importance of acknowledging our non-Ainu point of view, see Kitahara 2022.

 | DOI:10.1163/9789004524330_008

concepts of religion and religious freedom, including how these notions are understood differently in Japan than in Western societies. Next, I review how the Ainu have been impacted by colonization, assimilation, and discrimination over the course of Japan's modern history. The third section describes legal actions involving members of the Ainu community, while the fourth addresses the loss and adulteration of Ainu traditions. Finally, the chapter closes with an examination of contemporary issues affecting Indigenous religious rights.

But before proceeding, it is important to recognize the current state of Indigenous religious practice in Japan, as the situation does not necessarily align with widespread assumptions. Due to a long history of assimilation, discrimination, and legal prohibitions, as well as a government-imposed system of Japanese-language education, the Ainu no longer practice many of their religious traditions. In particular, the collapse and transformation of the *kotan* (the Ainu word for village), which provided a community structure for a society largely based on hunting and gathering, has profoundly disrupted traditional Ainu lifeways.

1 Understandings of Religion and Religious Freedom in Japan

Japanese conceptions of *shukyo* (宗教, generally translated as "religion") and religious freedom have significant implications for the Indigenous rights of the Ainu. Although outlooks can vary based on historical and cultural considerations, and despite the presence of diverse religious organizations in the country, the Japanese tend to downplay any public association with shukyo. In fact, the term has different connotations than "religion" in English and even the Japanese sometimes find it hard to articulate their relationship with the concept. For instance, despite portraying themselves as non-religious, many Japanese will still participate in New Year celebrations, mark the spring and fall equinoxes by visiting the graves of their ancestors, and join their children in observing O-bon, a traditional holiday dedicated to ancestral spirits returning home. As for legal guarantees of religious freedom in Japan, they are expressed in terms of *shinkyo no jiyu* (信教の自由). As opposed to shukyo, *shin* (信) refers to the inner psychological dimension of belief, suggesting that freedom of religion may not apply to outward manifestations of faith.

Religion and religious freedom were among the ideas brought to Asia by Western colonial powers. Indeed, although Buddhism, Confucianism, and a form of Shinto were widely practiced in Japan, the Japanese language lacked equivalent terms. It was only in the late nineteenth century, when the first diplomatic agreements were being negotiated with Western countries, that the notion of shukyo was introduced. In line with Western notions of religion, the new term reflected a new emphasis on doctrine: the first character, *shu* (宗), refers to a denomination or sect; the second, *kyo* (教), means belief, dogma, or teaching. For example, whereas Buddhism had previously been called *Butsu-do* (the way of Buddha), it came to be known as *Bukkyo* (the teaching of Buddha) after the word shukyo entered into use.

The notion of shukyo contributed to the development of a fundamental ambiguity in Japanese attitudes toward various religions. In 1882, the government had forbidden Shinto priests from teaching a range of tenets. The measure aimed to avoid conflicts between different Shinto schools and shrines by promoting a single dominant Shinto narrative that would support the state ideology of State Shinto. As a result, Shinto essentially became politicized. Then, in the post-war era, Shinto was formally established as an independent religion under the new *Religious Corporations Act*. But despite the fact that Shinto shrines and rituals are now officially considered forms of religious expression, most Japanese – including Shintoists – prefer to speak in terms of tradition or custom. Shukyo is also used to designate a variety of religious organizations founded since the late nineteenth century, including Kurozumikyo, Konkokyo, and Tenrikyo. Before the end of World War II, the Japanese government required these groups – as well as followers of older religious traditions, including Buddhism and various branches of Christianity – to incorporate Shinto practices. Some newly founded religions, such as Omotokyo, became targets of prosecution and repression at the hands of the government. For instance, Tsunesaburo Makiguchi, a founder of Soka Gakkai, died in prison.

Of course, notions of religious freedom and the separation of religion and the state were not entirely absent from Japan prior to the end of World War II. In fact, Article 28 of the 1889 Imperial Constitution declared: "Japanese subjects shall, within limits not prejudicial to peace and order, and not antagonistic to their duties as subjects, enjoy freedom of religious belief." However, this provision reflected an understanding of religious freedom not as a universal human right but as a limited right regulated by the state. In other words, duty prevailed over freedom. By contrast, the country's postwar constitution reflects a very different understanding. In chapter III, which is titled "Rights and Duties of the People," Article 20 states:

> Freedom of religion is guaranteed to all. No religious organization shall receive any privileges from the State, nor exercise any political authority. No person shall be compelled to take part in any religious act, celebration, rite, or practice. The State and its organs shall refrain from religious education or any other religious activity.

The terms of this provision are key to understanding the government's failure to protect Ainu religious rights. Prohibited from promoting any form of religion, Japanese officials have instead focused their efforts on preserving what they see as secular aspects of Indigenous culture. And yet, religion is at the very core of Ainu culture.

2 Colonization, Assimilation, Discrimination, and Loss: Ainu Culture under Japanese Law

From a legal perspective, the evolution of the Japanese state, both before and after World War II, has fundamentally shaped issues of religious freedom facing the Ainu today. The development of a Japanese nation state began in the second half of the nineteenth century, through the introduction of a modern political system and the notion of a Japanese people. As it was understood at the time, freedom of religion involved imposing restrictions on religious practices and beliefs (in contrast to prevailing interpretations in the United States and elsewhere). During the same period, Japan formalized its colonial policy toward the Ainu in the Hokkaido Former Aborigines Protection Act (HFAPA, *Hokkaido Kyu Dojin Hogo Ho*) of 1899. As noted above, Japan's democratic postwar constitution, which came into effect in 1947, provides for the separation of religion and the state as well as the comprehensive protection of religious freedom. As for the HFAPA, it was replaced in 1997 by the Ainu Culture Promotion Act (ACPA, *Ainu Bunka Shinko Ho*), thanks to the efforts of Shigeru Kayano, an Ainu member of the Diet's upper house. In 2019, the Ainu Policy Promotion Act (APPA) formally recognized the Ainu as an Indigenous people while providing for their economic and community development.

In 1868, the Meiji Restoration brought an end to the Tokugawa clan's warrior government. As it set about planning a modern social system, the new regime annexed Ezo Island – known to the Ainu as the Ainu Mosir ("land of humans") – to Japan and renamed it Hokkaido. Since the Japanese Matsumae clan had already subjugated and economically assimilated the local Ainu population, the government saw no need to obtain prior consent from the island's Indigenous inhabitants. Rather, Japanese officials saw Hokkaido as a vast land of opportunity that could lead the transition from feudalism to a modern society. Accordingly, the Hokkaido Development Commission was established and mandated to promote modernization, with an emphasis on the extraction of natural resources (Ichikawa 2019: 87).

Masato Ogawa (1991) has traced the history of how, in the years that followed the island's annexation, alien educational and legal systems were imposed on the Ainu, whose traditional way of life was progressively undermined by the Hokkaido Development Commission despite the latter's limited administrative authority (Ogawa 1991: 271). In 1871, use of the Ainu language was prohibited in favor of Japanese; Ainu families engaged in agriculture were provided with Japanese-style houses; and the Ainu custom of burning down a house where a death had occurred was prohibited, as were tattoos on women and traditional earrings. In 1872, the commission issued an order requiring the registration of land ownership. As a result, the Ioru – that territory held in common on which the Ainu had traditionally collected water, hunted game, gathered edible plants, etc. – came to be treated as unoccupied land and was made available to Japanese settlers. Meanwhile, officials outlawed the traditional Ainu method of hunting game with poison arrows. Instead, Indigenous hunters were encouraged to use guns.

Inhabitants of other parts of Japan were encouraged to move to Hokkaido. Still, as late as 1888, the number of Japanese settlers arriving on the island remained so small that they relied on the local Ainu population to greet them, teach them how to grow crops, and exchange food with them. During the same period, English missionaries began settling in Ainu communities with the aim of converting the Indigenous population to Christianity. Some of these missionaries gained sympathy for Ainu efforts to resist assimilation. In particular, the writings of John Batchelor reveal how, at the end of the nineteenth century, the Ainu were still holding out against Japanese and Western influences by practicing many aspects of their traditional religion.

However, as the settler population grew, new Japanese farms, villages, and towns sprang up throughout the island, significantly reducing the extent of land and resources available to the Indigenous population. Over-hunting became an issue in many areas, striking at the very heart of Ainu society. A drop in the animal population caused by heavy snowfall in the mountains during the winter of 1878–1879 led to a famine. Local Japanese officials responded by providing food aid and establishing a policy of renting land to the Ainu for cultivation. Adopted in 1899, the HFAPA was portrayed by the Japanese government as an attempt to protect the well-being of the Ainu. However, the act failed to recognize Ainu sovereignty over the Ioru and ultimately came to be seen as the source of tremendous harm. Provisions that severely weakened Ainu culture included the introduction of licenses for hunting deer and catching salmon; the prohibition of traditional rituals and the teaching of the Ainu language; and the forced adoption of Japanese names. Finally, the Ainu were subject to the authority of the Japanese emperor, meaning that many Ainu men had to serve in the Japanese military during the Russo-Japanese War of 1904–1905.

Despite the act having been repealed in 1997, the devastating impact of the HFAPA persists because of how it fundamentally shaped Japanese attitudes toward the Ainu. In the twenty-first century, individuals still report experiencing discrimination and financial difficulties due to their Ainu ancestry. Decades of bullying and humiliation led children and adults alike to hide their Ainu identity. Sometimes, they even kept their background a secret from subsequent generations. As a result, many Ainu children grew up without any knowledge of their Indigenous heritage, often becoming fully assimilated into mainstream Japanese society and lacking any affinity with Ainu culture. Nevertheless, some members of the community have sought to publicly proclaim their Ainu identity while actively seeking to revive Indigenous traditions.

3 Human Rights and Religious Freedom

3.1 *The Struggle for Legal Recognition of Ainu Human Rights*

The Ainu struggle for religious freedom forms part of a larger effort by the Indigenous population of Hokkaido to secure recognition of its human rights. Work currently underway can be traced to the immediate postwar period, when community members began to pay tribute to the struggles of their ancestors while taking stock of the cumulative impact of Japanese policy. The Ainu Association of Hokkaido (AAH, Hokkaido Utari Kyokai) was founded in 1946, with a mandate to improve Ainu life through social welfare and other measures, in collaboration with the island's municipalities (Kido 2019: 87). In the 1970s, the AAH began establishing connections with minority ethnic groups and Indigenous peoples in other countries, including China, Canada, and the United States. Through involvement in the consultations that would lead to the creation of the United Nations Working Group on Indigenous Populations in 1982, the AAH also developed proposals for new legislation to govern the relationship between the Ainu and mainstream Japanese society. In 1984, the organization demanded formal recognition of the Ainu as a separate ethnic group, with a distinct culture and the right to self-determination, while endorsing plans for the adoption of what would become known as the ACPA. Building on the momentum of the international movement for Indigenous rights, this legislation recognized Ainu rights in a range of areas. In 1993, AAH Chairperson Giichi Nomura was invited to address the ceremony at which the United Nations launched the International Year of the World's Indigenous Peoples.

While building an international profile and seeking changes to domestic legislation, the Ainu also fought to ensure that issues of Indigenous rights were addressed in various sectors of Japanese society. In 1985, an Ainu embroideress named Cikap Mieko filed a lawsuit against the editors (Ainu Bunka Hozon and Taisaku Kyogikai) and publisher (Daiichi Hoki Shuppan) of a book titled *Ainu minzokushi* (Ainu Ethnography). Having discovered that the book was using her photo without permission, she argued that the right to her image had been violated. Furthermore, she objected to how the book claimed that the Ainu were a vanishing people whose culture had been effectively erased through assimilation into mainstream Japanese culture. In 1988, the case was settled when the editors and publisher issued an apology.

Another highly significant case involving issues of Ainu rights was related to the Nibutani Dam, construction of which began in 1973 on the Saru River near Nibutani. The structure would submerge an area considered sacred by the local Ainu. Until about 1948, a new salmon fishing boat was ritually launched near the site once a year as part of a religious ceremony called Chipusanke. According to Hiroshi Tanaka, one of the lawyers who worked on the case, the first step in the project involved purchasing lands called *kyuyochi* (給与地) from their Ainu owners. Established under the HFAPA, the system of kyuyochi (給与地) provided five hectares (5町歩) of land to each Ainu person, with the aim of promoting the cultivation of rice and vegetables. At the time, the Ainu lacked a well-developed notion of land ownership, nor did they enjoy much in the way of land rights. The Japanese government had nationalized all land on Hokkaido in 1869, and although some of it was assigned to the Ainu, they could not sell it or borrow against it without permission from the Director of the Hokkaido Frontier Office (北海道開拓使長官) or, in the postwar period, the governor of Hokkaido. This framework remained in place until the repeal of the HFAPA in 1997. Driven by economic hardship exacerbated by the provisions of the HFAPA, forty-eight of the fifty Ainu individuals whose lands were needed for the dam agreed to sell, despite the area's religious significance. The two holdouts, Shigeru Kayano and Tadashi Kaizawa, chose instead to launch a lawsuit with the help of Hiroshi Tanaka.

In 1986, Prime Minister Yasuhiro Nakasone had notoriously stated that Japan was a monoethnic society. This remark reflected the extent to which the country's officials gave no regard to the rights of ethnic minorities, including the Ainu. The following year, the Ministry of Construction authorized the Hokkaido Development Agency to proceed with the expropriation of the lands belonging to Shigeru Kayano and Tadashi Kaizawa, under the provisions of the Land Acquisition Act (Fusagawa 1999: 250). The lawsuit these two men filed in response was not settled until 1997, by which time the dam had been completed and there was no practical way of overturning the land seizures. Nevertheless, the District Court of Sapporo recognized that the ancestors of the Ainu had inhabited Hokkaido while developing and maintaining a distinct culture long before Japan took control of the island. Furthermore, the court acknowledged that the Ainu had maintained their cultural identity despite the economic and political hardship suffered under Japanese government policy (Levin 1999: 394). According to Taniguchi (n.d.), the decision in the case covered four key points:

1. The Ainu are an Indigenous people.
2. Indigenous peoples have the right to the enjoyment of culture.
3. The Ainu had suffered a loss of culture due to Japanese policies of assimilation.
4. The expropriation of the Ainu men's lands had been illegal.

During the case, the plaintiffs had emphasized Nibutani's importance for Ainu history and culture (Fusagawa 1999: 256–257). In addition to being the home of the legendary cultural hero Okikurumi, the area formed part of the Iwor – the collective Ainu living space that served as a source of identity and belonging. Caught in a traditional manner, salmon swimming upstream in the Saru River were a primary source of nourishment for the Ainu population. Shigeru Kayano had even worked to revive the traditional Chipusanke festival to promote this aspect of Ainu culture among both the Indigenous and Japanese populations. The region was also home to twenty-seven *chashi* – multifunctional sites variously used as forts, watchtowers, and places of worship – built in locations high above bodies of water. Three local *chinomishiri* (a term that means "the space where we talk") provided the Ainu with everyday opportunities to seek out knowledge regarding fire, water, disaster, or sickness. Furthermore, as the setting for the *yukar* (traditional Ainu narratives), the regional landscape had a broader cultural significance. Its various features all corresponded to familiar legends or *kamuy* (divine beings). Finally, Shigeru Kayano sought to explain his people's reverence for the river by describing how, when nature called, the Ainu left the water and urinated along the shore; the Japanese, by contrast, urinated in the river itself (Matsumoto 2007).

Shigeru Kayano (1926–2006) was a pivotal Ainu figure in the second half of the twentieth century. Raised by his grandmother, who was one of the few remaining speakers of the Ainu language, he became bilingual in Ainu and Japanese. Dedicated to preserving the language and other aspects of his people's culture, he was a collector of traditional Ainu objects and narratives, the author of many books on Ainu traditions, and the director of the Ainu Cultural Museum (Nibutani Ainu Bunka Shiryokan) in Nibutani. In 1994, he became the first Ainu member of the Diet's upper house, after having already served multiple terms in the local municipal office of Nibutani. As noted above, his accomplishments as a politician included securing the repeal of the HFAPA and the adoption of the ACPA in 1997.

The ACPA included provisions for promoting the Ainu language as well as other aspects of Indigenous culture – including dance, handicraft, and music. But despite being hailed as the first Japanese law designed to improve quality of life for the Ainu, it was also criticized for failing to formally recognize the Ainu as an Indigenous people. Such recognition was only achieved in 2019, with the passage of the APPA. As Tsunemoto (2019) has explained, this legislation included "provisions for the implementation of measures to 'create an environment' conducive to cultural promotion from a national perspective, not just measures that will promote Ainu culture and disseminate knowledge about Ainu traditions." It also committed the government to building a "symbolic space for ethnic harmony," which materialized in 2020 with the opening of the National Ainu Museum (Kokuritsu Ainu Minzoku Hakubutsukan).

3.2 *The Struggle for the Freedom to Practice Indigenous Religion*

The traditional religion of the Ainu encompasses various elements, including narrative traditions, hunting rituals, the ceremonial killing of bears in a ceremony called *Iyomante* ("sending it off"), and ancestor worship. Here, I will focus on two issues central to the Ainu struggle for the freedom to practice Indigenous religion: salmon fishing and the repatriation of remains.

3.2.1 Salmon Fishing

Under current Japanese law, fishers must obtain a license and fish only in designated areas. Furthermore, under the provisions of the 1951 Act on the Protection of Fishery Resources, the Hokkaido Fishery Control Regulation prohibits the harvesting of salmon and trout from Hokkaido's rivers. Pollution in the Toyohira River had made salmon extinct in Sapporo by the 1950s. However, preparations for the 1972 Olympic Games included the installation of a new sewage system that greatly improved water quality. In 1978, the Come Back Salmon Movement released salmon fry and by 1981, adult fish were returning to the Toyohira River. The following year, the Ainu organized an Ashiri Chepnomi ceremony, during which salmon caught in the ocean were released into the river (Sapporo Ainu Bunka Kyokai, 2003). Over the years, the ritual became more complex – permission was received from municipal authorities to use a small number of salmon taken from the river itself – and eventually spread to other Ainu communities on Hokkaido.

Meanwhile, the Ainu sought to secure the right to pursue a traditional salmon fishery. In 2005, the government of Hokkaido amended local regulations to allow for catching salmon in inland waters for the purpose of performing traditional rituals. However, a special permit was required. In 2018, Satoshi Hatakeyama, an Ainu elder who chaired the Monbetsu Ainu Association, set out to assert his Indigenous rights by catching salmon for a ritual without applying for such a permit. Although he abandoned his plan in the face of objections from government officials, who threatened him with arrest, he did send a letter of protest to the governor of Hokkaido. The following year, he followed through on his threat despite renewed objections from the authorities. He was charged with illegal fishing and questioned at the local police station before being released. The police raided his home, confiscating a net and basket. After he had traveled to Tokyo for talks with cabinet officials, a government representative visited him in Monbetsu and suggested that the area be designated as a special salmon fishing zone. In 2020, Satoshi Hatakeyama wrote to the governor of Hokkaido to request that officials not interfere with the Ainu ritual of *kamuy chepnomi* (catching salmon) in the Monbetsu River. In response, the governor requested that anyone wishing to catch salmon apply for a permit beforehand. From the Ainu perspective, the right to catch salmon was protected under the UNDRIP and any Japanese restrictions on their ability to fish constituted outside interference in the traditional practices of the Indigenous inhabitants of the Ainu Mosir. By contrast, the authorities considered Satoshi Hatakeyama a Japanese citizen who was required to either obey the law (which allowed the Ainu to catch salmon so long as they applied for special permission) or face arrest.

In the context of this stalemate, it is important to remember that although the Japanese government has endorsed the UNDRIP, it only recognizes the cultural dimension of the Ainu's Indigenous rights, not the freedom to practice their traditional religion (Emory 2019). And although Satoshi Hatakeyama and other Ainu undoubtedly connect salmon fishing as a secular activity with the spiritual dimension of ritually releasing salmon into the river, they have refrained from appealing to religious rights in their interactions with government officials and police.[2] As a result, the government of Hokkaido has been able to focus exclusively on the enforcement of local laws and regulations regarding salmon fishing in inland waters. Resolving the conflict will likely require the full implementation of the UNDRIP by the Japanese government, in a way that comprehensively recognizes Ainu rights across the secular, cultural, and religious spheres.

2 Likewise, on August 17, 2020, an Uraho-based organization called Raporo Ainu Nation filed a lawsuit against the Hokkaido and Japanese governments in the Sapporo District Court, demanding recognition of their Indigenous right to catch salmon (Raporo Ainu Nation 2021). In his capacity as chair of the organization, Hiroki Nagane wrote that catching salmon and offering a prayer to the kamuy constituted an Ainu cultural tradition. Notably, he did not describe this tradition as a religious practice (Raporo Ainu Nation 2021: 169).

3.2.2 Repatriation of Remains

The opening of the National Ainu Museum in 2020 marked a new stage in a years-long effort to repatriate Ainu remains held by twelve Japanese universities (including Hokkaido University, Tohoku University, University of Tokyo, and Kyoto University) and research institutions in eight other countries (including Germany, England, Australia, and the United States). The Upopoy complex where the museum is located includes a memorial site for receiving such remains, which Japanese and foreign researchers removed from graves without permission. These acts of theft represent a violation of Indigenous religious rights since the Ainu pray to their ancestors at home or a ceremonial site other than a grave, the removal of remains is thought to prevent prayers from reaching the departed.

In 2017, Japanese diplomats negotiated the return of an Ainu bone stolen by a German in 1879 and kept as item number RV33 at the Berlin Society for Anthropology, Ethnology, and Prehistory. But because the village of the deceased no longer exists, the remains are being held by Hokkaido University until such time as they can be transferred to the memorial site at Upopoy. However, according to Hiroshi Oda (2018), this approach to repatriation fails to satisfy the need for "rehumanization." As an alternative, he has pointed to the process followed in 2016, when twelve Ainu bones stored at Hokkaido University's charnel house were returned to the Uraga grave site in Hidaka after repeated demands. The action was the result of a judicial settlement in a suit filed by Ekashi Kokichi Ogawa, and reflects the fulfillment of a prior commitment by the University of Tokyo and Hokkaido University to return Ainu remains to the Indigenous people of Hokkaido.

This controversy highlights one of several issues surrounding the repatriation of stolen Ainu bones. Despite Upopoy's generally laudable mission, the decision to store all unidentified remains at the memorial site stems from a very paternalistic government approach that has failed to prioritize Ainu interests or promote Ainu autonomy. To begin with, Japanese officials sought to appeal to foreign visitors by opening the Ainu National Museum in conjunction with the 2020 Tokyo Olympic Games (Upopoy opened in July 2020, although the Olympics were postponed due to the COVID-19 pandemic). Second, the development of both the museum and the larger complex remains under the control of the Council for Ainu Policy Promotion, which is chaired by the Chief Cabinet Secretary of Japan. Third, although Upopoy is intended as "a symbol of the building of a forward-looking vibrant society with a rich, diverse culture in which indigenous people are treated with respect and dignity, without discrimination,"[3] its mandate to facilitate research and exhibitions would appear

3 Upopoy National Ainu Museum and Park, https://ainu-upopoy.jp/en/about/, March 2, 2023.

to conflict with the other aspects of its mission, especially "fostering respect for spirituality."[4] Specifically, there have been objections to the fact that researchers can apply to extract DNA from bones held at the memorial site (Morris-Suzuki 2020), making it seem as supposedly repatriated remains are still in the hands of a research institution. Finally, Japanese politicians have failed to seize the opportunity offered by Upopoy to acknowledge the historical role of the Japanese government in dismantling the traditional Ainu way of life.

4 Loss, Adulteration, and Revival of Ainu Traditions

As explained above, the HFAPA devastated Indigenous Ainu culture. As the Ainu were forced to assimilate into Japanese society, with some converting to Christianity or Buddhism, traditional rituals ceased being observed at home and in the community. Likewise, there were fewer and fewer opportunities to pass down the Ainu language and traditional narratives to younger generations. The pace of change varied from one village to the next. In some places, performing dances and songs for tourists provided a means of keeping certain traditions alive. Also, many Ainu people began selling folk crafts as a means of generating income. But eventually, only a handful of elders retained the Ainu language, along with the culture's remaining ritual and narrative knowledge.

Meanwhile, as some Japanese scholars became interested in studying the Ainu, museums began to function as a cultural reservoir capable of supporting the revival of Indigneous traditions. The Ainu Ethnic Museum in Shiraoi has played an especially prominent role in this process. In 1992, when a reconstructed *poro-chise* (a large traditional Ainu house) on the museum grounds burned down (Zaidan 2000), the institution arranged for its reconstruction. With the help of both an Ainu elder and a Japanese scholar of Ainu culture, the museum organized a post-fire ritual to expel evil forces, followed by other traditional ceremonies associated with construction of a new house. Museum staff documented the entire process and published an account of the experience, thereby helping revive knowledge that had been lost since the Ainu began living in Japanese-style houses and abandoning their own house-building traditions. Iyomante was another traditional practice that had been gradually ceased. Under Japan's Wildlife Protection, Control, and Hunting Management Act, a license is required to hunt bears, and special permission is required to keep the animals in captivity. Nevetheless, the Ainu Ethnic Museum was able to organize an Iyomante ceremony, which it recorded to help keep traditional

4 Ibid.

knowledge alive. But once again, religious freedom was not explicitly cited as a justification for the activity.

Another example of cultural revival, as described by Irimoto (2004), similarly highlights how the adoption of the ACPA in 1997 had a positive impact on Ainu communities. In March 2002, Mr. P, an Ainu elder and recognized knowledge keeper, died at the age of 91. Since 1973, he had regularly led rituals throughout Hokkaido, drawing on his ability to offer prayers in the Ainu language. Through the years, he had mentioned that he disliked the idea of cremation – a common funerary practice in contemporary Japan – because it "looked hot." Upon Mr. P's death, his second son, Mr. Q, was inspired by the ACPA to insist on performing traditional Ainu funeral rites, which involve burial of the deceased. However, Mr. Q could not find anyone in the Ainu community with the necessary knowledge and language skills. He ended up asking a Japanese scholar, Mr. R, to organize and officiate at the funeral. The service was a mix of Buddhist and Ainu traditions, reflecting the social and family networks of Mr. P and Mr. Q. For instance, Mr. P had long been associated with the local Buddhist temple, which had offered free plots of farmland to him and other members of the public following World War II. Furthermore, his wife's funeral service had been performed at the Buddhist temple many years earlier. Mr. Q also had five sisters, some of whom were married to Japanese men. They generally objected to public displays of the family's Ainu heritage, and Mr. Q saw the inclusion of Buddhist elements in the ceremony as a way of avoiding any negative social repercussions on younger relatives.

It is interesting to note that when Irimoto discussed the question of ethnic belonging with Mr. Q, the latter did not raise the issue of religious freedom. Instead, he cast his efforts to provide his father with a traditional funeral solely in terms of the preservation of Ainu culture, while avoiding any direct reference to religion. As for the ACPA, its authors also had to avoid mentioning religion because of the constitutional prohibition on government support for any specific denomination or sect. As a result, public discourse surrounding the revival of Ainu traditions – including practices that might otherwise be described as religious – tends to focus exclusively on questions of culture. But as the case of Mr. P's funeral shows, even culturally focused efforts to assert Indigenous rights often require negotiations with family members who are immersed in mainstream Japanese culture, who may not fully grasp the ACPA's significance, and who may even object to being associated with the Ainu community. In addition to deviating from the accepted terms of public discourse, an appeal to Indigenous religious rights or freedom of religion by Mr. Q would have likely increased tensions with other members of the family. Given how strongly Japanese society views religion as a personal matter, a traditional

Ainu funeral would simply not be considered an appropriate occasion for exercising religious freedom. In any case, it would be hard to imagine a revival of Ainu religion in its original form, given the culturally hybrid social setting in which members of the Indigenous community currently live, not to mention widespread local variations in religious traditions.

5 Conclusion

Although the Ainu are known to have been active maritime traders in the past, their traditional rituals tend to be rooted in human-animal and human-plant relationships. Based on how their hunter-gatherer ancestors freely moved about the Iwor before Japanese colonization, the Ainu could certainly appeal to religious freedom in the contexts of demands for unrestricted access to their ancestral lands. As discussed above, Japanese laws and regulation currently prevent the Ainu from enjoying such access. However, the constitutional separation of religion and the state has meant that the ACPA and other state measures designed to promote Ainu traditions avoid any mention of religious practices, nor do they recognize Indigenous sovereignty. As a result, efforts to revive Ainu rites are consistently articulated in terms of culture including rituals, not religion.

The transformation of Ainu society under Japanese colonialism also needs to be considered. Most Ainu are no longer hunter-gatherers, and this change in the basis of subsistence has undoubtedly reshaped their religious views. Take the case of Mr. Akibe, an Ainu craftsman and activist who once kept a bear at home. When the bear was fully grown, Mr. Akibe considered performing Iyomante. But when the community learned of his plans, his older friends explained that observing a ritual they remembered from a time when they still practiced traditional hunting would be painful for them, since that way of life had now been lost (or was fast disappearing). Furthermore, because younger Ainu had been educated in Japanese and had grow up in a Japanese sociocultural context, they would have difficulty properly grasping the religious significance of traditional practices. Reflecting on his decision not to perform Iyomante, Mr. Akibe stated that life (*inochi* in Japanese) was essential. Most contemporary Japanese would accept this way of reconsidering the ritual killing of a bear based on respect for life. But his reasoning also meant not practicing an important Ainu tradition.

The struggle to preserve Ainu cultural traditions highlights the need to consider Indigenous rights from both collective and individual perspectives. Perhaps if large numbers of Ainu began hunting animals again, Iyomante and other forms of ritual killing could regain their spiritual significance. However, social, cultural, economic, and legal constraints make it highly difficult for present-day Ainu (and future generations) to base their efforts to promote Indigenous rights on the principle of religious freedom. Nevertheless, drawing on academic sources and the knowledge of elders, the Ainu community has been able to seize opportunities for reviving and documenting religiously significant traditional rituals, and even for teaching the Ainu language to younger generations, so such rituals can be performed in the future.

References

Batchelor, John. *The Ainu of Japan. The Religion, Superstitions, and General History of the Hairy Aborigines of Japan*. London: The Religious Tract Society, 1892.

Emori, Susumu. "'Ainu Shisaku Suishin Ho' no gaiyo to doho no seitei katei ni naizai suru shomondai." *Tohoku Gakuin Daigaku Touhoku Bunka Kenkyujo Kiyo* 51 (2019): 1–35.

Fusagawa, Yoshiki. "Ainu Minzoku no 'Shosu Senju Minzoku' sei ni kansuru kosatsu: iwayuru Nibutani damu hanketsu wo sozai toshite." *Hokudai Hogaku Kenkyuka junia risachi janaru* 6 (1999): 245–272.

Ichikawa, Morihiso. *Ainu no hoteki chii to kuni no fuseigi-ikotu henkan mondai to amerika Indian ho kara kangaeru Ainu senjuken, Hokkaido Bungaku Kenkyuka Kiyo*. Sapporo: Jurosha, 2019.

Irimoto, Takashi. "Ainu bunka niokeru shi no girei no fukko: funso kaiketsu, kyosei, kouishutai." *Hokkaido Daigaku Bungaku Kenkyuka kiyo* 113: 31–64.

Kido, Shirabe, "The Utari Association of Hokkaido no undo to ainu minzoku nno 'shutaisei': 1960 nenndai kara 1984 nenndai 'Ainu Shinpo (an) made.'" *Ajia shakai bunka kenkyu* 20 (2019).

Kojima, Kyoko. "Gendai no Ainu Bunkakan no yugami-kyosei no shiza to Genda." *Showa Joshi Daigaku Kokusai Bunka Kenkyusho kiyo* 6 (2001): 1–17.

Kurei, Giichi. "Ainu Minzoku to Jinken: Hoseido to gyosei no taio wo chusin ni." *Kansai Gaikougo daigaku Jinken kyoiku Shiso kenkyu* 12 (2009): 22–47.

Levin, Mark, A. "Kayano et al. v. Hokkaido Expropriation Committee, 'The Nibutani Dam Decision.'" *International Legal Materials* 38 (1999): 394–429.

Matsumoto, Takashi. "An essay on 'Iwor.'" *Ninchi Kagaku Kenkyu (Muroran Ninchi Kagaku kenkyukai)* 5 (2007): 11–29.

Kitahara, Mokottonashi. "Ainu, Wajin heno tegami (2) Ainu, Wajin no tojisha sei." *Ainu, Senjumin kenkyu* 2 (2022): 103–140.

Morris-Suzuki, Tessa. "Enshutsu sareta minzoku kyosei." In *Ainu No Kenri to Ha Nani Ka Shinpo Shocho Kukan Tokyo Gorin to Senjumin Zoku*, edited by Tessa Morris-Suzuki,

Morihiro Ichikawa and Hokudai Kaiji Bunsho Kenkyukai, 19–57. Kyoto: Kamogawa Shuppan, 2020.

Noguchi, Hiroya. "Sake girei 'ashiri chepnomi' kara mita Ainu minzoku no senjuken undo, Tanaka, Hiroshi." *Sapporo hogaku* 11 (2000): 1–39.

Oda, Hiroshi. "Hone kara Hitohe: aru Ainu ikotu no repatriation to sai ningenka." *Hopo jinbun Kenkyu* 11 (2018): 73–94.

Ogawa, Masato. "'Ainu Gakko' no secchi to 'Hokkaido Kyu Dojin Hogoho,' 'Kyu Dojin Jido Kyoiku Kitei' no Seiritsu." *Hokkaido Daigaku Kyoikugakubu Kiyo* 55 (1991): 257–325.

Raporo Ainu Nation and Hokudai Kaiji Bunsho Kenkyukai. *Samon pipuru: Ainu no sake hokakuken kaihuku wo mezashite*. Sapporo: Karinsha, 2021.

Sapporo Ainu Bunka Kyokai Niju nen no ayumi henshu iinnkai. *Sapporo Ainu Bunka Kyokai nijune no ayumi*. Sapporo: Sapporo Ainu Bunka Kyokai, 2003.

Taniguchi, Hiroshi, "Nibutani damu wo meguru hutatsu no saiban." Sapporo: The Law Office of Tanaka and Watanabe, n.d. http://tw-law-office.jp.

Tsunemoto, Teruki, "Overview of the Ainu Policy Promotion Act of 2019." Tokyo: Foreign Press Center, 2019. https://fpcj.jp/wp/wp-content/uploads/2019/11/b8102b519c7b7c4a4e129763f23ed690.pdf.

Yoshikawa, Hitoshi. "'Nibutani Damu jiken hanketsu' nit suite." *Kenpo Ronso* 8 (2002): 119–134.

Zaidan Hojin Ainu Minzokugaku Hakubutsukan. *Porochise no Kenchiku Girei, Densho Jigyo Hokokusho*. Shiraoi: Zaidan Hojin Ainu Minzoku Hakubutsukan, 2000.

Indigenous Religious Rights in the United States

Allison M. Dussias

The first freedom named in the U.S. Constitution's Bill of Rights – the Constitution's first ten amendments – is religious freedom. The priority given to religious freedom seems to promise a particularly strong commitment to ensuring the enjoyment of this freedom to all people. As this chapter reveals,[1] however, practitioners of Indigenous[2] religions continue to face obstacles to recognition of their religious rights.

1 Constitutional Provisions: The Religion Clauses

1.1 *Historical Refusal to Apply the Religion Clauses to Protect Indigenous Religions*

The First Amendment provides that "Congress shall make no law respecting an *establishment* of religion, or prohibiting the *free exercise* thereof."[3] In theory, these provisions protect the rights of all individuals against laws and government actions tending toward the imposition of a particular religion (the Establishment Clause), and against laws that significantly interfere with religious practices (the Free Exercise Clause). In reality, for many years, the U.S. government ignored both provisions where Indian religions were concerned. Beginning with the United States' founding and continuing into the twentieth century, federal laws and policies ignored the Establishment Clause and the Free Exercise Clause to the detriment of Indian religions and their practitioners. In the nineteenth century, for example, the Establishment Clause did not discourage the government from adopting a "Christianization" policy, expressly aimed at converting Indians and establishing Christianity as their religion. The policy was pursued through several means, such as by supporting missionary activities on reservations set aside for tribes and by funding schools run by religious groups for Indian children. Even when the government stopped directly funding schools

1 This chapter draws on the author's previous publications, including Dussias 1997; 2013; 2014.

2 The Indigenous peoples of the United States and their members most commonly refer to themselves by their tribal designations, and collectively use terms such as American Indian, Indian, and Native American (Carpenter 2020: 57, 57 n. 1). These terms are used in this chapter, along with "Indigenous" and "Indigenous peoples."

3 US Constitution amendment 1.

 | DOI:10.1163/9789004524330_009

run by religious groups, Protestant Christian religious indoctrination continued in government-run schools (Dussias 1997: 776–787).

Similarly, Indian religious practitioners were denied the First Amendment's protection of the free exercise of religion. The government designated religious rites such as ceremonial dances as "Indian Offenses" and punished those who took part in these dances and other religious practices. Punishments included the withholding of treaty-guaranteed food supplies and imprisonment. Some paid the ultimate price for practicing their religion, such as the hundreds of Lakota Sioux children, women, and men at the 1890 Wounded Knee Massacre, who were murdered by artillery fire while peacefully gathered for the Ghost Dance (Dussias 1997: 787–805). In short, when it came to the United States' First Peoples, historical government policy ignored both the Establishment Clause and the Free Exercise Clause, explicitly and unapologetically, and at times even in violent ways.

By the second half of the twentieth century these direct and overt government attacks on Indian religious rights had ended, and it became apparent that the government had failed to completely eradicate Indian religions. Because generations-old spiritual beliefs and practices lay at the heart of Indian cultures, they were not so easily stamped out. The abandonment of overt attacks did not mean, however, that henceforth Indian religious freedom would presumptively be protected when religious practitioners tried to rely on federal constitutional and statutory provisions. Moreover, the contemporary Indian religious freedom struggle has been made considerably more challenging by the government's success in pursuing another longstanding goal – separating tribes from as much of their land as possible. Over the course of the nineteenth century, lands were taken from tribes under the terms of treaties, which also created reservations. Pursuant to the Allotment Policy, many reservations were divided up into allotments of land for individual tribal members, with any land deemed "surplus" sold to non-Indians or retained by the United States (Dussias 1999: 671–680). In the western United States in particular, considerable areas that were taken from tribes are today held as federal lands, managed by government agencies such as the National Park Service (NPS) and the U.S. Forest Service (USFS).

The loss of millions of acres of land continues to have significant adverse impacts on religious freedom because of the intimate ties between Indian religions and land. Loss of land has meant loss of the ability to access, and to control and protect, many sacred sites, placing them at risk of disturbance, desecration, and even outright destruction. The loss of sacred lands, accompanied by the deleterious interpretations of constitutional and statutory provisions explored below, have meant that Indian religious practitioners continue to face an uphill battle in seeking the respect for their religious rights.

1.2 *The Adverse Impact of Free Exercise Clause Interpretations*

In two key cases – *Lyng v. Northwest Indian Cemetery Protective Association* (1988)[4] and *Employment Division v. Smith* (1990)[5] – the U.S. Supreme Court refused to apply the Free Exercise Clause in a way that would protect Indian religious freedom. In *Lyng*, the Court considered a challenge to a USFS plan to permit timber harvesting and to complete a logging road in California's Six Rivers National Forest. The plan affected the High Country, an area that contained the lands held most sacred by the Yurok, Karok, and Tolowa tribes.[6] Religious leaders preparing for religious activities, such as ceremonies aimed at renewal of the world, needed to travel to specific sites in the High Country to obtain the medicine necessary for successful renewal.[7]

Tribal members explained how the plan would impact worship and violate their Free Exercise rights. The Court rejected their claim, holding that the Free Exercise Clause did not prohibit the government's plan, even assuming that the challenged actions would "virtually destroy [their] ability to practice their religion."[8] The Court viewed the claim as a threat to government property rights[9] and did not require the government to justify its plan under the legal analysis (the compelling governmental interest test) that had been applied for decades to non-Indian Free Exercise claims.[10] Essentially, in the *Lyng* Court's view, the First Amendment did not protect Indian sacred sites on federal lands (Dussias 1997: 828–831).

4 485 U.S. 439 (1988). For a discussion of cases prior to *Lyng* involving Free Exercise claims related to sacred sites, see Dussias (1997: 823–828). *Lyng* was preceded by another Free Exercise case, *Bowen v. Roy*, in which the Court rejected a member of the Abenaki Tribe's challenge to the requirement that his daughter obtain a Social Security number to receive certain welfare benefits, which the child's parents believed would harm her spirit. *Bowen v. Roy*, 476 U.S. 693 (1986).

5 494 U.S. 872 (1990).

6 *Lyng*, 485 U.S. at 452.

7 Ibid 461 (Brennan, J., dissenting).

8 Ibid 451.

9 Ibid 453–54.

10 The test developed in *Sherbert v. Verner*, 374 U.S. 398 (1963), required the government to demonstrate that it had a compelling interest that was being advanced by the action that burdened Free Exercise rights and that the action was narrowly tailored to achieve that compelling interest. The Supreme Court elaborated on the test in *Wisconsin v. Yoder*, 406 U.S. 205 (1972).

The Court also rejected another objection to the plan: it was inconsistent with the American Indian Religious Freedom Act (AIRFA). Enacted in 1978, AIRFA provides that "it shall be the policy of the United States to protect and preserve for American Indians their inherent right of freedom to believe, express, and exercise the traditional religions of the American Indian, Eskimo, Aleut, and Native Hawaiians, including but not limited to: access to sites; use and possession of sacred objects; and the freedom to worship through ceremonials and traditional rites."[11] AIRFA seemed to commit the United States to breaking from past religious suppression. To be effective, the statute necessarily would provide protection for, and facilitate access to, places with sacred significance and for freedom to worship through traditional ceremonies, many of which are tied to particular sites. A site can be significant as, for example, the location of a ceremony or the source of plants or other ceremonial materials. The *Lyng* Court, however, rejected AIRFA as a source of judicially enforceable rights.[12]

The Court stated that its opinion should not be "read to encourage governmental insensitivity to the religious needs of any citizen" and that the government's property rights "need not and should not discourage it from accommodating religious practices."[13] However, as dissenting, Justice Brennan pointed out that it is "difficult [...] to imagine [a] conduct more insensitive to religious needs than the Government's determination to build a marginally useful road in the face of uncontradicted evidence that the road will render the practice of respondents' religion impossible."[14] *Lyng* demonstrated the skepticism and the lack of understanding of their religions that Indian religious practitioners all too often face in court.[15] The case also underscored land dispossession's devastating impact on Indigenous religious rights.

In *Smith*, the Court addressed Indian religious rights in another context. The Court rejected the religious freedom claim of Al Smith, a Klamath Indian who was denied unemployment benefits by Oregon after being fired for consumption of peyote in a Native American Church (NAC) ceremony.[16] NAC practices include sacramental ingestion of peyote, a small spineless cactus used in Indigenous religious ceremonies for millennia (Carpenter 2012: 405). Oregon criminalized peyote, with no exception for religious use. Smith argued that the

---

11 Pub. L. No. 95–341, § 1, Aug. 11, 1978, 92 Stat. 469, codified as amended at 42 U.S.C. § 1996.

12 *Lyng*, 485 U.S. at 454–55.

13 Ibid 453–54.

14 Ibid 477 (Brennan, J., dissenting).

15 Dussias (1997: 815–819), discussing challenges in explaining religious claims in court.

16 *Smith*, 494 U.S. at 874.

denial of unemployment benefits, based on engaging in a religious ceremony, violated the Free Exercise Clause.[17]

The *Smith* Court explicitly abandoned its existing analysis for most religious rights claims going forward, holding that when a generally applicable law that incidentally burdens religious conduct is challenged under the Free Exercise Clause, the government would no longer need to demonstrate that it had a "compelling interest" that justified infringing on religious exercise.[18] Oregon's peyote prohibition was constitutional under the Court's new approach, so denial of unemployment compensation for a dismissal based on sacramental peyote use was as well.[19]

Smith considerably weakened the Free Exercise Clause's protection for adherents of all religions. The Court noted, however, that practitioners of majority religions could rely on the political process to protect their worship through religious exemptions, while unapologetically acknowledging that this path might well be unavailable to minority religious practitioners like Al Smith.[20]

2 Statutory Provisions and Executive Agency Actions

Denied protection of their religious freedom under the Supreme Court's cramped Free Exercise Clause interpretation, Indian religious practitioners have turned to federal statutory provisions and administrative agency processes in the hope of finding more robust protection. This section explores these efforts in the context of several types of religious rights claims.

2.1 *Access to Ceremonial Materials*

2.1.1 Peyote

In response to *Smith*, Congress amended AIRFA to expressly protect sacramental peyote use against federal and state prohibitions.[21] Recognizing that "the traditional ceremonial use of the peyote cactus as a religious sacrament has for centuries been integral to a way of life, and significant in perpetuating Indian tribes and cultures," the statute provides that "the use, possession, or transportation of peyote by an Indian who uses peyote in a traditional manner for bona fide ceremonial purposes in connection with the practice of a traditional

17 *Smith*, 494 U.S. at 876–78.
18 Ibid 884–85.
19 Ibid 890.
20 Ibid.
21 42 U.S.C. § 1996a.

Indian religion is lawful, and shall not be prohibited by the United States or by any State."[22] Statutory protection is limited to members of federally recognized tribes.[23]

The amendment's enactment stands out as an explicit effort to protect an Indian ceremonial practice in the wake of an adverse judicial decision. NAC members' religious exercise remains threatened, however, by the decline in peyote habitat (Muneta 2020), which has prompted appeals to Congress for assistance with habitat protection (Thompson 2022).

2.1.2 Eagles

As the National Congress of American Indians has noted, "[e]agle feathers are of great spiritual and cultural significance to many tribal nations and their citizens."[24] Two federal statutes, the Bald and Golden Eagle Protection Act (BGEPA) and the Migratory Bird Treaty Act (MBTA), generally prohibit the taking and possession of bald and golden eagles, as well as feathers and parts,[25] thus creating barriers for religious practitioners who need eagles or eagle parts. In *United States v. Dion*, the Supreme Court held that the BGEPA abrogated the Yankton Sioux Tribe's treaty rights to hunt eagles on their reservation, barring their use as a defense to prosecution for on-reservation eagle hunting.[26] The Court noted that Congress knew of the importance of eagles "'in enabling many Indian tribes, particularly those in the Southwest, to continue ancient customs and ceremonies'" that hold deep religious significance and that the Secretary of the Interior has statutory authority to "permit the taking, possession, and transportation of eagles 'for the religious purposes of Indian tribes.'"[27] To implement this authority, the Interior Department developed a permitting system administered by the U.S. Fish & Wildlife Service (USFWS). The USFWS established a National Eagle Repository, which collects dead eagles salvaged from various sources.[28] Members of federally recognized tribes are eligible to apply for permits to obtain an eagle or eagle parts from the Repository for

---

22 Ibid, § 1996a(a), (b)(1).

23 Ibid, § 1996a(c)(1), (2).

24 https://www.ncai.org/news/articles/2012/10/15/ncai-statement-on-doj-announcement-of-department-wide-policy-on-eagle-feather-use-possession.

25 MBTA, 16 USC § 1703 et seq.; BGEPA, 16 USC § 668 et seq.

26 476 U.S. 734 (1986).

27 Ibid 740–41. The Supreme Court did not address a religious freedom claim that Dion had raised before the lower court but was not pursuing before the Court. Ibid 736 n. 3.

28 16 U.S.C. § 668(a); U.S. Fish and Wildlife Service, Possession of Eagle Feathers and Parts by Native Americans (Feb. 2009), https://www.fws.gov/sites/default/files/documents/PossessionOfEagleFeathersFactSheet.pdf.

religious purposes.[29] Permits for taking a live eagle for a religious ceremony have occasionally been granted.[30] Members of federally recognized tribes do not need permits simply to possess and use eagles and eagle parts (as opposed to obtaining them) or to collect molted feathers.[31]

Pursuant to a 2019 policy change stemming from tribal consultations, federally recognized tribes can retain, under certain conditions, deceased eagles found by tribal members on tribal lands, rather than sending them to the Repository. Tribes can apply for permits to retain found eagle remains for religious purposes. Following reporting of the discovery to tribal or USFWS officials, the tribe generally can retain possession of the remains, provided a permit is in place.[32] The permit process and Repository, though not perfect, support religious freedom by facilitating access to eagles and eagle parts that would otherwise not be available. Recent developments have shown greater willingness to heed tribes' concerns when developing eagle policies (Carpenter 2012: 462–466).

2.2 *Access to and Protection of Sacred Sites*

2.2.1 The Religious Freedom Restoration Act

The outcry from practitioners of many religions following the *Smith* decision led Congress to enact the Religious Freedom Restoration Act (RFRA) and to make clear its dissatisfaction with the decision's limits on religious freedom

29 16 U.S.C. § 668a; 50 C.F.R. § 22.60. The limiting of permits to federally recognized tribes has been challenged under the Religious Freedom Restoration Act (RFRA), discussed below. See, e.g., *United States v. Vasquez-Ramos*, 531 F.3d 987 (9th Cir. 2008) (rejecting a RFRA-based challenge to prosecution by two individuals who claimed that they had Indigenous ancestry and that their unpermitted eagle parts were received during Indigenous religious ceremonies); *United States v. Wilgus*, 638 F.3d 1274 (10th Cir. 2011) (reaching the same conclusion in a similar case). But see *McAllen Grace Brethren Church v. Salazar*, 764 F.3d 465 (5th Cir. 2014) (showing greater receptiveness to a similar claim by a member of the Lipan Apache Tribe – recognized by Texas (but not federally recognized) – which led to a settlement. https://becketpdf.s3.amazonaws.com/Exhibit-1-Settlement-Agreement-file-stamped.pdf).

30 The Northern Arapaho Tribe, e.g., received a permit to take two bald eagles for religious ceremonies, with the location of the take limited to Wyoming, outside the Wind River Reservation (shared with the Eastern Shoshone Tribe). *Northern Arapaho Tribe v. Ashe*, 92 F. Supp. 3d 1160 (D. Wyo. 2015) (holding that the location limitation, based on Eastern Shoshone objections, violated the Free Exercise Clause).

31 Office of the Attorney General, Possession or Use of the Feathers or Other Parts of Federally Protected Birds for Tribal Cultural and Religious Purposes (Oct. 12, 2012).

32 https://www.fws.gov/press-release/2019-08/service-announces-landmark-revision-eagle-retention-policy. See also Native American Tribal Eagle Retention Policy, https://www.fws.gov/service/3-1552-native-american-tribal-eagle-retention.

claims.[33] Under RFRA, the government may substantially burden a person's exercise of religion only if it

(1) Is in furtherance of a compelling governmental interest; and
(2) Is the least restrictive means of furthering that compelling governmental interest.[34]

A person whose religious exercise has been substantially burdened can bring a lawsuit to "assert that violation [...] and obtain appropriate relief against" the government. RFRA can also be raised as a defense in a judicial proceeding.[35] Notably, Congress did not enact a statutory repudiation of *Lyng*, which did not provoke the same outcry from adherents of mainstream religions as *Smith*. Indian religious practitioners have sought to use RFRA as a tool in efforts to access and protect sacred sites on federal land.

The trigger for the application of RFRA's compelling governmental test is that religious exercise is substantially burdened, yet the statute does not define what is a substantial burden. This omission has allowed room for courts to narrowly define the term, with adverse impacts on religious freedom. In *Navajo Nation v. U.S. Forest Service*, for example, several tribes sued under RFRA to challenge a USFS decision to allow snowmaking with treated sewage water at a ski resort on the San Francisco Peaks in the Coconino National Forest.[36] The water came from Flagstaff, Arizona and contained wastewater from homes, morgues, and hospitals.[37] The San Francisco Peaks are sacred to the plaintiff tribes, who explained that spraying the peaks with snow made from sewage water would interfere with specific practices and substantially burden their religious exercise.[38] The Diné Hataalii Association President, Anthony Lee, explained that the wastewater snowmaking would adversely affect Navajo prayers and offerings and would contaminate mountain soil bundles and ceremonies, while a Yavapai-Apache Nation Councilman Vincent Randall noted that "[t]he sacred Mountain is also a conduit for our prayers to travel into the unseen spiritual world" and that the proposed use of sewage water would

33 42 U.S.C. § 2000bb(a)(2)–(5).

34 Ibid, § 2000bb-1(a)–(b).

35 Ibid, § 2000bb-1(c).

36 535 F.3d 1058 (2008) (en banc), cert. denied, 556 U.S. 1281 (2009). The tribal plaintiffs were the Navajo Nation, the Hualapai Tribe, the Havasupai Tribe, the White Mountain Apache Nation, and the Yavapai-Apache Nation.

37 Plans also included building a 14.8-mile-long pipeline and daily pumping of 1.5 million gallons of artificial snow made from sewage water onto the mountains from November to February. Ibid 1030–31.

38 Ibid 1099–1106 (Fletcher, J., dissenting opinion; describing the religious practices and the adverse impact of the snowmaking plan).

"taint and scar the Mountain [...] essentially killing the spiritual force within it" (Dussias 2013: 387–388).

The Ninth Circuit Court of Appeals ruled that "a 'substantial burden' is imposed only when individuals are forced to choose between following the tenets of their religion and receiving a government benefit [...] or coerced to act contrary to their religious beliefs by the threat of civil or criminal sanctions."[39] Applying this narrow definition, the court dismissively stated that "the burden of the recycled wastewater can only be expressed by the Plaintiffs as damaged spiritual feelings" and held that the snowmaking plan did not impose a substantial burden on religious exercise (Dussias 2013: 387–388).

Dissenting from the court's decision, Judge Fletcher acknowledged the impact of land dispossession and recognized the decision's threat to Indian religions generally. He stated: "The United States government took this land from the Indians by force. The majority now uses that forcible deprivation as a justification for spraying treated sewage effluent on the holiest of the Indians' holy mountains [...]. If Indians' land-based exercise of religion is not protected by RFRA in this case, I cannot imagine a case in which it will be [...]. [T]he majority has effectively read American Indians out of RFRA."[40] Indeed, judicial interpretation of RFRA in a way that does not protect sacred sites on federal lands raises the question of why a category of claims would be excluded from RFRA's protection. *Navajo Nation* is significant because much of the federal land on which sacred sites are located lies within the Ninth Circuit.[41] A recent example of *Navajo Nation*'s deleterious impact is the summary rejection of the Fallon Paiute-Shoshone Tribe's RFRA-based challenge to approval of a Nevada geothermal project despite its impact on an area of sacred hot springs.[42]

Another court, based in the Tenth Circuit,[43] showed the potential impact on sacred sites claims of a different approach to identifying a substantial burden. In *Comanche Nation v. United States*, the tribe sued under RFRA, seeking an injunction against the construction of a warehouse for the U.S. Army's Fort Sill, Oklahoma military installation. The warehouse would adversely impact the viewscape of Medicine Bluffs, a landform that is frequently used by members of the Comanche, Kiowa, and Wichita Tribes for vision quests and healing ceremonies, and as a place of repose for deceased family members' remains

39 *Navajo Nation*, 535 F.3d at 1070.

40 Ibid 1113–14.

41 The Ninth Circuit hears appeals from district courts in Alaska, Arizona, California, Hawaii, Idaho, Montana, Nevada, Oregon, and Washington.

42 *Fallon Paiute-Shoshone Tribe v. Department of Interior*, 2022 WL 3031583 (9th Cir. 2022).

43 The Tenth Circuit hears appeals from district courts in Colorado, Kansas, New Mexico, Oklahoma, Utah, and Wyoming.

or ashes. By inhibiting the view of the three peaks of Medicine Bluffs to which religious practitioners orient themselves, the warehouse would prevent tribal members from exercising their religion as they had done for generations.[44]

Under the Tenth Circuit's RFRA analysis, for an action to be considered to substantially burden religious exercise, it must "'significantly inhibit or constrain conduct or expression' or 'deny reasonable opportunities to engage in' religious activities."[45] The court reasoned that the warehouse would impact an approach to Medicine Bluffs which is a Comanche sacred site and the situs of traditional religious practices that "are inextricably intertwined with the natural environment," and the warehouse's obstruction of the view would amount to a substantial burden.[46] Moreover, even if construction of the warehouse were in furtherance of a compelling governmental interest, there was no evidence that construction in the proposed location was the least restrictive means of furthering that interest. Following the court's determination that the plaintiffs' claim was likely to succeed,[47] the warehouse plan was abandoned (Dussias 2013: 409).

Thus, federal courts are split on how to define "substantial burden" and apply RFRA in sacred sites cases. If a court follows the Ninth Circuit's narrow approach to identifying substantial burdens on religious exercise, reliance on RFRA to protect a sacred site is unlikely to be successful.

2.3 *The National Historic Preservation Act and Executive Branch Orders and Policies*

Another legal tool for seeking protection of sacred sites is the National Historic Preservation Act (NHPA). NHPA Section 106 requires federal agencies to consider the adverse effects of proposed activities on historic properties, i.e., properties included, or eligible for inclusion in, the National Register of Historic Places (NRHP), administered by the NPS.[48] Tribal sacred sites may be eligible for inclusion and be covered by the Section 106 process. Many places that are religiously or culturally important for tribes fit within a category of historic properties called "traditional cultural properties" (TCPs) – properties that are eligible for inclusion on the NRHP because of their association with a living community's cultural practices or beliefs that are rooted in the community's history and important in maintaining its cultural identity (Parker and King

44 2008 WL 4426621, at *3–5 (W.D. Okla. 2008).
45 Ibid *3.
46 Ibid *17.
47 Ibid *18.
48 54 U.S.C. § 306108 & 300308.

1998). In addition to sacred sites' potential NRHP eligibility as TCPs, 1992 NHPA amendments explicitly state that "[p]roperties of traditional religious and cultural importance to an Indian tribe" are NRHP-eligible.[49] Agencies making decisions on projects that may affect religiously or culturally significant properties are required to consult with interested tribes and provide them a reasonable opportunity to: a) identify concerns about historic properties; b) advise on the identification and evaluation of properties; c) articulate views on a proposed project's effects; and d) participate in the resolution of adverse effects. Officials are to conduct consultation in a manner that is respectful of tribal sovereignty and that recognizes the government-to-government relationship between tribes and the federal government.[50] Section 106 consultation often takes place alongside the review process under the National Environmental Policy Act (NEPA)[51] for federal actions that could harm the environment, including sacred sites.[52]

Although the NHPA consultation process is the only statutorily mandated consultation specific to tribes (aside from more narrowly focused statutes, like the Native American Graves Protection and Repatriation Act[53]), some other statutes and policies related to federal lands management provide opportunities for tribal involvement in decision-making regarding sacred sites. The 1996 "Indian Sacred Sites" Executive Order requires federal land managers to "(1) accommodate access to and ceremonial use of Indian sacred sites by Indian religious practitioners and (2) avoid adversely affecting the physical integrity of such sacred sites."[54] The Sacred Sites Order's provisions are

49 54 U.S.C. § 302706(a).

50 Ibid, § 302706(b); 36 C.F.R. § 800.2(c)(2)(ii). See generally Advisory Council on Historic Preservation, *Consultation with Indian Tribes in the Section 106 Process: A Handbook* (June 2021), available at https://www.achp.gov/sites/default/files/2021-06/ConsultationwithIndianTribesHandbook6-11-21Final.pdf.

51 42 U.S.C. §§ 4321–4370h.

52 See Cook (n.d.: 19–26), discussing NEPA and tribal participation.

53 The Native American Graves Protection and Repatriation Act (NAGPRA), 25 U.S.C. § 3001 et seq., provides for the ownership or control of Native American human remains, funerary objects, sacred objects, and cultural patrimony excavated or discovered on federal and tribal lands, along with providing for the repatriation of these items from museums under specified circumstances. For a discussion of NAGPRA, see Dussias (2005: 74–87). The Interior Department has proposed revisions to the NAGPRA regulations that purportedly will "emphasize consultation in every step and defer to the customs, traditions, and Native American traditional knowledge," 87 Fed. Reg. 63,202 (Oct. 18, 2022).

54 Exec. Order No. 13007, Indian Sacred Sites, 61 Fed. Reg. 26,771 (May 24, 1996). https://www.doi.gov/sites/doi.gov/files/elips/documents/so-3403-joint-secretarial-order-on-fulfilling-the-trust-responsibility-to-indian-tribes-in-the-stewardship-of-federal-lands-and-waters.pdf.

triggered by identification of a site as being sacred by Indians themselves[55] (in contrast to TCP designations, which requires federal government involvement). Agencies with land management authority were directed to implement procedures to carry out the order and to report on procedures developed "to facilitate consultation with appropriate Indian tribes and religious leaders."[56] Drawing on the order, as well as AIRFA and Executive Branch actions related to the tribal-federal relationship, including Executive Order 13175, "Consultation and Coordination with Indian Tribal Governments"[57] (E.O. 13175), agencies with land management authority developed detailed policies and procedures for consulting with tribes when considering actions that could impact them (including actions impacting their sacred sites).[58]

2.4 *Examples of Results of Tribal Consultation*

Tribes have advocated for protection of sacred sites when federal officials are developing management plans and when they are considering proposed projects, such as projects that require a federal permit or approval, that will impact sacred sites. Tribal participation in consultation processes has led to some successes, with federal land managers taking actions aimed at protecting sacred sites in several national parks, forests, landmarks, and monuments. Consultations as to management plans for Devils Tower National Monument (known to tribes by the name "Bear's Lodge," and by other names indicating its traditional significance) and Medicine Wheel National Historic Landmark, for example, resulted in agreements involving relevant tribes, which were upheld against legal challenges based on the Establishment Clause.[59] Given the historical and contemporary Indian struggle for religious freedom, it is disturbing to see these attacks on federal actions that reflect tribal input on sacred sites.

---

55 "Sacred site" is defined to mean a specific location on federal land that is identified by a tribe or an authoritative religious representative "as sacred by virtue of its established religious significance to, or ceremonial use by, an Indian religion." Ibid, § 1(b)(iii).

56 Ibid, § 2.

57 65 Fed. Reg. 67,249 (Nov. 6, 2000). E.O. 13175 provides, among other matters, for federal agencies to engage in meaningful consultation with tribal officials in the development of policies that have tribal implications.

58 See, e.g., Bureau of Land Management, H-8120-1, Guidelines for Conducting Tribal Consultation (2004). See also https://www.blm.gov/sites/blm.gov/files/uploads/H-1780-1__0.pdf (2016 update).

59 The Devils Tower plan was upheld in *Bear Lodge Multiple Use Ass'n v. Babbitt*, 2 F. Supp. 2d 1448 (D. Wyo. 1998), *aff'd*, 175 F.3d 814 (10th Cir. 1999). The Medicine Wheel plan was upheld in *Wyoming Sawmills, Inc. v. U.S. Forest Service*, 179 F. Supp. 2d 1279 (D. Wyo. 2001), *aff'd*, 383 F.3d 1241 (10th Cir. 2004). For discussion of these, and similar, cases, see Dussias (2013: 360–384).

The controversy over plans for Montana's Badger-Two Medicine Area illustrates the challenges that can arise in implementation of a decision influenced by tribal consultation. Located in the Helena-Lewis and Clark National Forest, this area is a place of great sacred significance for the Blackfeet Nation. The area's 2002 designation as a traditional cultural district (a type of TCP), based on Blackfeet use of the area for traditional purposes for generations, led to Blackfeet Nation participation in a forest plan revision process. A May 2020 plan established the area's continuation as a sacred land and cultural touchstone as a goal and required tribal consultation to determine proposed uses' compatibility with that goal. The traditional cultural district designation played a role in an Interior Department decision to cancel a lease and drilling permit in the area; other leases in the area had previously been relinquished.[60] In September 2022, the D.C. District Court held that the Interior Secretary lacked authority to cancel the lease and ordered its reinstatement, along with the drilling permit.[61] An appeal of this decision is pending (Eggert 2022).

The ongoing efforts to save Chi'chil Bildagoteel ("Oak Flat" in English), a Western Apache sacred site in Arizona's Tonto National Forest, provide an additional example of the challenges related to tribal participation in consultation processes. In 2016, the Chi'chil Bildagoteel Historic District was added to the NRHP. The site is threatened with obliteration by the planned construction of a 2-mile-wide copper mine, due to a 2014 rider to a defense bill requiring the government to transfer the area to a mining company in exchange for other Arizona land. In 2021, the San Carlos Apache Tribe sued the USFS for failure to comply with the NHPA, as well as violation of RFRA, among other grounds. The physical destruction from the mine will prevent the tribe "from being able to physically practice and celebrate traditional religious and spiritual ceremonies [...] in the location where those ceremonies have been practiced for generations predating" European arrival and the United States' existence.[62] The USFS's attempts at Section 106 consultation had failed to examine the full range of the mine's operations, the Tribe argued, and were flawed by inadequate field work and by processing and reporting delays.[63] The lawsuit was stayed in 2021 after the Biden Administration withdrew a required environmental study, potentially providing an opportunity for more meaningful tribal

60 *Solenex LLC v. Bernhardt*, 962 F.3d 520 (D.C. Cir. 2020) (upholding the cancellation decision and remanding the case).

61 *Solenex, LLC v. Haaland*, 2022 WL 4119776 (D.D.C. 2022).

62 *San Carlos Apache Tribe v. U.S. Forest Service*, No. 21-00068, 5 (D. Ariz. Jan. 14, 2021).

63 Ibid 27 & 32–34.

participation in a new study. The Tribe is also supporting proposed legislation to rescind the land exchange mandate.[64]

An Apache grassroots group, Apache Stronghold, also challenged the project under RFRA. In June 2022, a divided Ninth Circuit panel rejected the claim, reasoning that under *Navajo Nation*, the land exchange did not impose a substantial burden, even if it makes worship on Chi'chil Bildagoteel impossible.[65] The dissenting judge highlighted the absurdity stemming from the majority's overly restrictive substantial burden test: "blocking Apaches' access to and eventually destroying a sacred site where they have performed religious ceremonies for centuries does not substantially burden their religious exercise."[66] In November 2022, the Ninth Circuit announced that the full court will consider the case.[67]

2.5 *Recent Executive Branch Developments and Summary*

In November, 2021, the Secretaries of Agriculture and the Interior issued a joint order aimed at ensuring that their departments, and component bureaus and offices, manage federal lands "in a manner that seeks to protect the treaty, *religious*, subsistence, and cultural interests" of federally recognized tribes, as well as being consistent with the nation-to-nation relationship between tribes and the federal government and in conformity with the government's trust obligation to tribes and their citizens. The order referenced the Sacred Sites Order and E.O. 13175.[68] Since the issuance of the order, several co-stewardship agreements have been signed, including an agreement for co-management of the Bears Ears National Monument among five tribes, the USFS, and the Bureau of Land Management (BLM).[69]

Also in November 2021, several federal agencies, including the Agriculture, Energy, Interior, and Transportation Departments and the Environmental

64 Save Oak Flat Act, introduced in the 117th Congress as H.R.1884 (Mar. 12, 2021) and S.1915 (Mar. 23, 2021).

65 *Apache Stronghold v. United States*, 38 F.4th 742, 766 (9th Cir. 2022).

66 Ibid 774.

67 https://www.reuters.com/markets/commodities/full-9th-us-circuit-tackle-complex-resolution-copper-mining-case-2022-11-18/.

68 Order No. 3403: Joint Secretarial Order on Fulfilling the Trust Responsibility to Indian Tribes in the Stewardship of Federal Lands and Waters (2021). See footnote 57.

69 Inter-Governmental Cooperative Agreement for the Cooperative Management of the Federal Lands and Resources of the Bears Ears National Monument (June 2022). https://www.blm.gov/sites/default/files/docs/2022-06/BearsEarsNationalMonumentInter-GovernmentalAgreement2022.pdf. The tribes are the Hopi Tribe, Navajo Nation, Ute Mountain Ute Tribe, Ute Indian Tribe of the Uintah and Ouray Reservation, and the Pueblo of Zuni.

Protection Agency, signed a Memorandum of Understanding (MOU) related to interagency coordination to protect sacred sites. The MOU affirmed the agencies' commitment to improve access to, and protection of, sacred sites through better interdepartmental collaboration and action, and stated their intention to demonstrate this commitment through early consideration of protection and access in decision-making and regulatory processes.[70] The Biden Administration is also working to strengthen tribal consultation generally, by requiring agencies to submit action plans to implement E.O. 13175, based on tribal input, and annually report on the status of actions in their plans.[71]

In September 2022, Deb Haaland, the first Native American Interior Secretary, announced that three Interior Department component offices – the BLM, the NPS, and the USFWS – had issued guidance outlining how each would implement the 2021 joint order. Secretary Haaland noted the Department's responsibility for managing millions of acres of lands that tribes previously owned and managed, which contain "cultural and natural resources of significance and value to Indigenous peoples, including sacred religious sites."[72]

Additional Biden Administration actions suggest a commitment to greater sacred sites protection. A 2021 proclamation restored Bears Ears National Monument, which was established by the Obama Administration and scaled down by the Trump Administration. The proclamation noted that "the entire Bears Ears landscape is profoundly sacred to sovereign Tribal Nations."[73] A legal

70 *Memorandum of Understanding Regarding Interagency Coordination and Collaboration for the Protection of Indigenous Sacred Sites* (Nov. 2021), https://www.doi.gov/sites/doi.gov/files/mou-interagency-coordination-and-collaboration-for-the-protection-of-indigenous-sacred-sites-11-16-2021.pdf.

71 *Memorandum on Tribal Consultation and Strengthening Nation-to-Nation Relationships* (Jan. 2021), https://www.whitehouse.gov/briefing-room/presidential-actions/2021/01/26/memorandum-on-tribal-consultation-and-strengthening-nation-to-nation-relationships/.

72 Department of the Interior, Press Release, *Interior Department Issues Guidance to Strengthen Tribal Co-Stewardship of Public Lands and Waters* (Sep. 13, 2022). The guidance documents are as follows: Bureau of Land Management, Permanent Instruction Memorandum No. 2022-011: *Co-Stewardship with Federally Recognized Indian and Alaska Native Tribes Pursuant to Secretary's Order 3403*; National Park Service, Policy Memorandum 22-03, *Fulfilling the National Park Service Trust Responsibility to Indian Tribes, Alaska Natives, and Native Hawaiians in the Stewardship of Federal Lands and Waters*; and U.S. Fish and Wildlife Service, Director's Order No. 227: *Fulfilling the Trust Responsibility to Tribes and the Native Hawaiian Community, and Other Obligations to Alaska Native Corporations and Alaska Native Organizations, in the Stewardship of Federal Lands and Waters*.

73 Pres. Proc. No. 10285, Bears Ears National Monument, 86 Fed. Reg. 57,321 (Oct. 15, 2021). The 1906 Antiquities Act empowers presidents to create national monuments. 54 U.S.C. § 320301.

challenge to the Bears Ears restoration is ongoing.[74] President Biden has also announced plans to protect Nevada's Avi Kwa Ame (Spirit Mountain), a religiously and culturally significant area for which tribes have sought national monument designation (Davenport, Freidman and Flavelle 2022).

In summary, tribal consultations pursuant to Section 106 and executive branch orders and policies have provided opportunities for tribes to play a meaningful role in shaping agency decision-making toward sacred sites protection in some instances. At the same time, the limitations on the effectiveness of consultation mechanisms are apparent in other tribes' experiences. Even though the NHPA includes the word "preservation" in its title, it does not prohibit destruction or require preservation of historic properties, so tribal participation in consultations provides no guarantee of sacred sites protection. Also, the NHPA consultation process is not a perfect fit with the goal of sacred sites protection given that these sites' primary significance is their ongoing religious, rather than historical, meaning (Barclay and Steele 2021). A 2020 government report highlighted some of the factors impacting tribal consultation effectiveness, including late initiation of consultation and inadequate consideration of tribal input.[75] In addition, to the extent that consultation rights are based on executive orders and agency policies, but do not have a statutory basis,[76] they are vulnerable to being eliminated when a new President takes office. The Biden Administration's actions show promise, but their impacts on specific sites and their long-term impacts are uncertain.

2.6 *Prison Inmates' Religious Freedom*

In 2000, following a Supreme Court decision holding that Congress lacked constitutional authority to impose RFRA on the states,[77] Congress enacted the Religious Land Use and Institutionalized Persons Act (RLUIPA).[78] Aimed at protecting the religious freedom of prison inmates and other institutionalized persons, RLUIPA provides that "[n]o government shall impose a substantial burden on the religious exercise of a person residing in or confined to an

74 *Garfield County v. Biden*, No. 4:22-cv-0059-DN (D. Utah Aug. 24, 2022) (also challenging restoration of Grand Staircase-Escalante National Monument, established in 1996 and reduced by about 50% in 2017).

75 Government Accountability Office, *Examples of Certain Federal Requirements that Apply to Cultural Resources and Factors that Impact Tribal Consultation* (2020).

76 In addition to statutes establishing consultation rights, a few statutes have authorized sacred site access and temporary closures. See, e.g., 16 U.S.C. § 460uu-47 (El Malpais National Monument).

77 *City of Boerne v. Flores*, 521 U.S. 507, 536 (1997).

78 Pub. L. No. 106-274, codified as 42 U.S.C. § 2000cc et seq.

institution, [...] even if the burden results from a rule of general applicability, unless the government demonstrates that imposition of the burden on that person –

(1) is in furtherance of a compelling governmental interest; and
(2) is the least restrictive means of furthering that compelling governmental interest."[79]

Religious exercise claims of state prison inmates are brought under the provisions of RLUIPA; federal prison inmates' claims are brought under RFRA, which protects the same scope of religious liberty.[80] Religious exercise includes "any exercise of religion, whether or not compelled by, or central to, a system of religious belief," and the concept is meant to "be construed in favor of a broad protection of religious exercise."[81] Once an inmate establishes that the prison is imposing a substantial burden on their religious exercise, the burden shifts to prison officials to show that imposition of the burden furthers a compelling interest, by the least restrictive means.

Indian inmates have sued under RLUIPA and RFRA when prison officials have burdened their religious exercise by imposing hair length regulations and by restricting access to devotional items, such as tobacco, and to smudging ceremonies and sweat lodges – with mixed results. For some Indigenous inmates, having long hair is part of their religious practice, but they may be subjected to a prison's short hair standards. About ten state prison systems impose long hair bans without providing for religious exemptions and federal courts are divided on whether religious exemptions are required.[82] In *Warsoldier v. Woodford*, a federal appeals court held that a hair length regulation imposed a substantial burden on an inmate's religious practice and was not the least restrictive means of achieving the asserted compelling interest in prison security.[83] In

79 42 § USC 2000cc-1. The definition of "institution" is in Section 2 of the Civil Rights of Institutionalized Persons Act (42 U.S.C. § 1997). In 2005, the Supreme Court rejected a claim that RLUIPA violated the Establishment Clause, holding it was a permissible accommodation of religion in view of the burden that incarceration imposed on religious rights. *Cutter v. Wilkinson* 544 U.S. 709 (2005).

80 RLUIPA amended RFRA to provide that the term "exercise of religion" in RFRA means religious exercise, as defined in RLUIPA. 42 U.S.C. § 2000bb-2(4).

81 42 U.S.C. §§ 2000cc-5(7)(A), 2000cc-3(g).

82 Native American Rights Fund, Submission to the United Nations Rapporteur on Freedom of Religion or Belief: *Indigenous Peoples and the Right to Freedom of Religion or Belief* 7 (July 11, 2022) (hereinafter NARF Submission).

83 418 F.3d 989 (9th Cir. 2005).

Thunderhorse v. Pierce, however, another appeals court upheld a hair length regulation as the least restrictive way to serve a compelling interest in security.[84] The Supreme Court declined the opportunity to create a national standard on this issue when it remanded *Knight v. Thompson*, in which an appeals court had rejected a challenge to a hair length regulation.[85]

The use of tobacco for spiritual and ceremonial purposes is accommodated in some prisons but prohibited in others, and legal challenges to tobacco bans have been decided inconsistently.[86] Courts have upheld indoor bans on smudging ceremonies, which are conducted for ritual purification. Some prisons allow outside smudging; other prisons do not, and inmates have sued to seek recognition of the right to smudge outdoors, without success.[87] Similarly, vindication of the right to engage in religious practices that requires access to sweat lodges, which make important contributions to inmate rehabilitation, is a work in progress. Some prisons provide sweat lodges;[88] other prisons do not, and courts have upheld sweat lodge bans.[89] Given the lack of uniformity in the treatment of inmates' religious freedom claims by prisons and courts, protection of inmates' religious practices has come to depend on where in the country they are incarcerated, even though it is federal law on which inmates are relying in these claims.

2.7 *Students' Religious Freedom*

Students have faced obstacles to practicing their religions in school, such as hairstyle restrictions and prohibitions on wearing regalia, including eagle feathers, in graduation ceremonies. In *New Rider v. Board of Education*,[90] three Pawnee students brought a Free Exercise Clause challenge to their suspension for violating an Oklahoma school rule that required them to cut their long, braided hair. Despite testimony as to the hairstyle's religious significance, the

---

84 364 F. App'x 141 (5th Cir. 2010).

85 797 F.3d 934 (11th Cir. 2015), remanded by *Knight v. Thompson*, 135 S. Ct. 1173 (2015). See also NARF Submission 7.

86 NARF Submission 6.

87 Ibid 7. *Hyde v. Fisher*, for example, rejected a RLUIPA-based challenge to a prison's refusal to allow outdoor smudging ceremonies, 203 P.3d 712, 729–30 (Idaho App. 2009). In another case, the fact that a prison permitted outdoor smudging played a role in the rejection of a challenge to a policy prohibiting indoor smudging. *Chance v. Tex. Dep't of Crim. Justice*, 730 F.3d 404, 417 (5th Cir. 2013).

88 *Yellowbear v. Lampert*, for example, was a successful RLUIPA-based claim by an inmate denied access to his prison's sweat lodge. 741 F.3d 48 (10th Cir. 2014).

89 NARF Submission 6–7.

90 480 F.2d 693 (10th Cir. 1973), cert. denied, 414 U.S. 1097 (1973), reh'g denied, 415 U.S. 939 (1974).

Tenth Circuit concluded that the claim did not implicate the exercise of constitutional rights[91] and commented on the benefit of public schools' "amalgamating children of various races, colors, cultural, ethnical and environmental backgrounds."[92] A later Texas decision, however, enjoined enforcement of a school hair length rule against members of the Alabama and Coushatta Tribes, based on First Amendment free exercise and free speech rights.[93]

In another case, a Lipan Apache student, whose exemption from a Texas school grooming policy did not allow him to wear his hair visibly long, challenged the exemption under the state's Religious Freedom Restoration Act, which prevents any Texas agency from "'substantially burden[ing] a person's free exercise of religion' unless it 'demonstrates that the application of the burden to the person [...] is in furtherance of a compelling governmental interest; and [...] is the least restrictive means of furthering that interest.'"[94] The court held that the exemption created a substantial burden on his exercise of his belief in wearing his hair visibly long and that the defendant had not shown any compelling interest justifying the burden.[95]

Each spring, Indian high school students seek to wear eagle feathers and other traditional regalia at their graduation ceremonies. Although many school districts allow students to wear the feathers, some do not.[96] In a 2022 case, a Ninth Circuit panel reversed a lower court's dismissal of a claim by a Sisseton Wahpeton Oyate member, Larissa Waln, that her free exercise and free speech rights were violated by a school district's denial of her request to wear a ceremonially blessed eagle feather on her cap during graduation. When she arrived wearing an eagle feather, she was prohibited from attending, while other students with secular messages on their caps were admitted. The court noted that an important part of Waln's religious beliefs is the sacred nature of eagle feathers and cited historical efforts to assimilate Indian children in boarding schools, including forcing them to discard traditional regalia. The case was remanded for a decision on the merits.[97]

---

91 Ibid 695–96.

92 Ibid 699.

93 *Alabama & Coushatta Tribes of Texas v. Trustees of Big Sandy Indep. Sch. Dist.*, 817 F. Supp. 1319, 1336 (E.D. Tex. 1993).

94 *A.A. ex rel. Betenbaugh v. Needville Indep. Sch. Dist.*, 611 F.3d 248, 257 (5th Cir. 2010).

95 Ibid 265–72.

96 Native American Rights Fund (NARF), *Wearing Eagle Feathers and Regalia at Graduation*, https://narf.org/cases/graduation/.

97 *Waln v. Dysart School District*, D.C. No. 2:20-cv-00799CDB (9th Cir. Dec. 9, 2022).

Several states have enacted statutes to ensure that students can wear eagle feathers and other significant objects at graduation ceremonies.[98] The National Eagle Repository has a process for requesting eagle feathers for presentation to tribal members at graduation ceremonies.[99] Given the history of suppression of Indian students' religions and cultures in educational institutions (Dussias 2001: 822–860), greater respect for their rights in the school setting is an important and long overdue step forward.

3 Conclusion

As this chapter has shown, the Indigenous peoples of the United States continue to face obstacles to recognition of their right to practice their religious beliefs. Barriers exist with respect to access to ceremonial materials; protection of, and access to, sacred sites; and religious exercise in prisons and schools. Constitutional protection is limited, leading to reliance on statutory provisions, administrative processes, and presidential initiatives in efforts to vindicate the right to the free exercise of religion. Although progress has been made, and the Biden Administration has voiced a stronger commitment to partnering with tribes and to protecting sacred sites, for the United States' First Peoples, complete attainment of religious freedom remains a work in progress.

References

Barclay, Stephanie Hall, and Michalyn Steele. "Rethinking Protections for Sacred Sites." *Harvard Law Review* 134, no. 4 (2021): 1294–1319.

Carpenter, Kristen Ann. "Religious Freedoms, Sacred Sites and Human Rights in the United States." In *UNDRIP Implementation: Comparative Approaches, Indigenous Voices from CANZUS*, 57–65. Waterloo: Centre for International Governance Innovation, 2020.

Carpenter, Kristen Ann. "Limiting Principles and Empowering Practices in American Indian Religious Freedoms." *Connecticut Law Review* 45, (2012): 387–405.

Cook, William John. *Preserving Native American Places: A Guide to Federal Law and Policies that Help Protect Cultural Resources and Sacred Sites.* National Trust for Historic Preservation, 2014.

98 NARF, *Wearing Eagle Feathers* (listing eight states with such protections).

99 https://www.fws.gov/program/national-eagle-repository/what-we-do.

Davenport, Coral, Lisa Friedman, and Christopher Flavelle. "Biden Promises Protections for Nevada's Spirit Mountain." *New York Times*, December 1, 2022. https://www.nytimes.com/2022/11/30/climate/biden-nevada-avi-kwa-ame.html.

Dussias, Allison M. "Room for a (Sacred) View? American Indian Tribes Confront Visual Desecration Caused by Wind Energy Projects." *American Indian Law Review* 38, no. 2 (2014): 333–420.

Dussias, Allison M. "Friend, Foe, Frenemy: The United States and American Indian Religious Freedom." *Denver University Law Review* 90, no. 2 (2013): 347–432.

Dussias, Allison M. "Kennewick Man, Kinship, and the 'Dying Race': The Ninth Circuit's Assimilationist Assault on the Native American Graves Protection and Repatriation Act." *Nebraska Law Review* 84, no. 1 (2005): 55–87.

Dussias, Allison M. "Let No Native American Child Be Left Behind: Re-envisioning Native American Education for the Twenty-first Century." *Arizona Law Review* 43, (2001): 819–865.

Dussias, Allison M. "Squaw Drudges, Farm Wives, and the Dann Sisters' Last Stand: American Indian Women's Resistance to Domestication and the Denial of Their Property Rights." *North Carolina Law Review* 77, no. 2 (1999): 637–680.

Dussias, Allison M. "Ghost Dance and Holy Ghost: The Echoes of Nineteenth-Century Christianization Policy in Twentieth-Century Native American Free Exercise Cases." *Stanford Law Review* 49, no. 4 (1997): 773–852.

Eggert, Amanda. "Groups Appeal Badger-Two Medicine Oil and Gas Lease Decision." *Montana Free Press*, November 2, 2022. https://montanafreepress.org/2022/11/02/badger-two-medicine-lease-appeal/.

Muneta, James D. "Peyote Crisis Confronting Modern Indigenous Peoples: The Declining Peyote Population and a Demand for Conservation." *American Indian Law Journal* 9, no. 1 (2020): 135–181.

Parker, Patricia L., and Thomas F. King. "Guidelines for Evaluating and Documenting Traditional Cultural Properties." *National Register Bulletin* 38, (1990; revised 1998). https://www.nps.gov/nr/publications/bulletins/nrb38.

Thompson, Darren. "Native American Church to Host Historic Field Meeting with House Natural Resources Committee." *Native News Online*, October 3, 2022. https://nativenewsonline.net/sovereignty/native-american-church-to-host-historic-field-meeting-with-house-natural-resources-committee.

The Colonial Overtones of Indigenous Religious Rights in Canada

Claude Gélinas

In the fall of 2021, Senator Mary Jane McCallum, of Cree descent, introduced a bill to recognize January 4 as National Ribbon Skirt Day across Canada. The bill describes the ribbon skirt as "a centuries-old spiritual symbol of womanhood" and representing "a direct connection to Mother Earth and its sacred medicines"[1] in Indigenous cultures. While noting the consistency of this approach with the United Nations Declaration on the Rights of Indigenous Peoples (UNDRIP) and the recommendations of the National Inquiry into Missing and Murdered Indigenous Women and Girls, the bill also recognizes that "Indigenous culture, tradition and ceremony, including Indigenous ties to language and the land, are critical to the vitality and well-being of Canada's First Peoples."[2] In many ways, this recent initiative characterizes the contemporary position of the Canadian state with respect to Indigenous spiritualities. As much as they are now widely recognized and even valued in certain contexts, their consideration remains largely confined to a symbolic level and is not integrated into the normative framework of the state.

Canada has three constitutionally recognized Indigenous (Aboriginal) peoples: Indian, Inuit, and Métis, with a total of 1.8 million people identifying as Indigenous in the 2021 census, representing 5% of the Canadian population. Under the Constitution Act, 1867, "Indians, and Lands reserved for the Indians" is a federal responsibility that tended to be limited to those recognized as "Indians" under the criteria set out in the Indian Act, to the exclusion of non-status Indians, i.e. people who claimed to be "Indians" without meeting the legal criteria, Inuit and Métis. In 1939, however, the Supreme Court of Canada ruled that the term "Indians" for constitutional purposes should include the Inuit,[3] and a similar ruling was made in 2016 with respect to non-status Indians and Métis.[4] Thus, while the historical relationship between the state and Indians, more commonly referred to today as First Nations, has been closer and largely

1 *An Act respecting a National Ribbon Skirt Day*, Senate of Canada, Bill S-219, First reading, November 24, 2021.

2 Ibid.

3 *In the Matter of a Reference as to whether the term "Indians" in Head 24 of Section 91 of the British North America Act, 1867, includes Eskimo inhabitants of the Province of Quebec*, [1939] SCR 104.

4 *Daniels v. Canada (Indian Affairs and Northern Development)*, 2016 CSC 12.

 | DOI:10.1163/9789004524330_010

defined by a specific legal framework, the relationship with Inuit and Métis has, until recently, been contingent and on the margins of the Indian Act.

In the wake of the Royal Commission on Aboriginal Peoples (RCAP 1996) and in parallel with other commissions of inquiry into the legacy of residential schools (TRCC 2015) and violence against Indigenous women (NIMMIWG 2019), the federal government has adopted and implemented a policy of reconciliation with Indigenous peoples that places particular emphasis on respect for their rights and cultures, greater political and financial autonomy for communities, and partnership and negotiation in good faith (Canada 2018b). Combined with the national policy of multiculturalism, which values and promotes cultural freedom and the preservation of ethno-cultural specificities, and an increased popular sensitivity to the colonial experience and legacy of Indigenous peoples, this has created a more favourable context for the recognition of Indigenous spiritualities by the Canadian state. This recognition has now taken many forms, from references to the importance of the spiritual dimension in the preambles of legislation and political agreements relating to Indigenous peoples, to the teaching of these spiritualities in a growing number of schools and curricula, to their inclusion in court proceedings and in ceremonial forms at various political events. Public services, particularly in the areas of health and justice, are also increasingly open to incorporating this spiritual dimension in order to provide a culturally safe environment for Indigenous beneficiaries.

However, beyond these forms of recognition, which are often superficial and left to the good will of the institutions or decision-makers concerned, the religious rights of Indigenous peoples in Canada still face numerous obstacles, whether in terms of access to sacred sites and heritage, the protection of the latter, or full autonomy to practice the beliefs and rituals they value. In this sense, I propose here an overview of the treatment of Indigenous religious rights in Canada, placing it in a historical perspective in order to highlight two persistent dimensions of the colonial regime, namely: a reluctance to consider Indigenous spiritual specificities to the point of attributing to them a normative value or scope, and a quasi-systematic subordination of Indigenous spiritual interests to the political and economic interests of the non-Indigenous majority.

1 The Limits of Recognition

At the time of the founding of the Canadian Confederation in 1867, there was certainly no unanimity among the political class as to whether Indigenous belief systems, often referred to as "pagan," should be considered recognizable religions. There was, however, a consensus that the adoption of Christianity was in the best interests of Indigenous people and communities. Christianization was, in fact, the moral component of the federal government's assimilation policy, which aimed to gradually integrate the Indians into the national society. In this context, the federal government reaffirmed its support for the religious congregations already active among the Indigenous communities, both in terms of evangelization and education. However, state officials had to operate within a broader normative framework that imposed a distance between political and religious powers and a duty of neutrality, which seems to have limited their ability to promote Christianization through legislation and coercion (Gélinas 2022).

First of all, the Indian Act of 1876 did not contain any explicit provision regarding the imposition of Christianity,[5] but rather a few provisions aimed at regulating the presence of missionaries on the reserves and indirectly facilitating their evangelization efforts, whether it was the prohibition of certain ritual practices beginning in the 1880's or the compulsory education of Indian children beginning in the mid-1890's. In addition, apart from the specific provisions of the Indian Act, Indigenous people enjoyed (in principle) the same rights as other Canadian citizens, including freedom of religion. Similarly, out of a concern for preventing discontent and uprisings that would be detrimental to social peace, as well as for avoiding defeat in the courts, most efforts to eradicate "pagan" beliefs and practices were based on persuasion rather than undue pressure. In the long run, and without denying the deplorable consequences of such an approach on the ability of Indigenous communities to freely make use of their traditional religious systems and to ensure their intergenerational transmission, this framework has also made it possible to preserve certain parts of these same religious systems, whether in their original form, in modified forms, or under the guise of or integrated with Christian beliefs and practices. More broadly, it has also allowed for the preservation of a specific cultural identity that Indigenous communities and nations throughout the country now display and affirm with conviction and pride.

At present, Indigenous spiritualities are not only recognized by the Canadian state, but in some respects valued. Recognizing the inherent right of Indigenous peoples to self-government, the Canadian government has committed to promoting rights that stem from, among other things, "their cultures, spiritual traditions, histories, laws, and philosophies" (Canada 2018b: 5). The 1996 Framework Agreement on First Nations Land Management, which allows First Nations to manage their own lands and resources, states that First Nations "have a profound relationship with the land that is rooted in respect for the Spiritual value of the Earth and the gifts of the Creator and have a deep desire to preserve their relationship with the land" (Canada 1996). As early as 1993, the Yukon

5 *The Indian Act*, 1876, S.C. 1876, c. 18.

Umbrella Agreement stated that the parties, the Crown and the affected First Nations, "wish to recognize and protect a way of life based on the economic and spiritual relationship between Yukon Indian People and the land" (Canada 1993a: preamble). In the same year, a parallel agreement recognized "the spiritual, cultural and religious importance of certain areas in the Nunavut Settlement Area to Inuit, [who] have special rights and interests in these areas" (Canada 1993b: 226). In addition to the land dimension, the spiritual connection that unites Indigenous peoples with certain cultural heritage resources, such as artifacts and other objects, is also recognized (Canada 1992: 124).

However, this form of symbolic recognition rarely proves sufficient when Indigenous religious rights are threatened, especially outside reserve or treaty lands, and it contrasts with the reception given to specific religious practices by the courts before which these rights are defended. Again, this is a notable advance, given that historically the courts not only ignored the spiritual dimension, but have been instruments of assimilation to combat it (Harring 1998: 217–238). Now, not only are traditional beliefs and practices considered religious in their own right, in which Indigenous people may sincerely believe, but these religious particularities and their roots in the land can be explicitly referred to by judges. For example, in *Delgamuukw v. British Columbia*, the Chief Justice of the Supreme Court of Canada stated that:

> when dealing with a claim of "aboriginal title," the court will focus on the occupation and use of the land as part of the aboriginal society's *traditional way of life*. In pragmatic terms, this means looking at the manner in which the society used the land *to live*, namely to establish villages, to work, to get to work, to hunt, to travel to hunting grounds, to fish, to get to fishing pools, to conduct religious rites, etc.[6]

In 2006, in *Platinex Inc. v. Kitchenuhmaykoosib Inninuwug First Nation*, regarding an Indigenous community's opposition to mineral exploration activities, Ontario Superior Court Justice Smith wrote:

> It is critical to consider the nature of the potential loss from an Aboriginal perspective. From that perspective, the relationship that Aboriginal peoples have with the land cannot be understated. The land is the very essence of their being. It is their very heart and soul. No amount of money can compensate for its loss. Aboriginal identity, spirituality, laws, traditions, culture, and rights are connected to and arise from this relationship to the

6 *Delgamuukw v. British Columbia*, [1997] 3 R.C.S. 1010, s. 194.

> land. This is a perspective that is foreign to and often difficult to understand from a non-Aboriginal viewpoint.[7]

A decade later, dissenting in *Ktunaxa Nation v. British-Columbia*, Justice Moldaver of the Supreme Court of Canada wrote:

> The connection to the physical world, specifically to land, is a central feature of Indigenous religions. [...] In many Indigenous religions, land is not only the site of spiritual practices in the sense that a church, mosque or holy site might be; land may *itself* be sacred, in the sense that it is where the divine manifests itself. Unlike in Judeo-Christian faiths, for example, where the divine is considered to be supernatural, the spiritual realm in the Indigenous context is inextricably linked to the physical world. For Indigenous religions, state action that impacts land can therefore sever the connection to the divine, rendering beliefs and practices devoid of their spiritual significance. Where state action has this effect on an Indigenous religion, it interferes with a believer's ability to act in accordance with his or her religious beliefs and practices.[8]

In a curious twist of fate, two recent cases in British Columbia were initiated by non-Indigenous citizens who felt, among other things, that certain forms of recognition of Indigenous spiritualities violated their freedom of religion. In *Servatius v. Alberni*, the British Columbia Supreme Court ruled that teaching about Indigenous spiritualities in schools, particularly to increase students' awareness and understanding of Indigenous cultures and languages, did not breach the duty of neutrality or interfere with the religious freedom of adherents of other faiths.[9] Recognizing the obvious need to make schools culturally safe for Indigenous students, Justice Thompson added: "I am satisfied that the classroom is rendered a safer place by having a Nuu-chah-nulth Elder visit the classroom, show students how a smudging is conducted, and explain the significance of smudging in Nuu-chah-nulth culture."[10] In *Redmond v. British Columbia*, the same court ruled in favor of the Ministry of Forests, Lands, Natural Resource Operations and Rural Development, which was being sued by the developer of a hydroelectric project to overturn a decision to deny it the necessary permit.

---

7 *Platinex Inc. v. Kitchenuhmaykoosib Inninuwug First Nation*, [2006] O.J. No. 3140, 272 D.L.R., s. 80.

8 *Ktunaxa Nation v. British Columbia (Forests, Lands and Natural Resource Operations)*, 2017 CSC 54, s. 127.

9 *Servatius v. Alberni School District No. 70*, 2020 BCSC 15, s. 5, 78, 95, 108.

10 *Servatius v. Alberni School District No. 70*, 2020 BCSC 15, s. 86, also 108.

This denial was based on the fact that the project would negatively impact the spiritual bathing practices of the Cheam First Nation. For the proponent, such a decision "violated the state's requirement to be religiously neutral by requiring him to meet religious criteria in the permitting process," thus violating his 2(a) Charter right to freedom of conscience and religion.[11] Indirectly, Justice Masuhara's dismissal of the challenge was beneficial to the Indigenous Nation (see Reguart Segarra 2021: 96–110).

However, although the cultural perspective of Indigenous people is now taken into account by judges, the courts have so far proved to be of little use in protecting religious rights, at least when spiritual elements are at the heart of the disputes. As a result, the courts have found it difficult to distance themselves from an ethnocentric approach that places religion in an individualistic, voluntary, and private framework and tends to favor a clear separation between the sacred and the secular (Gélinas 2021a; 2021b). This way of understanding religion has guided the interpretation of Section 2(a) of the Charter by the judges of the Supreme Court of Canada in matters of recognition of Indigenous religious and spiritual rights, where a separation is proposed between the fundamental right on the one hand and its possible forms of expression on the other. Such an interpretive context is difficult to reconcile with the collective and holistic dimensions that characterize Indigenous spiritualities, particularly with regard to their relationship to the land. For example, in *Cameron v. Ministry of Energy and Mines* (1998), in which Indigenous nations challenged the issuance of permits for gas exploration, the British Columbia Supreme Court held that the sacred concept of stewardship of a place of worship, on the basis of which the petitioners claimed a violation of their constitutional rights, was not protected under Section 2a of the Charter.[12] While acknowledging that it was "nevertheless clear on the evidence that this general area surrounding the Twin Sisters has a significant spirituality about it to First Nations people,"[13] and noting the argument that the prospecting activities would "defile an image of sanctuary that they are by their prophecies entrusted to preserve,"[14] the judge ruled, based on the lack of physical use of the site and significant restrictions on that use, that "there is no contemplated activity that inhibits or coerces the right to exercise religious beliefs or practices either on an actual basis or in an intellectual sense in this area as viewed by those who regard themselves as

11 *Redmond v. British Columbia (Forests, Lands, Natural Resource Operation and Rural Development)*, 2020 BCSC 561, s. 3, also 15.

12 *Cameron v. Ministry of Energy and Mines*, [1998] CanLII 6834 (B.C.S.C), s. 195.

13 Ibid, s. 23.

14 Ibid, s. 192.

stewards of it."[15] In the same year, however, a Saskatchewan Provincial Court judge took a more nuanced view in a case involving a prosecution for illegal hunting:

> Quite apart from its major importance as a food source, the area [Wapiti Lake] is strong in spirituality and tradition. People are buried there. It is where meetings, ceremonies and marriages have occurred. It is wilderness, precious and sacred. To accept the argument that the worth of this place to the Dene of Buffalo River is somehow less because the people cannot go there every day is untenable. To draw an analogy, this is akin to saying that, since a woman living and working in Vancouver cannot visit daily the grave of her mother, who is buried at Bay Bulls, Newfoundland, the grave holds no significance for her.[16]

More recently, in *Ktunaxa Nation v. British Columbia*, a British Columbia First Nation sought to overturn the approval of a recreational development project that would remove the spirit of Grizzly Bear living on a sacred mountain. The Ktunaxa claimed that the bear's spirit departure "would remove the basis of their beliefs and render their practices futile [... and] that the vitality of their religious community depends on maintaining the presence of Grizzly Bear Spirit in Qat'muk."[17] The Supreme Court of Canada, while recognizing alternately that "[t]he Charter protects all sincere religious beliefs and practices, old or new,"[18] the importance of protecting Indigenous religious beliefs and practices in order to achieve reconciliation,[19] and that "[i]t is undisputed that the Ktunaxa sincerely believe in the existence and importance of Grizzly Bear Spirit,"[20] held that the freedom of religion claimed was not infringed because the proposed development did not interfere with the ability of the Indigenous people to hold and manifest their religious beliefs,[21] and that although Section 2(a) has a communal aspect, "the communal aspects of freedom of religion do not, and should not, extend s. 2(a)'s protection beyond the freedom to have beliefs and the freedom to manifest them."[22] Unlike his majority colleagues, Justice

15 Ibid, s. 197.
16 *R. v. Catarat*, [1998] 4 CNLR 115, s. 145.
17 *Ktunaxa Nation v. British Columbia (Forests, Lands and Natural Resource Operations)*, 2017 CSC 54, s. 59.
18 Ibid, s. 69.
19 Ibid, s. 10.
20 Ibid, s. 11, also 69.
21 Ibid, s. 8, 70–72.
22 Ibid, s. 74.

Moldaver recognized that such an interpretation was too restrictive in the case of the Ktunaxa: "[t]he Minister's decision to approve the ski resort will render all of the Ktunaxa's religious beliefs related to Grizzly Bear Spirit devoid of any spiritual significance. Accordingly, the Ktunaxa will be unable to perform songs, rituals or ceremonies in recognition of Grizzly Bear Spirit in a manner that has any religious significance for them."[23] While adding that "[t]his approach also risks excluding Indigenous religious freedom claims involving land from the scope of s. 2(a) protection."[24]

In sum, although Indigenous spiritualities are now recognized and referred to by political and legal authorities as belief systems and practices as respectable as other mainstream religious traditions, their integration into the normative framework continues to clash with the culturally defined interpretative prisms of the majority (see for example: Beaman 2002; Borrows 2008; Shrubsole 2019; Gingras and Larregue 2019; Blair 2020; Carroll 2020). This is likely due in part to a certain lack of deep understanding of Indigenous spiritualities, but perhaps more importantly to a reluctance to move away from a comforting frame of reference, especially when the interests of the majority are at stake.

2 Dominance of Interests

As with other areas of their socio-economic and cultural life, the relationship of Indigenous people with Indian status to religion was subject to control by the federal government after Confederation. This control was exercised in different ways depending on whether the Indians were "pagans" or converts to Christianity, but it was always aimed at protecting the interests of the state and the majority. In the case of the "pagan" Indians, the political authorities certainly understood that conversion to Christianity was intended to benefit the Indigenous people themselves, but also the whole of society, insofar as it made it possible to win them over to the dominant moral values. However, the objectives of the Canadian state behind the criminalization of certain ritual practices such as the potlatch on the Northwest Coast or the Sun Dance on the Plains, were more pragmatic than ideological; beyond the indirect help they could provide to missionaries, they were linked to the project of colonization and development of the Canadian West, as well as to a recurrent concern to reduce the costs associated with Indian policy (Gélinas 2009). More specifically, it was the "give-away" component that accompanied these ceremonies,

23 Ibid, s. 118.

24 Ibid, s. 131.

namely the ritual distribution of goods, that was seen as economically harmful, not only to the populations involved, who were perceived as impoverished in this way, but ultimately to the state, which was at risk of having to meet material needs through relief measures. At the same time, the physical mutilations that sometimes accompanied some of these ceremonies were seen as immoral, of course, but also, and perhaps more importantly, as an obstacle to development because of the disturbing image of the West that they conveyed to potential settlers (Teasdale 2005). Both of these concerns would be explicitly reflected in the 1895 amendment to the Indian Act:

> Every Indian or other person who engages in, or assists in celebrating or encourages either directly or indirectly another to celebrate, any Indian festival, dance or other ceremony of which the giving away or paying or giving back of money, goods or articles of any sort forms a part, or is a feature, whether such gift of money, goods or articles, takes place before, at, or after the celebration of the same, and every Indian or other person who engages or assists in any celebration or dance of which the wounding or mutilation of the dead or living body of any human being or animal forms a part or is a feature, is guilty of an indictable offence and is liable to imprisonment for a term not exceeding six months and not less than two months; but nothing in this section shall be construed to prevent the holding of any agricultural show or exhibition or the giving or prizes for exhibits thereat.[25]

In short, it was not so much the ceremonies or rituals themselves, nor even their religious dimension, that the Canadian government wished to see disappear, but rather certain components of them that were deemed contrary to the immediate economic interests of the state and the nation as a whole. The effective repression of these cultural practices, which varied over time and according to circumstances, was reduced in the 1930s, while the legal provisions aimed at prohibiting them were abolished as part of the 1951 reform of the Indian Act.

For their part, Indians who converted to Christianity no longer appeared problematic on the basis of their religious beliefs and practices, and were accordingly treated differently in terms of religious rights in post-Confederation Canada. In this regard, Indian Affairs officials favoured an attitude of neutrality towards the various Christian denominations to which Indigenous people belonged, not only by avoiding interference in the choice of affiliation of

25 *An Act further to amend "The Indian Act,"* S.C. 1895, c. 35, s. 6.

individuals and communities, but also by acting fairly in the procedures surrounding the various forms of support for missionary congregations on reserves (Gélinas and Desruisseaux 2019). Moreover, by 1880, the Indian Act provided that the chief or chiefs of a band could designate "the religious communion to which the teacher of the school established on the reserve shall belong, – provided always that he shall be of the same communion as the majority of the band, and provided that the minority, Catholic or Protestant, may also establish a separate school,"[26] and Indian Affairs remained concerned with protecting the religious freedom of Indigenous people belonging to Christian religious minorities on reserves (Gélinas and Desruisseaux 2019). Thus, without minimizing the influence of the tutelage framework, which, for example, required government permission to set aside land and provide funds for the construction and maintenance of churches or cemeteries on reserves, and which at times proved to be restrictive of worship practices, the religious rights of Christian converts were one of the very few areas in which Indigenous people were treated relatively similarly to other Canadians, but precisely because, as Christians, they were reassuringly similar.

Since the late 1960s, Indigenous peoples in Canada have increased their demands on governments and through the courts to improve their living conditions and regain political autonomy. In this context, the responsibilities of local Indigenous political authorities have been expanded, agreements or "modern treaties" have been signed with almost one hundred nations representing approximately 5% of the Indigenous population, a constitutional guarantee of the aboriginal and treaty rights of the three peoples has been obtained, and a body of jurisprudence has been established that is more attentive and receptive to their rights and their historical and contemporary socio-cultural reality. Finally, since 2010, Canada has adhered to the principles set out in the UNDRIP, which affirms, among other things, the rights of these peoples to promote, practise, develop, transmit, protect and have access to their spiritual heritage (in particular Articles 11–12, 25 and 34), but it wasn't until 2021 that a law was passed to implement the Declaration.[27]

This political mobilization involves the assertion of a distinct cultural identity, including the expression, promotion and protection of spiritual symbols, beliefs, and practices. These are intended to serve both as markers of a distinct identity that reinforces the legitimacy of claims and as the basis for a healing process through which many communities seek to reverse the effects of colonialism and regain or strengthen collective pride. The emphasis on these

26 *The Indian Act, 1880*, S.C. 1880, c. 28, s. 74.1.

27 *United Nations Declaration on the Rights of Indigenous Peoples Act*, S.C. 2021, c. 14.

elements has led to certain forms of legal recognition of Indigenous spiritualities, although generally in a limited and eclectic manner. For example, federal and several provincial child welfare legislations recognize the importance of respecting and preserving the cultural and spiritual identities of Indigenous children in care, which may include a requirement that social workers acquire basic knowledge of these matters. The most recent federal legislation in this area states that "[t]o determine the best interests of an Indigenous child, all factors related to the circumstances of the child must be considered, including (a) the child's cultural, linguistic, religious and spiritual upbringing and heritage."[28]

Correctional facilities in Canada are required to provide for the spiritual needs off all inmates, within reasonable limits. Federal correctional facilities may, in the specific case of Indigenous inmates, offer the services of an Indigenous spiritual leader or elder, seek their advice in the provision of correctional services to an Indigenous inmate, and may even allow sweetgrass smudging, the use of any material used in an Indigenous spiritual ceremony led by an elder or cultural worker, or access to traditional medicines or healing practices. Opportunities to participate in a spiritual or ceremonial process or to receive teachings from an elder may also be offered as mitigation. All of this is based on the principle that "aboriginal spirituality and aboriginal spiritual leaders and elders have the same status as other religions and other religious leaders."[29] Finally, in the field of labour, provisions in a handful of statutes require respect for the beliefs, customs and values of Indigenous peoples, or the maintenance and provision of spaces for the spiritual needs of Indigenous workers, while exemptions may be provided for the use of tobacco in the workplace if it is for the purpose of cultural or spiritual practices and with the agreement of the appropriate authorities[30] British Columbia's provincial legislation also allows Indigenous persons to act as midwives in a manner consistent with traditional cultural and spiritual practices.[31]

Despite these sectorial advances, however, Indigenous peoples continue to face a number of obstacles to the expression of their religious beliefs and practices, particularly with respect to access to and autonomy over the free use of

---

28 *An Act respecting First Nations, Inuit and Métis children, youth and families*, S.C. 2019, c. 24, s. 10(3)a.

29 *Corrections and Conditional Realease Act*, S.C. 1992, c. 20, s. 83(1).

30 See *Fair Practice Act. Order Approving the Preferential Employment Programs in the Diavik Diamonds Project Socio-Economic Monitoring Agreement, Northwest Territories*, R-103-99, 2004, s. 1.2.4, Appendix (r); *The Occupational Health and Safety Regulations*, 2020, Chapter S-15.1 Reg 10, 2021, s. 6–14(3).

31 *Midwives Regulation*, BC Reg 281/2008, s. 4(2).

their heritage, such as sacred sites, ceremonial objects, ancestral remains, and other spiritually significant items. In many ways, this reality is the result of a political and legal framework that continues to normalize a form of control over Indigenous religious expressions.

By virtue of their autonomy on reserve lands or through political agreements, Indigenous nations can provide cultural and spiritual services to their members. However, these actions require some form of accommodation within the legal framework of the state. In the area of education, treaties provide that signatory nations may integrate the spiritual dimension into school curricula or, more broadly, develop educational content that is likely to preserve traditional culture and, in this sense, accredit teachers on the basis of linguistic, cultural, or spiritual criteria. In the same breath, however, it can also be stated that compatibility between local content and national education programs is required, for example, by ensuring that "curriculum, examination and other standards allow for the transfer of students between school systems and admission to post-secondary institutions" (Canada 2005a: 261–262). Whether or not such a provision can be considered justified, the scope of recognized rights remains limited by the need to adapt to the requirements of pursuing higher education in predominantly non-Indigenous educational institutions.

In the area of traditional medicine, Indigenous nations, in treaty territory, have recognized rights to provide services and to make laws or regulations, including the licensing of practitioners or healers (Canada 2003a: 44–45; 2005a: 262–263). However, it should be noted that this jurisdiction does not "include the authority to regulate [...] medical or health practices that, or practitioners who, require licensing or certification under Federal or Provincial Law; or [...] products or substances that are regulated under Federal or Provincial Law" (Canada 2010: 151). This tends to locate the use of traditional medicine, including its religious dimension, within a circumscribed framework that should not prejudice the field of "professional" medicine.

In the area of justice, Indigenous nations have also obtained the ability, through agreements, to provide or receive services and thus determine, in accordance with their cultural and spiritual values, sanctions, probation, parole, rehabilitation or aftercare for convicted persons. Indigenous communities can also contribute to the implementation of culturally appropriate programs in correctional facilities, as well as for offenders referred to facilities they supervise (healing lodges, Indigenous healing centers), in which cultural and spiritual dimensions can be integrated. However, these prerogatives are generally subject to the consent of the offender and must be consistent with other Canadian legal provisions.[32] As in the case of legislative jurisdiction over the solemnization of marriage rites and ceremonies and the establishment of rules regarding who may act as officiant (Canada 2003b: 28); such provisions do not exempt prospective spouses who wish to marry under the laws of their nation from possessing a valid marriage license as defined by state law (Canada 2012: 56), nor do they exempt officiants who must be appointed by provincial authorities (Canada 2018a: 172).

With respect to cultural heritage, most Indigenous nations are now able, within their economic means, to adopt the laws, regulations, and practices necessary to preserve and enhance the places, objects, and representations they consider to be of spiritual value on reserves or treaty lands. However, apart from the fact that these territories ultimately remain the property of the Crown, which, notwithstanding the duty to consult, can theoretically continue to infringe on Indigenous interests where justified, even on lands where Aboriginal title has been recognized,[33] certain provisions in the political agreements are intended to limit the exploitation of the natural resources found there for spiritual purposes. For example, the harvesting of plants for medicinal purposes in the areas covered by the agreements may be subject to the conservation standards in effect at the time (Canada 1992: 68, 70, 74; 2005a: 166; 2005b: 310).

Outside of Indigenous jurisdictions, the legal framework appropriate for the protection of spiritual heritage is limited to certain provisions requiring consultations or environmental impact assessments when development projects may affect Indigenous interests, or notification of affected nations in the case of archaeological discoveries. It is true that the scope of the normative framework for heritage protection in Canada has broadened over the years; some ordinary laws and political agreements include provisions that recognize a right of ownership or provide for the transfer of such objects or human remains to the Indigenous communities concerned, or at least require them to be informed of discoveries. Ultimately, however, heritage spaces and objects, including Indigenous human remains, located outside Indigenous jurisdictions or recognized cemeteries usually belong to the state or private owners, who can in principle dispose of them as they wish or determine the terms of access for Indigenous people (Bell 2017: 55).

Canada also lacks comprehensive legislation on the repatriation of Indigenous cultural property, and only a few provinces have enacted provisions to facilitate such procedures. Some political agreements provide that a First

32 *Corrections Act*, 2009 O.I.C 2009/250, s. 3(1f). See also Canada 2015: 60.

33 *Tsilhqot'in Nation v. British Columbia*, 2014 SCC 44, s. 2.

Nation may, under certain conditions, be informed of its heritage objects kept in certain museums, obtain the return of archaeological specimens, objects or human remains in the possession of the Crown or museums (national or provincial), or at least that requests and agreements to this effect may be made. In other cases, it is agreed that the federal government may or should facilitate the return of, or access to, heritage resources, objects or human remains outside Indigenous jurisdictions, provided that it is consistent with maintaining the integrity of national or territorial collections. Likewise, governmental and non-governmental museum institutions are now sensitive to and willing to respond to Indigenous needs and requests, albeit on a case-by-case basis, in accordance with their mission and the normative framework within which they operate. Decisions are ultimately made by those in authority.

As a result, there is no fundamental guarantee of religious rights for Indigenous people outside their jurisdictions. At this level, the fact remains that there is a form of state control over the ability of many Indigenous people to fully manifest their religious life, a situation that is not without conflict; let us recall that two major political crises in the country's recent history, Oka and Ipperwalsh, concerned, among other things, the protection of Indigenous cemeteries from economic activities. Admittedly, there are occasional initiatives by provincial, territorial, municipal, and sometimes even private authorities to protect and preserve Indigenous spiritual heritage, especially burial grounds, whether by denying development permits, recognizing burial grounds as cemeteries in their own right, or purchasing land from non-Indigenous people to ensure the protection of local heritage. However, there is nothing systematic about this, and the actions and decisions ultimately remain the prerogative of non-Indigenous decision-makers, which ultimately leads to a sense of injustice and unequal treatment among Indigenous people.

When such disputes are brought before the courts, Indigenous peoples must navigate an institutional framework that is guided by concepts and normative principles that are not necessarily consistent with those they value, and that is primarily concerned with reconciling conflicting claims of sovereignty (Stanton 2017). For example, the freedom of religion guaranteed by the Charter may be used by Indigenous peoples to protect what they see as their rights, but religious freedom is not envisioned as an absolute right and may be limited in order to balance individual rights with the interests of society. The burden is therefore on the state to prove that a restriction is justified and that it does not impose unfavourable conditions, and on the courts to assess this justification. To date, economic interests have tended to prevail over religious ones (Ross 2005), and it should be recalled that while Justice Moldaver found a violation of the Ktunaxa's freedom of religion, he agreed with his colleagues that the duty to consult and accommodate had been respected and that the decision to grant the permit was reasonable.

Another avenue available to Indigenous peoples is the use of Section 35(1) of the Constitution Act, 1982, which guarantees their Aboriginal and treaty rights, which may include rights of a religious nature. Aboriginal rights relate either to activities or practices that were integral to the particular way of life of an Indigenous group prior to contact with European colonizers, or to a right to the land (Aboriginal title), which includes a right to use it for a variety of cultural purposes, including religious activities (Otis 2007: 169). Again, these rights are not absolute. In addition to having to be proven on the basis of jurisprudential criteria established by the Supreme Court, the same court has recognized in Section 35 an objective of reconciliation between pre-existing Indigenous societies and the assertion of Crown sovereignty, while respecting historical treaty relationships. This stance has led to the Supreme Court' imposition of a duty of consultation on the part of the Crown, which requires the accommodation of Indigenous concerns before decisions are made on lands over which land claims have not yet been established, and which also has the potential to protect certain religious rights. At the same time, however, court rulings on these rights tend to revolve around the paradigm of reasonable balancing of harms. As the judges in Ktunaxa recalled: "[t]he s. 35 right to consultation and accommodation is a right to a process, not a right to a particular outcome [...]. While the goal of the process is reconciliation of the Aboriginal and state interest, in some cases this may not be possible. The process is one of 'give and take,' and outcomes are not guaranteed."[34]

On few occasions, Indigenous peoples have raised and attempted to defend these constitutional rights in relation to religious issues in the courts, whether in the context of applications for interlocutory injunctions to prevent or halt economic development activities detrimental to important sites, or to challenge laws or regulations that violate the free expression of beliefs and practices. Here too, the results have generally been disappointing, not only because the religious dimension is once again weighed against economic interests (Ross 2005), but also because the courts tend to value Aboriginal rights insofar as they are compatible with a normative framework and its values that are a priori exogenous to the Indigenous communities, apparently as a way of avoiding the implementation of a truly distinct Indigenous legal regime (Gélinas 2021b). In this sense, and in practice, the assessment of Aboriginal

34 *Ktunaxa Nation v. British Columbia (Forests, Lands and Natural Resource Operations)*, 2017 CSC 54, s. 114.

rights remains essentially dependent on the material and moral interests of the majority, not to mention the heavy burden of proof imposed on claimants.

3 Conclusion

The foregoing is not intended to deny certain advances in the recognition and protection of Indigenous religious rights in Canada, but only to show that the modalities surrounding the recognition or nonrecognition of these rights remain anchored in a certain colonial continuity, characterized by a significant lack of knowledge of Indigenous religious systems and a desire to exercise control over their forms of expression for the benefit of the dominant majority. The law relating to Indigenous religious rights remains under the aegis of a normative framework established and controlled by the latter, in such a way that, for Indigenous peoples, especially those who live off-reserves or outside the territories covered by modern treaties, the configuration and implementation of their religious way of life depends largely on the parameters of a common law that is not only exogenous, but which, in the event of conflict, tends more easily to give precedence to economic and private interests. As for the Indigenous communities which enjoy a greater degree of autonomy, their religious rights are no less largely inscribed in a dynamic of delegation of powers, rather than recognition of the specific and inherent nature of Indigenous normativities, which powers must also prove compatible with the normative framework of the state. The result is a set of Indigenous religious rights in Canada that is both limited and complex, eclectic and in itself a source of inequality, since it is not uniformly applicable and beneficial to all Indigenous peoples.

References

Beaman, Lori Gail. "Aboriginal Spirituality and the Legal Construction of Freedom of Religion." *Journal of Church and State* 44, no. 1 (2002): 135–149.

Bell, Catherine. "First Nation Control Over Archaeological Sites: Contemporary Issues in Heritage, Law, Policy and Practice." In *Comparative Law and Anthropology*, edited by James A.R. Nafziger, 55–84. Cheltenham: Edward Elgar Publishing, 2017.

Blair, Chase. "Indigenous Sacred Sites & Lands: Pursuing Preservation through Colonial Constitution Frameworks." *Appeal: Review of Current Law and Law Reform* 25, (2020): 73–88.

Borrows, John. "Living Law on a Living Earth: Aboriginal Religion, Law, and the Constitution." In *Law and Religious Pluralism in Canada*, edited by Richard Moon, 161–191. Vancouver: University of British Columbia, 2008.

Government of Canada. *Gwich'in Comprehensive Land Claim Agreement*. Ottawa: Minister of Indian and Northern Affairs Canada, 1992.

Government of Canada. *Umbrella Final Agreement Between The Government of Canada, The Council For Yukon Indians and the Government of the Yukon*. Ottawa: Minister of Indian and Northern Affairs Canada, 1993a.

Government of Canada. *Agreement Between the Inuit of the Nunavut Settlement Area and Her Majesty the Queen in Right of Canada*. Ottawa: Minister of Indian and Northern Affairs Canada, 1993b.

Government of Canada. *Framework Agreement on First Nation Land Management*. Ottawa: Minister of Indian and Northern Affairs Canada, 1996.

Government of Canada. *Westbank First Nation Self-Government Agreement Between Her Majesty the Queen in Right of Canada and Westbank First Nation*. Ottawa: Minister of Indian Affairs and Northern Development, 2003a.

Government of Canada. *Land Claims and Self-Government Agreement Among the Tłı̨chǫ and The Government of the Northwest Territories and the Government of Canada*. Ottawa: Minister of Indian Affairs and Northern Development, 2003b.

Government of Canada. *Land Claims Agreement Between the Inuit of Labrador and Her Majesty the Queen in Right of Newfoundland and Labrador and Her Majesty the Queen in Right of Canada*. Ottawa: Minister of Indian Affairs and Northern Development, 2005a.

Government of Canada. *The Carcross/Tagish First Nation Final Agreement*. Ottawa: Minister of Indian Affairs and Northern Development, 2005b.

Government of Canada. *Tsawwassen First Nation Final Agreement*. Ottawa: Minister of Indian Affairs and Northern Development, 2010.

Government of Canada. *Yale First Nation Final Agreement Act*. Ottawa: Minister of Indian Affairs and Northern Development, 2012.

Government of Canada. *Délı̨nę Final Self-Government Agreement: Our People, Our Future, Our Délı̨nę*. Ottawa: Minister of Indian Affairs and Northern Development, 2015.

Government of Canada. *Lheidli T'enneh Treaty*. Ottawa: Crown Indigenous Relations and Northern Affairs, 2018a.

Government of Canada. *Principles Respecting the Government of Canada's Relationship with Indigenous Peoples*. Ottawa: Department of Justice, 2018b.

Carroll, Michael P. "What Evicting Grizzly Bear Spirit Does (and Doesn't) Tell Us about Indigenous 'Religion' and Indigenous Rights." *Studies in Religion/Sciences Religieuses* 49, no. 1 (2020): 32–49.

Culhane, Dara. *Pleasure of the Crown. Anthropology, Law and First Nations*. Burnaby (B.C.): Talonbooks, 1998.

Gélinas, Claude. "L'État canadien et la répression des pratiques religieuses autochtones." In *L'État canadien et la diversité culturelle et religieuse, 1800–1914*, edited by Lorraine Derocher *et al.*, 93–116. Québec: Presses de l'Université du Québec/SoDRUS, 2009.

Gélinas, Claude. "Les tribunaux et la configuration des identités spirituelles autochtones: une comparaison des contextes canadien et australien." *Anthropologie et sociétés* 45, no. 3 (2021): 87–105.

Gélinas, Claude. "La reconnaissance étatique des droits religieux autochtones au Canada." *Canadian Journal of Law and Society/Revue Canadienne Droit et Société* 36, no. 2 (2021): 245–261.

Gélinas, Claude. "Droits ancestraux et réconciliation: quelques incompatibilités à la lumière de la décision *Hamilton Health Sciences Corp. v. D.H.*" *Recherches amérindiennes au Québec* 50, no. 3 (2021): 55–65.

Gélinas, Claude. "Assisting Indigenous Resistance Through Secularism: Legal Limits to Christianisation in Canada (1867–1939)." In *The Routledge Companion to Global Indigenous History*, edited by Ann McGrath and Lynette Russell, 550–568. London and New York: Routledge, 2022.

Gélinas, Claude and Caroline Desruisseaux. "Les Affaires indiennes et les lieux de culte sur les réserves, 1875–1940." *Bulletin d'histoire politique* 27, no. 2 (2019): 87–188.

Gingras, Yves and Julien Larregue. "L'Esprit de l'ours contre la station de ski: l'argumentation juridique face à un conflit épistémologique et ontologique." *Canadian Journal of Law and Society/Revue Canadienne Droit et Société* 34, no. 1 (2019): 13–32.

Harring, Sydney L. *White Man's Law. Native People in Nineteenth-Century Canadian Jusrisprudence.* Toronto: University of Toronto Press, 1998.

Hickling, James. "Religious Freedom in the New World? Indigenous Sacred Sites and Religious Beliefs in the Courts in British Columbia." *Oxford Journal of Law and Religion* 6, (2017): 544–579.

MMIWG (National Inquiry into Missing and Murdered Indigenous Women and Girls). *Reclaiming Power and Place: The Final Report of the National Inquiry into Missing and Murdered Indigenous Women and Girls*, 2 volumes. Ottawa, 2019.

Otis, Ghislain. "Revendications foncières, 'autochtonité' et liberté de religion au Canada." In *Les systèmes religieux amérindiens et inuit: perspectives historiques et contemporaines*, edited by Claude Gélinas and Guillaume Teasdale, 169–189. Québec/Paris: Muséologie In-Situ/L'Harmattan, 2007.

RCAP (Royal Commission on Aboriginal Peoples). *Report of the Royal Commission on Aboriginal Peoples*, 5 volumes. Ottawa, 1996.

Reguart Segarra, Núria. *Los pueblos indígenas de Canadá y la defensa de sus territorios sagrados. Análisis sociológico y jurisprudencial. Cuadernos Deusto de Derechos Humanos, no. 98.* Bilbao: Universidad de Deusto, Instituto de Derechos Humanos, 2021.

Ross, Michael L. *First Nations Sacred Sites in Canada's Courts*. Vancouver: University of British Columbia Press, 2005.

Shrubsole, Nicolas. *What Has No Place, Remains. The Challenges for Indigenous Religious Freedom in Canada Today*. Toronto: University of Toronto Press, 2019.

Stanton, Kim. "Reconciling Reconciliation: Differing Conceptions of the Supreme Court of Canada and the Canadian Truth and Reconciliation Commission." *Journal of Law and Social Policy* 26, (2017): 21–42.

Teasdale, Guillaume. "La politique autochtone du gouvernement canadien dans l'Ouest à la fin du XIXe siècle: une analyse de l'interdiction de la Danse du Soleil." Master's thesis, Religious Studies, Université de Sherbrooke, 2005.

TRCC (Truth and Reconciliation Commission of Canada). *Honouring the Truth, Reconciling for the Future. Summary of the Final Report of the Truth and Reconciliation Commission of Canada*. Ottawa, 2015.

The Fundamental Right to Freedom of Religion for Indigenous Peoples in Chile: Intersections with Territorial Rights and Cultural Integrity

Leslie Cloud

The right of Indigenous peoples to freedom of religion is amply protected under international human rights law, and such protections have been further strengthened by recent developments in international Indigenous rights law (Bellier et al. 2017: 19–84). In Chile, freedom of religion was enshrined in the Constitution of 1925. And yet, Indigenous peoples in that country[1] continue to struggle for the recognition and respect of their religious beliefs and practices, which reflect a cosmology based on the relationship between various elements that make up the universe and engender life. Based on the principle of reciprocity, Indigenous communities see their religious knowledge and religious practices as essential to the maintenance of life, to human health, and to the well-being of not only local ecosystems but also the visible and hidden biodiversity of all the different spaces that make up the universe. From this perspective, religious rights are bound up with the right to life, land rights, the right to natural resources, and cultural rights.

In his work on the anthropology of religion, Elio Masferrer Kan has noted the shortcomings of Western notions based on a dichotomy between the sacred and the secular, compared to Indigenous beliefs or worldviews that refrain from establishing boundaries between religion, spirituality, and other aspects of life. He has also observed the so-called ethnic nature of Indigenous religions, which support a system of identity construction and a shared worldview rather than seeking out converts (Kan 2002: 152). Likewise, José Martinez Cobo, in his role as Special Rapporteur of the United Nations Sub-Commission on Prevention of Discrimination and Protection of Minorities, took a decolonial perspective on Western concepts of religion and the need to protect Indigenous religious practices:

1 Adopted in 1993, the Indigenous Peoples Act (Statute no. 19253) formally recognized the Mapuche, the Aymara, the Rapa Nui, the Atacama (Lickan Antay), the Quechua, the Colla, the Chango, the Diaguita, the Kawésqar, and the Yagan. This legislation also addressed the protection, promotion, and development of Indigenous communities. Chile's Indigenous communities account for about thirteen percent of the country's population, with the Mapuche being the largest single group.

 | DOI:10.1163/9789004524330_011

> The concept of religion must include not only what have been considered the "world's great religions" but also other beliefs or creeds which essentially fulfil the same function. Within this wider view of religious rights and practices, recognition and protection must be given to all forms of religion which seek the moral improvement of human beings and foster understanding and brotherly love among them. (Martinez Cobo 1983, 3: par. 279)

These ideas resonate with a presentation on the Mapuche worldview and Christianity given by a *machi* (shaman) named Victor Caniullan. He emphasized the importance of protecting the Mapuche religion from cultural assimilation while warning against its appropriation by Western faiths.[2] Reflecting on whether the concept of religion has a functional homeomorphic counterpart in Mapuzugun (the Mapuche language), he settled on *nguilla mawun*. This term refers to an order of things, a spiritual logic that shapes a person's relationship with both the Füxakeche (the elders who are gone) and the wider environment (the components of the Wall Mapu, the universe).[3] Accordingly, the Mapuches' spiritual relationship with the Mapu is reflected in daily religious ceremonies that are performed individually or collectively and that facilitate a connection with the energies of the surrounding environment (Cloud 2009–2010: 513–516).

Colonialism struck at the roots and the very essence of Indigenous religious practices. And those affected continue to fight for their right to life, land rights, freedom of religion, and cultural rights. For instance, in an article on the struggles of Indigenous peoples to maintain their spirituality, Alexandra Tomaselli and Alexandra Xanthaki have described how religion was used as a tool of colonialism in Latin America, with dramatic consequences for Indigenous spirituality, belief systems, and worldview (Tomaselli and Xanthaki 2021: 869). Looking further north, the Truth and Reconciliation Commission of Canada has condemned the transgenerational trauma and cultural genocide imposed by the Catholic Church and other institutions on Indigenous children at residential schools (TRCC 2015). When the Pope visited Canada in

2 Caniullan, Machi Victor. 2016. Ponencia "Cosmovisión Mapuche y Christianismo," https://www.youtube.com/watch?v=hXQxkoRCkaw.

3 The concept of the Mapu, often translated as "the land," actually encompasses both spaces and beings. Beyond the surface of our planet, it also encompasses several other dimensions, including the Wenu Mapu (spaces and beings located "above"), the Ragiñ Mapu (the sun, the stars, different forms of wind, etc.), the Püji Mapu (everything that can be seen on Earth: trees, animals, stones, etc.) and the Miñche Mapu (all subterranean sources of energy: minerals, water, etc.).

July 2022, Indigenous groups took the opportunity to demand the repudiation of the Doctrine of Discovery, long used to dispossess Indigenous peoples of both their lands and their religions.

This chapter addresses the religious rights of Indigenous peoples living in Chile. Taking a historical perspective, it considers two dimensions of religious freedom: (1) the right of all human beings to their own beliefs and (2) the right to manifest such personal beliefs (individually or collectively, publicly or privately) without interference from third parties or the state. I begin by analyzing the religious rights of Indigenous peoples from Chilean independence in 1818 until the end of the military dictatorship in 1988, before looking at efforts to secure freedom of religion since the transition to democracy under a neoliberal constitution and economic model inherited from the Pinochet dictatorship. This periodization aligns with the local and international impact of the emergence of a body of international and comparative Indigenous law beginning in the 1980s. In tandem, a decolonization process began, at international level, to address infringements of Indigenous rights, especially the right to freedom of religion.

1 From Independence to the End of the Military Dictatorship

1.1 *Imposing Christianity*

In Chile, the impact of colonialism on the religious practices, institutions, and lands of Indigenous peoples long predates the country's independence. Furthermore, the process of colonization continued after independence, albeit through somewhat different means and on a different scale, with effects varying based on the Indigenous peoples involved and the location of their territories.

Catholic missions were established on Rapa Nui (Easter Island) beginning in 1864, 24 years prior to the island's annexation by Chile in 1888. In 1868, missionaries forcibly relocated those Rapa Nui families that continued to resist Catholicism, moving them to the missions of Hanga Roa and Vaihu. By October of that year, the entire population had been baptized and removed from its ancestral lands (Cristino 2011: 26). The missionaries left the island in 1871, taking 168 Rapa Nui with them to the Mangareva Mission in Tahiti. Following their departure, some aspects of the Rapa Nui religion reemerged, including certain ceremonies and rites of passage. In 1872, the island's Rapa Nui population stood at 157 (Cristino 2011: 29).

As for Indigenous peoples in northern Chile, they only came under the authority of the country's government in 1883, when the War of the Pacific was drawing to a close. But in the context of Spanish colonization efforts, representatives of the Catholic Church had arrived in the region as early as 1536. Later, they pursued a destructive campaign known as the Extirpation of Idolatry, designed to wipe away all traces of Indigenous beliefs, symbols, and idols, and in recognition of this process, some observers now speak in terms of an "Indigenous Andean Catholicism" when referring to some of the region's Indigenous communities (CVHNT 2008: 95). Finally, after the failure of initial evangelization efforts in Reche-Mapuche[4] territories not subject to the Spanish Crown, the Jesuits adopted a more defensive strategy. This involved a mix of fresh missionary incursions and the organization of *parlamentos*[5] between representatives of the Crown and Indigenous authorities (Contreras Painemal 2022). In this context, and without fully renouncing their own religious practices, the Mapuche began to adopt elements of Christianity.

1.2 *The Principle of Legal Equality*

Upon gaining independence, the Republic of Chile proclaimed the legal equality and freedom of all its citizens, regardless of origin. However, a strict interpretation of these principles and the adoption of specific provisions had the effect of infringing on the rights of Indigenous peoples to their lands, cultures, and religions. On the one hand, the decree issued by Bernardo O'Higgins on March 4, 1819, broke with the system of rights established under the Crown of Castile by granting the country's Indigenous and non-Indigenous populations equal rights under the law. On the other hand, while putting an end to indentureship and making members of the Indigenous population full legal persons, it also reflected an ignorance of their legal systems and institutions, in the context of a national program of cultural assimilation that had little consideration for their beliefs. Disregarding the traditional and communal ties between Indigenous peoples and their lands, the government established a legal framework for seizing control of their ancestral territories. An executive order dating from 1813 already provided for the sale of Indigenous lands by public auction. Legislation adopted on June 10, 1823, limited recognition of Indigenous ownership to property held by legal title; in all other cases, land used by Indigenous communities could be sold at auction. This progressive denial of judicial status, culture, and connections to the land

4 The term "Mapuche" was not used in the literature until the second half of the eighteenth century. Previously, the term "Reche" had been used to refer to the Indigenous people living in the Kingdom of Chile, from the Choapa River to the Chiloé Archipelago. See Boccara 1999: 90–91.

5 The Republic of Chile continued to organize such *parlamentos* until the end of the nineteenth century. See Contreras Painemal 2021.

was consolidated by the country's earliest constitutions, thereby enshrining assimilationist objectives and the invisibility of Indigenous peoples in the Constitution.

In fact, none of the constitutions adopted between independence and 1980 specifically recognized Indigenous rights[6] or even referred to Indigenous religious beliefs and customs. And although the issue of Indigenous peoples was raised at the constituent assemblies held in 1823 and 1828 (Cloud 2015a), discussions focused on promoting their assimilation and "internalizing" (Schulte-Tenckhoff 1997: 169) their status by withdrawing any acknowledgment of autonomy. Furthermore, Article 5 of the Constitution of 1833 (one of the so-called trial constitutions) established Catholicism as the state religion and forbade the public practice of any other faith. These provisions remained in force until the adoption of the Constitution of 1925, which established freedom of religion by guaranteeing the "[p]ractice of all beliefs, liberty of conscience, and the free exercise of all religions that may not be contrary to morality, good usage, and public order [...]" (art. 10, par. 2). This provision was retained in the Constitution of 1980, adopted under the military dictatorship.

A combined policy of "Chileanization" (assimilation justified in terms of the principle of equality) and evangelization also led to the seizure of the Aymara people's ancestral lands, devastating their religion and culture (CVHNT 2008: 288–290). In turn, the Quechua, Atacameño, and Colla peoples suffered a similar fate (CVHNT 2008: 283–444). At the same time, contrary to a strict interpretation of the principle of legal equality and in the wake of independence-era efforts to assimilate Indigenous peoples and erase their distinctiveness, Mapuche lands were directly targeted by a long series of legal measures adopted starting in 1927.[7] But although this body of legislation triggered the widespread loss of ancestral lands, it also contributed to the survival of Mapuche culture – including religious beliefs and customs – despite the upheavals associated with the resettlement of communities on Indigenous reserves (*reducciones*) (Le Bonniec 2020).

6 Specifically, the so-called trial constitutions of 1818, 1822, 1823, and 1828, as well as the constitutions of 1925 and 1980.

7 Measures supporting the policy of dividing collective land titles (*títulos de merced*) include statutes passed in 1927 (no. 4169), 1930 (no. 4802), 1931 (no. 4111), 1942, 1947 (no. 8736), 1961 (no. 14511), and 1972 (no. 17729), as well as an executive order issued in 1979 (no. 2568). See Cloud and Le Bonniec (2012: 29–30).

1.3 *Indigenous Reserves and the Preservation of a Mapuche Cultural Identity*

Until the end of the so-called Pacification of Araucania (1861–1883), a military effort to conquer the lands of the Reche-Mapuche, the latter maintained their own legal and political systems, meaning that Indigenous religious beliefs could be freely expressed. But even as it took control of the region, the Chilean government feared that a policy of outright cultural assimilation could provoke a Mapuche revolt. Accordingly, a statute adopted on December 4, 1866 recognized certain Indigenous institutions – such as customary unions and modes of inheritance. At the same time, the government established reserves, issuing a collective land title (*títulos de merced*) to the chief of each so-called *reducción* (Cloud and Le Bonniec 2012: 29–30). On the one hand, these titles facilitated the seizure of 90 to 95% of ancestral Mapuche lands. On the other hand, they paradoxically allowed for the persistence of not only Indigenous territorial rights, however limited the corresponding territory may have been, but also a Mapuche cultural identity based on, among other things, the continuation of religious practices on lands organized by *lof, rewe*, and *yjarewe*.[8] And although the collective land titles would later be divided into individual property titles as part of the Mapuche land division policy carried out from 1927 to 1988 (Cloud and Le Bonniec 2012: 29), an ongoing connection to the land allowed for Mapuche religious practices to persist, despite the growing influence of Catholicism and evangelical religions. However, new threats would emerge from the neoliberal economic framework established under the dictatorship.

1.4 *Case Law Relating to Mapuche Culture*

Most of the case law relating to the rights of the Mapuche people before 1989 were about land disputes involving collective property titles granted to Indigenous groups and the subsequent division of reserve lands (CVHNT 2008: 360–419, 430–443, 448–477). To verify whether special statutes were applicable to such cases, judges had to verify the "Indigenous status" of the litigants. In a case heard by the Court of Osorno in 1911, the lawyers representing a Mapuche woman named Maria Pichillanca sought the cancellation of a property transaction she

8 The term lof refers to a clan or extended family unit, which constitutes the basic structure of Mapuche society and provides a framework for the socio-spatial and ritual construction of a group of people who share a particular territory. In political and territorial terms, rewe refers to an area occupied by multiple related families and members of different lofs bound together by family, spiritual, social, political, and ritual ties. Finally, the term yjarewe refers to connections between multiple *gijatuwe*, which are sites for *gijatun* ceremonies. In sociopolitical terms, it refers to the integration of multiple rewe. See Bustos (2014: 160–163).

had made. They argued that since she was Indigenous, she was not authorized to sell land. The opposing party considered that, as a "respectable person and of Christian education," Pichillanca could not be considered Indigenous.

At the time, the issue of Mapuche spiritual beliefs was only raised in court on rare occasions. Specifically, the notion of an irresistible force was cited by those seeking to have Mapuche defendants found not criminally responsible. For example, in a well-known case from 1953, a Mapuche woman was absolved of criminal responsibility for murdering her grandmother, who was a machi, on the grounds that an irresistible moral, psychic, and ancestral force connected to the defendant's religious beliefs had compelled her to commit the homicide (Cloud 2009–2010: 525). In a controversial case, a similar legal justification was used by judges to exempt individuals from criminal liability after they were accused of throwing children into the sea to stop the earthquakes that caused a devastating tsunami in 1960 (Leiva Salamanca 2013). Although both instances involved some legal recognition of Indigenous beliefs and practices, the latter only served as a pretext for exempting individuals from criminal liability. There was no explicit recognition of the right of Indigenous peoples to religious freedom. Rather, the judgments in question reflect the integrationist spirit of the International Labour Organization's Indigenous and Tribal Populations Convention (ILO Convention no. 107), which essentially aimed to assimilate Indigenous populations while allowing them to retain certain cultural practices. Accordingly, an Indigenous person's degree of criminal responsibility depended on their degree of "cultural development," in a context where Indigenous religious beliefs and customs are deemed to reflect a lower level of development.

1.5 Te Pito Ote Henua*: Heritage Designation and the Infringement of Religious Rights*

After their conversion to Catholicism but before the annexation of Easter Island by Chile in 1888, the Rapa Nui were dispossessed of their lands (Tuki Huke and Leslie Cloud 2015) – including their sacred sites, burial grounds, cultural monuments, and other heritage locations (Teave and Cloud 2014; Tuki Huke and Cloud 2015) – as part of a process that progressively disconnected them from their ancestral beliefs and practices. In 1895, just a few years after the annexation treaty was signed, Chile leased part of the island to a French merchant named Enrique Merlet. In 1903, his eponymous company was sold to the Compañía Explotadora de Isla de Pascua, controlled by Williamson Balfour and Co., which converted the island into a sheep farm[9] producing wool

9 A similar measure had been implemented on Rapa Nui from 1872 to 1877, prior to the island's annexation on behalf of Chile by Dutrou-Bornier. This French citizen forced most of the island's Indigenous inhabitants to work on the reserve.

for the export market. In 1897, acting on Merlet's instructions, naval governor and company administrator Alberto Sanchez Manterola ordered that the Rapa Nui be driven from their lands and homes at gunpoint (Cristino 2011: 26–29). After burning their homes, Manterola confined the Indigenous inhabitants to a one-square-kilometer fenced reserve in Hanga Roa, now the island's main town.[10] Two years later, they plotted the assassination of Riro, the Rapa Nui king (Ko Riro A Ngure) (Cristino 2011: 32). Subsequently, Statute no. 3220, adopted in 1917, gave the navy full authority over the island and removed any protections granted under the Constitution of 1833 (Rochna-Ramirez 1996: 45). In 1933, Chile declared the island to be public land, in violation of the 1888 treaty that the Rapa Nui interpreted as having assigned ownership of the land and its resources exclusively to the Indigenous population (Teave and Cloud 2014: 407). Two years later, the government created a national park and historic monument covering the entire island.[11] In addition to dispossessing the Rapa Nui of their religious and cultural sites, these developments made preservation impossible. For more than three decades, no serious efforts were made to protect the island and its Indigenous heritage.

For decades to come, the Rapa Nui lived in captivity, forbidden to leave the reserve without authorization from the island's naval administrator. They were also subjected to abuse (including acts of physical and psychological torture) by naval authorities. It was not until 1966 that Statute no. 16.411 established the Department of Easter Island and recognized the civil and political rights of the Rapa Nui, who also received Chilean citizenship. This legislation allowed the state, deemed to be the island's sole landowner, to grant individual land titles to "native Chileans," defined as individuals born on the island to at least one parent who had also been born there. This included "non-Rapa Nui" Chileans.[12] Section 43 of the statute was the only one to deal with the island's cultural heritage. It empowered the Chilean president to authorize the removal of archaeological finds from the country. In the late 1960s, urban development and airport construction carried out within this new legal framework caused

10 This extremely violent episode – involving the assassination of resistance fighters, the rape of Indigenous women, the burning of crops and homes, the theft of animals, etc. – lasted three days.

11 Supreme Decree no. 103 (January 16, 1935), issued by the Ministry of Lands and Colonization; Supreme Decree no. 4536 (July 23, 1935), issued by the Ministry of Education.

12 The legislation forbade the granting of land titles to foreigners. However, Section 1 provided for the granting of land titles to Chileans who were not natives of the island, provided that their father or mother was born on the island, that they had resided there for at least five years, and that they practiced a profession or held an office or a permanent job there (Rochna-Ramirez 1996: 49).

irreparable damage to the island's natural archaeological heritage (Ramirez Aliaga 2004: 497) – and, by extension, to the cultural and spiritual heritage of the Rapa Nui.[13]

2 Legal Developments since Chile's Transition to Democracy

Starting in the 1980s, the constitutions adopted by Latin American countries transitioning to democracy tended to reflect a pluralist vision. The most progressive examples recognized the multinational character of the state, the rights of nature, and the rights of Indigenous nations to self-determination (including the right to their own legal systems and freedom of religion) (Yrigoyen Fajardo 2013: 209–228). By contrast, the Chilean Constitution of 1980, which remains in force, does not grant Indigenous peoples any specific rights. Furthermore, although ordinary legislation adopted since the end of the dictatorship has recognized some Indigenous rights, including the right of Indigenous peoples to practice their religions, such guarantees exist within a broader legal framework that remains largely incompatible with the broader protection of Indigenous religious beliefs and customs.

The Constitution of 1980 recognizes a limited number of fundamental rights and provides no protection for cultural rights (Faundes Peñafiel and Le Bonniec 2020: 167). It merely refers to a so-called third-generation right, the right to live in an uncontaminated environment. As in the Constitution of 1925 (see above), the right to practice beliefs, liberty of conscience, and the free exercise of religion are limited by a requirement not to contravene "morality, good usage, and public order" (art. 19, par. 6). And although designed to implement this constitutional provision, the so-called Religious Entities Act adopted in 1999 makes no reference to Indigenous religions. The

13 Under the Pinochet dictatorship (1973–1989), renewed efforts were taken to strengthen the island's heritage and tourism assets. However, the Rapa Nui were not involved, nor were their ancestral territorial rights or their spiritual ties to sacred sites on the island acknowledged. In response, a grassroots Indigenous movement established a Council of Elders. In 1988, with the support of 90% of adult Rapa Nui inhabitants, this body took legal action seeking control of the entire island. In support of these ongoing legal efforts, the Rapa Nui submitted a petition to the Inter-American Commission on Human Rights (IACHR) in 2015. In an admissibility report issued on July 14, 2021, the IACHR stated that allegations relating to the disregard of the collective property rights of the Rapa Nui over their lands and the island's natural resources, along with the restrictions imposed by Chilean law on access to their lands and archaeological sites, constituted violations of Articles 21 (Right to Property) and 12 (Freedom of Conscience and Religion) of the American Convention on Human Rights (ACHR).

Constitution of 1980 also governs the rights framework established under the Pinochet dictatorship with a view to implementing neoliberal economic policies designed to facilitate privatization and the wholesale exploitation of the country's natural resources. The resulting resource development efforts have led to many conflicts with Indigenous peoples seeking to prevent the destruction of ecosystems and religious or sacred sites on their lands. It is important to remember that among OECD countries, Chile has one of the economies most dependent on natural resource extraction. In 2021 alone, the country witnessed more than 130 environmental conflicts, 35% of which involved Indigenous lands.[14]

Signed on October 1st, 1989, toward the end of the military dictatorship, the Nueva Imperial Agreement committed the Coalition of Parties for Democracy (Concertación) to adopting an Indigenous Peoples Act and ensuring the constitutional recognition of Indigenous rights. Today, three infra-constitutional legal norms specifically address Indigenous peoples and their religious rights: the Indigenous Peoples Act, adopted in 1993 (see note 1); a separate statute governing Indigenous use of coastal areas; and ILO Convention no. 169, which was not ratified until 2008.[15]

Although the Indigenous Peoples Act does not specifically refer to religious rights, Section 7 does recognize "the right of indigenous peoples to maintain and develop their own cultural traditions," as well as the state's duty to promote Indigenous cultures as part of the Chilean nation's heritage. Meanwhile, the so-called Lafkenche Act provides for the temporary management of coastal areas by Indigenous people pursuing customary activities. It was drafted on the initiative of the Mapuche-Lafkenche people (*lafken*: of the sea, *che*: people). As cited in Section 6 of the statute, examples of customary uses include those related to fishing, recreation, medicine, and religion. Finally, in contrast to the integrationist spirit of ILO Convention no. 107, which had been adopted in 1957, ILO Convention no. 169 recognizes the rights of Indigenous peoples to their traditional lands or territories (arts. 13 to 18); to be consulted and to provide free, prior and informed consent (FPIC) on all legislative and administrative measures that affect their interests (arts. 6 and 7); and to the recognition and exercise of their cultural identity, including consideration of Indigenous institutions and legal systems (arts. 8 and 10). Adopted in 1989, the document

14 Instituto Nacional de Derechos Humanos, "Mapa de Conflictos Socioambientales," Instituto Nacional de Derechos Humanos, 2021, https://mapaconflictos.indh.cl.

15 In a decision delivered on January 23, 2013, the Constitutional Court of Chile declared that the provisions of ILO Convention no. 169 have supra-legal and infra-constitutional value within the country's constitutional order.

specifies that its provisions – including those respecting the right to development, land rights, territorial rights, and the right to natural resources – should be implemented in accordance with the religions, values, and spiritual practices of Indigenous peoples. It also requires state parties to grant reparations for cultural, religious, or spiritual property freely and knowingly given away or taken without the prior consent of Indigenous peoples or in violation of their laws, traditions, or customs.

3 Judicial Protection

The degree to which the religious rights of Indigenous peoples are protected by the courts in Chile depends on the contexts in which they are invoked. The cases discussed below illustrate three relevant aspects of case law, namely situations where Indigenous religious practices themselves appear to constitute criminal offenses; where Indigenous persons are held in detention; and where access to or the integrity of Indigenous lands is threatened.

3.1 *"Cultural Defenses" in Criminal Matters*

In criminal law, cultural defenses are either grounds for exclusion of criminal responsibility or extenuating circumstances based on a defendant's membership in an ethnic minority whose distinct culture, practices, and customs clash with those of the dominant cultural group (de Maglie 2012: 136). Often based on Section 54 of the Indigenous Peoples Act or on Articles 8 through 10 of ILO Convention no. 169, the use of cultural defenses has been fostered by cross-cultural facilitators who participate in court proceedings (Le Bonniec 2015). Many of the cases in question have involved Aymara and Quechua defendants found in possession of coca leaves and charged with offenses under the Drugs and Narcotics Act. Courts have found these individuals not guilty based on the medicinal and ceremonial uses of coca leaves within Aymara culture, the quality and quantity of coca leaves transported, and the over-representation of Indigenous Andeans among those arrested in possession of large quantities of coca leaves (Barrientos Pardo 2013). Furthermore, such decisions are aligned with a well-established body of case law (Cespedes Proto 2018); Article 27 of the UN Covenant on Civil and Political Rights; and Articles 2, 5, and 8 of ILO Convention no. 169. But although the judges involved have emphasized the religious aims of transporting coca leaves, none of them have expressly cited a violation of Article 19, paragraph 6 of the Constitution of 1980, which protects freedom of worship.

3.2 *Incarceration*

The Chilean state has actively criminalized the activities of movements seeking to protect Indigenous lands (Cloud 2020; Cloud and Le Bonniec 2019).

The resulting convictions have regularly raised the issue of an inmate's right to freedom of religion. Indeed, despite the large number of Mapuche individuals jailed for their role in so-called interethnic conflict, few standards have been implemented to ensure respect for the rights of Indigenous prisoners (Royo 2020).

In accordance with the United Nations Standard Minimum Rules for the Treatment of Prisoners, Indigenous inmates are deemed vulnerable persons who must be given special protection. With respect to applying national laws to Indigenous peoples and imposing criminal penalties on members of Indigenous communities, Article 8 of ILO Convention no. 169 requires that Indigenous customs and customary laws be considered, whereas Article 10 calls for taking account of the economic, social, and cultural characteristics of Indigenous peoples. In addition, the Religious Entities Act requires correctional institutions to adopt regulations for ensuring respect for the religious rights of prisoners. Article 6 of the regulations in question guarantees the ideological and religious freedom of inmates, whereas Article 10 requires that some form of pastoral care be provided "under conditions as close as possible to those outside of prison." The regulations also discuss the application of the principle of non-discrimination. Furthermore, a human rights training manual for prison staff was published in 2013 by the Chilean Gendarmerie. Based on the provisions of ILO Convention no. 169 and the United Nations Declaration on the Rights of Indigenous Peoples (UNDRIP), it specifies the need to show respect to traditional Indigenous spiritual leaders and states that "participation in religious rites or ceremonies is a universal human right applicable to all persons, without distinction. […] Incarcerated persons must be provided with the facilities required to attend such events, as long as they take place within the prison and do not compromise site security."[16] And yet, despite the standards of protection set out in the manual, a 2018 report issued by Chile's National Human Rights Institute denounced the wholesale neglect of the Indigenous prison population due to the absence of institutional policies adapted to its needs (INDH 2018: 137). Likewise, Manuela Royo has noted that while prisons provide for preaching by evangelical and Catholic clergy, no equivalent programs exist for meeting the spiritual needs of Indigenous inmates (Royo 2020).

These shortcomings have been met with public protests. Also, traditional Mapuche leaders held in prison have participated in hunger strikes to demand respect for their right to practice their religion. Specifically, they have called

16 Gendarmería de Chile, *Manual de Derechos Humanos de la Función Penitenciaria* (Unidad de Protección y Promoción de los Derechos Humanos, n.d.), accessed November 29, 2022, https://html.gendarmeria.gob.cl/doc/ddhh/Archivos_Adicionales/MANUAL_DDHH_GENCHI_FINAL.pdf.

for opportunities to participate in religious ceremonies, both in prison and in their communities (while on temporary release). Starting in 2016, sustained public pressure led to some improvements. In accordance with Articles 5 and 8 of ILO Convention no. 169, certain traditional leaders with the status of machi or *zugumachife* (the latter interpret for a shaman during a trance) were granted temporary release to visit their communities and rewe (sacred altars). They also had the opportunity to carry out traditional ceremonies, which are essential for restoring their health and maintaining balance within their communities.

When such cases have been heard in court, judges have recognized the connection between Mapuche prisoners' right to health and freedom of religion (Royo 2020). But despite these precedents, a request from a machi named Celestino Cordoba for the accommodation of his spiritual needs was denied by multiple courts. He had been sentenced to 18 years in prison after being accused of burning down the home of Werner Luchsinger and Vivianne Mackay in 2013. The couple, who had been involved in a decades-long territorial dispute with the community, were home at the time and died in the fire. A request by the machi to visit his community and care for his rewe was initially rejected by the institution where he was being held. Then, a legal action for protection (*recurso de proteccion*)[17] was made on the grounds that his imprisonment and separation from his rewe violated his right to life. However, the Supreme Court of Chile found that so long as the machi was not subjected to physical and mental abuse in detention, there was no infringement of his right to life. What the court failed to consider was that the Mapuche worldview perceives the separation of a shaman from his rewe as a serious threat to his life and health. Following a new 107-day-long hunger strike and mass demonstrations across Chile; with the support of the National Institute of Human Rights, the United Nations representative for South America and the Araucanía Regional Health Service; and with the consent of the Ministry of Justice, Cordoba was ultimately allowed 14 hours to visit his rewe, during which time he was able to perform a ceremony. The agreement reached with the Ministry of Justice also provided for the adoption of a resolution on the prison system, recognizing the need to protect freedom of religion in accordance with international Indigenous rights law. It authorized visits by traditional doctors and the use of traditional medicines in penitentiaries, and required the application of cultural relevance criteria, especially in matters of health and pastoral care. And although the agreement has yet to be fully implemented, it provides a framework for ensuring that Indigenous inmates can

17 In the Chilean court system, such applications are the most common means of protecting Indigenous rights. They allow judges to order a moratorium on the decision or project at issue, thereby immediately suspending the alleged violation of fundamental rights.

continue to practice their religions. In early May 2022, Cordoba was allowed to conduct a four-day Nguillatun (prayer ceremony) at the Temuco Prison, alongside some 200 participants.

3.3 *The Spiritual Connection to the Land*

As the Indigenous Peoples Act of 1993 was coming into force, Chile saw an escalation in environmental and territorial disputes related to infrastructure and natural resource projects in Indigenous territories (Cloud and Le Bonniec 2012; Cloud 2020). However, due to the poor recognition of Mapuche territorial rights under a system largely based on individual land ownership, some sites with special spiritual significance to Indigenous peoples are located on public lands or lands granted to third parties.

Prior to the ratification of ILO Convention no. 169, legal actions (*recursos de proteccion*) taken to protect Indigenous territories and sacred sites in Chile had consistently proven unsuccessful. These cases were largely based on the Indigenous Peoples Act of 1993 and environmental law (specifically, the constitutional right to live in an uncontaminated environment), rather than the constitutional rights to property and freedom of worship. This most likely reflected a belief that judges would find environmental arguments more convincing than cultural ones. Consider a case that highlighted the inability of the Indigenous Peoples Act, on its own, to safeguard religious beliefs and customs. It concerned the flooding of Indigenous lands and cemeteries at Ralco Lepoy, in the Andes, following the construction of a hydroelectric dam on the Bío-Bío River, which had once been a symbol of Mapuche independence. Rather than freedom of worship, the legal action taken in this instance cited the right to live in an uncontaminated environment and the special protection afforded to Indigenous lands under the Indigenous Peoples Act. The court ruled that efforts to generate electricity were in the national interest, and therefore took precedence over calls by "special interests" to protect Indigenous lands, including sacred or religious sites. The application then made its way to the IACHR, in the form of a petition citing a violation of Article 12 of the ACHR (which deals with freedom of religion):

> From our perspective, life, spirituality, and culture cannot be separated from our relationship with the land. They are bound together in a worldview based on respect for nature and communion with the spirits of our ancestors, who inhabit the volcanoes, rivers, canyons, and forests of Alto Bío Bío. Therefore, depriving us of our lands [...] is an assault on our identity as a people and as individuals, as well as on our beliefs and culture. The right to life and to physical, mental, and moral integrity encompasses not only the right not to be arbitrarily deprived of life and not to be

> subjected to torture or cruel treatment or punishment, but also the right to secure all conditions necessary for a dignified life, including respect for our beliefs and living environment, and especially respect for our cemeteries and ceremonial spaces, where we perform the Nguillatun, spaces that would be flooded and destroyed by the Ralco Power Plant project.[18]

In another case – this one dating from 2008 – a machi named Francisca Linconao took a legal action (*recurso de proteccion*) to protect a *menoko* (a sacred Mapuche site rich in biodiversity) that was threatened by logging operations undertaken by the company that held title to the land. In this instance, the application cited a violation of the constitutional right to live in an uncontaminated environment, without explicit reference to the constitutional right to freedom of religion (although Mapuche spirituality was mentioned). The court hearing the case approved the application on the grounds that the right to live in a healthy environment took precedence over the property rights of the forestry company, rights that in this case were restricted by the need to preserve environmental heritage. The decision also made specific reference to the territorial rights provisions contained in Article 15 of ILO Convention no. 169. Although the latter had not yet entered into force, Chile had already ratified it and the Supreme Court would subsequently confirm the lower-court ruling, in a decision rendered immediately before the convention took effect.[19]

Moreover, the implementation of ILO Convention no. 169 has facilitated new legal strategies for the promotion of Indigenous rights through efforts to protect the lands and, by extension, the sacred sites of Indigenous communities. A decision of the Constitutional Court handed down on April 3, 2008, confirmed that Article 6, regarding the right to consultation and FPIC, applies directly even in the absence of a regulatory framework. The ruling was initially upheld by appeals court judges and the projects of development or infrastructure targeted by the court action were suspended as a result. However, in many cases, the Supreme Court has overturned decisions favorable to Indigenous peoples by ruling, for example, that project proponents were merely required to follow the public consultation process set out in the Environment Act (Cloud 2018: 116). Building on their initial victories,

18 *Mercedes Julia Huenteao Beroiza et al. v. Republic of Chile*, Petition no. 4617/02, IACHR (December 10, 2022). For the Spanish-language version of the petition, see "Denuncia ante la Comisión Interamericana de Derechos Humanos en contra del Estado de Chile," accessed October 4, 2022, https://www.ciel.org/Publications/RALCO_Denuncia_CIDH.pdf.

19 Court of Appeal of Temuco, *Linconao Huircapan v. Sociedad Palermo Ltda* (September 16, 2009). The decision was confirmed by the Supreme Court on November 30, 2009. See Cloud (2009–2010: 529–530).

lawyers for Indigenous communities have continued to cite violations of the right to legal equality, alongside violations of the right to live in an uncontaminated environment, property rights, and, less frequently, the right to freedom of religion (Cloud 2018). And yet, the communities themselves were often motivated by the threat that such projects posed to their sacred sites and to their spiritual connection with the land. For the Mapuche, this connection with the Mapu is rooted in the Az Mapu, the law of the universe. Transmitted orally, the guiding principles of the Az Mapu dictate spiritual behaviors and practices, ways of understanding and experiencing religion, referred to as *pu Mapunche ñi Gijañmawün*. For example, individuals are required to carry out certain duties, such as giving offerings and prayers to the *ngen* (spiritual entities that protect the land) (Cloud 2009–2010: 508–511) when removing something from the land, insofar as such an act is permitted by the Az Mapu. The Mapuche are also expected to observe certain taboos, lest the ngen impose a *castigo-kuxan*, or "disease-punishment." When such illnesses occur, machi and other spiritual authorities serve as intermediaries between the different energies and forces present in the affected spaces to restore the harmony.

There are several possible reasons why freedom of worship has rarely been cited in court cases concerning threats to Mapuche religious practices. To begin with, Indigenous communities have often been reluctant to speak openly about the principles of the Az Mapu and other aspects of their spiritual connection to the land, out of fear that revealing the importance and exact location of certain sacred sites would facilitate intentional acts of destruction. In addition, as noted above, it has often been easier for legal representatives to cite environmental rights, appeals to which are more familiar to Chilean judges and lawyers alike, rather than Indigenous worldviews and the spiritual rights that stem from them. Moreover, it has taken time for activists, litigants, legal professionals, and judges to familiarize themselves with the provisions of ILO Convention no. 169 and the UNDRIP, with the IACHR procedures and precedents, and with Indigenous worldviews – and to adjust their approaches accordingly.

For instance, in 2011, the Valdivia Court of Appeals heard a case involving four Mapuche spiritual authorities, including two machi, who were seeking an injunction against logging at a site they considered sacred.[20] They also argued that, considering their worldview, the flooding caused by the construction of the Osorno hydroelectric plant threatened Mapuche spirituality due to its impact on the Ngen Kintuante religious complex. Accordingly, they cited the right

20 *Millaray Huichalaf Pradines et al. v. Juan H. Ortiz Ortiz*, case no. 501-2011 (4 May 2012). See Cloud 2015b.

to maintain their ancestral system of norms and laws (the Az Mapu), the natural balance between different forms of life inhabiting their lands (*itxofill mongen*), and the well-being of their environment (*küme mongen*). Furthermore, an anthropological report, commissioned by the National Corporation for Indigenous Development, explained how the site in question "embodies a person, namely the former owner of the site who was enchanted and removed to this physical space along with his brother, Kelen Wenxu." The presence of this spiritual entity was repeatedly noted in the arguments made before the court. Given that without the ngen, there can be no life and no Mapuche, the petitioners were able to directly associate the preservation of the site with the preservation of life itself. One machi explained how the location where a ngen resides provides strength and health to the whole community, to the entire region. Given that international Indigenous rights law recognizes the spiritual nature of the relationship between Indigenous peoples and their ancestral lands, the petitioners were careful to demonstrate their connection to the site, highlighting its role in ceremonies and emphasizing the duty of the ngen to protect local biodiversity for the well-being of future generations. They also noted that, according to the collective memory of the Mapuche living in the area, the home of the ngen corresponds to the Mapuche territory of Maihue-Carimallin. And although the petitioners did not cite any property rights violations, they did refer to freedom of religion and the right to live in an uncontaminated environment, as guaranteed under ILO Convention no. 169 (arts. 4.1, 5, and 8.2) and the UNDRIP.

On May 4, 2012, the Valdivia Court of Appeals found that the community's freedom of worship had been violated, without addressing the right to live in an uncontaminated environment. Giving ample consideration to the Mapuche worldview, the decision referred to provisions of ILO Convention no. 169 and the UNDRIP, as well as to IACHR procedures and case law. Although it did not recognize the petitioners' property rights, it did acknowledge how access to their traditional lands was essential to their religious practices and, by extension, to their cultural identity. Nevertheless, the decision was overturned on September 21, 2012, by a ruling based on reasons entirely unrelated to international Indigenous rights law. Declining to address the infringement of the Mapuche community's freedom of worship, the Supreme Court found that the request for access to the Ngen Kintuante religious complex infringed the property rights of the non-Mapuche party to the case.[21] And because they were constitutionally guaranteed (under Article 19, paragraph 24 of the Constitution of 1980), these property rights took precedence over Articles 5 and 8 of ILO Convention no. 169 (regarding freedom of worship).

21 Supreme Court of Chile, case no. 3863-2012 (21 September 2012).

Another case concerned the preservation of a pre-Hispanic cemetery in northern Chile that served as a place of worship for the Lickanantay, Aymara, and Quechua peoples. An Indigenous community took a legal action to stop a mining company from proceeding with prospecting work in a sacred place. The petitioners claimed that their rights to equality and freedom of religion had been violated, based on the fact that they had not been consulted and that they carried out religious practices at the site in question. In this instance, the Court of Appeals of Antofagasta initially rejected the application on the grounds that the petitioners had failed to prove that the work posed a risk to the heritage site. This decision was later overturned by the Supreme Court, which found that the petitioners' freedom of worship had been infringed. The judges observed that the case clearly concerned "a cemetery that, like historical memory, bears silent witness to countless traces of not only how the region's inhabitants lived before the Incas [...] but also various objects that reflect the practices, habits, and/or customs from the cultural peak of these ethnic groups, and to which their present-day representatives assign, [...] a superior and even sacred status [...]."[22]

Defenders of Indigenous lands were once again forced to rethink their legal strategies following the adoption, in 2013 and 2014, of two standards for meeting Indigenous consultation requirements.[23] In cases where no consultation had been carried out, applications began to be filed with infringements of freedom of religion as their primary claim. For example, in December 2021, the Indigenous community of Newen Lafken Mapu brought a case against a forestry company called Tubul SPA in the Court of Appeals of Concepción. The petitioners claimed that their right to freedom of religion had been violated by logging activities that threatened a site where they carried out ceremonies.[24] They argued that it was not merely shells, plants, trees, and the rewe that risked being destroyed. Rather the work threatened their very connection to the land and the energies that inhabit the site. In response, the forestry company referred to the Supreme Court ruling mentioned above, arguing that its property rights took precedence over the Mapuche community's religious rights. However, the earlier case had concerned a site whose religious nature was

22 Supreme Court of Chile, case no. 3.010/2013 (September 30, 2013).

23 Supreme Decree no. 40 (August 12, 2013), regulating the environmental impact assessment system and providing for a consultation mechanism to be implemented in connection with projects affecting Indigenous peoples; Supreme Decree No. 66 (March 4, 2014), regulating consultations with Indigenous communities.

24 Court of Appeals of Concepción, case no. 10489-2021 (December 14, 2021). The decision was confirmed by a judgment of the Supreme Court, case no. 95.908-2021 (January 24, 2022).

"physically invisible, intangible." In this instance, the National Monuments Council had identified the remains of an archaeological site that contained an ancient Indigenous burial ground. Accordingly, the agency had informed the company that work should not proceed without its permission. In turn, the court hearing the case ruled that by continuing its work without authorization from the National Monuments Council, the company had violated an Indigenous religious site and, by extension, the religious freedom of the Mapuche community.

This non-exhaustive analysis of case law regarding the religious rights of Indigenous peoples in Chile serves to highlight the difficulties facing those who seek to protect territorially rooted spiritual beliefs and practices. With rare exceptions and despite new measures designed to protect Indigenous and cultural rights, it has remained difficult to convince judges of the need to maintain the spiritual ties between Indigenous communities and their lands. Numerous factors are at play, starting with the fact that proponents of Indigenous rights have often neglected to formulate arguments based on freedom of religion. Second, judges have refused to recognize Indigenous communities as the owners of locations under threat, in cases where the property rights of other parties have taken precedence over Indigenous religious rights. Third, the courts have failed to recognize the religious significance of the sacred sites at issue. These challenges reflect both the legal culture of the professionals involved in such cases (Faundes Peñafiel and Le Bonniec 2020: 170–180) and the legal options available to litigants in terms of rights and remedies. In this regard, the Constitution of 1980 offers few legal or jurisdictional resources for the protection of either the rights of Indigenous peoples specifically or human rights in general. Based on a monocultural interpretation of fundamental rights, an interpretation shaped by the economic and ideological framework of the Pinochet dictatorship (as opposed to an intercultural interpretation of human rights capable of recognizing the religious rights of Indigenous peoples), property and economic rights have tended to take precedence over the right to a healthy environment and religious rights. Finally, the provisional nature of applications for protection means they cannot be relied upon to ensure the protection of Indigenous lands and the exercise of associated fundamental rights over the long term. For example, in many cases where the Supreme Court ordered the suspension of megaprojects on Indigenous lands due to a lack of consultation, the projects in question were able to resume once the consultation process was complete (Cloud 2020). This highlights the limitations of such legal remedies and the need for formal recognition of Indigenous territorial rights, a necessary step toward securing the religious rights of Indigenous peoples.

4 Final Considerations

The analysis presented above highlights the many challenges associated with decolonizing Indigenous rights in Chile, especially with respect to freedom of religion. The partial and ad hoc recognition of certain religious beliefs and customs has been achieved not through concerted government action, but instead through various legal strategies pursued by Indigenous communities to protect their religious rights. This underscores the need for a deeper understanding of the full range of Indigenous religious practices. The IACHR has recognized such practices as integral to Indigenous cultural identity, which it defines as follows:

> [...] the right of traditional communities and their members to live in accordance with their culture and to be recognized as different in their relations with others. [This] includes the right to maintain their own culture, spirituality, and cosmological references; their tangible and intangible cultural heritage; as well as their historical memory and their current identity. It also includes the right to respect and protection for their knowledge, languages, beliefs, arts, morals, religion, legal frameworks, and social structures. (Faundes Peñafiel and Le Bonniec 2020: 141)

Hence the importance of protecting the religious rights of Indigenous peoples alongside the protection of their languages, lands, heritage, and knowledge. All these elements are intrinsically connected. By guaranteeing the rights of Indigenous peoples and recognizing Chile as a plurinational, intercultural, ecological, and multilingual state, the proposed new constitution rejected in the referendum of September 4, 2022, would have been a great help in this regard. So long as the rights of Indigenous peoples are not fully enshrined in the Chilean constitution, various proponents will need to ensure that already recognized fundamental rights are interpreted through a dynamic and cross-cultural lens, and with reference to Indigenous rights recognized at the regional and international levels (Cloud 2020).

On the same subject, while recognizing that the courts have upheld certain cultural rights of Indigenous peoples, Juan Jorge Faundes Peñafiel and Fabien Le Bonniec have made the following observation:

> [...] the emergence of the right to cultural identity in Chile has been a source of tension between different stakeholders in the legal system. This reflects unresolved issues in our society insofar as the underlying development has triggered a paradigm shift in how we understand the right to

> difference and the injunction to respect culture and cultures. The result has been a clash with the principle of egalitarianism, which has traditionally consigned indigenous peoples – among other groups – to the shadows. (Faundes Peñafiel and Le Bonniec 2020: 180)

This assessment, which certainly applies to the recognition of Indigenous peoples' religious freedom, stands as a call not only to support and strengthen human rights and Indigenous rights in Chile, but also to develop the country's legal culture in a way that promotes acceptance of an intercultural form of constitutional democracy. Despite the work of the CVHNT, no reparations mechanism has been put in place to address the many violations of the right to religious freedom experienced by Indigenous peoples in Chile. Accordingly, the path forward requires the country to make a serious commitment to transitional justice, based on the principles of truth, justice, restitution, and non-repetition (Cloud 2021).

References

Bellier, Irène, Leslie Cloud, and Laurent Lacroix. *Les droits des peuples autochtones. Des Nations unies aux sociétés locales*. Paris: L'Harmattan, 2017.

Barrientos Pardo, Ignacio. "Licitud del porte y uso de la hoja de coca. Un caso de reconocimiento de la costumbre indígena en la jurisprudencia chilena." *Revista de derecho Penal y Criminología* 3, (2013): 79–100.

Antona Bustos, Jesús. *Los derechos humanos de los pueblos indígenas: el Az Mapu y el caso Mapuche*. Temuco: Ediciones Universidad Católica de Temuco, 2014.

Boccara, Guillaume. "Organisation sociale, guerre de captation et ethnogenèse chez les Reche-Mapuche à l'époque coloniale." *L'Homme* 150, (1999): 85–117.

Cespedes Proto, Rodrigo. "Religiones indigenas y jurisprudencia chilena." *Revista Latinoamericana de Derecho Y Religión* 4, no. 1 (2018): 1–8.

Cloud, Leslie. "Az Mapu, el derecho invisible o del derecho de los Mapuche." *Thule, Rivista italiana di studi americanistici* 26/27–28/29, (2009–2010): 501–543.

Cloud, Leslie. "Le droit à l'autodétermination du peuple mapuche au XIXème siècle: entre droit des gens et droit international classique." In *Les Mapuche à la mode*, edited by Ricardo Salas Astarin and Fabien Le Bonniec, 29–48. Paris: L'Harmattan, 2015.

Cloud, Leslie. "Derecho propio mapuche, derecho internacional de los pueblos indígenas y derecho chileno: Ilustraciones y desafíos de un des-encuentro de hoy, en las relaciones territoriales entre los Mapuche y el Estado de Chile." In *II Jornadas de debate y actualizacion en temas de antropologia juridica, dialogos entre antropologia y derecho*, edited by Morita Carrasco et al., 183–208. Buenos Aires: Eudeba, 2015.

Cloud, Leslie. "Los Tribunales chilenos y la protección de los territorios indígenas: los desafíos de una resolución jurisprudencial de la discronía entre el modelo económico neoliberal chileno y la efectivación de los derechos indígenas." In *Autodeterminação, autonomia territorial e acesso à justiça: povos indígenas em movimento na América Latina*, edited by Ricardo Verdum and Edviges Ioris, 99–124. Rio de Janeiro: Associação Brasileira de Antropologia, 2018.

Cloud, Leslie. "Le temps des droits autochtones au Chili: la jurisprudence comme mesure d'une interculturalité juridique émergente." In *Peuples et savoirs autochtones à l'épreuve des (dé)mesures*, edited by Sabrina Melenotte and Bruno Baronnet, 87–105. Paris: L'Harmattan, 2020.

Cloud, Leslie. "Entre invibilisation, injustices et vérités biaisée, les défis de la justice transitionnelle pour les peuples autochtones au Chili." In *Annuaire de justice transitionnelle – 2020*, edited by Marina Eudes et al., 67–95. Bayonne: Institut Francophone pour la Justice et la Démocratie, 2021.

Cloud, Leslie and Fabien Le Bonniec. "Entre logiques d'État et autochtonie: dynamiques de la territorialité mapuche à l'heure du droit à l'autodétermination des Peuples Autochtones." *Quaderns de l'Institut Catala d'Antropologia* 17, no. 1 (2012): 25–43.

Cloud, Leslie and Fabien Le Bonniec. "Dynamiques actuelles de criminalisation et de judiciarisation des droits autochtones au Chili." In *Échelles de gouvernance et peuples autochtones*, edited by Irène Bellier and Jennifer Hays, 235–254. Paris: L'Harmattan, 2019.

Contreras Painemal, Carlos. *Los Tratados celebrados entre la República de Chile y la Sociedad Mapuche*. Santiago: Centro de Documentación e Investigación Indígena RUCADUGUN, 2021. https://libros.uchile.cl/1283.

Contreras Painemal, Carlos. *Los tratados entre la Nación Mapuche y la Corona de España*. Santiago: Centro de Documentación e Investigación Indígena RUCADUGUN, 2022. https://libros.uchile.cl/1292.

Cristino, Claudio. "Colonialismo y neocolonialismo en Rapa Nui: una reseña histórica." In *La Compañia Explotadora de Isla de Pascua. Patrimonio, Memoria e Identidad en Rapa Nui*, edited by Claudio Cristino and Miguel Fuentes, 19–52. Concepción: Ediciones Escaparate, 2011.

CVHNT (Comisión Verdad Histórica y Nuevo Trato con los Pueblos Indígenas). *Informe de la Comisión Verdad Histórica y Nuevo Trato con los Pueblos Indígenas*. Santiago: Republic of Chile, 2008.

De Maglie, Cristina. *Los delitos culturalmente motivados ideologías y modelos penales*. Madrid: Marcial Pons, 2012.

Faundes Peñafiel, Juan Jorge and Fabien Le Bonniec. "Cultura juridica chilena y derecho a la identidad cultural: un acercamiento metodológico interdisciplinario." *Revista Chilena de Derecho y Ciencia Politica* 11, no. 1 (2020): 137–193.

INDH (Instituto Nacional de Derechos Humanos). *Estudio de las condiciones carcelarias en Chile. Diagnóstico del cumplimiento de los estándares internacionales de Derechos Humanos sobre el derecho a la integridad personal.* Santiago: Andros, 2018.

Le Bonniec, Fabien. "La culture mapuche à la barre: pouvoir et médiation linguistico-culturels des facilitateurs interculturels dans les tribunaux pénaux du sud du Chili." *Autrepart* 73, (2015): 55–71.

Le Bonniec, Fabien. "Cachez ce territoire que je ne saurais voir: la question du territoire au prisme des études sur la société mapuche durant le XXe siècle." *Nuevo Mundo Mundos Nuevos* (2020). https://doi.org/10.4000/nuevomundo.82962.

Leiva Salamanca, Ronny Alejandro. "Maremoto de 1960, sacrificio humano y restablecimiento del equilibrio en el Wallmapu." *Investigaciones Sociales* 17, no. 30 (2013): 35–45.

Martinez Cobo, José. *Study of the Problem of Discrimination Against Indigenous Populations.* New York: United Economic and Social Council, 1983.

Masferrer Kan, Elio. "Los derechos religiosos de las comunidades indígenas." In *Constitución y derechos indígenas*, edited by Jorge Alberto Gonzalez Galvan, 147–164. Mexico City: Universidad Nacional Autónoma de México, 2002.

Ramírez Aliaga, José Miguel. "Manejo del recurso arqueológico en Rapa Nui: Theoría y realidad." *Chungara, Revista de Antropología Chilena* 36 (2004): 489–497.

Rochna-Ramirez, Susana. *La Propriedad de la Tierra en Isla de Pascua.* Temuco: CONADI, 1996.

Royo, Manuela. "Libertad Religiosa y Pluralismo Cultural: Nuevos Desafíos Del Derecho Penitenciario." *Politica Criminal* 15, no. 29 (2020): 259–289.

Schulte-Tenckhoff, Isabelle. *La question des peuples autochtones.* Brussels: Bruylant, 1997.

Tomaselli, Alexandra and Alexandra Xanthaki. "The Struggle of Indigenous Peoples to Maintain Their Spirituality." *Religions* 12, no. 10 (2021): 869.

TRCC (Truth and Reconciliation Commission of Canada). *Honouring the Truth, Reconciling for the Future: Summary of the Final Report of the Truth and Reconciliation Commission of Canada.* Ottawa: Truth and Reconciliation Commission of Canada, 2015. https://publications.gc.ca/collections/collection_2015/trc/IR4-7-2015-eng.pdf.

Teave, Erity and Leslie Cloud. "Rapa Nui National Park, Cultural World Heritage: The Struggle of the Rapa Nui People for Their Ancestral Territory and Heritage, for Environmental Protection, and for Cultural Integrity." In *World Heritage Sites and Indigenous Peoples' Rights*, edited by Stefan Disko and Helen Tugendhat, 403–422. Copenhagen: IWGIA, Forest Peoples Programme, Gundjeihmi Aboriginal Corporation, 2014.

Tuki Huke, Tuhiira Terahi and Leslie Cloud. "Rapa Nui, un territoire placé sous régime patrimonial: les défis de sa restitution au peuple maori rapanui." In *Terres, territoires, ressources. Politiques, pratiques et droits des peuples autochtones*, edited by Irène Bellier, 271–290. Paris: L'Harmattan, 2015.

Yrigoyen Fajardo, Raquel. "Constitutionnalisme pluraliste et peuples autochtones en Amérique Latine. Du multiculturalisme à la décolonisation." In *Peuples autochtones dans le monde. Les enjeux de la reconnaissance*, edited by Irère Bellier, 209–228. Paris: L'Harmattan, 2013.

Exploring the Historical Impact of Colonialism on Indigenous Religious Rights in Nigeria

Abiodun Akeem Oladiti

In addition to freedom of religion, religious rights in Nigeria are based on freedom of thought and conscience. They include the right to adopt a new faith, as either an individual or a community, and to publicly or privately express religious belief through worship, teaching, ritual observance, dietary restrictions, modes of dress, or any other social habit that may have religious significance (Nwauche 2008).

Before the advent of colonial rule, the Nigerian population had belonged to independent groups with different political ideologies, languages, customary practices, and religions. Within each community, the ruler and the council of chiefs were responsible for providing welfare for the people. In terms of maintaining religious rights, these leaders essentially saw themselves as peacemakers, called upon to resolve disputes by reconciling divergent interests, while safeguarding the physical integrity and spiritual well-being of society (Adewoye 1977). At the community level, the Indigenous peoples of Nigeria traditionally safeguarded religious rights while tolerating differences in religious practices. They had no history of proselytization, perhaps because different communities shared certain basic beliefs and practices surrounding ancestors, sacrifices, offerings, prayers, invocations, blessings, and salutations. Their common aim was to maintain good relations between humanity and supernatural beings, as well as between the spiritual and physical worlds. Each community's religion expressed its culture and experience of nature in a distinct way, and it was understood that such expressions could not be transposed or imposed on another community (Mbiti 1969: 58–66).

By contrast, religious divisions feature prominently in the colonial history of Nigeria. As the southern states became predominantly Christian and Muslims continued to hold sway in the north, followers of Indigenous faiths could be found throughout the country (Ayandele 1968). However, as the foreign religions gained converts, the number of traditional worshipers dwindled (Ayandele 1992: 262). Within the colonial administration, Christianity enjoyed favored status. Associating imperial power with Christian and Islamic religious dominance, colonial officials prevented Indigenous priests from playing their traditional role in maintaining peace and social harmony. European

 | DOI:10.1163/9789004524330_012

missionaries gradually supplanted traditional leaders, who subsequently enjoyed little influence outside of local politics. This situation triggered significant changes to Indigenous religious practices and rights. For instance, human sacrifice was removed as a component of the burial tradition for the paramount ruler of Oyo, while the longstanding Igbo and Ogoni practice of using oracles for oath-taking and judicial decision-making was banned (Adekunle 2009). As Adewoye has argued, such restrictions on Indigenous rights had a number of objectives: maintaining the social status quo, ensuring the stability of the colonial regime, subjugating conquered groups, and reshaping Indigenous identity based on British political priorities (Adewoye 1977: 4–5). Likewise, colonial efforts to protect religious rights primarily sought to maintain peace and social equilibrium among the country's various ethnic groups.

Early in the colonial period, which lasted from 1850 to 1960, religious rights were enforced based on treaties. Between 1886 and 1904, a succession of colonial officials – Sir Alfred Moloney, Sir Gilbert Carter, Sir Henry McCallum, and Sir William Macgregor – oversaw the signing of numerous treaties with Indigenous populations in the hinterland of Lagos colony and beyond (Adewoye 1977: 15). Key to the British conquest of southern Nigeria, these documents focused on themes such as peace and friendship with Britain, freedom of trade, and assistance to British subjects in times of difficulty (Adewoye 1977). In terms of religious rights, the most significant treaty signed between colonial invaders and their conquered subjects granted Christian access to southern Nigeria, a provision that ran counter to agreements signed with the people of the country's north (Ayandele 1968: 162). By the second half of the nineteenth century, the colonial authorities were actively promoting the growth of Christianity in the south while blocking its spread into the Muslim-dominated north, where they sought to perpetuate the British system of indirect rule by maintaining Islamic political, judicial, and educational institutions (Adekunle 2009).

Historians have largely ignored the question of Indigenous religious rights in Nigeria. More specifically, they have failed to meaningfully address the impact of a half-century of British colonialism on such rights. This chapter seeks to help fill this gap in the historiography. Focusing on the lives and experiences of Indigenous peoples, it explores the negative impacts of the colonial social order and its legacy on religious rights. The chapter is divided into three main sections. The first discusses the governance of Indigenous peoples in colonial Nigeria. The second examines the status of Indigenous religious rights in Nigeria during the colonial period. Finally, the third section highlights legacy of colonialism and its impact on Indigenous religious rights in present-day Nigeria.

1 Governance of Indigenous Peoples in Colonial Nigeria

Captain Fredrick Lugard officially proclaimed the establishment of a British protectorate in northern Nigeria on January 1, 1900. This marked the culmination of a series of incursions, starting with the annexation of Lagos in 1861. In the decades that followed, the British maintained cordial and peaceful relations with the Sokoto Caliphate to the north while pursuing the transition from a society ruled by Indigenous leaders to one controlled by colonial administrators. Between 1900 and 1902, Lugard relied on various strategies to progressively conquer the emirate states of Bida, Kontagora, Yola, Bauchi, and Gombe. Katsina surrendered to save itself from British bombardment; its recalcitrant emir was arrested and exiled by the invaders. Zaria fell soon afterward, leaving only Kano and Sokoto, the region's two most powerful caliphate city-states, to carry on the military struggle (Afolayan 2009). Lugard then wrote to the Caliph of Sokoto demanding that he surrender peacefully to British protection and rule. The response proclaimed that the only possible relationship between an Islamic state and Britain was the one prescribed in the Holy Quran between the land of believers (*Dar-al-Islam*) and the land of infidels (*Dar-al Harb*). Lugard then launched an attack on Kano, which fell to the British in 1902. A year later, in a bitter battle fought outside the city walls of Sokoto on March 15, 1903, superior British weaponry overcame the army led by Caliph Attahiru I. Pockets of resistance would persist until 1906, in places like Hadejia and Satitu. However, the installation of a new caliph following Attahiru's death at the Second Battle of Burmi in July 1903 effectively marked the end of the caliphate's power, making way for the Pax Britannica (Afolayan 2009).

The Christian Missionary Society viewed the British conquest of northern Nigeria as a divinely ordained event that would allow it to spread the light of Christian civilization to what it saw as a morally and culturally backward region of the globe. The region's previous rulers had opposed missionary activity, sometimes persecuting, expelling, or even killing missionaries and their converts. Accordingly, missionaries worked in partnership with the conquerors, providing intelligence reports to British forces and helping complete the process of subjugation. But much to the disappointment of Christian missionaries, British rule did not usher in a new era of unrestricted access to northern Nigeria. In fact, the years that followed were marked by significant tensions and even open conflicts between missionaries, colonial officials, and Indigenous leaders (Afolayan 2009).

In southern Nigeria, the introduction of an English-style justice system proved to be a major means of consolidating imperial control. Between 1862 and 1914, a range of new legal institutions emerged in response to administrative and economic requirements. They allowed the British conquerors not merely to settle disputes according to their own rules, but also to dismiss any challenges to their power while punishing whatever they considered deviant patterns of behavior (Adewoye 1977: 18). H.S. Freeman, the first governor of Lagos Colony, was keenly aware of the significance of being able to punish crimes: "[t]he exercise of the power of life and death over Lagos people is the last seal on the establishment of British rule in this settlement."[1] Authorities in London empowered Freeman to appoint judges and other court officers, as well as establish prisons to hold those found guilty of crimes under British law (Awe 1968). But incarceration was also used to suppress Indigenous people's right to self-determination (Oladiti 2014), insofar as it served as a means of punishing resistance to colonial rule (Killingray 1986: 413–417). The prison network quickly spread to urban centers beyond Lagos, starting with Abeokuta (1880), Ado Ekiti (1894), Ibadan (1899), and Ilesha (1900). The year 1912 saw prisons established in Calabar, Asaba, Benin, Sapele, Degema, and Port Harcourt (Killingray 1999).

The turn of the twentieth century also brought the introduction of English legal processes to the Yoruba communities surrounding Lagos, with a view to protecting British economic interests and facilitating the day-to-day aspects of colonial administration. Officials were assigned to key communities like Ibadan, Ilesha, Oyo, and Ijebu-Ode, where informal councils were created to advise local authorities and settle disputes (Adewoye 1977). Quickly establishing the supremacy of English law was seen as particularly important for cases that pitted Europeans against Africans (whether from Nigeria or elsewhere). Indeed, British colonial officials had no confidence in the Indigenous justice system, whether in Yorubaland or other parts of southern Nigeria (Adewoye 1977). Consider the scathing assessment of the situation in Ibadan offered by Sir William MacGregor, who toured the region in 1903:

> The Ba[a]le's council is also the Supreme Court of Justice for the town and province. There is not a single, Enlightened man, not a man of new school, in the council. If there is one in Ibadan Justice, it is to be feared, is too often sold to the highest bidder that comes before the native tribunals. (Adewoye 1977: 22)

1 NAI (Nigerian National Archives, Ibadan), CSO 1/1, 1, Freeman to Newcatle, February 4, 1864.

Such statements reveal strong contempt for Indigenous systems of justice and an urge to strip local communities of their autonomy. In any case, MacGregor offered no evidence whatsoever to back up his claim that customary tribunals were selling justice to the highest bidder or issuing judgments that were unfair to non-Indigenous parties. Rather, the spurious suggestion that all members of the Baale's council were "utterly ignorant" reflects widespread discomfort with the growing number of legal disputes between Europeans and members of the Indigenous population. Indeed, European traders in Ibadan resented the very idea of Europeans being judged by an Indigenous court (Adewoye 1977: 22).

Persistent calls by colonial administrators and European commercial interests for the establishment of English-style legal institutions in Yorubaland led to the signing of judicial agreements with Alake and representatives of the Egba authorities in January 1904; with Ibadan and Oyo in August 1904; with Ife in September 1904; and with the Awujale of Ijebu in November 1908. Under these agreements, colonial authorities acquired the power to try all criminal offenses, to make and administer laws protecting the persons and property of British subjects trading in Yorubaland, and to adjudicate any disputes where the interests of British subjects were at stake. The Supreme Court of Lagos gained jurisdiction over virtually the whole of Yorubaland, and lower courts were established at Abeokuta, Oyo, Ijebu, and Ibadan. Henceforth, the laws of Lagos Colony relating to criminal and civil matters – i.e., English common law and principles of equity – would apply throughout the region insofar as local circumstances allowed (Adewoye 1977).

However, the impact of British rule on Indigenous peoples in Nigeria was not confined to the colonial era. Its legacies have continued to shape ideas in general and religious rights in particular. To begin with, colonial authorities promoted the ideals and religious values of Christianity while treating other religious traditions (Islam and Indigenous religions) as inferior. Missionaries offered opportunities to learn English, leading many members of the Indigenous population to convert. Indeed, Western education was and remains a prerequisite for state employment. Nor have the Nigerian political elites in charge of post-independence governments treated all religions equally. Instead, they have sought to structure partisan politics in terms of foreign religions – i.e., Islam and Christianity – while state officials have sternly opposed any public expressions of Indigenous religion at official events. The profound reluctance to showcase Indigenous prayers on occasions of national importance, such as Independence Day, and the lack of any national holidays marking traditional religious feasts not only alienates the corresponding communities from the nation-building process but also threatens the survival of many traditional beliefs and practices.

2 Indigenous Religious Rights during the Colonial Era

According to the working definition proposed by Martínez Cobo some four decades ago, Indigenous peoples are made up of individuals who self-identify with a larger community rooted in pre-colonial and pre-settler society. They are distinguished from mainstream society by their strong connection to the land and its resources, as well as by their distinct social groupings, economic and political systems, languages, cultures, and beliefs (Martínez Cobo 1987: 29). Approximately 250 distinct Indigenous peoples live in Nigeria, with the Yoruba, the Igbo, the Hausa, and the Fulani constituting the largest and most politically influential groups. Other examples include the Edo, the Ibibio, the Tiv, the Nupe, the Kanuri, the Ijaw, the Itshekiri, the Urhobo, and the Kalabari. Many of their customs are rooted in religious beliefs and practices established in present-day Nigeria before the British conquest and prior to the arrival of foreign religions (Oladiti 2009). Furthermore, the most distinctive aspects of their cultures – including their social and political institutions – were traditionally structured according to a body of traditional or customary law (Raja 2005). All Indigenous peoples in Nigeria share a firm traditional belief in the afterlife and, according to many of their religions, the spirits of the departed can intervene in the affairs of the living. An organized priesthood, whose members could mediate between humans and deities, oversaw each group's religious practices.

The land constitutes another fundamental component of the history and identity of Nigeria's Indigenous peoples, one that has shaped their participation in the country's social, economic, and political life. In this context, Odoemene has emphasized both the land's vital importance to the country's overall well-being and the social recognition enjoyed by those groups and individuals who own it. Nigeria's Indigenous systems of land tenure were based on collective and communal ownership by the male members of the society, with a strong and enduring emphasis on the connection between a group's traditional beliefs and the land of its forefathers. Accordingly, membership in an Indigenous community normally conferred "autochthonous rights" of ownership over such ancestral lands (Odoemene 2013). Each group's customary laws specified the means through which individuals or groups – defined in terms of ethnicity, identity, class, and gender – could negotiate the right to access and use ancestral lands (Korieh 2010: 15).[2]

2 By contrast, the authoritarian colonial regime facilitated land grabs and resource extraction by foreign interests (Oyeranmi 2018). During the colonial period, two broad systems of land tenure were imposed on the Indigenous population. In northern Nigeria, all lands previously

Before undertaking a more detailed exploration of how British authorities positioned themselves in relation to these Indigenous traditions and religious beliefs during the colonial era, I want to set the stage by describing the situation among some of the various ethnic groups concerned in the period leading up to the definitive establishment of British rule.

2.1 *The Hausa*

The Indigenous peoples of Hausaland traditionally organized their society on a clan basis, with a hereditary chief priest maintaining local shrines on behalf of each community. The Kano Chronicle describes how these traditional priests performed various rituals and sacrifices, often involving food and animals, to ensure collective peace and stability. The cult at the center of the Hausa belief system was based on a single deity, known as Tsumburburai or Ramaday (Oladiti 2009), who was venerated at shrines located in groves. Shobana Shankar has described Hausa religious practice, which also involved the use of charms for protection, as a synthesis of diverse spiritual traditions collectively referred to as Bori. As Islam gained influence in the region, the practice of Bori came to be not only discouraged but also condemned. Islamic objections to Bori inspired Usman dan Fodio's 1804 jihad, during which Fulani invaders violently destroyed the traditional Hausa political system and replaced it with an Islamic theocracy (Shankar 2005: 281–283). Once military resistance was overcome, Fulani missionaries forced many Hausa to recant their traditional Bori religion and embrace Islam – highlighting a lack of respect for Indigenous rights on the part of the Fulani following their arrival in northern Nigeria (Oladiti 2009).

2.2 *The Igbo*

The Igbo of eastern Nigeria traditionally had a strong attachment to ancestor worship, animal sacrifice, and ritual worship in groves. Sacrifices were performed in public to ward off evil spirits, seek redress, or express thanksgiving. For their part, ancestors were expected to help maintain community solidarity (Edmund 1974). The Igbo people believed in a supernatural being whom they worshiped through various deities or spirits, including Anyanwu (the god of

held under customary tenure were placed under the direct control of the colonial governor, who was empowered to grant rights of occupancy for definite or indefinite terms, setting rent and other conditions as he saw fit (Meek 1957). By contrast, the traditional lineage-based system of land ownership was maintained in southern Nigeria, although colonial authorities exercised exclusive rights over lands expressly acquired for public purposes by the Crown. Otherwise, local landholders were simply required to seek government approval before transferring ownership to someone else (Mabogunje 2010).

the sun), Igwe (the god of the sky), and Ala (the god of the earth). Individual communities worshiped different divinities – guardian spirits that were variously benevolent, mischievous, loving, or hostile (Oladiti 2009). They existed in physical form, as well as that of ancestral spirits or the spirits of national heroes. Shrines could be found along rivers, below trees, at road junctions, and in mountains or hills.

In the nineteenth century, Christian missionaries brought a new set of religious ideas to the region. In addition to embracing Christianity, converts were expected to adopt an entirely new understanding of morality and social organization. Viewing the Igbo religion as deeply inferior – they dismissed it as fetishism, idolatry, or juju – Europeans believed that the only way for the population of Igboland to enjoy the benefits of civilization was by abandoning traditional rites based on the worship of divinities and ancestral spirits (Adekunle 2009). As a result, those members of the Igbo community who sought out the educational opportunities and health-care services offered by Christian missions were required not only to embrace Christianity, but also to participate in the destruction of their traditional social structure and worldview (Adekunle 2009).

In this way, implementation of British colonial rule not only erased the right of the Igbo to self-determination, but also fundamentally undermined their right to practice their religion and maintain their belief system. Consider the fate of the cave called Arochukwu, which served as a sacred temple during the slave trade era. In addition to an oracular shrine named ukpabi, where rituals were performed, it also contained a dark chamber where people accused of offenses against others or abominable practices appeared before Chukwu (the supreme deity). In this way, the site served as the community's supreme court, and Chukwu's judgment was considered final and without appeal. According to oral tradition, the cave temple was one of the most sacred and mystically beautiful sites in Igboland. But in 1902, it was destroyed by the British to subjugate the Aro subgroup and neutralize the religious influence of the Ibini Ukpabi, an oracle also called the "Long Juju" (Anonymous 2015).

2.3 *The Yoruba*

In addition to a supreme being called Olodumare or Olorun, the Yoruba of southwest Nigeria believed in various lesser deities known as orisas, on which the community depended for peace, progress, stability, and success. Examples include Esu, a trickster associated with mischief;[3] Obatala (also known as

3 Esu, who also possesses protective and benevolent powers, should not be considered the equivalent of the devil or Satan in Islam and Christianity.

Oduduwa or Ogun), the god of iron and war; Sopona, traditionally associated with smallpox; Sango, the god of lightning; Sango's wife Oya, the goddess of thunderstorms; and Orisa Oko, the patron of hunters. Ifa, the oracle of the palm nut, was consulted regarding every social or political event with a view to promoting unity. For instance, this oracle's advice was sought when choosing a new leader, deciding whether to go to war, and planning marriages. It served as the court of the people, and all community members were bound by its judgments. The traditional Yoruba belief system also involved the veneration of natural phenomena such as rivers, trees, mountains, hills, iron, thunder, and lightning (Fadipe 1971: 265).

Victory by a coalition of Yoruba and Borgu forces at the battle of Osogbo in 1840 (Oladiti 2009: 24) halted the advance of Islamic invaders. Nevertheless, Islam continued to spread in Yorubaland through more peacefully means. Delegations of Muslims – including missionaries, traders, and merchants – visited the region for various purposes. They were greeted at the palaces of Yoruba chiefs and later granted lands on which to establish themselves in the community. These developments further increased the number of Indigenous inhabitants and communities renouncing their traditional religion for Islam or Christianity, both of which came to enjoy a certain level of acceptance in Yoruba culture (Oladiti 2010: 145–147). For instance, Chief Kuku of Ijebu-Ode accepted Islam on the basis that it permitted him to marry more than one wife. Christian missionaries, who feared that unrest would disrupt their evangelical activities, gained a reputation as mediators and peacemakers amid the armed conflicts engulfing the region. And as noted above, the Western educational methods practiced by Christian missionaries and the medical care they offered to the communities where they established themselves prompted many Indigenous residents of Yorubaland to embrace Christianity (Ayandele 1968: 162).

Beyond simply failing to protect Indigenous religion, the colonial authorities responsible for Yorubaland introduced legal measures facilitating its partial eradication. Like other Indigenous peoples in Africa, the Yoruba carefully maintained a tightly interwoven set of customary religious practices. Musical and dietary traditions, modes of dress and behavior, as well as other aspects of Yoruba culture were fundamentally shaped by the relationship with various deities. Sango, Oya, Obatala, Sopona, Ogun, and others were worshiped at festivals held in various towns. To appease these gods and avoid incurring their wrath, priests periodically performed rituals and sacrifices on behalf of kings and communities. As the god of smallpox, Sopona was the object of particularly strong devotion. Worshipers appealed to him by different names to avoid causing offense and triggering an epidemic. However, colonial authorities eventually outlawed the Sopona cult and its priests to encourage acceptance of smallpox immunization. Given the diverse range of cultural practices surrounding the worship of this deity, the measure did much more than simply remove a single name from the Indigenous pantheon. It profoundly disrupted the Yoruba people's beliefs and worldview (Oduntan 2012).

Similarly, Ayandele has described how, in the Yoruba town of Ijebu, British officials actively undermined the moral and social influence of religious traditionalists who had already lost their political role in the wake of the British conquest. The governor set the tone by banning the daylong Oro festival throughout Ijebuland (Ayandele 1992: 262). Attempts by some communities to proceed with the festivities were met with heavy fines and even prison sentences. It essentially became impossible to carry on the tradition when a subsequent order, issued in 1907, banned drumming on Sunday. As a result, the gods and their shrines were reduced to objects of ridicule, falling into neglect as the population of the town increased. In the 1930s and 1940s, Oro worshipers seeking to reassert themselves failed miserably while appeals from traditional rulers for the preservation of Yoruba cultural heritage fell on deaf ears. By 1932, even the sacred spot where the Awujale (king) received the Oro priest at Oju Offa (Porogun, Ijebu-Ode) had been abandoned, amid the growing belief that Oro was an "antiquated and barbarous practice." Once again, for British colonial authorities, dismissing an Indigenous tradition as "childish" or "stupid" proved merely to be the first step toward wholesale prohibition (Ayandele 1992: 263).

Between 1900 and 1959, the colonial regime also undermined Indigenous religious rights in various other ways. To begin with, authorities consistently dismissed Indigenous spiritual beliefs, values, and practices as heathen, backward, idolatrous, and uncivilized. They went on to use both legal and non-legal strategies to suppress a wide variety of individual practices, including cult initiation, witchcraft, juju charms and spells, the consultation of oracles, trial by ordeal, ancestor worship, human sacrifice, divination, and healing rituals. The fact that Indigenous religion covered a wide range of traditions and lacked a centralized structure or recognized leadership made it highly vulnerable to such piecemeal attacks (Raja 2005). Moreover, Mutua has shown how, during the colonial period, restrictions on Indigenous rights were commonly justified in terms of "social order," "public morality," and "public health" by a colonial regime that found the population's traditional belief system problematic and sometimes even abominable (Mutua 1999). Buttressing this point, Hackett has pointed out that accusations of witchcraft, ritual sacrifice, and charlatanism have caused tribal or folk religious groups to face exceptionally high levels of harassment in Africa (Hackett 2013).

Raja (2005) has detailed how, together with policy neglect and discriminatory measures, this sustained assault on Indigenous culture led to most traditional social and legal systems being eroded or erased. The colonial regime's refusal to fully or even partially recognize customary legal traditions left the people of Nigeria largely unable to exercise political and legal autonomy. In particular, the British swept away Indigenous ways of regulating social behavior, family relations (marriage, divorce, inheritance and child custody), land ownership, and the use of natural or sacred resources (forests, bodies of water, hills and mountains, shrines, sacred groves) (Raja 2005).

British efforts to eliminate extrajudicial means of dealing with disputes further undermined Indigenous religious rights. As the colonial era progressed, fewer and fewer cases involving matters of family law were handled by community elders, who lacked official recognition. Instead, they were heard by the Nigeria's newly established system of British courts, which considered Indigenous spiritual beliefs, values, and practices to be unreasonable, superstitious, and of no legal consequence. For example, Indigenous defendants were not allowed to take oaths according to their own cultural traditions. Furthermore, British judges decided cases involving spiritual matters on the basis of natural justice, equity, and good conscience. By contrast, Indigenous institutions considered the relevant conventions and traditions of different groups. For instance, depending on the community, a person who broke a taboo might be inflicted with sickness or death. The abolition of trial by ordeal, which had been prevalent in southern Nigeria, is another case in point. Talbot recorded the arguments of British administrators and jurists who believed that allowing the practice to continue, even in the context of customary law, would be regressive and primitive. However, given the great importance placed on trial by ordeal in the popular imagination as not only a dispute resolution mechanism but also a ritual observance, its abolition clearly represented a breach of Indigenous rights (Talbot 1926: 634–676).

The advent of colonialism in Nigeria also introduced new social practices that reshaped the population's understanding of education, marriage, justice, and, above all, community governance (Ekeh 1983). For example, colonists introduced the concept of a "white wedding" celebrated in the Church. Among the Indigenous population, respect for the traditional marriage system waned as the Western-educated, Christianized elite embraced the European practice as the "right" way of getting married, one that was formally endorsed by newly introduced marriage registry laws. Meanwhile, the criminalization of child betrothal, levirate marriage, and marriage by abduction served to further suppress Indigenous marriage practices. Other related regulations directly targeted the Indigenous population's freedom of religion. For instance, colonial official prevented anyone married according to customary law from marrying someone else in the Church, and anyone married in the Church from marrying someone else according to customary law. Men married in the Church were prevented from practicing polygamy and Christian wives were given the legal right to a monogamous marriage, a right enforced by the colonial court system (Adesina 2005).

Another major impact of colonialism in Nigeria was the removal of traditional taboos and cultural restrictions on the use of forests (Omosini 1970). Previously, only powerful hunters, priests, or medicine men responsible for ensuring the spiritual well-being of their communities enjoyed access to the forest. For the Benin people of Nigeria, the forest represented the home of their ancestors, who were believed to have transformed themselves into bodies of water (streams, rivers, and lakes). Eken (the fifth day of the week) was reserved for these ancestral spiritual beings, and no one was permitted to enter the forest lest they bring misfortune and disaster on themselves or their communities. However, colonial authorities took advantage of the weak position of the Oba (ruler) of Benin to induce him to give the British control over forest resources that had traditionally been reserved for social, cultural, and religious activities. In this way, the establishment of forest reserves represented a key aspect of colonial power in Nigeria (Hellermann and Usanlele 2012).

But even as it undermined the foundations of Indigenous religion in Nigeria, the colonial regime acknowledged the right to practice it. From the government's perspective, Indigenous belief systems were meant to be practiced at the level of the family, clan, or community – where they served to promote peace, social solidarity, and happiness – but not protected by the state. Accordingly, officials made no effort to consult followers of Indigenous religions on matters of public policy. In fact, they tended only to discuss such religions in the context of petitions from followers of Christianity and Islam. Consider what happened in 1938, when Indigenous authorities in Ibadan notified colonial officials of calls to abolish the town's traditional Oke-badan festival. Leaders of the local Christian and Muslim communities had prepared separate petitions complaining about vulgar songs and obscene performances. However, the resident officer responded that it was not a matter of government concern, explaining that people had the right to practice the religion of their choice. In addition to highlighting the formal policy of neutrality vis-à-vis religion adopted by the colonial regime (Oladiti 2010), the incident also shows how Christians and Muslims were inclined to disparage traditional beliefs and seek to suppress associated cultural practices. In other words, it was not only or always British authorities who criticized, undermined, or attacked Indigenous religion.

In today's Nigeria, Indigenous religions are only practiced irregularly in some states of the federation, and not at all in others. Meanwhile, the government provides them with little in the way of legal protection or even recognition. For example, Indigenous religions are not listed on the official forms used for school enrollment, public service recruitment, or passport and identity card applications. While boldly acknowledging Islam and Christianity, such forms will, at best, provide an option for "Other" religions – leaving the impression that Indigenous belief systems are either alien or non-existent. Since Nigeria gained independence, Osun has been the only state to establish a public holiday recognizing followers of Indigenous religions. Otherwise, governments at both the state and national level have consistently overlooked Indigenous belief systems. Whereas holidays are observed for both Muslim and Christian festivals, celebrations associated with Indigenous religions receive virtually no such recognition. Moreover, Indigenous religious practices tend to be entirely absent from Independence Day ceremonies and national prayer services broadcast on television and radio stations. Insofar as it reflects an assumption that citizens are either Muslims or Christians – and that the exceptions to this rule are uncivilized, heathen idol worshipers – the general refusal to formally recognize and protect the practice of Indigenous religion clearly contradicts the principle of religious freedom and represents an attack on Indigenous rights.

3 Conclusion

Colonialism has had a lasting impact on freedom of religion and religious rights in Nigeria. The colonial regime's political structure, legal system, and cultural values all served to deprive the Nigerian people of not only their land and natural resources, but also their cultural value systems. Any Indigenous beliefs or practices seen as inimical to British economic, commercial, or moral interests were swiftly outlawed. Examples range from traditional marriage practices to taboos preventing access to forests on the fifth day of the week. Furthermore, independence failed to inspire any real effort to address colonial encroachments on Indigenous religious rights. For instance, the Federal Republic of Nigeria lacks any constitutional provisions specifically protecting the religious rights of Indigenous groups in the country. Nor are Indigenous religious beliefs and practices recognized on official forms, through public holidays, during national prayer services, or in the context of election campaigns and anti-crime measures – all of which portray the population as essentially a mix of Muslims and Christians.

In theory, the Nigerian constitution protects religious rights. But in practice, authorities essentially ignore the rights and needs of citizens who follow Indigenous religions, including by dismissing them as members of so-called secret societies. Article 38.4 of the constitution categorically states that no person is "entitled to form, take part in the activity or be a member of a secret society," a provision that contradicts the rights to free assembly and religious freedom. For instance, secrecy is an important aspect of the Egbe Ogboni and Osugbo cults, practiced by the Ijebu-Ode, as well as the Ekpe cult, practiced by the Ibibio. And although such groups regularly face violent and sometimes deadly attacks, the government has failed to make any significant effort to protect their security or religious culture. Likewise, among the Yoruba, there have been frequent clashes between followers of the Oro cult and those who practice Islam, Christianity, or another religion. Meanwhile, individual politicians and officials often focus on promoting their own belief system at the expense of others, to the extent that a person who commits a crime may be able to evade justice based on its affiliation with a specific religious group. In particular, the courts do not seem to have taken a firm stand on violent crimes committed by followers of rival religions, crimes that constitute a major threat to Indigenous religious rights in Nigeria. This all leave followers of Indigenous religions largely unsupported and unprotected in their efforts to maintain their distinct forms of worship and systems of belief.

References

Adekunle, J.O. "Introduction: Religion and Politics in Transition." In *Religion in Politics: Secularism and National Integration in Modern Nigeria*, edited by J.O. Adekunle, 3–17. New Jersey: Africa World Press, 2009.

Adesina, Oluwakemi. "Marriage and Divorce in Yorubaland: Between Colonial Impositions and African Reality." Unpublished paper presented at the Postgraduate conference at the Centre for Research in Arts, Social Sciences and Humanities, Cambridge University, March 13–15, 2005.

Adewoye, Omoniyi. *The Judicial System in Southern Nigeria, 1854–1954. Law and Justice in a Dependency*. New Jersey: Humanities Press, 1977.

Afolayan, Funso. "Religion and Politics in Colonial Nigeria: The Life and Career of Sir Walter Miller, 1782–1952." In *Religion in Politics: Secularism and National Integration in Modern Nigeria*, edited by J.O. Adekunle, 37–66. New Jersey: Africa World Press, 2009.

Awe, Bolanle. "The History of the Prison System in Nigeria." In *The Prison System in Nigeria*, edited by Taslim Olawale Elias, 4–25. Lagos: University of Lagos Bookshop, 1968.

Ayandele, Emmanuel Ayankanmi. *The Missionary impact on Modern Nigeria: A Political and Social Analysis, 1842–1914*. London: Longman, 1968.

Ayandele, Emmanuel Ayankanmi. *The Ijebu of Yorubaland: Politics, Economy and Society 1850–1950*. Ibadan: Heinemann Educational Books, 1992.

Edmund, Ilogu. *Christianity and Igbo Culture*. Leiden: Ball, 1974.

Ekeh Peter Palmer. "Colonialism and Social Structure." Inaugural lecture, University of Ibadan, 1983.

Fadipe, Nathanie Akinremi. *The Sociology of the Yoruba*. Ibadan: Ibadan University Press, 1971.

Hackett, Rosalind I.J. "Traditional, African, Religious, Freedom?" In *Politics of Religious Freedom*, edited by Winnifred Fallers Sullivan, Elizabeth Shakman Hurd, and Saba Mahmood, 89–98. Chicago: University of Chicago Press, 2015. https://doi.org/10.7208/chicago/9780226248646.003.0009.

Killingray, David. "The Maintenance of Law and Order in British Colonial Africa." *African Affairs* 85, no. 340 (1986): 413–417.

Killingray, David. "Punishment to Fit the Crime? Penal Policy and Practice in British Colonial Africa." In *Enfermement, prison et châtiments en Afrique du 19e siècle à nos jours*, edited by Flurence Bernault, 181–203. Paris: Karthala, 1999.

Korieh, Chima J. *The Land Has Changed: History, Society and Gender in Colonial Eastern Nigeria*. Calgary, Alberta: University of Calgary Press, 2010.

Mabogunje, Akin L. "Land Reform in Nigeria: Progress, Problems and Prospects." Presented at the Annual Bank Conference on Land Policy and Administration, Washington DC, April 26–27, 2010.

Martínez Cobo, José R. *Study of the Problem of Discrimination Against Indigenous Populations. Volume V: Conclusions, Proposals and Recommendation*. New York: United Nations, 1987. E/CN.4/Sub.2/1986/7/Add.4.

Meek, Charles Kingsley. *Land Tenure and Administration in Nigeria and the Cameroons*. London: HMSO, 1957.

Mbiti, John S. *African Religions and Philosophy*. London: Heinemann Books, 1969.

Mutua, Makau. "Returning to my Roots: 'African Religions' and the State." In *Religion and Human Series, Proselytisation and Communal Self-Determination in Africa*, edited by Abdullahi Ahmed An-Na'im, 169–190. New York: Oasis Books, 1999.

Nigeria, *Constitution of the Federal Republic of Nigeria, 1999*.

Nwauche, Enyinna S. "Law, Religion and Human Rights in Nigeria." *African Human Rights Law Journal* 8, no. 2 (2008): 568–595.

Odoemene, Akachi. "Competing Rhetoric in the Context of Foreign Land Acquisitions: The Case of 'New Nigeria.'" In *Africa for Sale? Positioning the State, Land and Society in Foreign Large-Scale Land Acquisitions in Africa*, edited by Sandra J.T.M. Evers, Caroline Seagle, and Froukje Krijtenburg, 259–274. Boston: Brill, 2013.

Oduntan, Babatunde Oluwatoyin. "Beyond 'The Way of God:' Missionaries, Colonialism and Smallpox in Abeokuta." *Lagos Historical Preview* 12, no. 1 (2012): 1–22.

Oladiti, Abiodun Akeem. "Religion and Politics in Pre-colonial Nigeria." In *Religion in Politics: Secularism and National Integration in Modern Nigeria*, edited by J.O. Adekunle, 21–36. New Jersey: Africa World Press, 2009.

Oladiti, Abiodun Akeem. "Islamic Literacy and Cultural Influence in Ibadan c.1945–1995." PhD diss., Institute of African Studies. University of Ibadan. 2010.

Oladiti, Abiodun Akeem. "The Role and Historical Development of Nigerian Prisons Sevice, 1935–1985." *Ado Journal of History and International Studies* 1, no. 1 (2014): 190–205.

Omosini, Olufemi. "Background to the Forestry Legislation in Lagos Colony and Protectorate, 1897–1902." *Journal of the Historical Society of Nigeria* 9, no. 3 (1970): 45–69.

Oyeranmi, Soji. "Land Use Act 1978 and the Question of Environmental Justice in Nigeria." In *Socio-Political and Culture History of Nigeria: Festschrift in Honour of Professor Akin Alao*, edited by Victor Osaro Edo and Dolapo Z. Olupayimo, 18–38. Ibadan: John Archers Publishers, 2018.

Raja, Devasish Roy. *Traditional Customary Laws and Indigenous Peoples in Asia*. London: Minority Rights Group International, 2005.

Shankar, Shobana. "Religion, State and Society in Hausaland: History and the Politics of Incorporation in the Kano Chronicle." In *Precolonial Nigeria, Essays in Honor of Toyin Falola*, edited by Akinwumi Ogundiran, 281–283. Trenton: Africa World Press, 2005.

Talbot, Percy Amaury. *The Peoples of Southern Nigeria. Vol. 3*. London: Oxford University Press: 1926.

"Unique Nature of Arochukwu Long Juju." *The Nation Newspaper Nigeria*, May 23, 2015.

Von Hellermann, Pauline, and Uyilawa Usanlele. "The Owner of the Land: The Benin Obas and Colonial Forest Reservation in Benin Division, Southern Nigeria." In *The Third Wave of Historical Scholarship on Nigeria: Essays in Honour of Ayodeji Olukoju*, edited by Saheed Aderinto and Paul Osifodunrin, 154–182. Cambridge: Cambridge Scholars Publishing, 2012.

Recognition and Denial of Indigenous Religious Rights in East and Central Africa

Guy Bucumi

Although a certain number of common themes emerge from efforts to protect the rights of Indigenous peoples around the globe, thorough socio-historical and legal analysis requires strong familiarity with regional contexts. With reference to Africa, Solomon Dersso has noted how minority and Indigenous rights "are more about the accommodation of the interests and needs of members of different ethno-cultural groups than about protecting some groups by carving out a certain space for their protection against domination by and assimilation into the majority" (Dersso 2010: 15). Accordingly, any in-depth analysis of Indigenous rights in Africa will depend on a commitment to probing those aspects of human rights that are rooted in national contexts and local realities. Specifically, this chapter will focus on the religious rights of Indigenous peoples in East and Central Africa, as well as the effectiveness of measures to protect such rights.

Because indigeneity remains a controversial concept in Africa, the first issue faced by those researching Indigenous rights on the continent tends to be semantic in nature. Some scholars, especially anthropologists and historians, have defined Indigenous persons as "members of a dominated population that settled in a given territory before any other groups and that has established a specific, enduring, and still-relevant relationship with the territory and its environment, in addition to maintaining their own distinct customs and culture" (de Lespinay 2016). Based on this definition, some argue that all Africans should be considered Indigenous, given their shared experience as a dominated people during the long colonial period (see Bellier 2006). Others only associate indigeneity with African peoples that still live according to so-called traditional values and age-old customs.

The issues associated with defining indigeneity are also reflected in the various reports of the Working Group on Indigenous Populations/Communities in Africa, established by the African Commission on Human and Peoples' Rights (ACHPR) in 2001. Ultimately, the African Court of Human and Peoples' Rights provided some guidance, in the context of a dispute between the Ogiek people, who consider themselves Indigenous to Kenya, and the Kenyan government. Granted, the court failed to clearly define what constitutes an "Indigenous

 | DOI:10.1163/9789004524330_013

people" in the African context, preferring to leave that up to individual states.[1] Nevertheless, it did define a set of criteria for recognizing Indigenous peoples in Africa, drawing on certain provisions of the International Labor Organization's 1989 Indigenous and Tribal Peoples Convention. Known as Convention 169, it confers the status of Indigenous or tribal people on the following groups:

> (a) tribal peoples in independent countries whose social, cultural and economic conditions distinguish them from other sections of the national community, and whose status is regulated wholly or partially by their own customs or traditions or by special laws or regulations;
> (b) peoples in independent countries who are regarded as indigenous on account of their descent from the populations which inhabited the country, or a geographical region to which the country belongs, at the time of conquest or colonisation or the establishment of present state boundaries and who, irrespective of their legal status, retain some or all of their own social, economic, cultural and political institutions.[2]

In addition, the ruling issued by the African Court of Human and Peoples' Rights refers to "self-identification as well as recognition by other groups, or by state authorities that they are a distinct collectivity."[3] Based on the criteria set out in this decision, East and Central Africa are home to many peoples recognized as Indigenous by the various states concerned, although the exact wording used varies from one country to the next.[4]

In Central Africa, recognized Indigenous peoples mainly live in and around the Congo rainforest.[5] They include the Bambenga in Congo-Brazzaville and Gabon, the Baka in Cameroon and the Central African Republic (CAR), the Mbuti in the Democratic Republic of Congo (DRC), and the Twa in the eastern part of the Democratic Republic of Congo and in the remaining forested areas of Rwanda and Burundi. Still commonly and collectively referred to as

1 *ACHPR v. Republic of Kenya*, Application no. 006/2012, Judgment, African Court on Human and Peoples' Rights (27 May 2017), https://www.escr-net.org/sites/default/files/caselaw/ogiek_case_full_judgment.pdf.

2 International Labor Organization, *Indigenous and Tribal Peoples Convention, 1989 (no. 169)*, art. 1, http://www.ilo.org/dyn/normlex/en/f?p=NORMLEXPUB:12100:0::NO::P12100_ILO_CODE:C169.

3 *ACHPR v. Kenya*, pars. 106–8.

4 For more on the presence of Indigenous peoples in East and Central Africa, see Gazel 2018.

5 Covering nearly three million square kilometers, this rainforest crosses multiple countries in East and Central Africa.

"pygmies,"[6] the Indigenous peoples of Central Africa are largely hunter-gatherers. Meanwhile, the Indigenous peoples of East Africa – including the Ogiek, the Endorois, and the Maasai – primarily live in Kenya, Tanzania, and Uganda.

East Africa and Central Africa, regions that both straddle the equator and that together encompass the Congo rainforest,[7] are home to numerous and often highly mobile Indigenous peoples. In many cases, the territory inhabited by a particular Indigenous group straddles the two regions, covering multiple countries and therefore multiple legal systems. Such a situation can make it difficult for the groups in question to secure respect for their religious rights.

Questions of religion have always been of central importance to the Indigenous peoples of East and Central Africa. They believe in a God who refrains from intervening in everyday life. Instead, this role is reserved for helpful and wise ancestral spirits, to whom people pray for intercession. Ancestor worship is seen as a means of both ensuring a successful hunt and protecting against disease. In both regions, Indigenous peoples have maintained a "clear" awareness of the existence of this Supreme Being, who goes by various and multiple names, depending on the area (Mary 2010). Each East or Central African matriarchal Indigenous lineage has its own totem, a sacred animal it venerates and that normally symbolizes a positive attribute such as daring, bravery, hardiness, vigor, etc. Finally, a variety of religious rituals mark the everyday lives of Indigenous Africans, including rites associated with coming of age, healing, fertility, and death.

Across East and Central Africa, Indigenous religious rights are based on the general notion of the universality of human rights in a multicultural context, as set out in the 1993 Vienna Declaration and Programme of Action.[8] This document reaffirms "the commitment of the international community to ensure [Indigenous peoples'] enjoyment of all human rights and fundamental freedoms

---

6 Use of the term "pygmy" has been prohibited by new legislation designed to promote and protect Indigenous rights in Congo-Brazzaville (see further). Nevertheless, it remains in widespread use as a generic term for diverse ethnic groups scattered around the Congo rainforest, including in the legislation of other Central African countries, in official reports, and in academic work. Indeed, its use has not been a major subject of debate in other countries. However, it is important to note that the term refers to groups with significant linguistic and sometimes cultural differences. In this chapter, I will use it where appropriate, to reflect the content of my sources, especially legislative sources.

7 This explains why the DRC is a member of both the Economic Community of Central African States (ECCAS) and the East African Community (EAC).

8 Office of the United Nations High Commissioner for Human Rights (OHCHR), *Vienna Declaration and Programme of Action* (June 25, 1993), https://www.ohchr.org/en/instruments-mechanisms/instruments/vienna-declaration-and-programme-action.

and to respect the value and diversity of their cultures and identities."[9] It also emphasizes the contribution of Indigenous peoples to social development and diversity while calling for their full participation in all aspects of society. These key provisions have led to the adoption, by East African and Central African countries, of several pieces of special legislation that I analyze below to assess the effectiveness of Indigenous peoples' rights and the extent to which such rights have been protected within the different legal systems concerned. I also discuss how the circumstances surrounding the land law implementation can shed light on the nature of interactions between domestic legislation and customary Indigenous law.

1 Indigenous Religious Rights in the Domestic Legislation of East and Central African Countries

In the heart of the Congo rainforest, which extends into all Central African countries, Pygmy peoples practice ancestor worship and pay respect to Zèngi or Jengi, a protective spirit that mediates between God and humanity. The constitutions of all Central African states guarantee freedom of religion, even if the relevant provisions do not usually refer to Indigenous peoples specifically. For instance, freedom of belief and religion is guaranteed in the preambles of the Cameroonian and Gabonese constitutions, as well as by Article 18 of Congo-Brazzaville's constitution and Article 22 of that of the DRC. The preamble to the CRA's constitution, which was adopted in 2015, commits the country to implementing international conventions "concerning the prohibition of all forms of discrimination against [...] indigenous and tribal peoples." In addition, Article 6 assigns the state responsibility for ensuring "enhanced protection for the rights of minorities [and] indigenous peoples [...]."[10]

Alongside such constitutional guarantees, other Central African countries have adopted specific legislation to promote and protect the fundamental rights of Indigenous peoples, including their religious rights. In 2011, Congo-Brazzaville adopted a statute defining use of the term "pygmy," in reference to the Indigenous population, as a criminal insult due to its pejorative connotations.[11]

9 OHCHR, *Vienna Declaration*, preamble and par. 11.

10 CRA, *Décret n° 160218 portant promulgation de la constitution de la République Centrafricaine* (March 30, 2016), https://www.ilo.org/dyn/natlex/docs/SERIAL/104713/127839/F1101593134/CAF-104713.pdf.

11 Republic of the Congo (Brazzaville), *Loi n° 5-2011 portant promotion et protection des droits des populations autochtones* (February 25, 2011), s.1, par. 2, https://pcpacongo.files.wordpress.com/2016/04/loi-05-2011-peuples-autochtones.pdf.

The same legislation protects the religious and spiritual property of Indigenous peoples while assigning responsibility to the state for protecting "the integrity of the sacred or spiritual sites of indigenous peoples and guaranteeing them free access to such sites."[12]

For its part, the DRC recently adopted a special statute designed to protect the rights of Indigenous Pygmy peoples. Having entered into force on November 14, 2022, the legislation's preamble explicitly recognizes that "the indigenous Pygmy peoples have not always received special consideration as an indigenous group."[13] A subsequent provision states that "the cultural, intellectual, religious and spiritual assets of the indigenous Pygmy peoples are protected and promoted by the laws of the Republic."[14] Furthermore, public authorities are given responsibility for "identifying and protecting the sacred sites of indigenous Pygmy peoples for the preservation of their endogenous culture and knowledge," and for doing so in close collaboration with the Indigenous communities concerned.[15] The statute goes on to grant the country's Indigenous peoples "the right to access objects of worship and any other relics and, where necessary, to restore them."[16] Finally, it prohibits "any expropriation of cultural, intellectual, religious, or spiritual works."[17] Billed as historic, this was the first legislative effort to officially recognize and protect the Indigenous population of the DRC. Meanwhile, the CAR has also adopted a special statute protecting Indigenous religious rights, in a legal context where Indigenous peoples are considered ethnic minorities.[18] Designated the Cultural Charter of the Central African Republic, this legislation includes an article clearly stating that "freedom of association, conscience, culture and religion is guaranteed."[19] These various legislative measures appear to reflect the political will of certain

12 Congo-Brazzaville, *Loi n° 5-2011*, s. 16, par. 2.

13 DRC, *Loi n° 22/030 portant protection et promotion des droits des peuples autochtones pygmées*, (July 15, 2022), http://extwprlegs1.fao.org/docs/pdf/cng213451.pdf.

14 DRC, *Loi n° 22/030*, s. 28.

15 DRC, *Loi n° 22/030*, s. 29.

16 DRC, *Loi n° 22/030*, s. 33.

17 DRC, *Loi n° 22/030*, art. 31.

18 Indeed, legislation passed by the CAR rarely refers to "Indigenous" peoples. Instead, the country's legislators tend to opt for the term "ethnic minority." This reflects the constitution's emphasis on the indivisibility of the country's people, alongside recognition of ethnic diversity. Accordingly, the preamble to the constitution opens with a reference to "the sovereign people of the Central African Republic, proud of its national and linguistic unity and of its ethnic, cultural and religious diversity, which serves to enrich its character." CRA, *Décret n° 160218*.

19 CRA, *Loi n° 06-002 portant Charte culturelle de la République Centrafricaine* (May 10, 2006), s. 6.

Central African countries to breathe new life into efforts for the promotion and protection of Indigenous religious rights.

By contrast, other countries in the region have refused to adopt any legislation focused on the protection of Indigenous peoples' rights. For example, Gabonese authorities have expressed a fear that such measures would threaten national unity by giving "indigenous people a status different from other citizens."[20] For their part, legislators in Cameroon have avoided the term "Indigenous peoples" in favour of "marginal peoples," to reflect "their departure from the socio cultural identity of the majority of their fellow citizens."[21] In fact, this approach violates international law, which recognizes the right of Indigenous peoples to self-identify as such.[22] Accordingly, in 2010, the ACHPR's Working Group on Indigenous Populations/Communities recommended that Cameroonian authorities adopt terminology and legislation that better support the protection of Indigenous peoples.[23]

Like those of Central African nations, the constitutions of East African states guarantee freedom of religion, but usually without mentioning Indigenous peoples specifically or providing them with any special protections. Nevertheless, Uganda's constitution commits the state to taking "affirmative action in favour of groups marginalised on the basis of gender, age, disability or any other reason created by history, tradition or custom [...]."[24] This constitutes the legal basis for efforts by the Ugandan government on behalf of recognized Indigenous peoples, including provisions of the 1998 *Land Act* and the 1995 *National Environment Statute* designed to protect customary land interests and traditional uses of the country's forests, where many Indigenous peoples live.[25]

As for Burundi, it recognizes the existence of an Indigenous people on its territory, one that enjoys the same religious protections as other segments of the

20 ACHPR, *Report of the African Commission's Working Group on Indigenous Populations/Communities: Research and Information Visit to the Republic of Gabon, 15–30 September 2007*, 18, https://www.iwgia.org/images/publications/ACHPR_Gabon_ENG.pdf.

21 Second periodic report of Cameroon to the African Commission, par. 342, as cited in Centre for Environment and Development (CED), Réseau Recherches Actions Concertées Pygmées (RACOPY), and Forest Peoples Programme (FPP), *Indigenous Peoples' Rights in Cameroon: Supplementary Report Submitted in Connection with Cameroon's Second Periodic Report* (May 2010), 12, https://www.forestpeoples.org/sites/default/files/publication/2010/08/cameroonachprsubmissionmay10eng.pdf.

22 For instance, Article 2 of the International Labour Organization's 1989 Indigenous and Tribal Peoples Convention states that: "Self-identification as indigenous or tribal shall be regarded as a fundamental criterion for determining the groups to which the provisions of this Convention apply."

23 CED, Racopy, and FPP, *Indigenous Peoples' Rights in Cameroon*, 1.

24 Republic of Uganda, *Constitution* (1995), art. 32, https://www.parliament.go.ug/documents/1240/constitution.

25 Uganda, *Land Act* (1998), s. 2, and *National Environment Statute* (1995), s. 46.

population. The country's constitution not only recognizes the need to respect the Indigenous population's "ethnic and religious diversity,"[26] but also states that "the rights and duties proclaimed and guaranteed by duly ratified international protocols on human rights form an integral part of the Constitution."[27] As a result, the 2007 United Nations Declaration on the Rights of Indigenous Peoples (UNDRIP) and all other international and regional frameworks for the protection of Indigenous peoples ratified by Burundi are constitutionally binding. Moreover, the 2000 Arusha Accords, which brought an end to the Burundian Civil War and provided for power sharing between the country's various ethnic groups, reserved one ministry and between two and three senate seats for members of the Indigenous population.[28] Successive governments have consistently honored this commitment, allowing the officials concerned to speak on behalf of the entire Indigenous population with respect to questions relating to the protection of Indigenous rights.

In contrast to Uganda and Burundi, and despite having voted in favour of the UNDRIP, Tanzania has systematically refused to recognize an Indigenous presence on its territory. As a result, the country has no policies or statutes specifically protecting the religious rights of its Indigenous population. Nevertheless, court challenges to government policy on land use and other matters have produced some relevant legal precedents (see below). Likewise, Rwanda has no legislation specifically addressing Indigenous rights. Furthermore, authorities have avoided using the term "Indigenous" or even acknowledging an Indigenous presence, even though several studies have documented the country's large Batwa community.[29]

All things considered, across these two regions of Africa, the extent to which specific legislation has been adopted to protect Indigenous rights in general and Indigenous religious rights in particular highlights the presence of human populations that have yet to benefit from the transformative power of the 1948 Universal Declaration of Human Rights and other human rights frameworks. Indeed, it is precisely with the aim of addressing this disparity and achieving "formal" equality that some jurisdictions have taken such legislative measures.

The comparative analysis provided above illustrates two trends present in both East and Central Africa. Whereas some countries have shown an interest

26 Republic of Burundi, *Constitution de la République du Burundi* (2018), http://www.presidence.gov.bi/wp-content/uploads/2018/07/constitution-promulguee-le-7-juin-2018.pdf.

27 Burundi, *Constitution*, art. 19.

28 Burundi et al., *Arusha Peace and Reconciliation Agreement for Burundi*, Protocol II, art. 6, par. 15, https://peacemaker.un.org/node/1207.

29 Among other sources, see Musilikare 2015; and the various reports issued by the International Work Group for Indigenous Affairs (IWGIA), https://www.iwgia.org/en/rwanda/3502-iw2019-rwanda.html.

in protecting and ensuring the effectiveness of Indigenous religious rights through specific legal measures, others refuse to even recognize the presence of Indigenous peoples on their territories. In some cases, this denial even extends to a ban on the use of the term "Indigenous." These divergent trends are also reflected in foreign policy matters: whereas a handful of states have shown a commitment to implementing the different international declarations and conventions concerning Indigenous peoples, most have not. But regardless of the policy positions taken and the legislative agendas pursued in these two regions of Africa, the main threat to Indigenous religious rights continues to come from the uncertainty surrounding land policy and land rights. This shifting legal landscape has seen Indigenous peoples deprived of their ancestral lands, thereby undermining traditional ways of life and disrupting religious practices that remain inseparable from the surrounding natural environment.

2 The Challenge Posed to Indigenous Religious Rights by African Land Law

In East and Central Africa – two regions where the forest constitutes the traditional living environment of Indigenous peoples – economic and infrastructure development has placed increasing pressure on woodland resources. Furthermore, the turn of the millennium saw a dramatic increase in direct Chinese investment, primarily tied to natural resource development, across all regions of Africa (see Gazibo and Mbabia 2010). New land legislation introduced to facilitate such development has posed an explicit threat to the religious rights of Indigenous peoples in both regions. In addition to prompting the repeated expulsion of Indigenous peoples from their ancestral lands, land reforms have also threatened Indigenous religious rights through the privatization of land in natural areas, which can then no longer serve as places of worship. In this way, nature, which remains at the heart of Indigenous spirituality, has been "soiled" by a series of policy initiatives designed to prepare land for development. Accordingly, in those rare cases where affected lands have been returned to Indigenous peoples, the latter have carried out purification rites and ceremonies on what they perceive as desecrated ground.

Not only have the land policies of many East and Central African countries failed to address the needs of Indigenous peoples, but they have often proven incompatible with Indigenous cultural realities, thereby rendering compliance impossible. For example, although Cameroon's current land law does not formally discriminate against Indigenous communities, many of its provisions tend to marginalize them. Consider the 1974 ordinance (still in force) that makes ownership of any land or estate conditional on its registration with the Registry of Lands.[30] Although "usage rights" may exceptionally be granted to Indigenous peoples, unregistered lands and estates are deemed to be the property of the state. However, anyone wishing to register land or an estate must provide proof of "development," a very difficult condition to meet for Indigenous peoples who mainly engage in subsistence activities – hunting and gathering – that do not necessarily require the type of specialized structures that would reflect development as defined in the ordinance.

Alongside issues of land law, the religious rights of Indigenous peoples have also been threatened by the criminalization of witchcraft, especially in Cameroon. In fact, the Cameroonian penal code prohibits "the practice of witchcraft, magic or divination likely to disturb public order, threaten the public peace, or cause harm to persons."[31] And given that Indigenous worship sometimes involves rites associated with the occult, it may constitute a crime. However, in the absence of a modern and reliable framework for investigations, accusations of witchcraft are often made to settle scores, out of vengeance or jealousy. As a result, the law is prone to abuse,[32] sometimes at the expense of Indigenous peoples.

In Gabon, authorities have refused to recognize the nomadic way of life practiced by the Indigenous Pygmy population. As a result, ancestral Indigenous lands remain unprotected. Like that of several other Central African countries, Gabonese land law deems all lands and underground resources to be the property of the state, with provisions for usage rights in the case of "visible" occupation. In other words, such rights depend on the pursuit of economic activity. Meanwhile, the state may seize, for various uses, lands that are not "visibly occupied." In many cases, this involves dispossessing Indigenous peoples of lands they have long inhabited – in some cases, since time immemorial – but not in a way aligned with settler notions of development.[33]

---

30 Republic of Cameroon, *Ordonnance n° 74-2 fixant le régime domanial* (July 6, 1974), http://www.cvuc-uccc.com/minat/textes/35.pdf.

31 Cameroon, *Loi n° 2016/007 portant Code pénal* (July 12, 2016), s. 251, https://www.wipo.int/edocs/lexdocs/laws/fr/cm/cm014fr.pdf.

32 For more information on the criminalization of witchcraft in Cameroon and related abuses, see Geschiere 1997; Fisiy and Geschiere 1990; Fisiy 1998; Tchoukou 2018.

33 For examples of relevant measures, see Republic of Gabon, *Ordonnance n° 52/PR relative à l'expropriation des terrains insuffisamment mis en valeur* (October 12, 1970); Gabon, *Ordonnance n° 01/76/PR relative à l'expropriation des terrains insuffisamment mis en valeur* (January 6, 1971); DRC, *Loi n° 80-008 modifiant et complétant la Loi n° 73-021 du 20 juillet 1973 portant régime général des biens, régime foncier et immobilier et régime des sûretés* (July 18, 1980); Congo-Brazzaville, *Loi n° 10-2004 fixant les principes généraux applicables aux régimes domanial et foncier* (March 26, 2004); and Congo-Brazzaville, *Loi n° 16-2000 portant Code forestier* (November 20, 2000).

More generally, in the land tenure systems of Central African countries, the coexistence of property rights rooted in either positive law or customary law can introduce significant complications. Indeed, the overlap between the two legal systems often leads to disputes regarding how the law should be applied. To begin with, political authorities often view customary or traditional rights, which by their very nature are based on an oral tradition rather than written documents, as outdated. Only Congo-Brazzaville, which distinguishes between the customary rights of Indigenous and other communities, has sought to implement policies designed to reconcile the different forms of land law in operation on its territory.[34] Moreover, recognizing that Indigenous customary rights are characterized by "extreme vulnerability,"[35] Congo-Brazzaville's land law includes special provisions giving such rights preeminence over those derived from any competing sources of law.

In East Africa, the land law of Uganda allows the government to prohibit human activities in certain forested regions by designating such woodlands as "protected areas," a measure that appears to override the customary rights of Indigenous peoples to use such spaces.[36] Since 2019, the Ugandan state has repeatedly relied on this provision to forcibly evict groups from areas earmarked for the creation of "conservation areas."[37] Often accomplished through violent means, these government operations have been undertaken without any consultation whatsoever, let alone the provision of adequate compensation to the affected Indigenous communities – all in violation of existing expropriation law.[38] Such actions run roughshod over Indigenous cultural and religious life, increasing the marginalization and social exploitation of Indigenous groups in relation to other local communities.

---

34 Congo-Brazzaville, *Loi n° 10-2004 fixant les principes généraux applicables aux régimes domanial et foncier* (March 26, 2004), s. 31; and Congo-Brazzaville, *Loi n° 5-2011 portant promotion et protection des droits des populations autochtones* (February 25, 2011). In the case of a dispute involving land, the legislation specifies that Indigenous customary sources take precedence over the customary sources of other communities.

35 Congo-Brazzaville, *Loi n° 5-2011*, s. 1, par. 1.

36 Uganda, *Land Act*, ss. 2 and 44; and Uganda, *National Environment Statute*, s. 46.

37 The official designation of national parks in Uganda.

38 For example, the Uganda National Land Policy, first adopted in 2013, provides for consultation with affected families and communities, as well as subsequent compensation for properties destroyed or expropriated during the creation of protected areas. Uganda, *The Uganda National Land Policy Implementation Action Plan, 2015/16–2018/19* (March 5, 2015), https://mlhud.go.ug/wp-content/uploads/2015/10/National-Land-Policy-Implementation-Action-Plan-2015-16-to-2018-19.pdf. Meanwhile, the issue of expropriation in Uganda has reemerged as a key concern for human rights organizations, following a 2017 constitutional reform designed to facilitate the process. A challenge launched by the Uganda Law Society is currently pending before the East African Court of Justice. For more on the topic, see RFI 2017.

In 2017, Kenya adopted a statute based on the community land provisions set out in the country's constitution, stating that "a registered community [which can include Indigenous communities] may reserve special purpose areas including areas for [...] the promotion or upgrading of public interest."[39] It has proven a highly problematic piece of legislation for Indigenous peoples by creating a "land market" that mainly covers areas inhabited by members of the Indigenous population.[40]

3 Jurisprudence and the Protection of Indigenous Religious Rights

Amid the simultaneous denial and recognition of Indigenous religious rights across East and Central Africa, national and regional courts have held firm. In addition to consistently condemning land policies that deprive Indigenous peoples of their most fundamental rights, African judges have also sought to establish principles protecting such communities. Accordingly, Indigenous groups and human rights organizations have not hesitated to initiate legal action in response to policies and legislation adopted by the various countries discussed above. Such cases include national and regional court challenges by the Maasai, the Ogiek, and the Endorois in response to evictions carried out under Tanzanian and Kenyan land law.

In Tanzania, three landmark cases with repercussions for Indigenous religious rights were launched in 1987, 2010, and 2013. In 2015, the High Court of Tanzania ruled that granting northern lands occupied by the Indigenous Maasai people to Tanzania Breweries Limited for a business expansion violated the fundamental rights of the affected Indigenous community. Specifically, the court cited the community's right to religion, property, and culture.[41] As a result of this decision, part of the land was returned to the Maasai, marking an important step forward in the struggle to protect Indigenous peoples' religious sites against the impact of land reforms. Given the lack of government

39 Kenya, *The Community Land Act*, no. 27 (2016), s.3, https://faolex.fao.org/docs/pdf/ken160984.pdf; and Kenya, *Constitution* (2010), art. 63, http://www.parliament.go.ke/sites/default/files/2017-05/The_Constitution_of_Kenya_2010.pdf.

40 This issue was extensively analyzed and addressed by the Ndungu Commission, established in 2003. Kenya, *Report of the Commission of Inquiry into the Illegal/Irregular Allocation of Public Land* (2004), http://kenyalaw.org/kl/fileadmin/CommissionReports/A_Report_of_the_Land_Commission_of_Inquiry_into_the_Illegal_or_Irregular_Allocation_of_Land_2004.pdf.

41 *Mondorosi Village Council et al. v. Tanzania Breweries et al.*, High Court of Tanzania, Land Case no. 26 of 2013 (October 28, 2015), https://old.tanzlii.org/tz/judgment/court-appeal-tanzania/2018/303-0. For a discussion of the case, see Minority Rights Group International, "Tanzania: Protecting Maasai Right to Land" (November 11, 2016), https://minorityrights.org/2016/11/11/.

commitment to the protection of Indigenous rights, it is important to recognize efforts in civil society, including the creation of leadership forums to mobilize Maasai community members across Tanzania. In the context of various court cases, such efforts have facilitated the rapid organization of community consultations and the development of a common legal strategy. Furthermore, non-governmental organizations like the Minority Rights Group (MRG) have worked to raise awareness of Indigenous rights within the legal profession.[42] For instance, in 2014, the MRG organized training for members of the judiciary on issues and challenges facing Indigenous groups in Tanzania. That year, nineteen higher-court judges and clerks attended training sessions.

In Kenya, the Endorois Indigenous people went to court to assert their fundamental rights by challenging the government's decision to take away part of their land, including all access to Lake Bogoria. The expropriations were to make way for tourism development in the region, including the construction of hotels and other recreational infrastructure. A lack of response from judicial and political authorities in Kenya prompted the ACHPR to take up the case. In a 2010 ruling, the commission found that several of the Endorois community's rights had been violated, including the right to freely practice its religion and the right to property, as protected by the African Charter on Human and Peoples' Rights. In response to the Kenyan government's arguments that expropriating the land was in the public interest, the ACHPR stated that:

> [...] the Respondent State has not only denied the Endorois community all legal rights in their ancestral land, rendering their property rights essentially illusory, but in the name of creating a Game Reserve and the subsequent eviction of the Endorois community from their own land, the Respondent State has violated the very essence of the right itself, and cannot justify such an interference with reference to "the general interest of the community" or a "public need."[43]

42 Since 2009, Africa's Indigenous population has enjoyed significant legal and financial support from this international human rights organization focused on the interests of religious, linguistic, and ethnic minorities. The MRG regularly engages in international advocacy work on behalf of Indigenous peoples in Africa. It produces annual reports dealing with legal, political, economic, and social concerns. The efforts of international organizations like the MRG serve to showcase the struggles of Indigenous groups in Africa – not only to promote their rights at the national level but also to pressure African states for a meaningful commitment to promoting and respecting Indigenous rights.

43 *Centre for Minority Rights Development (Kenya) and Minority Rights Group International (on behalf of Endorois Welfare Council) v. Kenya*, ACHPR Communication no. 276/2003 (November 25, 2009), par. 215, https://www.escr-net.org/sites/default/files/Endorois_Decision.pdf.

The commission recommended that Kenya "ensure that the Endorois community has unrestricted access to Lake Bogoria and surrounding sites for religious and cultural rites and for grazing their cattle."[44] The decision was hailed as a great victory for the Indigenous peoples of Africa. Indeed, it was the ACHPR's first unequivocal assertion of Indigenous rights on the continent.[45]

The ACHPR referred a similar case involving the Ogiek to the African Court on Human and Peoples' Rights, having determined that the Kenyan government had extensively violated Indigenous rights by expropriating land for a forest reserve.[46] In 2017, after eight years of legal proceedings, the court ruled in favor of the Ogiek, condemning the Kenyan government for depriving them "of the right to enjoy and freely dispose of the abundance of food produced by their ancestral lands" and for pursuing evictions that "have adversely impacted on their economic, social and cultural development."[47] In all, the judgment lists eight violations of the African Charter, including the fact that "the evictions of the Ogieks from the Mau Forest rendered it impossible for the community to continue its religious practices and is an unjustifiable interference with the freedom of religion of the Ogieks."[48] But despite this historic victory, the Kenyan government has yet to implement the court's decision; the Ogiek community has had to continue fighting for the return of its ancestral lands.

Ultimately, the effectiveness of a judicial body depends on its ability to enforce its judgments, and Kenya's repeated inaction reflects the absence of a monitoring and follow-up mechanism. The fact that the task is entrusted to a political body – in this case, the African Union's Assembly of Heads of State and Government is responsible for following up on the court's decisions[49] – helps explain the prevailing sense of stagnation.[50]

44 *Centre for Minority Rights Development v. Kenya*, 80.

45 It is important to remember that an African legal framework for the protection of human rights has been in place since 1981. Although the African Charter does not specifically refer to "Indigenous peoples," it continues to provide a legal basis for the protection of such communities across the continent. ACHPR, *African Charter on Human and Peoples' Rights* (June 27, 1981), https://www.achpr.org/legalinstruments/detail?id=49.

46 *ACHPR v. Kenya*.

47 *ACHPR v. Kenya*, pars. 201 and 210.

48 *ACHPR v. Kenya*, par. 169.

49 On the division of responsibilities within the African Union, see the *Constitutive Act of the African Union* (2022), art. 5, https://au.int/en/constitutive-act; and the *Protocol to the African Charter on Human and Peoples' Rights on the Establishment of an African Court on Human and Peoples' Rights* (June 10, 1998), art. 29(2), https://au.int/en/treaties/protocol-african-charter-human-and-peoples-rights-establishment-african-court-human-and.

50 Observers have repeatedly noted the need for reform in this area. Among other examples, see Hébié 2017.

4 Conclusion

The different regional and national realities analyzed above show how Indigenous religious rights remain a matter of concern in both East and Central Africa. The situation varies from one country to the next, and the effective enjoyment of such rights is far from universal. Although there are encouraging signs in countries like Congo-Brazzaville and Burundi, where the positive impact of special legislation can be observed, significant obstacles remain. To begin with, states have struggled to reconcile customary Indigenous law, which is fundamental to Indigenous religious practices, with domestic law, which is often more favorable to economic development. Furthermore, despite the remarkable commitment of some governments to protecting minority rights, Indigenous communities continue to face very real threats. Dwight Newman has argued that the resistance of some governments to recognizing Indigenous rights is "rooted in a number of historical-structural characteristics of the post-colonial African state," including borders established with "little regard to prior existing communities and identities and not even any particular regard to material and physical realities," along with the resulting "challenges in terms of state building and identity formation" (Newman 2010: 145–147). This perspective highlights the need to approach the interpretation and application of Indigenous rights in a manner that engages "with the specific characteristics of the African context, including the persistent legacy of colonialism" (Labadie 2012: 226). Finally, beyond legal issues, Indigenous communities face a significant material threat to the enjoyment of their religious rights, namely the growing climate of insecurity in East and Central Africa. Indeed, even in the absence of unfair expropriation policies, armed conflicts have forced different Indigenous peoples to abandon their lands and religious sites in favour of more secure locations.[51]

References

Bellier, Irène. "Identité globalisée et droits collectifs: les enjeux des peuples autochtones dans la constellation onusienne." *Autrepart* 2, no. 38 (2006): 99–118. https://doi.org/10.3917/autr.038.0099.

51 United National Permanent Forum on Indigenous Issues, "Backgrounder: Indigenous Peoples in the African Region" (May 23, 2013), https://www.un.org/esa/socdev/unpfii/documents/2013/Media/Fact%20Sheet_Africa_%20UNPFII-12.pdf.

de Lespinay, Charles. "Le concept d'autochtone (*indigenous*) et de minorité (*minority*)." *Droit et Cultures* 2, no. 72 (2016): 19–42. https://doi.org/10.4000/droitcultures.3870.

Derssso, Solomon Ayele. "Introduction." In *Perspectives on the Rights of Minorities and Indigenous Peoples in Africa*, edited by Solomon Ayele Dersso, 3–19. Pretoria: Pretoria University Law Press, 2010. https://www.pulp.up.ac.za/component/edocman/perspectives-on-the-rights-of-minorities-and-indigenous-peoples-in-africa.

Fisiy, Cyprian F. "Containing Occult Practices: Witchcraft Trials in Cameroon." *African Studies Review* 41, no. 3 (1998): 143–163. https://doi.org/10.2307/525357.

Fisiy, Cyprian F., and Peter Geschiere. "Judges and Witches, or How is the State to Deal with Wichcraft? Examples from Southeast Cameroon." *Cahiers d'Études africaines* 30, no. 118 (1990): 135–156. https://www.jstor.org/stable/4392259.

Gazel, Hervé. "Le peuplement de l'Afrique centrale et orientale. Logiques héritées et développement urbain actuel." *Espace populations sociétés* 3, (2018). https://doi.org/10.4000/eps.7909.

Gazibo, Mamoudou, and Olivier Mbabia. "La politique africaine de la Chine montante à l'ère de la nouvelle ruée vers l'Afrique." *Études internationales* 41, no. 4 (2010): 521–546. https://doi-org.qe2a-proxy.mun.ca/10.7202/045561ar.

Geschiere, Peter. "The State Attacks: A Judiciary Offensive Against Witches." In *The Modernity of Witchcraft: Politics and the Occult in Postcolonial Africa*, translated by Peter Geschiere and Janet Roitman, 169–197. Charlottesville and London: University of Virginia Press, 1997.

Hébié, Mamadou. "L'exécution des décisions de la Cour africaine des droits de l'homme et des peuples." *Revue générale de droit international public* 121, no. 3 (2017): 689–724.

Labadie, Camille. "Compte rendu de [Solomon A. Dersso, ed, *Perspectives on the Rights of Minorities and Indigenous Peoples in Africa*, Pretoria, Pretoria University Law Press, 2010]." *Revue québécoise de droit international* 25, no. 2 (2012): 223–229.

Mary, André. "La preuve de Dieu par les pygmées." *Cahiers d'Études africaines*, nos. 198–199–200 (2010): 881–905. https://doi.org/10.4000/etudesafricaines.16411.

Musilikare, Jérémie. *La vie des pygmées Batwa au Rwanda*. Paris: L'Harmattan, 2015.

Newman, Dwight G. "Africa and the United Nations Declaration on the Rights of Indigenous Peoples." In *Perspectives on Minority and Indigenous Peoples' Rights in Africa*, edited by Solomon Dersso, 141–154. Pretoria: Pretoria University Law Press, 2010.

Tchoukou, Julie Ynes Ada. "Malleus Maleficarum: Scrutinizing Sorcery in Cameroon." *Journal of African Law* 62, no. 1 (February 2018): 129–146. https://doi.org/10.1017/S0021855317000328.

Indigenous Religious Rights in Taiwan: The Invisibility of Animism in Modern State Law

Scott E. Simon

In memory of Rabay Lowbing, who passed away on January 11, 2022

On September 8, 2021, as part of a public relations campaign to get access to the United Nations General Assembly (UNGA), the Ministry of Foreign Affairs (MOFA) of the Republic of China (ROC) on Taiwan launched a four-minute YouTube video entitled "To Freedom."[1] The video begins with an LGBTQ+ pride parade, appropriately so because Taiwan is the first country in Asia to legally recognize same-sex marriage. Religious freedom is highlighted through the testimony of a Muslim devotee in the Taipei Grand Mosque, images of temples and churches, and even a spinning dreidel to symbolize Taiwan's tiny Jewish community. Beginning at 2 minutes 51 seconds, a 17-seconds segment, labeled "equal rights for ethnic minorities," depicts a lone young man in a red and white woven gown on a cliff overlooking the Pacific Ocean. He sits alone at a table, pours rice wine into glass cups and weighs a *daran* (a divinatory bamboo baton) in his hand. A hawk, perhaps representing the ancestors, soars above him and looks down in approval. In Sediq (Truku) language, he says, "As a 10th generation shaman in my community, I feel the spirit of my ancestors gave me my vocation. I will continue to study to continue this culture of rites."[2]

MOFA, in a bilingual posting on its Facebook page, explained that this man is 19-year-old Lowbing Miyu from the Sediq Toda Indigenous community of Dgarung in Hualien.[3] At the age of 14, he discovered that the daran clings to

1 Technically, there is no state called "Taiwan," even though that is the name by which most of the world relates with the ROC. In this chapter, I use the term Formosa to refer to the main island, Taiwan to refer to the contemporary society that inhabits the geography (country) of the entire archipelago of islands under ROC control, and ROC to refer to the State.

2 The video is available here: https://www.youtube.com/watch?v=lRSgdmfjn6E. The quote is taken directly from the English subtitles. The subtitles do not include the last sentence, when the man says, "Thank you all," presumably in thanks for MOFA including him in the film.

3 https://www.facebook.com/mofa.gov.tw/posts/1147802369077737.

 | DOI:10.1163/9789004524330_014

his hand, indicating his vocation as a *msabuh*, or shaman. He thus began an apprenticeship with his grandmother, becoming the youngest shaman in his community.[4] There is much for an anthropologist to unpack in this brief representation of Taiwan's Indigenous religion, but for now it suffices to remark that MOFA, out of nearly limitless other possibilities, chose Lowbing to portray Taiwan as a country that recognizes religious freedom and Indigenous rights. In this chapter, I will likewise use the Sediq-Truku as a case study of Indigenous religious rights in Taiwan.[5] What does attention to religion reveal about Indigenous-State political relations since the 1970s? What space does State law (formal normativity) give to Indigenous religious practice? What happens in daily practice on the ground (informal normativity)? Looking forward, how can Taiwan, arguably among the freest countries in the world for religion, further strengthen religious rights for Indigenous peoples? I will begin with an introduction to Taiwan's Indigenous peoples. Because Taiwan is unique in having had a major shift in ruling powers, from Japan to the ROC at the conclusion of World War II, I will briefly explain changes that happened at that point before concentrating on political relations since the 1970s. I then explore formal and informal normativity related to Indigenous religions before providing my own personal standpoint and a conclusion.

1 Introduction to Formosan Indigenous Peoples

The peoples recognized as Indigenous in Taiwan are speakers of various Austronesian languages, a vast linguistic family ranging from Taiwan in the North to the Māori of Aotearoa/New Zealand in the South; from Madagascar in the West to Rapa Nui (Easter Island) in the East. Austronesian peoples inhabited the islands of Formosa (Taiwan's main island) and Ponso no tao (Orchid Island) for millennia before Chinese settlement began on Formosa's western

4 When Lowbing was only three years old, I was conducting field research in the adjacent village. People took me to see his grandmother, who welcomed me ritually into the community by giving me the Truku name of Walis Watan. She said that my personality reminds her of a classmate with that name during the Japanese period, as he also enjoyed reading and studying.

5 I have interacted with Sediq and Truku Indigenous peoples since I taught anthropology at National Dong Hwa University (Hualien) in 2000–2001. I have done research in their communities continually since 2004, and (until the pandemic) made annual return visits, including field research courses with Canadian students. I maintain daily contact with these communities using social media. I have published and commented widely on Indigenous hunting rights, including in 2021 as a panelist on a webinar hosted by the Taiwan Association for Human Rights.

plains in the early 17th century, after the Dutch East India Company established a trading colony around what is now Tainan (Andrade 2008). Although the coastal Indigenous (*pingpuzu*) were subjugated to Han (Chinese) control in a violent history of conquest from the 17th to the 19th century, Indigenous peoples of the central mountains and most of the East Coast maintained effective political autonomy until after Japan acquired the island from Qing Dynasty China in the 1895 Treaty of Shimonoseki. The Japanese quickly realized that the Qing had no effective authority to transfer Indigenous lands, as they faced armed resistance until 1914. In that year, the Truku of Hualien, after 90 days of fierce battles, were the last peoples to surrender. Japan, basing their policies partially on the American frontier model, governed Indigenous and Han populations under very different legal institutions (Barclay 2018), thus laying the foundation for the Indigenous political claims of the 20th and 21st centuries.

Residential separation during the fifty years of Japanese administration, as well as for the first decades of ROC rule, followed by the multiculturalist policies during democratization, kept Indigenous languages and cultures alive. Now recognized by the ROC as 16 "tribes," each group still seeks to maintain and negotiate the limits of their own sovereignty. Out of Taiwan's population of 23.5 million, nearly 580,000 (2.4%) people have Indigenous status. Taiwan's demographic majority are Han Taiwanese, often called "Native Taiwanese" in anthropology, descendants of settlers who came from China beginning in the 17th century. Many of them are the results of *métissage*, as Chinese settlers took Indigenous women as wives. Among these settlers, speakers of Hoklo and Hakka constitute respectively about 65.3% and 19.3% of the population. The remaining 13% are "Mainlanders" who came from China with the ROC beginning in 1945.[6] As I explore in this chapter, traditional religion has not emerged as a point of contention between Indigenous peoples and the State, perhaps because the social movement formed initially around Christian networks, allowing traditional practices to fade into the background. Traditional religion, however, provides new perspectives on Indigenous-State relations and religious rights. The non-Indigenous populations are mostly Buddhist, Taoist, or an amalgam of "folk religion." Some of the most prominent Mainlanders were

6 These population figures are approximate. Only the Indigenous population is carefully monitored as an ethnic group, with household registration data updated monthly (https://www.cip.gov.tw/zh-tw/news/data-list/940F9579765AC6A0/index.html?cumid=940F9579765AC6A0). The statistics given here are from October 2021. In 2016, a Hakka Affairs Council study estimated that 19.3% of Taiwan's population are Hakka (https://www.hakka.gov.tw/File/Attach/37585/File_73865.pdf). Baidu, a Chinese equivalent to Wikipedia, estimates the Mainlander population (https://baike.baidu.hk/item/外省人/2281150).

Christian, which helped build relations with the United States during the Cold War. They also gave Christianity a new form of prestige in Taiwan.

The Sediq peoples, including the Sediq (pop. 10,771) and Truku (pop. 33,162), call their way of life *Gaya*. Although this word is usually glossed as "law," it includes a rich oral tradition of stories, rituals, and above all, an ethical framework for seeking equilibrium in relations between people, between communities, between the living and the dead, and between humans and non-human beings of the mountain forests. Even the most fundamentalist of Christians, who reject traditional rituals and practices of msabuh such as that now claimed by Lowbing, agree that their moral and ethical lives are regulated by Gaya. In spite of the political debates of recognition that have divided communities and even families (to be discussed below), Gaya remains at the core of pluralistic Sediq-Truku ontologies, lifeworlds, and identities.

2 Indigenous-State Political Relations since the 1970s

For over two decades after Taiwan's defeat in WWII as part of Japan, Formosa had become the last refuge of the ROC, which was itself defeated in the 1949 Chinese Civil War. Although the ROC had U.S. support and maintained its seat in the United Nations Security Council and General Assembly until October 25, 1971, the Taiwanese people experienced ROC rule as a colonial imposition and were discretely developing their own oppositional form of nationalism (Mendel 1970). Ever since an anti-ROC rebellion in 1947, the ROC security apparatus was concerned about the possibility that the Native Taiwanese and Indigenous people could collaborate and use the mountains for guerrilla warfare. ROC Indigenous policy thus became a bricolage of residential separation, political institutions that tied Indigenous leadership to the ROC State and Chinese Nationalist Party (Kuomintang, KMT), and cultural assimilation. The idea was to create a Mainlander-Indigenous alliance that would foreclose the possibility of pan-Taiwanese resistance to the ROC. The ROC, eager to show the world they were better to their minorities than the People's Republic of China (which had just invaded Tibet), was a signatory party to the International Labour Organization (ILO) *Indigenous and Tribal Populations Convention 107* in 1962.

As part of the "Mountain People's Lifestyle Improvement Movement," Indigenous people were forced to learn Mandarin and adopt modern Chinese lifestyles. This included exhortations to abandon "superstition" and ban shamans from healing (Harrison 2001: 73). Indigenous communities converted *en masse* to Christianity. Although some Christian churches, especially the Presbyterian Church, encouraged the use of Indigenous languages, Indigenous people themselves seemed willing to abandon many ritual practices and to adopt a religion that was compatible with Chineseness, yet simultaneously justifying certain differences from Han communities on apparently non-ethnic terms (Harrison 2001: 76). At the same time, the ROC government integrated Indigenous populations into State structures *as Indigenous people*, albeit with the nomenclature of "mountain compatriots." This included the creation of 30 "mountain townships" in which the magistrate by law must be Indigenous, the modernization of usufruct regulations on Indigenous reserve land (which had been created under Japanese administration), and a quota for Indigenous political representation in the Taiwan Provincial Assembly. Indigenous affairs were governed through the Taiwan Province Bureau of Civil Administration. These institutions, a blend of cultural assimilation with political integration under the slogan of "local autonomy," created a KMT-loyal political Indigenous elite that was beholden to State and party (Rudolph 2003: 403). The goal was to transform Japanese Imperial subjects, the men having even proudly served in the Japanese military, into modern citizens of a Chinese State that was itself under threat of extinction. The KMT party-State, fearful of the threats to their power posed by both Communism and Taiwanese nationalism, kept most outsiders at bay by requiring visitors to Indigenous communities to obtain "mountain entry passes." They encouraged subaltern Mainlanders to settle in Indigenous communities and take Indigenous wives.

The 1970s marked an important turning point in Taiwan's history. After losing its international position as government of China, the ROC intensified nation-building at home, part of which included the creation of national parks. This process began in 1972, with the *National Park Law* creating six national parks on mountain-forests that had been under State control since the Japanese period. These parks, which now cover 8.58% of Formosa as part of 19.19% of the island dedicated to wildlife and natural preservation (Chinese Taipei Mountaineering Association n.d.), are concentrated on Indigenous traditional territory. The national parks brought the State and non-Indigenous people into Indigenous territories in new ways that endangered Indigenous rights. Most importantly for the Indigenous people, the *National Park Law* unilaterally made hunting on large swaths of Indigenous traditional territory illegal, with fines and possible imprisonment. The 1989 *Wildlife Conservation Act* (WCA) restricted hunting across the island, making most hunting and trapping practices illegal (Simon 2013: 221). In 1983, a study commissioned by the Taiwan Province Bureau of Civil Administration and administered by the Institute of

Ethnology at Academia Sinica, took stock of "mountain administrative policy," concluding that the policies did not meet the standards of "progressive integration" instituted by the ILO Convention 107, but instead tended toward "artificial assimilation" (Li 1983: 91). Among the many issues raised was the fact that Indigenous men, even those who live in cities and return home only on the weekends, valorize hunting and are troubled by its criminalization. The report cautiously encouraged deepening political self-government (Li 1983: 50).

The Indigenous peoples themselves were able to claim more rights after the end of martial law in 1987 and the subsequent democratization created more space for an autonomous Indigenous rights movement. The Alliance of Taiwanese Aborigines, created in 1984 around Presbyterian networks (Allio 1998, Rudolph 2003: 86–87), was at the forefront of the movement. A quota of Indigenous legislators was included in the Legislative Yuan when direct elections began in 1992. Among the early successes of the social movement were convincing the State to include their own terminology for Indigenous rights in the constitutional revisions of 1994 and 1997 (see below). In 1996, the cabinet-level Council of Indigenous Peoples was founded, effectively moving Indigenous administration from the provincial to the national level.

Awi Mona and Huang Chia-yuan divide the history of the Indigenous movement into three waves. The first wave, described above, focused on name rectification, Return Our Land,[7] and opposition to nuclear waste storage and dam construction on Indigenous lands. The second wave began after the election of Chen Shui-bian as president of the Democrat Progressive Party (DPP), with hopes for a "new partnership" or "government-to-government relationship" between the State and Indigenous peoples. Although many government promises remained unfulfilled, the 2005 *Indigenous Peoples Basic Law*, which Indigenous activists perceived to be subordinate only to the ROC Constitution, laid the foundation for subsequent pro-Indigenous legislation. The third wave began when newly elected DPP President Tsai Ing-wen made a historical apology on August 1st, 2016, for 400 years of colonialism (Awi and Huang 2021: 213–214). On that day, Tsai also created the Presidential-level Indigenous Historical Justice and Transitional Justice Committee. In summary, the State in the 2020s has embraced a policy oriented toward truth and reconciliation, inspired by precedents in South Africa and Canada. Across all three waves, Indigenous political claims have remained rooted in the core value of inherent sovereignty.

7 This was the slogan for a political movement that called for a return to Indigenous peoples of land that had been "nationalized" under Japanese rule and remained under ROC State control.

Awi and Huang are hopeful that Tsai's government will introduce a new legal paradigm that recognizes Indigenous legal traditions and constitutionalizes Indigenous rights (Awi and Huang 2021: 214).

On May 7, 2021, Indigenous activists were disappointed by ruling Interpretation 803 of the Constitutional Court of the Judicial Yuan about one of the most important Indigenous rights issues. In 2013, Talum Suqluman, from the Indigenous Bunun group, went hunting for his 92-year-old mother, returning with one Formosan serow (a kind of mountain goat) and one Reeve's muntjac (a small deer). On his way home, he was arrested and charged with using a "modified firearm," rather than the permitted homemade front-loading muskets, and with killing two protected animals. He was convicted in 2015, initially sentenced to prison for 3.5 years, and lost an initial appeal, but had his prison term suspended after domestic and international outcry. The case was turned over to the Constitutional Court for legal interpretation. The court made four interpretations. First, it ruled that provisions in the *Controlling Guns, Ammunition and Knives Act* (CGAKA) exempting Indigenous hunters from punishment if they use self-made rifles meet constitutional standards of clarity and proportionality. Second, it declared that the relevant *Regulations Concerning Weapons* regarding "self-made hunting guns" are insufficiently standardized. Third, provisions for Indigenous rights to hunt as "traditional culture" in the WCA do not justify hunting protected or endangered species. Finally, the court ruled that regulations requiring hunters to report in advance the species and number of animals they intend to catch are unreasonably inflexible (Simon 2021). The court thus upheld Talum's sentence but did make some practical concessions to Indigenous hunters. President Tsai, in her first ever presidential pardon, granted him amnesty.

Indigenous activists, however, were especially disappointed that the judges did not even consult or mention the *Indigenous Peoples Basic Law* (see below) in their deliberations.[8] They noted that many others remain in prison or have criminal records that render their lives difficult. Bunun activist Savungaz Valincinan pointed out that listing the name and number of animals hunters plan to catch "goes against their beliefs," as trying to predict the outcome of a hunt can anger the forests and mountains, with dangerous consequences to the hunter (Savungaz 2021). This points to the fact that Indigenous hunting rights

8 Since 2005, Indigenous activists assumed that the *Basic Law* was subordinate only to the Constitution, and that all other laws and regulations are subordinate to it. By excluding the *Basic Law* from the deliberations, the judges signaled that it has equal or even less importance than existing legislation.

are, at the core, an issue of religious rights. The problem is that Indigenous traditional religion is poorly understood and under-protected.

3 Formal Normativity Related to Indigenous Religions

Without a doubt, Taiwan is one of the freest countries in the world in terms of religion. Taiwan is even ranked first in the world in the Humanists International *Freedom of Thought Report*, which includes freedom from religion (Humanists International 2018). As argued by André Laliberté (2009), it took Taiwan four decades after the ROC retreated to attain this much lauded freedom. State-religion relations are managed by the Religious Affairs Bureau of the Department of Civil Affairs of the Ministry of the Interior. The Taiwan Provincial Police initially targeted Japanese religious associations out of concern that they sympathized with Japan. Many elites, including President Chiang Kai-shek, promoted the notion that Christianity is more "modern" than other beliefs. They had a particular disdain for Taiwanese local religions and folk beliefs, which led to restrictions on some local religious practices. Organized religions were better able than folk religions to assert their rights. As Taiwan democratized, the State embraced the principles of freedom of conscience and separation between religion and State. This has led to a situation in which religious organizations contribute to social welfare without compulsion, and the State avoids interference in religion. Because most Indigenous people are Christian, this framework protects their most prominent and visible Indigenous religious institutions and practices. This created conditions in which the Presbyterian Church emerged as the main proponent of Indigenous rights (Stainton 1995). I argue, however, that a blind spot in the law obscures traditional religious practices that Japanese anthropologist Kiyoto Furuno called "invisible churches" (Furuno 1971: 370). It is challenging for the State to regulate this kind of religion in the ROC tradition of civil law which, in contrast to common law jurisdictions, is based on explicit legislation rather than on legal precedents derived from life practices.

State law protects religious freedom. The Constitution of the ROC, promulgated in Nanjing in 1947, guarantees in Article 7 that all citizens are equal before the law, irrespective of "sex, religion, race, class, or party affiliation." Article 13 guarantees freedom of religious belief. It is important to note that the Constitution was written in China, by people who had little knowledge of Taiwan or Formosan Indigenous peoples. It instead established principles of local self-government and quotas for minority representation in the legislature regarding Tibet and Mongolian Leagues and Banners. This was a legal precedent for subsequent institutions of indigeneity in Taiwan. As Taiwan emerged from martial law 40 years later as the only region under ROC constitutional authority, the State had to revise the constitution to enable elections limited to Taiwan and to make the law conform to local realities. Seven series of revisions, known as the "Additional Articles," were made between 1991 and 2005.

Article 10, defining State responsibilities, brought Indigenous rights into constitutional law. The official English version reads:

> The State affirms cultural pluralism and shall actively preserve and foster the development of aboriginal languages and cultures.
>
> The State shall, in accordance with the will of the ethnic groups, safeguard the status and political participation of the aborigines. The State shall also guarantee and provide assistance and encouragement for aboriginal education, culture, transportation, water conservation, health and medical care, economic activity, land, and social welfare, measures for which shall be established by law. The same protection and assistance shall be given to the people of the Penghu, Kinmen, and Matsu areas.[9]

The evolving vocabulary in Chinese reveals the negotiations that occurred between the Indigenous social movement and the National Assembly between 1994 and 1997. Having participated in international Indigenous rights forums, Indigenous activists insisted on "name rectification": changing the assimilationist vocabulary of "mountain compatriots" (*shandi tongbao*) to one that better translates the international legal concept of "Indigenous." In 1994, they succeeded in getting their chosen translation for this term, *yuanzhumin* (which means "original inhabitants"), inserted in the Additional Articles. At the time, the UNGA proclaimed the International Year of the World's Indigenous People (1993) and then, from 1994, the International Decade of the World's Indigenous People. Arguing that the term "people" is assimilationist and grants rights to individuals as citizens, Indigenous groups insisted on the term "peoples," which has connotations of collective sovereignty in international law, and protested in Geneva with signs carrying only the letter "s." In the UN system, the break-through happened only in the Second International Decade of the World's Indigenous Peoples, in 2007, when the plural was accepted in the UN Declaration on the Rights of Indigenous Peoples (UNDRIP). In Taiwan, the 1994 version of the additional articles of the Constitution, in Article 9, accorded

9 https://law.moj.gov.tw/ENG/LawClass/LawAll.aspx?pcode=A0000002.

yuanzhumin status, the right to political participation, and State support for their needs. The 1997 version of the additional articles changed the Chinese vocabulary to *yuanzhu minzu* ("original peoples," so equivalent to adding the final -s in English), lengthened the list of items to be funded, and added two important clauses. The clause on cultural pluralism and fostering development of languages and cultures was entirely new, as was the wording "in accordance with the will of the ethnic groups." This is a good example of the "vernacularization" of international law (Merry 1996), as ideas from international law took on new form when adopted in a local context. Indigenous activists have told me that all members of the National Assembly did not fully understand the radically different meaning of adding the character -zu. The fact that the article promises the same protection and assistance to the Chinese inhabitants of Penghu, Kinmen, and Matsu, who are in no way Indigenous, gives credence to this argument. But, by affirming cultural pluralism and promising to foster Indigenous cultures, this article enabled subsequent legislation. However, considering that Indigenous activism first emerged from the Presbyterian church, Indigenous religion was scarcely a priority to either the legislators or the social movement.

In 2005, the Legislative Yuan passed the *Indigenous Peoples Basic Law* with the goal of aligning all legislation with the Constitution and draft versions of the UNDRIP. The *Basic Law* promised to amend, make, or repeal all legislation relevant to Indigenous peoples by 2008, which in hindsight was overly optimistic. The *Basic Law* itself, now with 35 articles, was modified in 2018. Five of those articles can be interpreted to include Indigenous religious rights. Article 10 requires the government to "keep and maintain indigenous cultures," albeit couched in a neo-liberal vocabulary of "cultural industry." Article 23 mentions that the government shall "respect indigenous peoples' rights to choose their lifestyle, customs, clothing, modes of social and economic institutions," etc., surely includes religion.[10] Article 30 requires the government to respect "traditional customs" when dealing with Indigenous affairs, making laws, or implementing judicial procedures. Article 33 specifically calls for the government to promote exchanges and cooperation with international Indigenous peoples and ethnic minorities on a list of issues that includes religion.

Article 19 is the most important for Indigenous religion. While legalizing hunting for Indigenous persons, it explicitly makes the link between hunting and ritual. The text in its integrity reads:

---

10 The non-capitalization of the word "Indigenous" here reflects usage in the original document. https://law.moj.gov.tw/ENG/LawClass/LawAll.aspx?pcode=D0130003.

> Indigenous persons may undertake the following non-profit seeking activities in indigenous peoples' regions and the sea areas be promulgated by the central indigenous competent authority:
> 1. Hunting wild animals.
> 2. Collecting wild plants and fungus.
> 3. Collecting minerals, rocks and soils.
> 4. Utilizing water resources.
>
> The central indigenous competent authority shall consult with the central relevant authority before promulgate the sea areas in the preceding paragraph.
>
> The activities in Paragraph 1 can only be conducted for traditional culture, ritual or self-consumption.

The stipulation that hunting can only be done for traditional culture, ritual, and self-consumption calls for a better understanding of religion and ritual related to hunting, which Savungaz Valincinan (see above) thought of in terms of beliefs.

The WCA, under the authority of the Council of Agriculture, was revised in 2013 in conformity with the *Basic Law*. Article 21–1 states:

> Wildlife may be hunted or killed for traditional cultural or ritual hunting, killing or utilization needs of Taiwan aborigines, regardless of Article 17, Paragraph 1; Article 18, Paragraph 1; and Article 19, Paragraph 1.
>
> Hunting, killing or utilizing wildlife in the condition listed above shall be approved by authorities. The application process, hunting method, hunted species, bag limit, hunting season, location, and other regulations shall be announced by the NPA and the national aborigine authority.[11]

In 2020, probably due to attention brought to Indigenous hunting by the legal case of Talum Suqluman (see above), the CGAKA provided guidelines from the Ministry of the Interior to implement the WCA. Article 5-2 specifies that until the WCA is further modified, Indigenous people shall not be punished for hunting for "traditional culture, ritual hunting, or non-profitable utilization."[12] The main purpose of this law is to restrict Indigenous hunters to using home-made front-loading rifles.

These legal protections suggest a need to clearly define Indigenous religions and rituals. The 2015 *Administrative Rules on the Capture, Slaughter and Use of*

11 https://law.moj.gov.tw/ENG/LawClass/LawAll.aspx?pcode=M0120001.

12 https://law.moj.gov.tw/ENG/LawClass/LawAll.aspx?pcode=D0080047.

Wild Animals Based on Needs of Indigenous Traditional Culture and Rituals attempts to do this.[13] This regulation defines traditional culture as values, norms, religions, art, ethics, systems, language, customs, and all other life content that have existed for a long time in Indigenous society and are passed down from generation to generation to this day. It defines rituals as ritual activities and behaviors that are repeatedly practiced through generations based on religion, beliefs, or habits. These rules are applicable only in Indigenous areas as defined by the *Basic Law*, and do not apply in areas where hunting is prohibited (as in national parks). The law requires an individual, community, or legally recognized organization to apply to local authorities for permission 20 days in advance with information about the hunters, the name of the "traditional culture," as well as details on the place of the hunt, the species, and numbers of animals to be caught. The regulations include an annex with a list of permitted festivals and rituals, classified according to ethnic group and locality, with details on dates, hunting tools to be used, animal species, and information specific to certain communities. The Council of Agriculture consulted with all local communities to make this list, but the regulations conflict with other laws, especially since some of the species listed in the law as potential elements of rituals are protected or even endangered. It is noteworthy that ritual is defined as collective festivities, usually those that are organized by villages or associations, and even sometimes with a tourist audience in mind. It assumes that religion is collective, organized, and distinct from other dimensions of life. This excludes informal ad hoc rituals by individuals, even if those are arguably the core of Indigenous religion.

To sum up so far, ROC constitutional law provides religious freedom and calls for protection of Indigenous religion. Following the *Indigenous Peoples Basic Law*, which calls for revision of all legislation in recognition of Indigenous rights, laws regarding firearms and wildlife have been revised with the goal of exempting Indigenous hunters from these laws, for purposes of ritual and self-consumption. Other laws, such as the National Park Law, which prohibits hunting over vast swaths of Indigenous traditional territory, have not been revised to provide similar exemptions. Although the laws claim to protect Indigenous ritual and religion, the actual regulations limit Indigenous hunting more than they permit it, most notably by restricting it to a formal list of recognized rituals. Indigenous hunters and activists say that the lawmakers simply do not understand the nature of Indigenous rituals and religions. If anything, they render animism invisible.

---

13 https://law.moj.gov.tw/LawClass/LawAll.aspx?pcode=M0120007. No English translation is available.

4 Informal Normativity Related to Indigenous Religions

Ever since the Japanese period, Indigenous religion has been either rendered invisible or stigmatized, a historical burden that makes MOFA's film with Lowbing Miyu mentioned in the introduction of this chapter remarkable. Since the 19th century, various States have promoted the story of Wu Feng, a Confucian settler and trader with the Tsou Indigenous people near Chiayi. In the story, Wu Feng befriended the Tsou, who were addicted to head-hunting and constantly raided Taiwanese settler communities. The Tsou loved and respected Wu Feng but refused to give up head-hunting. One day, he instructed the Tsou warriors to attack a person who appeared at dawn on horseback wearing a red cloak. When they did so, they opened the cloak of the deceased and, to their horror, discovered it was their beloved Wu Feng. They were so emotionally moved that they decided to give up head-hunting forever. Taiwanese settlers glorified this story as the triumph of Chinese civilization over savages. In 1820, they constructed a temple in his memory in Chiayi, and since 1950, they have erected statues of him across the island, and taught the story in primary school. One textbook even said: "Wu Feng was the first Han Chinese to give the mountain compatriots human rights" (Cheung 2017: 8). To Indigenous people, however, this story, which essentially reduced their traditional religion as wanton homicide, became a source of shame. As a result, removing this hagiography from State-sponsored curricula was one of the first goals of the Indigenous rights movement in the 1980s (Rudolph 2008: 49).[14]

Considering the diversity of Indigenous religions across Formosa, all of which can be considered as variants of animism, I focus on the Sediq and Truku groups with whom I have done field research. These peoples, along with the Atayal, see themselves as the people of the law which, in Truku and Tgdaya is called Gaya.[15] Korean anthropologist Kim Kwang-ok put Gaya in its ecological context, defining Gaya as "firstly that of natural order and secondly of life and action in agreement with this order" (Kim 1980: 181). Gaya is an ethical framework for the regulation of relations between human individuals,

14 All Indigenous groups on Formosa, but not on Orchid Island, did in fact have rituals that involved taking a human head. Skull racks were prominent features in all Indigenous villages until the 1920s. In the 1980s, the Indigenous movement first protested the abusive appropriation of this history in the public sphere. Beginning in the 1990s, writers and others in a genre of Indigenous resurgence began to re-appropriate these ritual traditions as a source of Indigenous pride. This all lies beyond the scope of the current chapter. See Simon 2012 and Simon 2023.

15 The word in Atayal is Gaga. In Teuda, it is Waya. Both the State-recognized Sediq and Truku include speakers of Truku, Tgdaya, and Teuda.

between communities, between the living and the dead, and between humans and animals. Among the central rituals of Gaya are the pig sacrifices called "powda Gaya" (moving through Gaya) that happen at every life transition, notably at marriage and divorce, as celebrations of blessings and atonement for violation of Gaya (Lin 2011: 34). The over-arching framework is that, in Gaya, humans sacrifice domestic pigs to the ancestors, who in generalized reciprocity, give wild boars to hunters in return (Simon 2015). Hunters who uphold Gaya through carrying out correct rituals and sharing with others, developing a "spirit" of moral righteousness called *bhring*, will be rewarded with successful hunting by the ancestors (Huang 2000: 57). These Formosan beliefs are variants of Southeast Asian animism, which posit an intersubjective and personalized universe, full of spirits, where animals and plants also appear as intentional subjects and persons (Århem 2015: 3). Gaya thus stands as a counterpoint to the hegemonic ontology of modernity.

People have worked diligently to reconcile traditional religion with Christianity. Some Christians reject all old practices as idolatry; whereas a small number of traditionalists refuse to step into a church because they see it as a colonial religion. But most people live with some form of syncretism. Some see the ancestral spirits and God as co-existing in parallel, as they move between the spirits (*utux*) of the mountain-forests and the church. No less than Lowbing's grandmother Rabay Lowbing suggested a combination of "God above" (*utux baraw*) and the ancestral spirits (*utux rudan*), nonetheless insisting that God alone is the "root" (*pusu*) (Kaji 2011: 31–32). The easily recognizable rituals of Gaya include shamanic healing rituals, which are now conducted in live performances by Lowbing. There are also practices of interpreting messages from the ancestors that come through dreams or divination by bird behavior (Simon 2018). Hunters tend to blend the two religions quite well. They believe that the ancestors provide game animals and watch for signs from them. They also carry out discrete rituals to the ancestors, sometimes leaving some betel nuts or rice wine in sacrifice before entering the mountain-forest. And, most importantly, they share the meat with others after they return to the village. Sharing meat is itself an important ritual.

Gaya has very little in terms of material culture, beyond the shaman's bamboo stick or daran, as the sacrifices are done with everyday items. The rituals happen outdoors, mostly in the mountain-forest, but pig sacrifices also happen in the courtyards in front of homes, which is why Kiyoto Furuno spoke of "invisible churches." What is perhaps most difficult for State actors and other outsiders to understand is that the act of hunting is *itself* a ritual. Talum Suqluman, as Bunun, would have other words to describe it, but the basic principle is the same. Hunting is the primary way in which living people communicate with the spirits of the deceased and with the deities of the mountain-forests. If Talum's mother had only needed protein, it would suffice, and it would have been easier to purchase meat at the supermarket. In fact, muntjacs can also be raised by farmers, and are legally sold in "mountain product" restaurants. Most importantly, she was asking him to carry out a very sacred traditional ritual. He had a moral obligation to fulfill his elderly mother's wishes.

5 Discussion

Over the past two decades, while doing field research in Sediq and Truku communities, I have found that the most wide-spread grievance against the State is interference in hunting, especially the criminalization of hunting practices. In Hsiulin Township Hualien, people are frustrated most of all by the Taroko National Park. In all the neighbouring communities, each clan (*alang* in Truku) has staked out collective hunting territories that predate the establishment of the park. Elderly men carve out traplines in those territories. They share the territory with other men who hunt at night with hand-crafted muskets, using headlamps to identify the reflective eyes of mammals in the forest.[16] Locally generated rules about hunting exist across Taiwan, also in forests managed by the Forestry Division of the Council of Agriculture. Some experienced hunters, like Lowsi Rakaw (Huang Chang-hsing), see a weakening of Gaya because hunters can less effectively manage their own territories (Huang 2000). Although most people say they hunt only in their traditional territories, older men say that the presence of State police and wildlife conservation authorities undermines their ability to exclude others. Some say that this even allows non-Indigenous poachers to get away with illegal hunting and even cutting down trees. Some young people, who generally only shoot flying squirrels, have told me that they can hunt anywhere they wish, if they avoid being arrested. Such sentiments show that hunters perceive the risk of a tragedy of the commons, which is ironically exacerbated by State actions to limit hunting. They nearly always frame it as an issue of sovereignty, saying that they have the right to hunt on the land that their ancestors used for those purposes long before the arrival of any State on Formosa.

16 There is nothing traditional about using headlamps or other new technologies in hunting. The Indigenous peoples seek nothing less than full sovereignty over their territories and life practices, and reject being enclosed by the State in externally imposed notions of tradition.

I have argued elsewhere (Simon 2013) that Indigenous rights and sustainability of wildlife populations would be best protected through legislative change, but most importantly by the creation of hunting institutions in which hunters themselves can regulate their practices. I was encouraged by the research of wildlife biologist Kurtis Pei, who found that Rukai hunting practices in southern Taiwan contribute to sustainable wildlife populations by: 1) hunting only in the winter and for hoofed animals with high reproduction rates; 2) scattering distribution of hunting territories; and 3) limiting the numbers of hunters in each territory (Pei 1999). Following Fikret Berkes, I argued that members of each community must be able to exclude outsiders and make and reinforce their own rules. I maintain that effective use of Indigenous knowledge must include recognition of what Berkes calls "world view," including religion, ethics, and belief systems (Berkes 2008: 17–18). For the Sediq and Truku, this is the form of animism they call Gaya. I even think that the Indigenous rights movement can include religious rights as part of their arguments for further decriminalization of Indigenous hunting. These practices are part and parcel of animism, a form of religion that is invisible to State law, and marginalized. But animism provides ways of living in the world that all of humanity might need as we struggle to deal with issues of climate change and biodiversity decline. From a socio-anthropological perspective, tensions in Taiwan about Indigenous religion and hunting reveal a lot about the nature of State law.

6 Conclusion

The legal framework that encapsulates Indigenous religion on Formosa is unique because it is a hybrid of both Japanese and Chinese modernity. The foundations of indigeneity, the "bifurcated sovereignty" of Japanese biopolitics that placed Han Taiwanese and Indigenous Formosans under two systems of colonial governance (Barclay 2018), remain firm. Han and Indigenous have different property regimes and different political institutions. All Indigenous people are enumerated, not only as citizens, but as members of Indigenous groups, the borders of which were first defined by Japanese anthropologists. Japanese authorities forced the Indigenous to pray in Shinto shrines that were built for them in their new, modern villages. The Japanese period saw the end of certain religious practices, most notably the facial tattooing, that was essentially a coming-of-age ceremony, and the human sacrifices of head-hunting. The Indigenous people welcomed some of these changes. As one Truku elder told me, they are thankful that the Japanese brought them modern lifestyles and extracted them from "the worst kind of feudalism." But, in the Japanese era, they continued to hunt in the mountain-forests according to Gaya. The Japanese, whose own Shinto beliefs include awe to the spirits across mountain-forests, were perhaps more accommodating to such practices than those who came afterwards.

The ROC, beginning when it ruled in China-proper, but not in Taiwan, had a more aggressive approach to the modernization of religion. China, faced with a heritage of folk religions that could turn into massive anti-State rebellions (e.g. the 1851–1864 Taiping Rebellion or the 1899–1901 Boxer Rebellion) as well as missionary activities, was more eager to control religion. In 1936, the ROC adopted rules for the registration of temples that sought to give local governments more authority over Buddhism and Taoism (Laliberté 2009: 68). This itself emerged from ROC, and even late Qing, policies that hoped to provide freedom to religion, while eliminating anything classified as "superstition." In China, this led to the appearance of nationwide associations claiming to represent Taoism, Buddhism, Islam, Christianity, and Confucianism. Christianity was in some ways the normative model, as the State permitted religion with strong organization, official hierarchies, and written texts (Goossaert 2008). After the ROC came to Taiwan, the new rulers were quick to place restrictions on many Taiwanese folk religious practices and in the "Mountain People's Lifestyle Improvement Movement," to stamp out shamanic healing rituals and other Indigenous practices they defined as superstitious. This certainly set the stage for massive Indigenous conversion to Christianity, which simultaneously promised modernity and an identity distinct from the Han Taiwanese. From Indigenous perspectives, this was only a new wave of colonialism.

Even as they adapted to new rulers and State governance, the Indigenous peoples never abandoned their sovereignty over the mountain-forests or their own agency. Most people adopted new religions in a syncretic fashion in which they might, for example, pray in church while in the village but make sacrifices to the ancestors before entering the mountain-forests to hunt. Because of the resilience of these latter practices, one could even say that hunting itself is the central ritual in Formosan Indigenous religion. This, however, is very difficult to even perceive because of the way State law on religion shapes even everyday popular perception of what is and what is not religious.

The ontological turn in anthropology puts this in a new perspective. Beginning with the ground-breaking work of Philippe Descola (2005), there has been renewed interest in anthropology in animism as a counterpoint to naturalism. Naturalism, the hegemonic cosmology of naturalism, assumes a fundamental dichotomy between an objective nature and subjective culture, and thus between animals and humans. This is the ontology that posits nature as composed of resources beyond human society, that can be thus extracted, domesticated, and dominated to the benefit of humans. This is the modernist ontology that led to the creation of national parks, ideally as pristine wilderness untouched by humans. Colonialism, says Descola, brought this ontology to populations around the world (Descola 2011: 91). This is also the ontology that posits religion as part of human culture, as a question of subjective, personal beliefs, and rituals. In Asia, competing Japanese and Chinese modernities also vernacularized this naturalist ontology and imposed it upon Indigenous peoples. If naturalism is indeed the cause of ecological destruction at a planetary scale (Descola 2011: 77), animism may provide moral and ethical lessons for all of us.

Animism has been very resilient, and the hunting practices of Formosan Indigenous peoples are paradigmatic examples of that. The Sediq peoples inhabit a world in which forests are hallowed spaces, the ancestors are the overseers of the living, and birds become sacred texts that reveal the mechanisms of Gaya. Because of bhring, success or failure at hunting indicates whether an individual meets the standards of Gaya. Without hunting, this meshwork of lives would dry up and fade from existence. The naturalist assumptions behind laws about everything, from religion and hunting to national parks and mining, obscure this way of inhabiting the world. Lawmakers, judges, and social activists are all aware of this reality, and struggle to describe it through a vocabulary of ritual and beliefs. Dressing animism up as multiculturalism, as in the MOFA film, is far from sufficient. It is far more important to recognize animism as an Indigenous religious right. Full religious rights are possible only when all variants of religion are made visible and recognized as central in the lifeworlds of sovereign Indigenous peoples.

References

Allio, Fiorella. "L'autochtonie en terre taïwanaise." *Recherches amérindiennes au Québec* 28, no. 1 (1998): 43–57.

Andrade, Tonio. *How Taiwan Became Chinese: Dutch, Spanish, and Han Colonization in the Seventeenth Century*. New York: Columbia University Press, 2008.

Århem, Kaj. "Southeast Asian Animism in Context." In *Animism in Southeast Asia*, edited by Kaj Århem and Guido Sprenger, 3–30. London: Routledge, 2015.

Awi Mona and Huang Chia-yuan. "Conflict and Reconciliation between Civil Law and Indigenous Legal Traditions." In *Taiwan's Contemporary Indigenous Peoples*, edited by Chia-yuan Huang, Daniel Davies, and Dafydd Fell, 128–146. London: Routledge, 2021.

Barclay, Paul D. *Outcasts of Empire Japan's Rule on Taiwan's "Savage Border," 1874–1945*. Oakland: University of California Press, 2018. https://doi.org/10.1525/luminos.41.

Berkes, Fikret. *Sacred Ecology, 2nd Edition*. London: Routledge, 2008.

Cheung, Han. "Taiwan in Time: The Drastic Downfall of Wu Feng." *Taipei Times*, September 10, 2017. https://www.taipeitimes.com/News/feat/archives/2017/09/10/2003678150.

Chinese Taipei Mountaineering Association. "台灣山岳資源知多少列七:國家公園。." Accessed January 3, 2022. http://www.alpineclub.org.tw/front/bin/ptdetail.phtml?Part=yw_184-1&Rcg=221.

Descola, Philippe. *Par-delà nature et culture*. Paris: Gallimard, 2005.

Descola, Philippe. *L'écologie des autres: L'anthropologie et la question de la nature*. Paris: Éditions Quae, 2011.

Furuno, Kiyoto (古野清人). 原始宗教の構造と機能 [*The Construction and Function of Primitive Religion*]. Yokohama: Yūrindō Shuppan 横浜:有隣堂出版, 1971.

Goossaert, Vincent. "Republican Church Engineering: The National Religious Associations in 1912 China." In *Chinese Religiosities: Afflictions of Modernity and State Formation*, edited by Mayfair Mei-hui Yang, 209–232. Berkeley: University of California Press, 2008.

Harrison, Henrietta. "Changing Nationalities, Changing Ethnicities: Taiwan Indigenous Villages in the Years after 1946." In *In Search of the Hunters and their Tribes: Studies in the History and Culture of the Taiwan Indigenous People*, edited by David Faure, 50–78. Taipei: Shung Ye Museum of Formosan Aborigines, 2001.

Huang, Chang-xing 黃長興. "東賽德克群的狩獵文化 [Hunting culture in eastern Seediq groups]." 民族學研究所資料彙編 [*Field materials of the Institute of Ethnology*] 15, (2000): 1–104.

Humanists International. "Ranking Index 2018." Accessed January 4, 2022. https://fot.humanists.international/ranking-index-2018/.

Kaji Cihung 旮日羿 吉宏. 太魯閣族部落史與祭儀樂舞傳記 [*Truku Tribal History and Memoir of Ritual Music and Dance*]. Taipei: Shan-hai, 2011.

Kim, Kwang-Ok. "The Taruko and their belief system." PhD diss. Institute of Social Anthropology, University of Oxford, 1980.

Laliberté, André. "The Regulation of Religious Affairs in Taiwan: From State Control to Laisser-faire?" *Journal of Current Chinese Affairs* 38, no. 2 (2009): 53–83.

Li, Yih-yüan, et collab. 李亦園. *Shandi xingzheng zhengce zhi yanjiu yu pinggu baogaoshu* 山地行政政策之研究與評估報告書 [Rapport de recherche et évaluation des politiques administratives montagnardes]. Nantou: Taiwan sheng zhengfu minzheng ting 南投:臺灣省政府民政廳, 1983.

Lin, Ching-Hsiu. "The circulation of labour and money: Symbolic meanings of monetary kinship practices in contemporary Truku society, Taiwan." *New Proposals: Journal of Marxism and Interdisciplinary Inquiry* 5, no. 1 (2011): 27–44.

Mendel, Douglas. *Politics of Formosan Nationalism*. Berkeley: University of California Press, 1970.

Merry, Sally Engle. "Legal Vernacularization and Ka Ho'okolokolonui Kanaka Maoli, The People's International Tribunal, Hawai'i 1993." *PoLAR: Political and Legal Anthropology Review* 19, no. 1 (1996): 67–82.

Pei, Kurtis. "Hunting system of the Rukai Tribe in Taiwan, Republic of China." *Proceedings of the International Union of Game Biologists XXIV Congress, Thessaloniki, Greece*, (January 1999). https://www.researchgate.net/publication/228934804_Hunting_System_of_the_Rukai_Tribe_in_Taiwan_Republic_of_Chinas.

Rudolph, Michael. *Taiwans multi-ethnische Gesellschaft und die Bewegung der Ureinwohner: Assimilation oder kulturelle Revitalisierung?* Münster: LIT Verlag, 2003.

Rudolph, Michael. *Ritual performances as authenticating practices: Cultural representations of Taiwan's aborigines in times of political change*. Hamburg: LIT Verlag, 2008.

Savungaz Valincinan. "Taiwan's Indigenous Peoples Hunt for Justice." *Asia Democracy Chronicles*, November 23, 2021. https://adnchronicles.org/2021/11/23/taiwans-indigenous-peoples-hunt-for-justice/.

Simon, Scott. "Politics and Headhunting among the Formosan Sejiq: Ethnohistorical Perspectives." *Oceania* 82, no. 2 (2012): 164–185.

Simon, Scott. "Of Boars and Men: Indigenous Knowledge and Co-Management in Taiwan." *Human Organization* 72, no. 3 (2013): 220–229.

Simon, Scott. "Real people, real dogs, and pigs for the ancestors: The moral universe of 'domestication' in indigenous Taiwan." *American Anthropologist* 117, no. 4 (2015): 983–709.

Simon, Scott. "Penser avec des oiseaux: L'ornithomancie et l'autochtonie à Taïwan." *Anthropologie et Sociétés* 42, no. 2–3 (2018): 151–169.

Simon, Scott. "The Limits of Indigenous Hunting Rights in Taiwan." *East Asia Forum*, June 30, 2021. https://www.eastasiaforum.org/2021/06/30/the-limits-of-indigenous-hunting-rights-in-taiwan/.

Simon, Scott E. *Truly Human: Indigeneity and Indigenous Resurgence on Formosa*. Toronto: University of Toronto Press, 2023.

Stainton, Michael. "Return our Land: Counterhegemonic Presbyterian Aboriginality in Taiwan." Master's thesis in social anthropology, York University, Toronto, 1995.

Integration or Separation? Religious Freedom in Post-authoritarian Indonesia: The Case of the Indigenous Kaharingan Religion in Central Kalimantan

Mirza Satria Buana

Some aspects of Indonesian governance still reflect the priorities of the authoritarian Soeharto regime, which consistently emphasized national unity over cultural pluralism. For instance, the government still officially recognizes only five religions – Islam, Christianity (Catholic or Protestant), Hinduism, and Buddhism – that are considered "modern systems of faith" based on their monistic beliefs. Granted, Indonesian authorities have often avoided the term "official religions." Consider the 1965 Blasphemy Act, the first section of which somewhat ambiguously refer to "religions that are embraced by Indonesians." In any case, the government's narrow definition of religion has had a major impact on Indigenous peoples like the Dayak, who inhabit Central Kalimantan Province and practice a local animistic religion called Kaharingan. To satisfy administrative and social requirements, followers of Kaharingan have routinely had to associate themselves with Hinduism. Among the so-called modern religions recognized by Indonesian authorities, Hinduism is widely seen as the one whose beliefs and practices are most closely aligned with Kaharingan (Schiller 1996).

Local and Indigenous peoples began demanding the right to manage their own affairs when the Soeharto regime was overthrown in 1998. The following year saw the adoption of the Decentralization Act, which significantly increased the degree of autonomy enjoyed by local governments. More broadly, the period from 1999 to 2004 – the early years of the reform era (*era reformasi*) – brought a radical process of decentralization to what had previously been considered the most centralized country in Asia (Alm et al. 2001: 85). Like other ethnic minorities in Indonesia, the Indigenous peoples of Central Kalimantan seized on the opportunity to revive their cultural and religious traditions. Adopted in 2008, Central Kalimantan Provincial Regulation No. 16 was just one of many pieces of local legislation designed to formally recognize Indigenous institutions.

Meanwhile, two landmark decisions of the Indonesian Constitutional Court facilitated Indigenous advocacy in general and the recognition of traditional religious beliefs in particular. To begin with, Decision No. 35/PUU-XI/2013

 | DOI:10.1163/9789004524330_015

ordered that the 1999 Forestry Law be amended to distinguish between *adat* (traditional) forests and state-owned forests. This would allow Indigenous peoples to autonomously manage local woodlands, including by applying their traditional systems of land tenure. Second, Decision No. 97/PUU-XIV/2016 provided for identifying the local or traditional religions of members of minority groups on national identification cards (the Kartu Tanda Penduduk, or KTP). It is important to note that these were not self-executing decisions; they required legislative approval and administrative implementation to be fully enforced. Nevertheless, they inspired some followers of Kaharingan, especially Indigenous rights activists, to demand an end to their affiliation with Hinduism. Others, who were more comfortable with the association between Hinduism and Kaharingan, dismissed such calls as politically motivated. To some extent, these differences of opinion reflect the fact that not all followers of Kaharingan are Dayak, while other live in urban areas and lack any spiritual connection to their ancestral lands.

Based on a socio-legal methodology that supplements legal research with socio-cultural and political insights gained through fieldwork or drawn from non-legal literature (Banakar & Travers 2005), this chapter addresses two main questions. First, to what extent does the status of Kaharingan and its followers' religious freedom depend on national legislation and the recognition of human rights? Second, how has the clash between those who seek to end the association with Hinduism and those who seek to maintain it played out among followers of Kaharingan, from both social and political perspectives?

1 Kaharingan: A Traditional Religion among the Dayak

Also known as Helo, Kaharingan is practiced by the Dayak and other Indigenous peoples living in Central Kalimantan. Theologically, it promotes universal values that transcend familial, tribal, or ethnic identities. Conversion to Kaharingan, which mainly occurs through marriage, involves stating five principles and taking a ritual bath in coconut water.[1] Among the Dayak, the religion is rooted in Indigenous social customs that reflect a worldview based on humanity's connectedness to cosmic and ancestral realms. These connections depend on a combination of divine revelations (*godsdienst*) and mystical-animistic beliefs (*bijgeloof*). Like other Indigenous religions in Indonesia, it has been frequently described as religio-mystical (Schiller 1996). And as is often the case with Indigenous belief systems, followers of Kaharingan have

1 Interview with Christiana Bangkang, Palangkaraya City, December 3, 2019.

an animistic ecological view of the relationship between humans and nature, whereby nature will not destroy humanity so long as humans preserve it.[2]

Still, some have rejected the idea that Kaharingan constitutes a religion, dismissing it as a collection of traditional values, ancestral stories, and fanciful myths. In Weberian terms (Coe 1904), these critics see Kaharingan as a distinctly unmodern belief system. And yet, it shares many characteristics with so-called modern religions. For instance, it features a holy scripture (the Panaturan), a human origin story like those told in the Bible and the Quran, and holy places such as the Hill of Tantan Sama Tuan and the Hill of Raya.[3] Followers of Kaharingan visit formal places of worship, called *balai*, where they perform special chants, called *kandayu*.[4] It is even a monistic and monotheistic faith, whose sole god (Ranying Hatalla Katamparan) is associated with the beginning and end of creation, as well as the four elements that make up the universe.[5] Based on these various components, Kaharingan clearly meets the criteria used to identify modern religions, including the capacity to provide effective moral guidance and promote self-awareness (Weber 1930; Coe 1904). There is no objective reason for it not to be placed on an equal footing with Indonesia's other religions. Indeed, Kaharingan has reached a stage of development where followers can grow and strive through self-expression, based on well-established norms of conduct and an internalized belief in the sanctity of human subjectivity (Berger 1990: 44).

2 The Constitutional Court's View on Indigenous Religious Rights

In 2016, Indigenous followers of traditional religions brought a judicial review case before the Indonesian Constitutional Court. They aimed to challenge certain provisions of the 2006 Citizenship Act, according to which the "Religion" section of the KTP was kept blank in the case of individuals who reported following an Indigenous or traditional belief system. Instead, the relevant

2 Ibid.

3 Ibid. The first human beings were Manyamei Tunggul Garing (husband) and Kameluh Putak Bulau (wife).

4 Ibid.

5 Ibid. The four elements are Langit Katambuan (the sky), created by Ranying Hatalla and under which all human beings live; Petak Tapajakan (the earth), the place where humans strive, develop, and procreate; Nyalung Kapanduian (rivers and oceans), an eternal source of life that benefits all humankind and can cleanse sin; and Kalata Padadukan (the womb), from which human beings enter the world, where they are nurtured by a mother who shows them the path to paradise in return for respect and obedience.

information would only be recorded in the National Population Database. In Decision No. 97/PUU-XIV/2016, the court found that freedom of religion and the right to equal treatment with respect to public services constitute inalienable human rights under the Indonesian constitution, as opposed to rights granted by the state (KTP Case: 138–139). Applying this principle to the administration of public services, the court went on to nullify specific provisions of the Citizenship Act that discriminated against followers of Indigenous or traditional religions. For instance, Section 61 (1) and (2), as well as Section 64 (1) and (5) wrongly portrayed freedom of religion as a right granted by the state. Also, Section 27 (1), and Section 28D (1) violated constitutional human rights provisions respecting equality and equal treatment under the law, irrespective of race, religion, or political affiliation. But the court placed special emphasis on how Section 28E (1) and (2) as well as Section 29 (2) violated religious freedom by creating an administrative mechanism that diminished the ability of citizens to express and assert their religious affiliations and beliefs (KTP Case: 147). Finally, the court's decision reflected a view of human rights as interrelated and interdependent norms, insofar as it recognized how the government's failure to protect the religious rights of certain citizens in the delivery of public services – due to its insistence on recognizing only a handful of so-called official religions – represented a threat to a whole range of social, economic, and cultural rights.

From the perspective of the complainants, the decision had two drawbacks. First, by referring to the notion of "Indonesian experiences," the court drew a distinction between religion and belief – although it concluded that both are equal before the law (KTP Case: 141). Second, despite being final and binding, the decision was not self-executing. Its implementation depends on the adoption of legislation and administrative action by authorities who still tend to consider religion as far more important than belief. Moreover, the standard for applying religious rights equally remains very much open to interpretation by the ministries separately responsible for religious matters and issuing KPTs: the Ministry of Religious Affairs and the Ministry of Home Affairs. Which one will take the lead in protecting the rights of followers of Indigenous or traditional religions?

But whatever approach the government takes in implementing the court's decision, it is clear that the formal recognition of only certain religions is the key issue at play. If political authorities find a way of complying with the decision while maintaining the status quo, minority religious rights will remain under threat. Although modern states commonly adopt policies for recognizing religious groups, the process can have serious consequences for Indigenous or traditional religions that fail to meet the established criteria. In particular, such policies tend to be implemented in a way that glosses over the social complexities characterizing the semi-autonomous social field of Indigenous communities (Moore 1973). As a result, the court's decision has sparked communal discord, especially in Central Kalimantan where anti-Kaharingan discrimination is a prominent issue.

3 Separation or Integration? A Clash of Perspectives

Central Kalimantan is home to groups that hold opposing views on whether followers of Kaharingan should emphasize the distinctiveness of their religion or seek closer ties with Hinduism. I gathered perspectives and opinions from activists on both sides of the debate through interviews and observation. Given the sensitive nature of the issues involved, some informants asked to remain anonymous.

3.1 *Opposition to Hindu Hegemony*

As a minority group, followers of Kaharingan have long suffered discrimination at the hands of the government. As noted above, the Soeharto regime's emphasis on unity and uniformity continues to shape official attitudes toward religion.[6] In 1980, national authorities decreed that Kaharingan and Hinduism would be treated as a single religion – Hindu-Kaharingan – for administrative purposes. Beyond a desire to streamline religious categories, this measure reflected the widespread influence of Hindu practices and beliefs among followers of Kaharingan. This was especially true for economically and socially marginalized rural populations – including the Dayak. Nevertheless, some members of the Dayak community saw the association with Hinduism as a short-term means of preserving their religious traditions. Indeed, they believed the measure was only meant to be temporary.[7] Meanwhile, a mere nine days after the integration with Hinduism was announced, some followers of Kaharingan sought government recognition of their belief system as a separate religion. Not surprisingly, the authorities refused to expand the list of officially recognized faiths.

Dayak demands for increased autonomy began to emerge in 1987, although a lack of political consensus prevented the movement from gaining momentum.[8] The fall of the Soeharto regime in 1999, coupled with the rise of the international

6 Interview with Suel, Palangkaraya City, September 24, 2020.

7 Ibid.

8 Interview with Christiana Bangkang, Palangkaraya City, September 28, 2020.

Indigenous rights movement, provided a fresh opportunity to push for decentralization and local self-governance. In 2000, an independence-minded group called the Indonesian Kaharingan Religious Council (MAKI) was established in Palangkaraya, Central Kalimantan. Avoiding any references to Hindu-Kaharingan, its leaders insisted on Kaharingan's status as a separate religion (Banjarmasin Post 2010). Emphasizing theological differences with Hinduism, they argued that those who sought to unify the two belief systems were motivated by political and economic interests. The Ministry of Religious Affairs responded that distinguishing between Hinduism and Kaharingan could pose a threat to security and social stability, especially in Central Kalimantan. One official at the Directorate of Hindu Religious Affairs went so far as to argue that, as a universal religion, Hinduism could not be divided along ethnic or racial lines – meaning that the Hindu-Kaharingan religion should be considered Hinduism, full stop (Kompas 2006). At the time, proponents of integration also occupied strategic positions in the provincial administration as well as at state institutions under the direct authority of the Ministry of Religious Affairs.[9] For instance, the State Hindu Institute in Palangkaraya City had stopped using the word "Kaharinga" altogether. And according to some anonymous research participants, students from the institute regularly visited rural areas to teach at elementary schools, where they gave instruction on Hinduism without any reference to Kaharingan as an Indigenous spiritual tradition. In the eyes of some, this reflected an effort by the Directorate of Hindu Religious Affairs to gradually eradicate Kaharingan practices and beliefs, while spreading mainstream Hinduism to rural areas.[10]

3.2 *Hindu-Kaharingan Integration: Maintaining Social Order and Cultural Integrity*

I also interviewed proponents of Hindu-Kaharingan integration to gain a clearer idea of the issues at play. They emphasized the need to honor the commitment made in 1980 and the fact that integration had been broadly supported by followers of Kaharingan – including those who later came to oppose it. From this perspective, efforts to have Kaharingan recognized as a separate religion were a political tactic used by supporters of the Indigenous rights movement and enjoyed no grassroots support.[11]

The informants concerned were also keen to place integration in a broader historical context. For instance, they argued that when the Union of Kaharingan

9 Ibid.

10 Interview with anonymous informants, Palangkaraya City, September 29, 2020.

11 Interview with Sisto Hartati, Palangkaraya City, October 23, 2020.

Dayaks of Indonesia (SKDI) was established in 1950, the Kaharingan religion was considered inseparable from the Dayak people.[12] Then, in 1969, when the Soeharto regime's approach to religious affairs threatened to undermine the civil rights of followers of Indigenous religions (by leaving the "Religion" section blank on their KPTs), the Council of Indonesian Kaharingan Pious Scholars (MBAUKI) discussed the best means of securing respect and recognition. One approach involved ensuring that Kaharingan met the criteria used to identify modern religions. Accordingly, religious leaders set about compiling the Panaturan as a holy scripture.[13] Then, in 1980, followers of Kaharingan were required to associate themselves with one of the country's officially recognized religions. They chose Hinduism because, compared to Islam or Christianity, it seemed more compatible with Kaharingan's animistic-ancestral traditions. Furthermore, proponents argued that, far from promoting the eradication of Kaharingan practices and beliefs, integration helped ensure their survival[14] by fostering their modernization. Specifically, they cited the benefits of having Hindu-Kaharingan books distributed in rural areas, as well as the contributions of the many religion teachers and theology lecturers trained at the Hindu-Kaharingan Institute after its founding in 1983.[15]

Research participants who supported integration also stressed the highly pluralistic nature of Kaharingan. For instance, across the thirteen districts of Central Kalimantan, each tribal chief tends to interpret the associated traditions differently; whereas some believe they constitute a religion, others prefer to describe them as a set of Indigenous practices and beliefs. Likewise, the Dayak are split into multiple sub-tribes across a number of river valleys. And although the Panaturan and the authority of tribal chiefs (*damang* and *mantir*) are recognized in Ngaju areas, including Palangkaraya City,[16] this is not the case for all segments of the Dayak population. As a result, when Dayak-Ngaju leaders have risen to power in certain districts, Kaharingan institutions have become highly politicized.[17] Indeed, such leaders – including the charismatic former governor of Central Kalimantan, Tjilik Riwut, and large numbers of local bureaucrats – have been at the forefront of efforts not only to promote recognition of Kaharingan as a separate religion but to impose a Dayak-Ngaju identity throughout the region. According to a research participant named Nali Eka, this highlights the political nature of the movement for recognition of

12 Interview with Walter S. Peyang, Palangkaraya City, October 23, 2020.

13 Ibid.

14 Interview with Pranata, Palangkaraya City, October 23, 2020.

15 Interview with Walter S. Peyang, Palangkaraya City, October 23, 2020.

16 Interview with Nali Eka, Palangkaraya City, September 20, 2020.

17 Interview with Sisto Hartati, Palangkaraya City, October 23, 2020.

Kaharingan as a separate religion.[18] Another informant responded to the accusation that proponents of integration are pursuing a process of Hinduization in rural areas of Central Kalimantan by asserting that opponents of integration are pursuing their own process of Ngajunization.[19]

Informants who supported integration were also keen on addressing what they saw as three widespread misconceptions. To begin with, they rejected the idea that the Council of Hindu-Kaharingan was failing to respect religious freedom as enshrined in the Indonesian constitution. They explained that, notwithstanding certain administrative implications for the recording of demographic and religious information, people who no longer wish to be associated with Hinduism are entirely free to identify solely as followers of Kaharingan.[20] Second, these research participants dismissed allegations that the State Hindu Institute exclusively uses Hindu materials, claiming that 40% of the curriculum covers Kaharingan traditions (with 70% focused on Hinduism). Not only is the Sangiang Indigenous language taught alongside Sanskrit, but students learn about Dayak traditions and ceremonies such as the Panaturan, *tandak*, *balian*, and *lawang sekepeng*.[21] Finally, this group of informants insisted that the institute's reluctance to use the word "Kaharingan" reflects the administrative preferences of the Ministry of Religious Affairs, which considers Hinduism (but not Kaharingan) to be an official religion. However, in practice, students are allowed to worship in *Balai Kaharingan*, along with other shrines.[22]

Of particular interest is the concern expressed by proponents of integration regarding the Constitutional Court's decision on KTPs. They feared it would be used by their political opponents to foment civil unrest and potentially undermine the recognition of Hindu-Kaharingan as an official religion. Without Hinduism, they argued, Kaharingan would no longer constitute a religion but merely a belief.[23] Furthermore, these research participants argued that although the court's decision required the government to ensure respect for the rights of all citizens, especially followers of Indigenous belief systems, it in no way created an obligation to recognize such belief systems as official religions. Accordingly, they contended that the only ministry that should be involved in implementing the decision is the Ministry of Home Affairs, and that the Ministry of Religious Affairs is in no way concerned.[24] Unlike their

18 Interview with Nali Eka, Palangkaraya City, September 20, 2020.

19 Ibid.

20 Ibid.

21 Ibid.

22 Ibid.

23 Interview with Pranata, Palangkaraya City, October 23, 2020.

24 Ibid.

political opponents, who favor recognition of Kaharingan as a separate religion, these informants portrayed the integration policy adopted in 1980 as reasonable and pragmatic, while accepting the need for the current government to make certain administrative adjustments to promote the rights of marginalized groups. However, they were much less comfortable with the connection between demands for religious freedom and the larger movement for local autonomy based on Indigenous identity.

4 Local Identity Politics

Both sides of the debate on the status of Kaharingan have been accused of injecting political issues of identity into debates on religious affairs. One opponent of integration argued that the government's role in officially recognizing only certain religions naturally made the fight for religious freedom into a political struggle. However, she claimed that her side was merely seeking justice, not aiming to overthrow the political status quo.[25] In any case, followers of Kaharingan have been closely aligned with the Indigenous rights movement in Indonesia, and especially in Central Kalimantan. In the early years of the reform era, decentralization gave provincial and district authorities extensive power to govern their own affairs. Until recently, this drove a strong trend toward the formalization of Indigenous institutions and traditions, in the context of which many unofficial leaders, such as tribal chiefs and shamans, were also appointed to positions in local state institutions. The fact that these appointments were made by local officials, rather than according to community or traditional procedures (*musyawarah*), made them highly politicized.[26] They also provide an example of state law pluralism (a weak form of legal pluralism), insofar as the appointments provided state authorities with an opportunity to appropriate aspects of local or Indigenous non-state legal traditions, with a view to promoting the legitimacy of official institutions.

Between July 20 and 24, 2019, Indigenous groups supporting the recognition of Kaharingan as a separate religion gathered to commemorate the 1894 Tumbang Anoi Agreement, which had ended tribal warfare and headhunting among the Dayak. Those present claimed that supporters of integration did not show up, despite being invited;[27] supporters of integration dispute this,

25 Interview with Christiana Bangkang, Palangkaraya City, September 29, 2020.
26 Interview with Nali Eka, Palangkaraya City, September 20, 2020.
27 Interview with Christiana Bangkang, Palangkaraya City, September 29, 2020.

claiming they were never invited.[28] Regardless, participants capitalized on the opportunity to consolidate their political position by issuing a set of three declarations. First, they expressed support for the Indonesian government's plan to move the national capital to Kalimantan. Second, they called for an affirmative action policy in favor of the Dayak, especially in the education sector. Third, they demanded that a restitution process be implemented with a view to restoring Dayak control over Indigenous lands.[29] Then, on August 29, the SKDI helped organize a Dayak delegation to Jakarta with the aim of presenting three main demands: that the president appoint a Dayak to head a government ministry; that he formally recognize Kaharingan as a separate religion; and that the government fulfill its pledge to move the capital to Kalimantan by 2024. Although the delegation failed to secure a meeting with President Joko Widodo (Jokowi),[30] supporters of Dayak autonomy see themselves as politically aligned with the ruling Partai Demokrasi Indonesia Perjuangan (PDI-P), a nationalist party that received strong support among the Dayak in the 2019 presidential election. Indeed, Jokowi performed impressively in Central Kalimantan and West Kalimantan, two provinces seen as Dayak strongholds. And as one informant explained, the delegation was intended to lay the groundwork for the 2020 local election in Central Kalimantan by letting it be known that Indigenous electors would only support Indigenous leaders and would refrain from voting for non-Indigenous candidates.[31] Claiming the president's support, the MAKI and its Indigenous allies announced a Dayak Consolidation Meeting for October 5, 2019. However, the event was canceled due to opposition from supporters of Hindu-Kaharingan integration, who claimed such a meeting would cause civil unrest by deepening divisions within the Dayak population, especially in Central Kalimantan.[32] Nevertheless, the organizers claimed to enjoy the support of virtually all regional and district heads in the province.[33]

Meanwhile, given the tactics adopted by their Ngaju and Christian Dayak political opponents in earlier years, proponents of integration reacted defensively to these developments. For instance, under Christian governors Reinout Sylvanus and Teras Narang, the government of Central Kalimantan Province had introduced policies that discriminated against those who identified as Hindu-Kaharingan. Moreover, the governor interfered in the conduct of the 2010 population census by allowing followers of Kaharingan to be counted separately

28 Interview with Walter S. Peyang, Palangkaraya City, October 23, 2020.
29 Interview with Christiana Bangkang, Palangkaraya City, September 29, 2020.
30 Ibid.
31 Ibid.
32 Interview with anonymous informants, Palangkaraya City, September 30, 2020.
33 Interview with Christiana Bangkang, Palangkaraya City, September 29, 2020.

from followers of Hinduism, under "Other Believers." In response, the Council of Hindu-Kaharingan demanded that the census results be revised.[34] Political debates surrounding religious affairs have been further stoked by the activities of a charismatic Christian movement based in Palangkaraya City. According to a Christian Dayak research participant, this group portrays beliefs and practices associated with Hindu-Kaharingan as misguided expressions of paganism that can only be corrected through alignment with Christianity.[35] Despite an ongoing reconciliation process, it will no doubt take decades to resolve tensions between the two main factions, especially if local and national governments fail to implement the decision of the Constitutional Court in a fair manner that respects the rights of the various groups involved.

5 Legal Centralism in Religious Affairs

From the perspective of legal centralism, the laws adopted by the national government take precedence over other forms of regulation, such as informal law and rules established by non-state entities. It is a paradigm rooted in the Cartesian's school of philosophy, which emphasizes self-sufficiency, independence, and neutral science (Villa 1997). Efforts to secure the recognition of Kaharingan as a separate religion testify to the power of this viewpoint, insofar as followers of the belief system feel bound by the state's management of religious affairs. The state's reliance on rules and procedures to assert its legitimacy and sovereignty is often described in terms of instrumentalism. Accordingly, Austin (1954) held that the state is sovereign because its rules are created by political authorities and enforced by sanctions. Once again, this perspective places the state as the center of legal and political analysis by emphasizing its power to incorporate non-state entities into "the cycle of the State" (Barkin & Cronin 1994).

In short, proponents of legal centralism argue that rules create sovereignty, not the other way around. However, they disagree somewhat on what is meant by "rules," which are not necessarily limited to "rules stipulated by the State" (Hart 1994: 119–132). For instance, Hart identified two different categories of rules. On the one hand, primary rules are normative rules of conduct governed by a sense of moral obligation. Such sociologically defined rules can include customary or traditional laws and religious values that shape the development of both individuals and entire societies (e.g., the Marxist concept of religion as

34 Interview with Sisto Hartati, Palangkaraya City, October 23, 2020.

35 Interview with Alfianus Rinting, October 3, 2020.

"ideology"). On the other hand, secondary rules relate to the state's official recognition of certain primary rules in the context of its formal legal system. Hart (1958) described the state's endorsement of primary rules in terms of "rules of recognition," which serve to resolve the ambiguity surrounding primary rules, a drawback that makes the latter unsuitable for the exercise of sovereignty. For instance, each religion or belief system can have distinct – and sometimes contradictory – interpretations of how society should operate. Granted, such normative uncertainty does not pose a major problem for societies characterized by mechanical solidarity supported by ethnic homogeneity, a simple division of labor, and strong bonds of kinship (Hart 1958). Indeed, traditional Indigenous societies have been able to thrive under such rules. However, heterogeneous societies and ones where individualism prevails require a more explicit legal system based on secondary rules. In such contexts, the state treats primary rules as crude ingredients of law, which are then refined according to the neutral application of the rule of recognition and rational parameters.

I would argue for adopting a different outlook that recognizes the limits to this understanding of state neutrality and rationality. Of course, in many ways, social stability depends on the active involvement of the state, especially through its interactions with the public sphere, which help preserve the integrity of the private sphere. However, the public interest may not justify state neutrality in certain matters where equality and justice are at stake. From an ideological perspective, neutrality becomes inherently political insofar as the neutral state always takes the side of the status quo in the political sphere. As a result, rather than seeking to actively undo problematic realities (e.g., unjust and discriminatory practices), the state consistently opts for pragmatism. Moreover, I would contend that the perception of the rule of recognition as the basis of state sovereignty is ahistorical in cases where it is used as an instrument of power. In such situations, it becomes co-opted and loses its historical and sociological significance. This is the point of view from which I will discuss the human rights issues associated with the status of Kaharingan in Central Kalimantan.

6 Human Rights: The State's Responsibilities in Religious Affairs

Where human rights are concerned, the state should eschew neutrality in favor of protecting citizens in general and marginalized or minority groups in particular. I would argue that the idea of a system of state law that accommodates rights is both historically and sociologically valid, insofar as the law acknowledges social realities, beyond merely providing for the implementation of general provisions through legislation. From this perspective, state law has an emancipatory potential that can be realized through the application of universal human rights instruments in a way that recognizes local diversity.

Soon after Soeharto's regime was overthrown at the end of the 1990s, the post-authoritarian government of Indonesia quickly ratified several international human rights covenants and conventions. However, implementation has proven more of a challenge amid deeply rooted beliefs regarding the relative legitimacy of different cultural traditions, especially where sensitive topics like religious freedom are concerned.

For example, Indonesia has ratified the International Covenant on Civil and Political Rights (ICCPR), which guarantees freedom of religion and belief (art. 18, par. 1):

> Everyone shall have the right to freedom of thought, conscience and religion. This right shall include freedom to have or to adopt a religion or belief of his choice, and freedom, either individually or in community with others and in public or private, to manifest his religion or belief in worship, observance, practice and teaching.

Meanwhile, Article 27 of the ICCPR makes the following stipulation regarding minority rights:

> In those States in which ethnic, religious or linguistic minorities exist, persons belonging to such minorities shall not be denied the right, in community with the other members of their group, to enjoy their own culture, to profess and practice their own religion, or to use their own language.

These international norms are well aligned with those enshrined in the 1945 Indonesian constitution – especially in Article 28E (1) and (2), as well as Article and 28I (1) – which guarantees the freedom to choose a religion and to express one's faith, point of view, and ideas:

> Every person shall be free to choose and to practice the religion of his/her choice [...]
>
> Every person shall have the right to the freedom to believe his/her faith, and to express his/her views and thoughts, in accordance with his/her conscience.

Moreover, the constitution deems this right to be inalienable: "[...] freedom of thought and conscience, freedom of religion [...] are all human rights that cannot be limited under any circumstances."

Generally speaking, under the country's constitution and founding principles (Pancasila), the relationship between the state and religion is accommodative, meaning the government ensures that any privileges granted to the majority religion (Islam) are also granted to the four other so-called official religions. Nevertheless, religious affairs remain highly politicized, leading some to describe Indonesia as a theistic-secular democratic state (Khanif 2015). I contend that upholding the right to believe in a religion or faith in accordance with one's conscience is more than a matter of establishing Indonesia as "the Godly state" (McGovern 2007) by officially recognizing certain religions. In particular, such recognition should not be implemented in a way that discriminates against religious minorities. Instead, the government should also take fair and unbiased measures to protect believers regardless of their religious traditions, ethnicity, and social status. With a view to realizing the emancipatory potential of state law, such measures would make it possible to abandon an instrumentalist approach to religious affairs in favour of one based on three fundamental principles of human rights.

The first of these principles would be that of the inherent dignity of humans, as enshrined in the Universal Declaration of Human Rights (UDHR). It serves as the foundation of freedom, justice, and peace in the world, while also providing a moral justification for the state's efforts to recognize and protect the equal and inalienable rights of all human beings. In terms of religious freedom, this means that followers of Indigenous or minority religions have an equal and inalienable right to practice their beliefs even in the absence of official recognition. Accordingly, the state is obliged to recognize and protect the religious freedom of all citizens in accordance with their personal conscience, free of coercion or intimidation.

Second, religious freedom also needs to be based on the principle of equality. Treating all individuals and groups fairly means not only maintaining a level playing field for those who enjoy favorable conditions but also providing targeted support to those facing marginalization (Minow 2021). To begin with, this would involve recognizing that all believers are equally entitled to follow their chosen religion, regardless of whether the latter enjoys formal recognition from the state. However, the very notion of official religions implies that non-official beliefs – whose status often reflects a lack of institutional power compare to their official counterparts – enjoy a lesser legal status, potentially leading to unequal treatment. In this regard, attempts to distinguish between the concepts of religion and belief pose a serious threat to religious equality and, by extension, to religious freedom. ICCPR General Comment No. 22 on Freedom of Thought, Conscience and Religion (Article 18) directly addresses the issue by broadly interpreting belief to encompass not only monistic and non-monistic traditions, but also atheism: "The right to religion which includes the freedom to hold beliefs is far-reaching and profound; it encompasses freedom of thought on all matters […] The terms 'belief' and 'religion' are to be broadly construed." Ultimately, the right to culture – which encompasses all forms of human expression, including language, philosophy, religion, and ideology – depends on rejecting the dichotomy between religion and belief. Human societies must be allowed to thrive in accordance with their authentic moral guidelines, which include those expressions of the sacred through which religion becomes internalized (Berger 1990).

Finally, religious freedom depends on the principle of non-discrimination, which applies to situations where similar cases are treated differently, or distinct cases are treated similarly (Minow 2021). Followers of minority religions often face direct or indirect discrimination at the hands of followers of majority and/or official religions. Accordingly, ICCPR General Comment No. 23 on the Rights of Minorities (Article 27) insists on the need to provide religious minorities with legal protections:

> In those States in which ethnic, religious or linguistic minorities exist, persons belonging to such minorities shall not be denied the right, in community with the other members of their group, to enjoy their own culture, to profess and practice their own religion, or to use their own language.

7 Conclusion

Although Indonesia has ratified several international human rights covenants and conventions since 2005, the country continues to face issues related to their implementation – especially where religious freedom is concerned. To begin with, rather than promoting the free exercise of religious rights, the post-Soeharto policy of decentralization has tended to engender new forms of discrimination against marginalized groups. Second, the decision of the Indonesian Constitutional Court regarding the identification of religious affiliation on KTPs constitutes a major step in the right direction. However, the decision needs to be interpreted and implemented by legislative and administrative authorities, especially the ministries of Home Affairs and Religious Affairs, in a manner that reflects the government's duty to develop policies and procedures that are fair to all religious groups, including followers of Indigenous belief systems. Finally, among followers of Kaharingan, clashes between proponents of integration with Hinduism and supporters of recognition as a separate religion reflect the state's mismanagement of religious affairs and its failure to accommodate the needs of Indigenous groups. Accordingly, the government needs to interpret and implement the Constitutional Court's decision in a way that not only respects but also promotes the religious rights of those on both sides of the debate. Meanwhile, all levels of government need to address the underlying tensions without resorting to litigation and with a view to preserving the social bond that unites the Dayak people.

Acknowledgment

This study was funded by the Center for Religious and Cross-Cultural Studies (CRCS), Universitas Gadjah Mada, in 2019–2020.

References

Alm, James, Robert Aten, and Roy Bahl. "Can Indonesia decentralize successfully? plans, problems and prospects." *Bulletin of Indonesian Economic Studies* 37, no. 1 (2001): 83–102.

Austin, John. *The province of jurisprudence determined.* London: Weidenfeld and Nicolson, 1954.

Banakar, Reza, and Max Travers. *Introduction to theory and method in socio-legal research.* Oxford: Hart Publishing, 2005.

Barkin, John Samuel, and Bruce Cronin. "The state and the nation: Changing norms and the rules of sovereign in international relations." *International Organization* 48, no. 1 (1994): 107–130.

Berger, Peter Ludwig. *The sacred canopy: Elements of a sociological theory of religions.* New-York: Open Road Media, 1990.

Coe, George Albert. "Religion as a factor in individual and social development." *The Biblical Word* 23, no. 1 (1904): 37–47.

Hart, Herbert Lionel Adolphus. "Positivism and the separation of law and morals." *Harvard Law Review* 71, no. 4 (1958): 529–593.

Hart, Herbert Lionel Adolphus. *The concept of law.* Oxford: Clarendon Press, 1994.

"Kaharingan Desak Jadi Agama." *Banjarmasin Post*, June 2, 2010.

Khanif, Al. "Questioning a theistic-secular Pancasila to protect religions." *Jakarta Post*, June 1, 2015. https://www.thejakartapost.com/news/2015/06/01/questioning-a-theistic-secular-pancasila-protect-religions.html.

McGovern, John. "Fundamentalism: The Godly State." In *Modern State*, edited by John McGovern, 1–18. Edinburgh: Edinburgh University Press, 2007.

Minow, Martha. "Equality vs Equity." *American Journal of Law and Equality*, no. 1 (2021): 167–193.

Moore, Sally Falk. "Law and society change: the semi-autonomous social field as an appropriate subject to study." *Law & Society Review* 7, no. 4 (1973): 719–746.

Schiller, Anne. "An 'old' religion in 'New Order' Indonesia: notes on ethnicity and religious affiliation." *Sociology of Religion* 57, no. 4 (1996): 409–417.

Villa, Vittorio. "A definition of legal positivism." In *Legal Systems and Legal Science, ARSP*, edited by Marijan Pavcnik and Gianfrancesco Zanetti, 23–35. Berlin: IVR, 1997.

Weber, Max. *The Protestant Ethic and the Spirit of Capitalism.* Oxford: Routledge, 1930.

From Marginalization to Self-Determination: The Long Walk of First Nations' Religious Rights in Bolivia

Raphaël Mathieu Legault-Laberge

> La autodeterminación, expresada en la lucha histórica de los pueblos indígenas por la liberación de toda forma de dominación, implica el respeto a las diversas formas de autogobierno de las naciones y pueblos indígena originario campesinos. [...] desde la concepción indígena existe una conexión entre el cosmos y la humanidad ...[1]

At the beginning of the 2000s-decade, Bolivia's population was composed of about 30% of *mestizaje*; Quechua and Aymara were 28% and 19% of the total, respectively, with the remainder consisting mainly of Europeans (12%) and other ethnic communities (11%) (Library of Congress – Federal Research Division 2006: 9). Spanish was the most widely spoken language, with Quechua and Aymara dialects. Catholicism was the predominant religion, with 95% of the population identifying as Roman Catholic (Library of Congress – Federal Research Division 2006: 10). According to the 2012 census, these data were almost identical, with a slight increase in the number of people identifying as Aymara (25% in 2012). However, Catholicism has lost much of its base, as 82% of the population identified as Roman Catholic at that time. In 2012, only 0.1% of the Bolivian population claimed to belong to a First Nation religion or spirituality.[2] These data do not do justice to the place and the role of the

1 *Patricia Mancilla Martínez c. Asamblea Legislativa Plurinacional*, Tribunal Constitucional Plurinacional, Sala Plena, 0206/2014, Sucre, 5 de febrero de 2014, expediente 00320-2012-01-AIA (Acción de inconstitucionalidad abstracta).

2 "Population 10,027,254 (2012 Census); Ethnic makeup: Quechua – 30 percent, Mestizo – 30 percent, Aymara – 25 percent, White – 15 percent; Language: Spanish (official), Quechua (official), Aymara (official); Religion: Roman Catholic – 81.8 percent, Protestant – 12.9 percent, Historic/Mainline Protestant – 2.6 percent, Pentecostal/Evangelical – 10.3 percent, Jehovah's Witnesses and Latter-Day Saints – 1.7 percent, Other (Jewish, Muslim, Eastern

 | DOI:10.1163/9789004524330_016

Pachamama in Bolivia,[3] nor do they give a proper idea of the nature of the syncretic manifestations of religiosity that can be observed in the country – which are the fruit of the hybridization of European and South American traditions – such as the *Diablada*[4] or the Virgin of Copacabana.[5]

Belonging to a First Nation in Bolivia is based on a social division that implies, on the one hand, a postcolonial culture that mostly denies manifestations of Indigenous identities, such as religious or spiritual expressions and their political recognition, and, on the other hand, a search for legitimacy and authenticity within a culture that has been denied its own roots and reduced to slavery.[6] Paradoxically, this search can turn into a politico-religious instrumentalization by Natives seeking political privileges (Healey 2009; Lucero 2006). The situation of the First Nations in Bolivia is very specific, since the colonial context has resulted in the majority of the population belonging to a First Nation or being *mestizaje*.[7] Despite this fact, since the arrival of the

religions) – 0.4 percent, Native religions – 0.1 percent, None/None specified – 3.3 percent" (Morales Cruz 2014: 133).

3 "In the indigenous cultures of the Andes, the Pachamama represents Mother Earth, concerned with plenty, fertility, crops, and generosity. She symbolizes the human environment in all its aspects and in recent decades ecological concerns have brought her greater attention. Under Evo Morales's government, the state has recognized the importance of the Pachamama and has accorded the environment equal rights under the law" (Morales Cruz 2014: 149).

4 "During Carnival festivities in Oruro, *La Diablada* (Dance of the Devils) combines Christian and indigenous traditions dating to pre-Colombian times. On the one hand, it is connected to dances in honor of the Uru god Tiw, protector of mines, rivers, and lakes, as well as to the Aymara rituals to Anchanchu, a demon spirit inhabiting caves. On the other hand, the elaborate devil costumes worn are reminiscent of medieval Spanish plays depicting the battle of Saint Michael the Archangel against Lucifer and his demons. Today, the dance continues to be held in honor of the Virgin of Socavón, patron saint of miners" (Morales Cruz 2014: 147). This dance, which honours the patron saint of the cave workers, underlines the importance of the mining industry in Bolivia's economy.

5 "Our Lady of Copacabana, a sixteenth-century four-foot image of the Virgin Mary made by sculptor Francisco Tito Yupanqui, is the patron saint of Bolivia. Carved with indigenous features and dressed in garments reminiscent of an Inca princess, she is housed in the Basilica of Copacabana on the shores of Lake Titicaca, an area sacred to the Aymara and Quechua who have lived there for ages. She was crowned queen of Bolivia in 1925" (Morales Cruz 2014: 149). Other similar syncretic representations were developed elsewhere in Latin America, see for example Our Lady of Guadalupe in Mexico.

6 The comparison with Canadian First Nations may be interesting in this respect. See Simard 2003.

7 "Indigenous peoples constitute a slight majority of Bolivia's total population. The Aymara and Quechua are the principal indigenous peoples in the highlands. The Bolivian lowlands are home to over 30 ethnic groups, including the Guarani, Chiquitano and Moxeño peoples" (Rice 2014: 59).

Europeans, Bolivia's Fist Nations have been constantly marginalized, as they have been placed in a state of apartheid-like domination. Prior to the election of Evo Morales in 2006, their demographic dominance was never met with satisfactory political recognition (Kohl 2010; Postero 2010).

As the first Indigenous president ever elected in Bolivia, Morales took steps very soon after taking office to improve the political and religious recognition of the country's First Nations. This event represents a historical milestone for the Indigenous population, and especially for the Aymara, since Morales belongs to this First Nation. This chapter seeks to address this context by asking the following questions: how can the recognition of Indigenous religious rights in Bolivia be conceived and understood, before and after the election of Evo Morales? What did this historical change mean for Bolivia's Indigenous population at the political and religious levels? What did it mean? The hypothesis underlying this study is that only after 2006 did Bolivia's First Nations move from a position of marginalization to one of self-determination. The recognition of their religious rights followed the same curve, as they were subjected to colonial and foreign religious (Christian) powers for centuries and were recognized only under the government of Evo Morales.

Under the Morales government, Bolivia has moved from a political model based on assimilation – which has always marginalized the country's First Nations –, to one based on pluralism and recognition of social diversity (Van Cott 2000). This was a major paradigm shift that had a direct impact on the Indigenous population. This dynamic also brought greater recognition of their religious and/or spiritual rights. In fact, these rights were part of the strategy of constructing Indigenous self-determination in Bolivia, on a legal and formal level, but also as a public and more informal element of identity affirmation. In other words, the state's recognition of Indigenous religious rights in Bolivia became part of the *ethos* of a marginalized, but majority population that succeeded in regaining its place, a place that had undoubtedly been diminished by the power of a minority in an apartheid-like context.

Moreover, the concept of self-determination may be the central aspect of all Indigenous' claims: "[…] la affirmación del derecho de autodeterminación solidaria de los pueblos es el corazón del movimiento indigena" (Girardi 1996: 35). Girardi adds:

> Reivindicando este derecho, los pueblos pretenden rescatar su identidad y affirmarse como sujetos, fente a una organización de la sociedad y del mundo, que ellos caracterizan como colonialista, orientada a expropiarlos de su mismo ser.

> La importancia vital de este derecho resulta más evidente, en la medida en que se explicitan sus múltiples aspectos e implicaciones, en el campo político, económico, ecológico, cultural, educativo, religioso, etc. (Girardi 1996: 35–36)

Demands for the recognition of Indigenous religious rights are closely linked to this principle of self-determination. They confront colonial realities that foster marginalization, which is still the fate of many Indigenous peoples around the world. In post-colonial contexts, understanding this dialectic between marginalization and self-determination seems to be central to grasping the various dynamics raised by First Nations claims.

This chapter begins with a historical chronology of Indigenous marginalization in Bolivia. The historical context that will be considered goes back to the time of colonization by the Spanish authorities until the election of Evo Morales. Then, some cases of expression of informal Indigenous religious or spiritual manifestations will be presented, all of which were part of the political (ontological?) strategy of Morales. Then, the formal recognition of Indigenous religious rights under the Morales government is presented in more detail. The chapter concludes with some remarks on the political instrumentalization of religiosity as a means of legitimizing Indigenous claims.

1 Historical Background

Before colonization, historians believe that the Inca kingdom took over the current Bolivian territory around 1450.[8] The Indigenous religions and spiritualities were the only ones that could be found in this geographical area at that time.

1.1 *From Colonization to 1970*

Between 1530 and 1540, when Spain defeated the Inca Empire and imposed its rule, Christianity was imported from Europe and implanted in South America. Between 1534 and 1536, Dominican and Franciscan friars contributed

8 "Advanced Indian societies inhabited the Andes region of South America long before the arrival of Europeans. Ruins of these societies, especially the Tiwanaku civilization, dot the high-altitude Bolivian countryside, serving as reminders of the first great Andean empire. Tiwanakan dominance lasted until 1200, when the regional kingdoms of the Aymara subsequently emerged as the most powerful of the ethnic groups living in the densely populated region surrounding Lake Titicaca. Power struggles continued until 1450, when the Incas incorporated upper Bolivia into their growing empire" (Library of Congress – Federal Research Division 2006: 1).

to European missions in the territory of present-day Bolivia, imposing foreign religions on the Indigenous population, which had millennial traditions.[9] Immediately after colonization, Bolivia was incorporated into the diocese of Cusco (Peru). In 1570, an inquisition was initiated in Cusco and extended to Bolivian territory, with disastrous consequences for the Indigenous religious and spiritual traditions. Christianity was a tool of the colonizers, and other forms of religiosity or spirituality were not tolerated. The marginalization of Indigenous religiosity and spirituality in South America was effective immediately after the Spanish colonization and it was operationalized through an alliance between religion and politics that served the will and desires of the invader who ruled over the traditions of the local population.

However, the marginalization of Indigenous peoples affects a number of areas that go far beyond religion and spirituality. The assimilation of the Indigenous population was the goal of the Spanish conquistadors' policy, using all possible means, especially the economic system.[10] In 1572, a regime of slavery, the *mita* system,[11] was established,[12] which forced every Indigenous man to work in the silver mines.[13] In response to this state of marginalization, the local populations found ways to maintain their cultural and religious vitality, especially by incorporating some Indigenous features into Christian religiosity. In 1576, Francisco Tito Yupanqui carved the Virgin of Copacabana, giving to the Bolivian culture one of its first manifestations of syncretic religiosity. From

9 Coca, for example, has been in use since the third millennium BC. The plant was an element of the traditional medicine of South American Indigenous populations (for more information on these traditional medicines, see Bouso and Sánchez-Avilés 2020), as was peyote, a traditional medicine of Central American Indigenous populations (Anderson 1980; Steward 1987). According to the cosmological and ontological vision of Indigenous people, which assumed a complete unity between humans and nature, these plants were part of a social tradition, but they also possessed strong spiritual virtues. We will see later what role coca played in the self-determination of Bolivia's Indigenous people.

10 Capitalism, which had just appeared in Europe around in the 16th and 17th centuries, also found its way to Latin America, and the process of colonization was closely linked to the imposition of this economic system on a global scale, both in Europe and elsewhere in the world. The mining industry was predominant in the development of capitalism in both Europe and Latin America.

11 A similar system existed at the time of the Inca Empire. It could be said that, in the same way, the Spaniards tried to indigenize colonialism, see Murra 1982.

12 "In the 1570s, Viceroy Francisco de Toledo introduced a coercive form of labor, the *mita*, which required Indian males from highland districts to spend every sixth year working in the mines. The *mita*, along with technological advances in refining, caused mining at Potosí to flourish" (Library of Congress – Federal Research Division 2006: 2).

13 "The *mita* [...] [was] a compulsory labor system that forces able-bodied male Indians to work the silver mines of Potosí for months at a time" (Morales Cruz 2014: 134).

a historical point of view, this almost simultaneous appearance of the mita and the creation of the Virgin of Copacabana is an important fact: it shows the vitality of Indigenous religiosity and spirituality, which, with a surprising impulse, finds a way of expression that overturns the assimilationist worldview imposed by Spain. It also affirms the merging of two cultural systems into one. By the decade of the 1570s, Bolivia's First Nations undoubtedly knew that the colonial process and asymmetrical power dynamics were irreversible. By then, they also knew that the path of syncretism and mixed cultures was also inevitable.[14] The cultural mix led to original expressions of religiosity and spirituality, and allowed the emergence of the notion of *mestizaje* and its corollary, *mestizo*.[15]

The Bolivian territory was not independent from the diocese of Cusco until 1776, when a royal court was established in La Plata. A few years later, in 1781, the Spanish army defeated the uprising led by Tupac Katari, an Aymara who was fighting against the colonial authorities (Strobele-Gregor, Hoffman and Holmes 1994: 108).[16] The struggle was against Spanish rule, but probably also for emancipation from Peruvian control. Bolivian independence was finally achieved in 1825: "[l]ed by 'El Libertador,' Simón Bolívar Palacios, Bolivia gained complete independence from Spanish and Peruvian control" (Library of Congress – Federal Research Division 2006: 1).[17] The political system that was then adopted in Bolivia was an identical copy of the European one, and it was completely under the rules of the colonizers. However, one of the first political measures taken by Bolivar was the abolition of the mita. In January of the following year, presidential powers were transferred to Antonio José de

14 This situation led to religious syncretism, but also to the hybridization of legal systems: "[…] the centuries-long, asymmetric interplay between these orders resulted in modifications and a hybridization of indigenous law, thereby revealing the non-statist and adaptive nature of indigenous legal practices" (Barrera 2011: 6).

15 See Strobele-Gregor, Hoffman and Holmes 1994. These authors emphasize that the notions of *Indio* and *Mestizo* are social constructs.

16 This rebellion took place at the same time as the one led by Tupac Amaru II: "In 1780 the Inca descendant, Túpac Amaru II, led nearly 60,000 Indians against the Spaniards near the Peruvian city of Cuzco. Spain put down the revolt in 1783 and executed thousands of Indians as punishment, but the revolt illustrated the precarious nature of Spanish colonial rule in the Andes" (Library of Congress – Federal Research Division 2006: 2).

17 According to Bolivar, state did not have to adopt an official religion: "Simón Bolívar's proposed articles for the new constitution, however, while retaining for the national government the rights of patronage, made no mention of an official religion. He believed that the law had no role in governing consciences and had no desire of returning to a time when the state scrutinized people's religious convictions and practices" (Morales Cruz, 2014, p. 142).

Sucre Alcalá.[18] As soon as he became president, Sucre adopted measures that targeted religion: he forced the closure of monasteries with fewer than twelve monks; he also confiscated the dime and ecclesiastical lands, and declared that the Roman Catholic Church would be the only religion recognized and tolerated by the Bolivian Republic. This dominance of Christianity was only possible within the limits set by the state (Ward Loughran 1940). It was limited and without any real influence on the politics. Catholicism became the official religion in Bolivia without any consideration for the religious or spiritual traditions of the Indigenous people, who were the numerical majority of the population. During the 19th century (especially between 1860 and 1900), the Roman Catholic Church continued to assimilate the First Nations of Bolivia by carrying out some evangelical missions in Indigenous territories. The rest of the century was marked by wars, upheavals and Indigenous revolts. Political and social instability were the order of the day in Bolivia. In 1880, however, the domination of the Roman Catholic Church was challenged:

> In 1880 the article prohibiting the exercise of non-Catholic religions was amended to allow for the toleration of such religions in the colonies – that is, for immigrant groups – but not for Bolivian citizens. The Roman Catholic Church retained its privileged position. In 1905 the article was amended yet again to allow freedom of religion throughout the country, an act that was opposed by the Catholic hierarchy. (Morales Cruz 2014: 143)

Consequently, this new "freedom or religion" opened the door to Protestant missions in Bolivia's Indigenous territories. Although this freedom did not take into account the religions or spiritualities of the First Nations, it became the first step in the recognition of religious pluralism in the country. The *mestizaje* culture also gained more visibility and, in 1925, the Virgin of Copacabana was crowned as the patron saint of Bolivia. It should be emphasized that it was more the *mestizaje* culture that was recognized, and less the "*indigenousness*" in itself.

In 1952, Bolivia entered a new era. A major restructuring took place in both the political and economic sectors.[19] On the political level, the military regime

18 "Bolívar served five months as Bolivia's first president before being succeeded by Sucre in January 1826" (Library of Congress – Federal Research Division, 2006, p. 3).

19 "The Nationalist Revolutionary Movement (*Movimiento Nacionalista Revolucionario* – MNR) ushered in Bolivia's nationalist 'revolution' on April 9, 1952, when it launched an armed takeover of La Paz by mine workers in collaboration with disaffected elements of the National Police. […] the MNR was a loose coalition of mine workers, Indian subsistence farmers, and middle-class mestizos. Once in power, the MNR moved quickly to

that had prevailed since the founding of the country, was replaced by a democratic mechanism. This was accompanied by major changes in education and agriculture, which in turn affected the entire Bolivian economy.[20] The social influence of the Roman Catholic Church remained the same. Since the end of the 1960s, the theology of liberation gained momentum (Libanio 2005), which fueled socialist political parties throughout Latin America, including Bolivia. This social movement did not allow Indigenous peoples to revive their religious or spiritual traditions or to gain self-determination. Until then, they were still severely marginalized.

1.2 *From 1970 to 2006*

In the mid-1960s, a military regime was reinstated in Bolivia. The country adopted a new constitution that guaranteed the protection of religious freedom:

> The Constitution of 1967 grants official status to the Roman Catholic Church but also guarantees the public exercise of all other religions. It states that the relationship between the Roman Catholic Church and the Bolivian government will be agreed upon by both the state and the Vatican. The position of under-secretariat of religious affairs was created in 1971 to supervise and approve programs for the public ceremonies and broadcasts of non-Catholic churches. (Morales Cruz 2014: 143)

At the time, political stability was quite fragile. For example, Ernesto "Che" Guevara was captured on Bolivian territory in 1967 while trying to incite uprisings among the local population. The military regime maintained political control until the mid-1980s, when an economic crisis hit the country. The civilian government that took power in 1985 imposed the most austere policies ever seen in Bolivia. The government of Paz Estenssoro, supported by the left and popular movements, was elected for the fourth time since 1952. But

---

establish its populist credentials, decreeing universal suffrage, nationalizing mining and export industries, and reapportioning large tracts of farmland among Indian smallholders" (Library of Congress – Federal Research Division 2006: 4).

20 "Initially, the MNR governments garnered multi-class support, but rampant inflation and declining farm productivity resulting from inadequate capital investment in agriculture held back economic growth. In 1964 Paz Estenssoro ran for and won re-election, only to be deposed by armed forces members concerned over the threat of Cuban-style revolutionary violence in the Andes. Although fundamental changes remained in place, many observers on the left lamented that the Bolivian revolution remained as yet 'unfinished.'" (Library of Congress – Federal Research Division 2006: 4).

he turned away from his supporters and adopted a neoliberal tendency that would remain untouched for the next 20 years (Arce and Rice 2009).[21]

Around the same time, the United States of America began to actively promote the eradication of the coca culture.[22] In the late 1990s, the Dignity Plan was implemented: "[a]lthough temporarily successful in its limited aims of eradicating coca fields, the Dignity Plan increased rural poverty and sparked a new generation of social protest movements among the largely Indigenous coca farmers (*cocaleros*) of the Chapare region" (Library of Congress – Federal Research Division 2006: 6). Many Indigenous people in Bolivia, for whom coca was a part of their cultural and spiritual traditions, were deprived of one of their most basic resources. It was among the *cocaleros* that Evo Morales began his career, as a member of their syndicate. Economic pressure fueled the Indigenous opposition, but overall the Indigenous people of Bolivia were still highly marginalized.

Thus, it was mainly in the 1980s and 1990s that Bolivia's First Nations began to assert their self-determination.[23] As the international law focused more directly on the issues related to indigeneity,[24] the "Indigenous question" was reintroduced into the country's political agenda.[25] The first Indigenous march was held in 1990. Indigenous rights were recognized by the Bolivian state. In 1994, the *Ley de Participación Popular* (LPP) allowed Indigenous communities to form autonomous legal entities.[26] In 1996, the *Ley INRA* (*Instituto Nacional de Reforma Agraria*)[27] led to the creation of Indigenous communal territories. In this socio-legal context, the mobilization of Bolivia's First Nations took shape

21 "[…] la década de 1990 significó la adopción de una serie de ideas y reformas que Charles Hale ha descrito como el paradigma del «multiculturalismo neoliberal»" (Rousseau and Manrique 2019, on line: http://journals.openedition.org/bifea/10314).

22 "Coca farming has existed in parts of Bolivia since Inca times, but it took on increased importance and spread to new areas of the country as the international drug trade expanded during the 1980s and 1990s" (Library of Congress – Federal Research Division 2006: 6).

23 "Desde los años 1980, una corriente del movimiento indígena boliviano, asociado al Consejo Nacional de Ayllus y Markas del Qullasuyu (CONAMAQ), empezó a reconstruirlos como una forma de ejercer autonomía, fuera de la institucionalidad oficial" (Rousseau and Manrique 2019, on line: http://journals.openedition.org/bifea/10314).

24 This question is considered bellow.

25 "[…] la noción de «indigenidad» entró en la agenda nacional en los años 1990" (Rousseau and Manrique 2019, on line: http://journals.openedition.org/bifea/10314); "[e]l Estado reconoció en los años 1990 los derechos de los pueblos indígenas y procedió a institucionalizar mecanismos de participación política para ellos" (Rousseau and Manrique 2019, on line: http://journals.openedition.org/bifea/10314).

26 *Ley Nº 1551, Ley de Participación Popular, 20 de abril de 1994.*

27 *Ley Nº 1715, Ley del servicio nacional de reforma agraria, 18 de octubre de 1996.*

as a concrete political-economic project. A new wave of confrontations intensified at the beginning of 2000. The *Movimiento al Socialismo* (MAS) party, founded in 1997,[28] presented Evo Morales for the 2002 presidential elections,[29] which he lost by a small margin. At that moment, the dynamics of re-empowerment and self-determination for Bolivian's First Nations were well underway. The following years were marked by violence, revolts, and upheavals, as the Indigenous peoples challenged government projects (Ho 2004). New elections were called in 2005, and this time Morales won the presidency: "Morales was elected with 53.7 percent of the vote, becoming the first president of Indian ethnicity in Bolivia's history as well as the first majority president since the revolution. A high turnout of more than 80 percent of eligible voters lent added legitimacy to the results" (Library of Congress – Federal Research Division 2006: 7). This situation reversed the entire power struggle that had plagued the Indigenous peoples of Bolivia since the colonization. From a marginalized population, they had the opportunity to gain more self-determination. From this point on, the recognition of their religious and/or spiritual rights also gained momentum through informal and formal normativity.

2 Informal Normativity

Indigenous spirituality is expressed in many ways that can be seen as creating an "informal normativity." This was the case in Bolivia before and after the election of Evo Morales. This kind of spirituality is similar to a lived religion, as it is experienced by the Indigenous population on a daily basis, more as a way of life. Three examples of these practices are presented here to illustrate this informal normativity: traditional meals, traditional music, and religious rituals that accompanied important political events.

---

28 "[…] creación de un nuevo partido político, el Instrumento Político por la Soberanía de los Pueblos, que adoptará el nombre de Movimiento al Socialismo (MAS) por conveniencia electoral. Formado en 1997 en el departamento de Cochabamba por varias organizaciones sociales, el MAS lanzó candidaturas a elecciones municipales, luego al congreso nacional y finalmente a la presidencia del país con Evo Morales" (Rousseau and Manrique 2019, on line: http://journals.openedition.org/bifea/10314).

29 "The May 2002 presidential elections became a contest between former president Sánchez de Lozada and Evo Morales, an Aymara Indian and *cocalero* leader who headed the ticket of the Movement Toward Socialism (*Movimiento Al Socialismo* – MAS) party" (Library of Congress – Federal Research Division 2006: 6).

2.1 *Traditional Meals*

As an element of their way of life, food, and especially the sharing of the food as a form of communion, is part of the spirituality of Indigenous peoples. In Bolivia:

> Men and women in Mizque say that they prepare traditional ritual meals to "*convidar a la Pachamama.*" Pachamama is a feminine spiritual-natural force with pre-Columbian roots, associated throughout Andes with the fertility of plants and animals. *Convidar*, a verb used to invite someone to share food and drink, relates conceptually and conversationally with ideas of "*compartir*" (commensality) and "*convivir*" (cohabitation) as well as "*communion.*" (Paulson 2006: 652)

For the First Nations of Bolivia, traditional meals as a part of a celebration called *qhopuyus* become an element of belonging, which in turn refers to a pre-colonial religiosity: "[p]articipants say that through *qhopuyus* they return the care, gifts, and hospitality of Pachamama" (Paulson 2006: 655). This long history of food use underscores how Indigenous people view food as spiritual. These celebrations, held in February or March, include food, but also music, dancing, and the wearing of traditional clothing.[30] Since the 1980s and 1990s, they have become better known internationally. Since the 2000s, these celebrations have become increasingly popular, especially among young people. They have become a must for any gathering dedicated to Indigenous identity.

In this context, as Paulson notes, it is the experience of embodiment through the sharing of the meal that takes on symbolic and spiritual significance.[31] This experience is part of a way of life that involves a close relationship with the environment and the territory from which the food is taken. Food takes on spiritual significance because it sustains physical and spiritual life. When food is prepared collectively, it is spiritualized and symbolized:

30 "[...] *qhopuyus* are tangibly and consciously about managing vital economic resources, both in the immediate sense of obtaining foodstuffs, organizing labor, and producing meals to feed people during a harvest festival and in the long-term sense of sacralizing bonds of reciprocity with Pachamama and with local and extralocal social relations to assure continued access to social and natural resources throughout the agricultural and migration cycle" (Paulson, 2006, p. 662).

31 About the body and symbolism, see Legault-Laberge 2022. About the embodiement of religious experience, see Martin and Laplantine 1991, Zwilling 2019, and Feuillet-Liger and Rissel 2021.

> Through collaborative labor, they transform this produce into meals that constitute them as communities. In this process, individuals, products, places and spiritual-natural forces are forged into a kind of communal substance that, like the Eucharist, mysteriously joins different essences. [...] the ritual process of becoming part of a collective body provides specific types of strength and meaning. (Paulson 2006: 652)

Traditional meals began to appear in Bolivian public and media space during Evo Morales's electoral campaigns as celebrations dedicated to the Pachamama: "[c]onsubstantiation – the process of uniting people, places, and forces in common substance through ritual meals – is among a constellation of practices gaining prominence in Bolivia" (Paulson 2006: 662). Politicians also began attending these traditional meals, a fact that was promptly reported in the press: "[p]residential candidates make themselves more Bolivian by confessing publicly to carnal and spiritual weakness for Indigenous food" (Paulson 2006: 662). This practice became an informal norm of Indigenous spirituality in Bolivia. Included in the agenda of the presidential campaign, Evo Morales himself would have said that he prefers traditional Indigenous food. From a political point of view, this is quite strategic, since Morales rallied the local population to win the elections, taking a step back from the country's elite. But it also shows a real concern for Andean's spiritual practices, giving them full public recognition.

2.2 *Traditional Music*

In an apartheid-like context of marginalization, where every aspect of the cultures of Indigenous peoples was discriminated against, even traditional arts were subject to shame. This can be the case with traditional clothing, and certainly with traditional music.[32] Stobart wrote about it: "[...] before Morales' presidency rural native people used to hide their origins, by avoiding the use of local dress when they came to town, and would feel shame for the local musical traditions they played" (Stobart 2019: 204). The religious or spiritual nature of music is related to the experience of oneness with all of creation as lived and expressed in Indigenous traditions. In this context, music is not entertainment. It is played, listened to, and used to pay respect to the creation, territory, nature, etc. It is not surprising, then, that the reappropriation of traditional music has become a way for the First Nations of Bolivia to reaffirm their self-determination. During an event dedicated to the fight against discrimination and racism held in Santa Cruz in 2017, Evo Morales himself

32 These observations may also apply to traditional Indigenous dances.

emphasized the religious or spiritual aspect of traditional music in his speech. Stobart describes the event as follows:

> The second national meeting of this organisation, held in Santa Cruz in May 2017, was attended by more than 2,000 school students from around the country and officially opened by Evo Morales. In his speech, Morales claimed that Bolivia had 'managed to recover its identity through recognising its 36 native-peasant nations in the constitution as well as through respect for their culture, clothing, music, dance and language.' He went on to observe that 'the only way to decolonise ourselves is through recovering our dress, our lifeways, and our music. The music's content that is sung is for unity, for the Mother Earth.' Thus, in the context of a major national event dedicated to combatting racism and discrimination, it was cultural expressions that Morales highlighted, pointing in particular to the unifying nature of native music and its connection with the environment. (Stobart 2019: 194)

The spiritual or religious aspect of the music is well emphasized here by Stobart.

Morales was aware of the importance of traditional music, and he consciously used it in his political agenda. The example of Gregorio Mamani Villacorta speaks volumes in this regard.[33] Mamani was a famous musician and Indigenous activist, both in Bolivia and internationally. Embodying the Indigenous identity of his tradition, which traces its roots back to Tomás Katari, Mamani played an important role in Morales' politics: "Gregorio played an active part in Morales' election campaign and in the MAS party, releasing a music video of influential campaign songs" (Stobart 2019: 199). This musician embodied belonging to Bolivian indigeneity while also criticizing the appropriation of traditional music by the *mestizaje* culture. In this creation of an Indigenous identity, the possession of cultural capital is highly valued. It became a way of overcoming marginalization, discrimination, and racism, and an expression of self-determination: "[d]espite ongoing silent and sometimes explicit racism, under Morales, indigeneity and ethnicity shifted from always being viewed as obstacles to being seen as economic, social and political opportunities, and even as a qualification for certain rights, privileges or government support" (Stobart 2019: 204). Traditional music was an element of Morales' political agenda, and it helped create a sense of belonging and unity among the First Nations of Bolivia.

---

33 "He was an outspoken campaigner for *originario* musicians and against media piracy, and often presented himself as a revolutionary" (Stobart 2019: 199).

2.3 *Religious Rituals and Political Events*

The clearest expression of the informal normativity associated with Indigenous spirituality or religion relates to the incorporation of religious rituals into Bolivian public and political life. Before his inauguration as president, Morales received a kind of blessing from the Aymara priests: "[i]n January 2006, Evo Morales assumed office in what has become a well-known story: the first Indigenous president of Bolivia, accepting the *bastón de mando* from Aymara priests at the pre-Columbian site of Tiwanaku the day before being sworn into office at the presidential palace" (Kohl 2010: 107). By receiving the "wand of command" from the Aymara high priests, Morales himself became a priest of public life, basing his power on his traditional Indigenous spirituality. About the same event, Alvizuri mentions: "Desde su primer día de gobierno, el presidente Evo Morales ha demostrado su religiosidad, consagrándole tiempo, practicándola con regularidad y con fasto. Ha participado en rituales de diversa índole: eucaristías inculturadas, libaciones para la Pachamama, cultos solares y ceremonias ancestrales" (Alvizuri 2017: 83). On the one hand, Morales received a kind of blessing from the Aymara priests before he was appointed to the presidency and before he was sworn in. These events were scheduled one after the other. The fact that the ritual with the priests came first clearly demonstrates the importance and recognition of spirituality in this context. On the other hand, Morales participated in rituals of many religious traditions, such as "intercultural" ceremonies including the Eucharist, which also points to the importance of Catholicism in Bolivia.

Morales repeated the same scenes throughout his political career: "[l]a tercera y última tuvo lugar el 21 de enero de 2016. Evo Morales cumplió una década en el poder, inició su tercer mandato presidencial consecutivo y dio gracias a la Pachamama en un Te Deum 'inculturado,' oficiado por yatiris" (Alvizuri 2017: 83). In 2016, when he was re-elected, six religious ceremonies of different nature were celebrated by Morales:

> Al día siguiente protagonizó la ceremonia ancestral. Un total de seis rituales fueron concebidos para la ocasión: Morales fue limpiado de las energías negativas; luego, vestido; unas mujeres ritualistas convocaron las energías terrenales. Seguidamente, unos varones captaron la energía cósmica y, después de una última libación, lo conectaron con el presente. El espectáculo de la devoción presidencial terminó con una escena digna del cine. Morales de pie delante de la escalinata de la Puerta de Kalasasaya, vestido con un pantalón blanco, unas sandalias del mismo color, un poncho de vicuña beige con una enorme pechera de oro y una cofia. El atuendo del presidente costó 30 000 bolivianos,

> esto es 16 veces el salario mínimo. La ceremonia tuvo un costo de 3,4 millones de bolivianos. (Alvizuri 2017: 83–84)

These cinema scenes refer to the performance of an Indigenous (authentic?) identity that includes religious and spiritual elements. Fabricant highlights this dynamic:

> [...] performances of indigenous identity through public theatrical political events, music, costume, and language also contributed to the success of Evo Morales and MAS in the recent elections. Morales's administration mobilized discourses and performances of Andean culture to reorder or cleanse Bolivian society of the colonial legacy of racism and the more contemporary evils of capitalism and neoliberalism. (Fabricant 2009: 780)

The "*mise en scene*" of spirituality in the public sphere sought and succeeded in attracting the attention of public opinion in such a way as to strengthen Indigenous identity against colonialism, which completely negated and evaded this religiosity by imposing Christianity. This public enactment of their spirituality is an element of their reappropriation of this identity: "[w]hen we return to the question of what *recovery* of native-peasant traditions might mean, and who the *we* Morales invokes might – or might not – include, it quickly becomes apparent that expressions of native music, dance and dress are deeply interwoven with the politics of identity and alterity" (Stobart 2019: 195). The public enactment of Indigenous spirituality can be seen as a politico-religious strategy that aimed at regaining self-determination. It was also a tool for winning votes and elections. As much as the self-determination of Indigenous peoples rests on this re-appropriation of their traditions, including their religious or spiritual traditions, as much as it passes through the political and democratic system of the West to be seen and legitimized. To a large extent, it is mostly or only a matter of gaining power to transform marginalization into self-determination, a dynamic that is expressed through formal normativity.

3 Formal Normativity

If informal normativity in matters of spirituality or religiosity helped the Indigenous peoples of Bolivia to regain their self-determination, it was formal normativity that achieved this self-determination. This national recognition of the religious and spiritual rights of the First Nations of Bolivia had been preceded by the international law. It was then incorporated into national law, both the Constitution and the ordinary laws. There are also jurisprudential cases to be considered in this regard.

3.1 *The International Law*

To understand the importance of international law in recognizing the spiritual or religious rights of Indigenous people in Bolivia, one must go back a few decades before the election of Evo Morales.[34] In 1991, Bolivia was one of the first countries to sign Convention 169.[35] This document of the International Labour Organisation lists guidelines for a better recognition of Indigenous values, traditions, and their political, economic and social rights:[36] "[e]l Convenio núm. 169 tiene dos postulados básicos: el derecho de los pueblos indígenas a mantener y fortalecer sus culturas, formas de vida e instituciones propias, y su derecho a participar de manera efectiva en las decisiones que les afectan."[37] Spiritual or religious matters are indeed mentioned in some articles of the Convention. In its preamble, the Convention takes into account the "aspirations of these peoples to exercise control over their own institutions, ways of life and economic development and to maintain and develop their identities, languages and religions, within the framework of the States in which they live." Indigenous spirituality or religiosity is also mentioned in Articles 5, 7, 13, and 32. Not only did Bolivia sign Convention 169, but the country immediately passed an ordinary law to enforce the international law on its territory.[38] At that time, the self-determination of the Indigenous peoples of Bolivia was already beginning to appear on the horizon, although the economic context of the country at that time was disastrous and the marginalization of the Indigenous peoples was still their daily reality.

34 Bolivia did not sign the C107 – Convention (No. 107), 1957.

35 C169 – Convention (No. 169), 1989. The first countries to sign the Convention were: Norway (June 19, 1990), Colombia (August 7, 1991), Mexico (September 5, 1990), and Bolivia (December 11, 1991).

36 This convention is quite important in Bolivia, considering the mita system that has been imposed on the Indigenous male population for so many centuries.

37 Derechos indígenas, Droit international, *Convenio N° 169 Organización Internacional del Trabajo Sobre Pueblos Indígenas y Tribales en Países Independientes*, on line: http://www.ftierra.org/index.php/derechos-indigenas/100-derechos-indigenas.

38 "El Estado boliviano aprobó el convenio mediante la Ley N° 1257 del 11 de julio de 1991," Derechos indígenas, Droit international, *Convenio N° 169 Organización Internacional del Trabajo Sobre Pueblos Indígenas y Tribales en Países Independientes*, on line: http://www.ftierra.org/index.php/derechos-indigenas/100-derechos-indigenas.

A few decades later, the United Nations Declaration on the Rights of Indigenous Peoples (UNDRIP), adopted in 2007,[39] also placed Bolivia in a leading role in the recognition of Indigenous peoples. The Declaration contains several provisions regarding the recognition of the spiritual or religious rights of Indigenous peoples (Articles 11, 12, 25, 34, and 36) as part of their self-determination. This self-determination (as stated in Article 3 of the Declaration – "Indigenous peoples have the right to self-determination") includes the recognition of this spiritual and religious heritage, especially with regard to their relationship with their traditional territory and nature. Bolivia immediately passed national legislation to implement the Declaration in the country: "En Bolivia tiene el rango de ley gracias a la Ley N° 3760 de 7 de noviembre de 2007."[40]

3.2 *The 2009 Constitution*

The laws of 1991 and 2007, which allowed the incorporation of international law into Bolivian legislation, were only ordinary laws. In other words, they were not the supreme law of the land.[41] Another step towards the full recognition of the Indigenous peoples of Bolivia was taken in 2009, with the adoption of a new Constitution:[42] "[...] the 2009 constitution employs the hybrid term 'first peoples Indigenous peasants' [las naciones y pueblos indígena originario campesinos]. The term includes the first peoples of the highland plateau, the Indigenous peasants of the highland valley region and the Indigenous peoples

39 "Es una Resolución aprobada en la 107a sesión plenaria de la Asamblea General de Naciones Unidas, el 13 de septiembre de 2007," Derechos indígenas, Droit international, *Declaración de las Naciones Unidas sobre los derechos de los pueblos indígenas*, on line: http://www.ftierra.org/index.php/derechos-indigenas/100-derechos-indigenas.

40 Derechos indígenas, Droit international, *Declaración de las Naciones Unidas sobre los derechos de los pueblos indígenas*, on line: http://www.ftierra.org/index.php/derechos-indigenas/100-derechos-indigenas.

41 "La Constitución es la norma suprema del ordenamiento jurídico boliviano y goza de primacía frente a cualquier otra disposición normativa," art. 410II. For more details on constitutional theories, see Kelsen 1962 and 1992.

42 "The new constitution also recognizes all 36 Indigenous languages as official languages of the state [...] and guarantees the proportional representation of indigenous peoples in the national legislature" (Rice 2014: 60). "Son idiomas oficiales del Estado el castellano y todos los idiomas de las naciones y pueblos indígena originario campesinos, que son el aymara, araona, baure, bésiro, canichana, cavineño, cayubaba, chácobo, chimán, ese ejja, guaraní, guarasu'we, guarayu, itonama, leco, machajuyai-kallawaya, machineri, maropa, mojeño-trinitario, mojeño-ignaciano, moré, mosetén, movima, pacawara, puquina, quechua, sirionó, tacana, tapiete, toromona, uru-chipaya, weenhayek, yaminawa, yuki, yuracaré y zamuco," art. 5I. The 2009 Constitution was adopted after a referendum, with the approval of the majority of the Bolivian people.

of the lowlands" (Rice 2014: 59). Although Bolivia's Indigenous communities are numerous, their *Weltanschauung* converges in a shared vision of spirituality and religiosity associated with the Pachamama.

In 2009, Bolivia became a leader in the recognition of Indigenous rights: "Bolivia was the first country in the world to incorporate the 2007 UNDRIP into domestic law and later into its constitution" (Rice 2014: 59). From this point on, the transformation of the assimilationist model, which was at the core of the marginalization of Bolivia's Indigenous peoples, into a pluralist model of the state was fully effective (Gustafson 2009).[43] As Barrera notes:

> With a nod to the concurrent adoption of the United Nations Declaration on the Rights of Indigenous Peoples (UNDRIP) in 2007, which established the right of indigenous peoples to self-determination [...], the constitutional assemblies of both Bolivia and Ecuador accepted a key demand of their domestic indigenous organizations: they agreed to transform their states from assimilative nation-state models into *plurinational* state models. (Barrera 2001: 7)

The election of Evo Morales played an important role in this great political transformation. The convergence of international law with the election of an Indigenous president created the right moment to fully valorize the self-determination of Bolivia's First Nations, including their cosmovision and religiosity/spirituality.[44] With Morales, the recognition of Indigenous rights was extended to all areas of government (Vargas Gamboa and Gamboa Alba 2014). This emphasis on self-determination includes explicit references to religious and spiritual rights. Officially, the Bolivian state is plurinational (Article 1). Religious freedom and secularism (*"laïcité"*) are part of the general provisions of the Constitution.[45] In particular, freedom of religion is recognized

43 "It replaces the unilateral system of domination with bilateral relations of mutual respect and consideration. In short, plurinationality posits a new set of indigenous-state relations" (Rice 2014: 60).

44 "Dada la existencia precolonial de las naciones y pueblos indígena originario campesinos y su dominio ancestral sobre sus territorios, se garantiza su libre determinación en el marco de la unidad del Estado, que consiste en su derecho a la autonomía, al autogobierno, a su cultura, al reconocimiento de sus instituciones y a la consolidación de sus entidades territoriales, conforme a esta Constitución y la ley," Article 2.

45 "El Estado respeta y garantiza la libertad de religión y de creencias espirituales, de acuerdo con sus cosmovisiones. El Estado es independiente de la religión," Article 4. Religious discrimination is prohibited by the Constitution (Article 14), an element that also affects the religions and spiritualities of Indigenous peoples.

as a fundamental civil right (Article 21). If these provisions may seem somewhat general, they may well find ways to be applied to Indigenous peoples.

More specifically, several articles of the Bolivian Constitution explicitly address the recognition of Indigenous religious rights. In the preamble, we find the mention: "Cumpliendo el mandato de nuestros pueblos, con la fortaleza de nuestra Pachamama y gracias a Dios, refundamos Bolivia." The references to "our people" and "our Pachamama" constitutionally established an unbreakable link between the Indigenous people of Bolivia and traditional Andean spirituality. A very good example of this can be found in Article 30:

> I. Es nación y pueblo indígena originario campesino toda la colectividad humana que comparta identidad cultural, idioma, tradición histórica, instituciones, territorialidad y cosmovisión, cuya existencia es anterior a la invasión colonial española.
> II. En el marco de la unidad del Estado y de acuerdo con esta Constitución las naciones y pueblos indígena originario campesinos gozan de los siguientes derechos:
> 1. A existir libremente.
> 2. A su identidad cultural, creencia religiosa, espiritualidades, prácticas y costumbres, y a su propia cosmovisión.
>
> […]
> 9. A que sus saberes y conocimientos tradicionales, su medicina tradicional, sus idiomas, sus rituales y sus símbolos y vestimentas sean valorados, respetados y promocionados.
>
> […]
> 14. Al ejercicio de sus sistemas políticos, jurídicos y económicos acorde a su cosmovisión.

Articles 35 to 42, which deal with health and social security, refer directly to traditional Indigenous medicine, an element also linked to their spirituality and their cosmovision. This spirituality is also mentioned and recognized in relation to education (Articles 80, 83, 86, and 95II). Several articles relating to cultural rights contain references to the rights of Indigenous peoples, including their religious and spiritual rights (Articles 98II, 99, 100, and 101). The entire fourth chapter of the Constitution is devoted to an independent Indigenous justice system (Articles 190–192). If the spirituality or religiosity is not present in this section of the Constitution, it can be assumed that the cosmovision of the Indigenous peoples includes a particular conception of justice.

The self-determination of Bolivia's Indigenous peoples is described in greater detail in Chapter Seven of the Constitution.[46] It is based on the traditional Indigenous territory of each First Nation (Articles 290–296, and 304),[47] resulting in a real decentralization of governmental powers. Although their religious rights are not explicitly mentioned in this section of the Constitution, the relationship with their traditional territories is marked by religious and spiritual aspects.[48] It is also worth noting that Article 384 of the Constitution protects coca as a traditional medicine of Bolivia's Indigenous peoples.[49]

With all these articles of the Bolivian Constitution that directly and indirectly refer to Indigenous religious rights, it is clear that, after 2007 these rights have been positively recognized by the Bolivian state. This recognition is present in every area of Bolivian constitutional law, as well as in several of the country's ordinary laws.

3.3 *The Ordinary Laws*

Many ordinary laws have been passed that confirm the constitutional provisions on the religious and spiritual rights of the Indigenous peoples of Bolivia. These laws affect all areas of the socio-political sphere.

3.3.1 Education

In the field of education, the law approved in 2010 affirms,[50] in its general dispositions (Article 2), the respect for the administrative rights of religious institutions. This provision primarily concerns the Roman Catholic Church, but also the other forms of religiosity present in Bolivia. Article 3 concerns

---

46 "La autonomía indígena originaria campesina consiste en el autogobierno como ejercicio de la libre determinación de las naciones y los pueblos indígena originario campesinos, cuya población comparte territorio, cultura, historia, lenguas, y organización o instituciones jurídicas, políticas, sociales y económicas propias," Article 289.

47 "El gobierno de las autonomías indígena originario campesinas se ejercerá a través de sus propias normas y formas de organización, con la denominación que corresponda a cada pueblo, nación o comunidad, establecidas en sus estatutos y en sujeción a la Constitución y a la Ley," Article 296.

48 "El territorio indígena originario campesino comprende áreas de producción, áreas de aprovechamiento y conservación de los recursos naturales y espacios de reproducción social, espiritual y cultural," Article 403II. See also Article 405.

49 "El Estado protege a la coca originaria y ancestral como patrimonio cultural, recurso natural renovable de la biodiversidad de Bolivia, y como factor de cohesión social; en su estado natural no es estupefaciente. La revalorización, producción, comercialización e industrialización se regirá mediante la ley," Article 384.

50 *Ley Nº 070, Ley de la educación "Avelino Siñani – Elizardo Pérez,"* 20 de diciembre de 2010.

the principles of education and is more directly aimed at the religious rights of the Indigenous peoples. Paragraphs 6,[51] 10,[52] and 11[53] all affirm the right to teach Indigenous religion and/or spirituality. Article 4, paragraph 5,[54] insists on respect for the different cosmovisions that coexist in Bolivia. Articles 5 and 6 mention that the goal of education in Bolivia includes respect for Indigenous culture (and religion/spirituality).

3.3.2 Health

In the field of health, the law adopted in 2013[55] also includes intercultural measures (Article 2) concerning the First Nations. This law recognizes their traditional medicine, which is linked to religious/spiritual practices. Article 6 also guarantees the access to traditional plants used in the preparation of medicines.[56] In 2019,[57] an amendment to the 2013 law is even clearer on the complementarity of modern and traditional Indigenous medicine (Article 2, paragraphs 5 and 6). This law also guarantees universal access to the health system, without discrimination based on religious affiliation or spirituality (Article 2, paragraph 12).

51 "Es laica, pluralista y espiritual, reconoce y garantiza la libertad de conciencia y de fe y de la enseñanza de religión, así como la espiritualidad de las naciones y pueblos indígena originario campesinos, fomenta el respeto y la convivencia mutua entre las personas con diversas opciones religiosas, sin imposición dogmática, y propiciando el diálogo interreligioso," Article 3(6).

52 "Es científica, técnica, tecnológica y artística, desarrollando los conocimientos y saberes desde la cosmovisión de las culturas indígena originaria campesinas, comunidades interculturales y afro bolivianas, en complementariedad con los saberes y conocimientos universales, para contribuir al desarrollo integral de la sociedad," Article 3(10).

53 "Es educación de la vida y en la vida, para Vivir Bien. Desarrolla una formación integral que promueve la realización de la identidad, afectividad, espiritualidad y subjetividad de las personas y comunidades; es vivir en armonía con la Madre Tierra y en comunidad entre los seres humanos," Article 3(11).

54 "Contribuir a la convivencia armónica y equilibrada del ser humano con la Madre Tierra, frente a toda acción depredadora, respetando y recuperando las diversas cosmovisiones y culturas," Article 4(5).

55 *Ley Nº 475, Ley de prestaciones de servicios de salud, integral del estado plurinacional de Bolivia,* 30 de diciembre de 2013.

56 "[...] la provisión de medicamentos esenciales, insumos médicos y productos naturales tradicionales," Article 6 I.

57 *Ley Nº 1152, Ley modificatoria a la ley Nº 475 de 30 de diciembre de 2013, de prestaciones de servicios de salud integral del estado plurinacional de Bolivia, modificada por Ley Nº 1069 de 28 de mayo de 2018,* 20 de febrero de 2019.

3.3.3 Law against Racism and Discrimination

In 2010,[58] the Bolivian Parliament adopted a law against racism and discrimination, which must be respected by all Bolivian citizens, including the members of Indigenous communities (Article 4). Discrimination on religious grounds is explicitly prohibited, as defined in Article 5. The prevention of racism in education is explicitly mentioned, including racism against Indigenous cultural and religious traditions (Article 6). The recognition of important historical figures of Bolivia's First Nations is also included in the law,[59] which also establishes a Commission to deal with issues of racism and discrimination, in which the Indigenous communities have a seat (Article 8). This law has penal implications and anyone who does not respect the measures included, in matters of discrimination (Article 281 ter.) or racism (Article 281 bis.), is exposed to a prison sentence ranging from one to five years.

3.3.4 Law for the Protection of Indigenous Peoples in a Situation of Great Vulnerability

In 2013,[60] a law was passed to protect Bolivia's Indigenous peoples in a situation of great vulnerability. This law includes several measures that give some recognition to their traditions. In the event of an epidemic, traditional medicine can be prescribed alongside modern medicine (Article 7). Some of the law's mechanisms concern the regeneration of habitats. Other measures are aimed at revitalizing their cultural identity and the vitality of their religious and spiritual traditions.[61] At the state level, some mechanisms are also

58 *Ley Nº 045, Ley contra el racismo y toda forma de discriminación*, 8 de octubre de 2010.

59 "Promover el reconocimiento de los héroes y las heroínas nacionales pertenecientes a las naciones pueblos indígena originario campesinos, el pueblo afroboliviano y de comunidades interculturales," Article 6II(g); "El Comité contra el Racismo y toda forma de Discriminación tendrá como tareas principales: [...] Promover el reconocimiento de los héroes y heroínas bolivianas y bolivianos, pertenecientes a las naciones pueblos indígena originario campesinos, el pueblo afroboliviano y de comunidades interculturales," Article 9(i).

60 *Ley Nº 450, Ley de protección a naciones y pueblos indígena originarios en situación de alta vulnerabilidad*, 4 de diciembre de 2013.

61 "Ante las diferentes situaciones de alta vulnerabilidad que debiliten las capacidades de regeneración y reproducción de los sistemas de vida de los titulares de la presente Ley, se activarán los siguientes mecanismos de fortalecimiento: 1. Ejecutar estrategias y acciones para mantener y fortalecer las identidades culturales propias, la vitalidad lingüística de los idiomas, cosmovisiones, religiones, creencias y cultos, así como lugares sagrados. [...] 4. Fortalecer el ejercicio de sus sistemas políticos, jurídicos y económicos acorde a su cosmovisión. [...] 9. Desarrollar acciones de conservación, restauración y custodia de todo el patrimonio material e inmaterial. [...] 11. Promover el rescate de las costumbres milenarias vinculadas a la ritualidad, la medicina tradicional, las expresiones religiosas y festivas, apoyando su conservación y difusión como estrategia del 'Vivir Bien,'" Article 15.

developed to ensure the preservation of Indigenous traditions, including their religious aspects (Article 16). The scope of this legislation is very important since it includes penal consequences (15 to 30 years of imprisonment[62]) for anyone who proposes to destroy part or all of the Indigenous peoples of Bolivia. This measure also affects the religious aspects of the Indigenous population.

3.3.5 Law for the Protection of the Country's Cultural Heritage

In 2014,[63] Bolivia also passed a law to protect the country's patrimony and cultural heritage, including that of the Indigenous peoples, according to an intercultural approach of decolonization.[64] Article 5 clearly states that this heritage is related to the diversity inherent to the plurinational state of Bolivia. This historical heritage includes both material and intangible elements (Article 7), and the religious and spiritual traditions of the Indigenous population are included in the protection guaranteed by this legislation. In this regard, any expression of the religious/spiritual elements of the identity of Bolivia's First Nations can be considered part of this intangible cultural heritage.[65] Article 36 also mentions that the administrative bodies of Indigenous communities may have authority over the protection of cultural heritage.[66]

62 "Quien o quienes con propósito de destruir total o parcialmente a la población boliviana, nación o pueblo indígena originario campesino, comunidades interculturales, afrobolivianas, o segmento de ellos, o grupos de un credo religioso, diere muerte o causare lesiones a sus miembros, o los sometiere a condiciones de inhumana subsistencia o de asimilación forzosa, o les impusiere medidas destinadas a impedir su reproducción, o realizare con violencia el desplazamiento de niños o adultos hacia otros grupos, será sancionado con privación de libertad de quince (15) a treinta (30) años," first additional disposition of the law, that modifies the Articles 138 and 216 of the Bolivian Penal Code.

63 *Ley Nº 530, Ley del patrimonio cultural boliviano,* 23 de mayo de 2014.

64 "Es el conjunto de bienes culturales que como manifestación de la cultura, representan el valor más importante en la conformación de la diversidad cultural del Estado Plurinacional y constituye un elemento clave para el desarrollo integral del país. Se compone por los significados y valores atribuidos a los bienes y expresiones culturales, inmateriales y materiales, por parte de las naciones y pueblos indígena originario campesinos, comunidades interculturales y afrobolivianas y las comunidades que se autodefinen como urbanas o rurales, migrantes, espirituales o de fe, transmitidos por herencia y establecidos colectivamente. Estos significados y valores forman parte de la expresión e identidad del Estado Plurinacional de Bolivia," Article 4.

65 "Cualquier expresión o bien cultural que se considere portador de identidad de las naciones y pueblos indígena originario campesinos, comunidades interculturales urbanas o rurales y pueblo afroboliviano, puede ser reconocida como Patrimonio Cultural," Article 34II.

66 "Los Órganos Legislativos de los Gobiernos Autónomos Departamentales, Municipales e Indígena Originario Campesinos, en razón del interés que revista un bien o manifestación cultural, podrán emitir declaratorias de Patrimonio Cultural, en el marco de su jurisdicción y competencia," Article 36I.

3.3.6 Freedom of Religion Law

In 2019,[67] the government of Evo Morales passed a law on religious freedom. Article 1 states that religious freedom is guaranteed to all Bolivian citizens, regardless of their beliefs, practices or affiliations.[68] As in the international legal instruments, the Bolivian law guarantees the freedom to practice and to teach one's religion or spirituality (Article 61). In this regard, Indigenous religions and spiritualities are directly mentioned in the law.[69] This law is the most direct expression of the formal recognition of Indigenous religions and spiritualities in Bolivian ordinary legislation.

3.4 Court Decisions

According to its plurinational paradigm, the Bolivian state includes several jurisdictions that are considered equal. The Constitution clearly mentions the equality between the jurisdiction of the country's Indigenous peoples and the "ordinary" jurisdiction of the state (Hammond 2011).[70] There is a strong interest in examining how the "ordinary" jurisdiction of Bolivia considers the cases related to the Indigenous peoples and whether the courts recognize their religious or spiritual rights in any way. Decisions from two of Bolivia's highest courts, the Tribunal Supremo de Justicia and the Tribunal Constitucional Plurinacional, are considered here.

The Tribunal Supremo de Justicia is the highest court in Bolivia for ordinary cases in all areas of law, both civil and criminal. A brief review of the cases related to the Indigenous peoples will quickly show how the tribunal considers their rights in general. In a family law case, the tribunal, while enumerating the pertinent legislation related to the case, considers that a "judicial competence" can be directly assumed by the Indigenous authorities, stating: "art. 12 de la *Ley Nº 025 Ley del Órgano Judicial* [...] define a la competencia como o autoridad indígena originaria campesina para ejercer la jurisdicción en

67 *Ley Nº 1161, Bolivia: Ley de libertad religiosa, organizaciones religiosas y de creencias espirituales*, 16 de abril de 2019.

68 "La presente Ley tiene por objeto establecer un marco jurídico de derechos y deberes para el ejercicio de la libertad religiosa y de creencias espirituales de acuerdo a sus cosmovisiones, de culto, de conciencia y de pensamiento de forma individual o colectiva, pública o privada; y el reconocimiento institucional de las organizaciones religiosas y de creencias espirituales en el Estado Plurinacional de Bolivia," Article 1. See also Article 4.

69 For example, Article 61(i) of the Act states: "Practicar libremente los saberes, conocimientos, cosmovisión ancestral de las naciones y pueblos indígena originario campesinos y afrobolivianos." See also Article 611(j), 7(d), and 1311.

70 According to the Bolivian Constitution, "[l]a jurisdicción ordinaria y la jurisdicción indígena originario campesina gozarán de igual jerarquía" (Article 17911).

un determinado asunto."[71] The tribunal fully recognized the judicial authority of the First Nations, on an equal footing with its jurisdictional authority. This is particularly emphasized in the following quotation: "es la facultad del Estado Plurinacional de administrar justicia emanada del pueblo boliviano (art. 178 de la CPE) a través de los órganos competentes [...] y la jurisdicción indígena originaria campesina."[72] This recognition of the Indigenous autonomy in judicial matters not only guarantees their positive rights, but also, in a broader sense, ensures that their own judicial systems and mechanisms or procedures are fully recognized and protected at the state level. This means that Indigenous justice systems are fully competent in the eyes of the Bolivian state. Again, this fact is rooted in the plurinational model of the state that has been implemented in Bolivia under the leadership of Evo Morales. The recognition of the judicial pluralism that accompanies this paradigm is even clearer in a 2021 case related to a claim for the space of a building in La Paz. The decision of the tribunal mentions:

> Con todo esto, la adopción y el reconocimiento del pluralismo jurídico permite un dialogo intercultural entre derechos y fortalece el proceso de irradiación de contenido en las normas infra-constitucionales, ya que permite que los actos de la vida social y en particular los actos jurídicos y procesales, no solamente comprendan las normas positivizadas, sino

---

71 *Martín Serrudo Huaylla c. Gabriela Alarcón Reyes*, Tribunal Supremo de Justicia, Sala Civil, Auto Supremo 464/2017, Sucre, 08 de mayo 2017, expediente CB-46-16-S, p. 6. Another case states: "A decir de Ramiro Molina Rivero, la jurisdicción indígena, es definida como la unidad espacial sociocultural y jurídica donde se establecen las competencias de las autoridades tradicionales o sindicales indígenas campesinas originaria. Es decir, las jurisdiccionales indígenas son aquellas jurisdicciones políticas que combinan ciertos elementos organizativos importantes que hacen a la unidad tanto socioeconómica como sociocultural. Por lo general, estas unidades jurisdiccionales recaen en las denominadas markas, centrales agrarias o capitanías, que coinciden muchas veces con el nivel cantonal de la estructura estatal. Sin embargo, con el reconocimiento de los municipios rurales, que corresponde a la sección como parte de la estructura estatal. El municipio ha coincidido también en muchos casos con las markas subcentrales o capitanías. Las markas, a su vez, son las unidades políticas que sobrevivieron desde los tiempos prehispánicos de manera fragmentada, y hoy están conformadas generalmente por dos parcialidades (de arriba y abajo), y éstas, por un número determinado de ayllu," *Ministerio Público y otro c. Aquilino Jaldín Ferrufino y otros*, Tribunal Supremo de Justicia, Sala Penal, Auto Supremo 295/2019-RRC, Sucre, 02 de mayo de 2019, expediente, Cochabamba 63/2018, p. 12.

72 *Vivian Mónica Velásquez Orihuela c. Claudia María Canaza Jorges y otros*, Tribunal Supremo de Justicia, Sala Civil, Auto Supremo 956/2019, Fecha, 24 de septiembre de 2019, expediente CB-54-19-A.

> también, las normas y procedimientos no escritos que comúnmente pertenecen a las naciones y pueblos indígena originario campesinos.[73]

Meanwhile, the tribunal also imposed some restrictions on the religious rights of Bolivia's Indigenous peoples. In a criminal case involving the rape of a minor,[74] the Court did not consider the fact that the defendant belonged to a First Nation to be a legitimate reason for hearing the appeal. The appeal was granted, but on other grounds. In an appeal of a usucapion case, in which a religious group claimed a space it considered sacred, the tribunal declared that the case was not well-founded, even though the religious group had demonstrated in its grounds for appeal that the lower court's decision had restricted its property rights as well as its religious identity: "la sentencia restringe su derecho a la propiedad y a al identidad y respeto a la espiritualidad y religión amauta."[75] In a criminal case involving the possession and transportation of illegal substances (91 kilos of cocaine),[76] the defendant appealed arguing that, as a member of a First Nation, he had a constitutional right to coca, which was deeply linked to the cultural and religious customs and traditions of the Indigenous population of Bolivia. The tribunal upheld the defendant's conviction, emphasizing that even if the Constitution protects coca, that protection cannot be extended to drug trafficking. The Court drew limits to the protection of Indigenous cultural and religious traditions.

The Tribunal Constitucional Plurinacional, which is specializes in constitutional matters, takes a similar position to the Tribunal Supremo de Justicia regarding Indigenous religious rights. A brief review of recent cases shows the extent to which the recognition of these rights is effective in the decisions of the Constitutional Court. It is worth noting that a decision of the Tribunal Constitucional Plurinacional recognizes the collective nature of Indigenous rights.[77] The same decision also recognizes the great importance of the

---

73 *Margarita Quevedo Alcón c. Gregorio Mario Nina Bravo*, Tribunal Supremo de Justicia, Sala Civil, Auto Supremo 455/2021, Fecha, 26 de mayo 2021, expediente LP-50-21-S, p. 4.

74 *Justino Montero Gutiérrez c. Ministerio Público*, Tribunal Supremo de Justicia, Sala Penal, Auto Supremo 299/2022-RA, Sucre, 03 de mayo de 2022 (*Análisis de Admisibilidad*).

75 *Movimiento Místico Espiritual "KURMI-A CONSEJO DE RELIGIOSIDAD MILENARIA INDÍGENA DE AMAUTAS" c. María Carmen Beatriz Loza y Otro*, Tribunal Supremo de Justicia, Sala Civil, Auto Supremo 144/2015, Sucre, 06 de marzo 2015, expediente: LP-165-14-S, p. 2.

76 *Ministerio Público c. Serapio Quispe Pérez*, Tribunal Supremo de Justicia, Sala Penal, Auto Supremo 120/2012, Sucre, 22 de mayo de 2012, expediente La Paz 68/2012.

77 *Zacarías Reyes Andrade y Remigio Córdova Andrade, representantes legales de la Organización Territorial de Base (OTB) "Comunidad Villa Flor de Pucara" c. Grover Vallejos Zárate, Alcalde del Gobierno Autónomo Municipal de Anzaldo del Departamento de*

anti-colonial struggles waged by the Indigenous peoples of Bolivia for their self-determination and the recognition of their rights and identity.[78] The same recognition is present in another decision of the Court.[79]

However, in a labor case also related to the best interests of the child,[80] a case that has nothing to do with Indigenous affairs, the Court refers to the holistic worldview of Bolivia's Indigenous peoples to explain the meaning of "*suma qamaña o vivir bien*,"[81] one of the central elements of the plurinational paradigm

---

Cochabamba, Tribunal Constitucional Plurinacional, Sala Tercera, 0176/2012, Sucre, 14 de mayo de 2012, expediente 00053-2012-01-AP (*Acción popular*).

78 "Asimismo, cuando advierte, que el pueblo boliviano, de composición plural, desde la profundidad de la historia, construye el nuevo modelo de Estado, inspirado en las luchas del pasado, en la sublevación indígena anticolonial, en la independencia, en las luchas populares de liberación, en las marchas indígenas, sociales y sindicales, en las guerras del agua y de octubre, en las luchas por la tierra y territorio," *Zacarías Reyes Andrade y Remigio Córdova Andrade, representantes legales de la Organización Territorial de Base* (OTB) *"Comunidad Villa Flor de Pucara" c. Grover Vallejos Zárate, Alcalde del Gobierno Autónomo Municipal de Anzaldo del Departamento de Cochabamba*, Tribunal Constitucional Plurinacional, Sala Tercera, 0176/2012, Sucre, 14 de mayo de 2012, expediente 00053-2012-01-AP (*Acción popular*).

79 *Epifanía Ferrel García y otros c. Agapito, Secretario General, Sergio, Secretario de Relaciones y Paulino, Corregidor, todos García Saldaña, del Sindicato Agrario Laimiña*, Tribunal Constitucional Plurinacional, Sala Liquidadora Transitoria, 1941/2012, Sucre, 12 de octubre de 2012, expediente 2011-23255-47-AAC (*Acción de amparo constitucional*).

80 *Ángel Delgado Araona c. Oscar Julio Terán Ayala y Melisa Puerta Kramer*, Tribunal Constitucional Plurinacional, Sala Segunda, 2065/2012, Sucre, 8 de noviembre de 2012, expediente 01559-2012-04-AAC (*Acción de amparo constitucional*).

81 The same phenomenon also occurs in the following cases: *Haidy Vaca Chávez c. Frans Días Conorio, Alcalde Municipal de Santa Rosa del Abuná del departamento de Pando*, Tribunal Constitucional Plurinacional, Sala Segunda, 1479/2012, Sucre, 24 de septiembre de 2012, expediente 01333-2012-03-AAC (*Acción de amparo constitucional*); *Emir Sejas Justiniano c. Mauricio Calvo Rioja, Secretario de Desarrollo Vial y Obras Públicas del Gobierno Autónomo Departamental de Beni*, Tribunal Constitucional Plurinacional, Sala Tercera, 2148/2013, Sucre, 21 de noviembre de 2013, expediente 04190-2013-09-AAC (*Acción de amparo constitucional*); and in *Acción de inconstitucionalidad abstracta interpuesta por Rolando Villena Villegas, Defensor del Pueblo del Estado Plurinacional de Bolivia*, Tribunal Constitucional Plurinacional, Sala Plena, 0260/2014, Sucre, 12 de febrero de 2014, expediente 02895-2013-06-AIA, which makes even more explicit the "cosmic" caracter of the Indigenous worldview: ("El suma qamaña, es la 'filosofía de la vivencia cósmica' de los pueblos ancestrales, que hace referencia no sólo a la vida biológica del ser natural, sino también a la vida espiritual, económica, social, cultural, etc., en sus diferentes dimensiones. Además, no sólo se refiere al ser humano, sino también se incluye en esta filosofía de vivencia conjunta y compleja, a otros seres como los animales, vegetales, cerros, agua, etc. El suma qamaña, es entendido como una 'filosofía de convivencia colectiva,' pacífica, armónica, consustancial al entorno que es parte del todo y en similar dimensión es definido por la filosofía del pueblo quechua como el sumajkawsay y/o qhapajñan.") This last excerpt is also cited in *Acción de amparo constitucional interpuesta por Rolando*

adopted by the state, which de facto implies some religious or spiritual aspects. This situation represents a general recognition of Bolivian Indigenous religiosity or spirituality in the decisions of the Court, which goes beyond a recognition that could be limited to cases that directly affect Indigenous persons or communities. Otherwise, in a case of violation of religious rights, in which a man took the body of his deceased mother from a hospital in order to give her a "Christian burial," the Court goes into a very interesting constitutional analysis that takes into account in some detail the struggles of the Bolivian First Nations that led to their self-determination. The decision emphasizes the plurinational paradigm of the state, which implies a plurality of conceptions of life and death. This analysis leads the judges to expose the Indigenous population's concept of death: "Esta forma de concebir la vida, ratifica que para las naciones y pueblos indígena originario campesinos no hay muerte; simplemente es el 'paso de un espacio a otro del cosmos."[82] Again, even when the case does not involve Indigenous persons or communities per se, references to their worldview are included in the tribunal's decision.

Other cases decided by the Tribunal Constitucional Plurinacional concern some Indigenous communities more directly. These cases also include references to their religiosity or spirituality. In a case of violence against an Indigenous community,[83] the Takana El Turi Manupare II, who wanted access to their ancestral territory, the tribunal sometimes refers to their spiritual tradition. The Indigenous group won the case, an outcome that shows, to some extent, that religious rights may have played a role in the tribunal's recognition of the Indigenous community's territorial rights. In another territorial case, in which an Indigenous community, the Pacahuara, had lost their access to its ancestral lands, which were being economically exploited by corporations,[84] the tribunal recognized the legitimacy of their claim. Spirituality is mentioned

---

Villena Villegas, Defensor del Pueblo del Estado Plurinacional de Bolivia, Tribunal Constitucional Plurinacional, Sala Segunda, 0173/2014, Sucre, 20 de enero de 2014, expediente 03218-2013-07-AAC.

82 *Victoriano Velarde Alcoba c. Gastón Osorio Oporto y Magaly Gloria Ávalos Zamudio*, Tribunal Constitucional Plurinacional, Sala Tercera, 2007/2013, Sucre, 13 de noviembre de 2013, expediente 04162-2013-09-AL (*Acción de libertad*).

83 *Duri Mar Merelis Genaro, Presidente de la Central Indígena de Pueblos Originarios de la Amazonía de Pando (CIPOAP) en representación sin mandato de la Comunidad indígena "Takana El Turi Manupare II" c. Miguel Ruiz Cambero*, Tribunal Constitucional Plurinacional, Sala Primera Especializada, 0572/2014, Sucre, 10 de marzo de 2014, expediente 02889-2013-06-AP (*Acción de amparo constitucional*).

84 *Lucio Ayala Siripi, Presidente de la Central Indígena de Pueblos Originarios de la Amazonía de Pando (CIPOAP) c. Julio Urapotina Aguararupa y otros*, Tribunal Constitucional Plurinacional, Sala Liquidatora Transitoria, 0014/2013-L, Sucre, 20 de febrero de 2013, expediente 2009-20773-42-AP (*Acción popular*).

several times in the decision, treated as one of the elements of the holistic Indigenous way of life.

In Bolivia, the right to access to drinking water is enshrined in the Constitution. It is considered a fundamental right, even more so for First Nations (Constitution, Article 374). In a case where an Indigenous community, Ayllu[85] Jesús de Machaca, was without adequate water, the Constitutional Court of Bolivia ruled that the access to drinking water was a basic service that the city of Potosi had to provide to the Indigenous community.[86] In another case challenging the constitutionality of a legislative decree that reduced the Bolivian state's consultation obligations,[87] the decision declared the decree unconstitutional. The decision refers to Convention 169 and to the UNDRIP.[88] The decision also refers to the spirituality of the Bolivian peoples. Another case, this time involving a conflict of jurisdiction between an Indigenous community, the Yuracaré-Mojeño, and a criminal court in Santa Cruz, shows that the Tribunal Constitucional Plurinacional has a high regard for the jurisdiction of First Nations.[89] Their spirituality is mentioned several times in the decision.

85 "Ayllu: es la unidad territorial conformada por varias comunidades; es el cargo que se asume a nivel del Ayllu como unidad territorial, con muchas más responsabilidades en el ejercicio de sus roles y funciones conforme a su cosmovisión, maneja la multidimensionalidad espiritual, social, económica y política todo se encuentra a su cargo," *Benedicto López Villca y Josefina Churqui de López c. Sabino Mollo Luna y otros*, Tribunal Constitucional Plurinacional, Sala Liquidadora Transitoria, 1574/2012, Sucre, 24 de septiembre de 2012, expediente 2010-22873-46-AAC (*Acción de amparo constitucional*).

86 *Martín Tijra López, Regulo Tapia Tijra, Julián Tarqui Tijra y Tomás Mamani Tapia en representación del Ayllu "Jesús de Machaca" c. Williams Roger Cervantes Beltrán, Gerente General de la Administración Autónoma para Obras Sanitarias (AAPOS) Potosí*, Tribunal Constitucional Plurinacional, Sala Primera Especializada, 0169/2014-S1, Sucre, 19 de diciembre de 2014, expediente 06988-2014-14-AP (*Acción popular*).

87 *Acción de inconstitucionalidad abstracta interpuesta por Pedro Nuny Caity, Diputado de la Asamblea Legislativa Plurinacional*, Tribunal Constitucional Plurinacional, Sala Plena, 2056/2012, Sucre, 16 de octubre de 2012, expediente 00213-2012-01-AIA.

88 "[...] sin embargo esta ley, introdujo regulación ajena, como es el de la Consulta Previa y Obligatoria totalmente modificada, tanto para los pueblos indígena originario campesinos en relación a la afectación de su territorio y a la población en general cuando su medio ambiente sea afectado por un emprendimiento; asimismo, contradice el Convenio 169 de la Organización Internacional del Trabajo (OIT) sobre Pueblos Indígenas y Tribales en Países Independientes y la Declaración de las Naciones Unidas sobre los Derechos de los Pueblos Indígenas, instrumentos ratificados por el Estado Plurinacional de Bolivia," *Acción de inconstitucionalidad abstracta interpuesta por Pedro Nuny Caity, Diputado de la Asamblea Legislativa Plurinacional*, Tribunal Constitucional Plurinacional, Sala Plena, 2056/2012, Sucre, 16 de octubre de 2012, expediente 00213-2012-01-AIA.

89 *Jueza Segunda de Instrucción en lo Penal del departamento de Santa Cruz c. Consejo Indígena del Pueblo Yuracaré-Mojeño (CIPYM)*, Tribunal Constitucional Plurinacional, Sala Plena, 0698/2013, Sucre, 3 de junio de 2013, expediente 01570-2012-04-CCJ (*Conflicto de competencias jurisdiccionales*).

The decision emphasizes their holistic view of the world and their way of life, which cannot separate the spiritual aspects of conflict situations. In particular, the "political and spiritual" traditions of the Yuracaré-Mojeño people are directly recognized by the tribunal and presented in great detail. In this case, the judges concluded the legitimacy of the Indigenous jurisdiction.

Finally, in a case concerning women's sexual and reproductive rights,[90] specifically abortion, the Tribunal Constitucional Plurinacional took into account in great detail the religious and cosmic vision of life of the Indigenous population of Bolivia. Several references to the Pachamama and their cosmical view of the world are presented in the tribunal's decision. However, Article 263 of the Bolivian Penal Code, which prohibits and punishes abortion, was declared constitutional by the Court; the judges also urged the Parliament to consider revising the sexual and reproductive rights of the Bolivian women.

From this brief review of the decisions of two of Bolivia's highest courts, a very clear line of recognition of Indigenous communities and of their religious rights emerges. Although there have been some limitations imposed by the courts, and although this judicial review is limited to the years following the election of Evo Morales, which means that it is still difficult to say whether this line of recognition goes back earlier, it does appear that the Bolivian courts of "ordinary" jurisdiction have made a significant recognition of Indigenous rights in general, and Indigenous religious or spiritual rights in particular.

4 Discussion and Conclusion

My concluding remarks will be brief. From what has been presented, it can be said that the (informal and formal) recognition of Indigenous religious and spiritual rights has undergone a dramatic change under the leadership of Evo Morales. It is true that a paradigm shift took place in Bolivia at the turn of the 21st century. But Evo Morales was also caught up in political and economic games (Tockman and Cameron 2014), and he could not escape these dynamics. He faced strong opposition from (right-wing) capitalists in the agricultural sector. His social policies did not live up to their expectations. Authors such as Strobele-Gregor, Hoffman and Holmes (1994), or Hollender (2016), have clearly shown that the opposition to Evo Morales also came from some factions of

90 *Patricia Mancilla Martínez c. Asamblea Legislativa Plurinacional*, Tribunal Constitucional Plurinacional, Sala Plena, 0206/2014, Sucre, 5 de febrero de 2014, expediente 00320-2012-01-AIA (*Acción de inconstitucionalidad abstracta*).

the Indigenous peoples themselves. The polarization within the Bolivian Indigenous communities resulted from some paradoxical actions of the government of Evo Morales (paradoxical because it staged this dialectic between marginalization and self-determination). For example, the TIPNIS project aimed to build a highway through Indigenous territories. After many protests, the project was suspended. One can understand that this kind of project is harmful to the environment. Given that the religious and spiritual rights of Indigenous peoples are intertwined with the territory in which they live, this type of project is simply a pragmatic way of circumventing the formal legal texts that recognize these religious and spiritual rights. As Hollender notes: "[m]any scholars eagerly grasp the colorful discourse and personae of Evo Morales, magnifying his image as a champion of Indigenous social movements and the Rights of Nature, while neglecting the underlying contradictions and failures of MAS" (2016: 71). There is no easy way out for contemporary political leaders, whether they are Indigenous or not, who must face the economic pressures of our time (Regalsky and Ortega Breña 2010). In this regard, and as Alvizuri (2017) has noted, Indianness may be a pragmatic category and religious and spiritual rights, in their informal and formal manifestations, may have been used as means to construct the representation of an "authentic Aymara" president (see also Lucero 2006), like ingredients in the making of a politics of identity.

My final comment will recontextualize the place of Indigenous religious and spiritual rights in the plurinational state of Bolivia. As a secular republic, all forms of religiosity should be tolerated in the country and no preference should be given to any particular faith. However, international reports on religious freedom over the past decade underscored the criticism of Christian groups who believe that the separation between state and religion is not well established or respected. For example, the 2017 report states: "Catholic and evangelical Protestant leaders said the government continued to favour an Andean spiritual philosophy, especially the philosophy of the ethnic Aymara community, over other religious beliefs, for government use in public statements and ceremonies. They stated this was a violation of the constitution's separation of religion and state" (Bolivia 2017 International Religious Freedom Report 2017: 6–7). In a post-colonial context, where Indigenous peoples are just regaining their self-determination, there is no easy way to create a harmonious *buen vivir* or *convivir*, free from all the tensions of the past. Will it be possible in Bolivia? Will it last? Perhaps, but only within the limits of recognition and tolerance of religious freedom for every citizen of the country.

References

Alvizuri, Verushka. "Indianismo, política y religión en Bolivia (2006–2016)," *Caravelle*, vol. 108 (2017), on line: journals.openedition.org/caravelle/2282.

Anderson, Edward F. *Peyote. The Divine Cactus*. Tucson: The University of Arizona Press, 1980.

Arce, Moisés and Roberta Rice. "Societal Protest in Post-Stabilization Bolivia," *Latin American Research Review*, vol. 44, no. 1 (2009): 88–101.

Bouso, José Carlos, and Constanza Sánchez-Avilés, "Traditional Healing Practices Involving Psychoactive Plants and the Global Mental Health Agenda," *Health and Human Rights*, vol. 22, no. 1 (2020): 145–150.

Barrera, Anna. *Turning Legal Pluralism into State-Sanctioned Law: Assessing the Implications of the New Constitutions and Laws in Bolivia and Ecuador*. German Institute of Global and Area Studies, 2011.

Fabricant, Nicole. "Performative Politics: The Camba Countermovement in Eastern Bolivia," *American Ethnologist*, vol. 36, no. 4 (2009): 768–783.

Feuillet-Liger, Brigitte, and Aurélien Rissel (eds.). *Corps et religions. Panorama international*. Rennes: Presses universitaires de Rennes, 2021.

Girardi, Giulio. *El derecho indigena a la autodetermination politica y religiosa*. Quito: Ediciones Abya-Yala, 1996.

Gustafson, Bret. "Manipulating Cartographies: Plurinationalism, Autonomy, and Indigenous Resurgence in Bolivia," *Anthropological Quarterly*, vol. 82, no. 4 (2009): 985–1016.

Hammond, John L. "Indigenous Community Justice in the Bolivian Constitution of 2009," *Human Rights Quarterly*, vol. 33, no. 3 (2011): 649–681.

Healey, Susan. "Ethno-Ecological Identity and the Restructuring of Political Power in Bolivia," *Latin American Perspectives*, vol. 36, no. 4 (2009): 83–100.

Ho, Tin-Yun. "Mass Movement: Indigenous Turmoil in Bolivia," *Harvard International Review*, vol. 26, no. 1 (2004): 10–11.

Hollender, Rebecca, "Capitalizing on Public Discourse in Bolivia – Evo Morales and Twenty-first Century Capitalism," *Consilience*, no. 15 (2016): 50–76.

Kelsen, Hans. *Théorie pure du droit*. trad. Charles Eisenmann, 2e éd. Paris: Dalloz, 1962 (original publication in German in 1934).

Kelsen, Hans. "Qu'est-ce que la théorie pure du droit?," *Droit et société*, no. 22 (1992): 551–568.

Kohl, Benjamin. "Bolivia under Morales: A Work in Progress," *Latin American Perspectives*, vol. 37, no. 3 (2010): 107–122.

Legault-Laberge, Raphaël Mathieu. *Quatre essais d'anthropologie des religions*. Québec: Presses de l'Université Laval, 2022.

Libanio, Joao Batista. "La théologie de la libération," *Études*, vol. 5, tome 402 (2005): 645–655.

Library of Congress – Federal Research Division, "Country Profile: Bolivia," January 2006.

Lucero, José Antonio. "Representing 'Real Indians': The Challenges of Indigenous Authenticity and Strategic Constructivism in Ecuador and Bolivia," *Latin American Research Review*, vol. 41, no. 2 (2006): 31–56.

Martin, Jean-Baptiste, and François Laplantine (eds.). *Corps, religion, société*. Lyon: Presses universitaires de Lyon, 1991.

Morales Cruz, Joel. *The Histories of the Latin American Church. A Handbook*. Minneapolis: Fortress Press, 2014.

Murra, John. "The Mit'a Obligations of Ethnic Groups to the Inka State," in *The Inca and Aztec States: 1400–1800*, edited by George A. Collier, Renato I. Rosaldo and John D. Wirth, 237–262. New York: Academic Press.

Paulson, Susan. "Body, Nation, and Consubstantiation in Bolivian Ritual Meals," *American Ethnologist*, vol. 33, no. 4 (2006): 650–664.

Postero, Nancy. "Morales's MAS Government: Building Indigenous Popular Hegemony in Bolivia," *Latin American Perspectives*, vol. 37, no. 3 (2010): 18–34.

Regalsky, Pablo, and Mariana Ortega Breña. "Political Processes and the Reconfiguration of the State in Bolivia," *Latin American Perspectives*, vol. 37, no. 3 (2010): 35–50.

Rice, Roberta. "UNDRIP and the 2009 Bolivian constitution: lessons for Canada." *The Internationalization of Indigenous Rights, UNDRIP in the Canadian Context*: 59–63. Centre for International Governance Innovation, 2014.

Rousseau, Stéphanie, and Hernán Manrique. "La autonomía indígena 'tutelada' en Bolivia," *Bulletin de l'Institut français d'études andines*, vol. 48, no. 1 (2019) en ligne: http://journals.openedition.org/bifea/10314.

Simard, Jean-Jacques. *La réduction: l'Autochtone inventé et les Amérindiens d'aujourd'hui*. Sillery: Septentrion, 2003.

Stewart, Omer C. *Peyote Religion: A History*. Norman: University of Oklahoma Press, 1987.

Stobart, Henry. "Bolivia's anti-racism law: transforming a culture?," in *Cultures of Anti-Racism in Latin America and the Caribbean*, edited by Peter Wade, James Scorer and Ignacio Aguiló, 191–212. London: University of London Press/Institute of Latin American Studies, 2019.

Strobele-Gregor, Juliana, Bert Hoffman, and Andrew Holmes. "From Indio to Mestizo... to Indio: New Indianist Movements in Bolivia," *Latin American Perspectives*, vol. 21, no. 2 (1994): 106–123.

Tockman, Jason, and John Cameron. "Indigenous Autonomy and the Contradictions of Plurinationalism in Bolivia," *Latin American Politics and Society*, vol. 56, no. 3 (2014): 46–69.

Van Cott, Donna Lee. "A Political Analysis of Legal Pluralism in Bolivia and Colombia," *Journal of Latin American Studies*, vol. 32, no. 1 (2000): 207–234.

Vargas Gamboa, Nataly Viviana, and Shirley Gamboa Alba. "El Derecho de los 'Pueblos y Naciones Indígena Originario Campesinos' en la Constitucíon Política del Estado Purinacional de Bolivia," in *Derechos Humanos de los Grupos Vulnerables. Manual*, edited by Jane Felipe Beltrão et al., 405–430. Barcelona: Red de Derechos Humanos y Educación Superior, 2014.

Ward Loughran, Elizabeth. "The Rôle of Catholic Culture in Bolivia," *The Catholic Historical Review*, vol. 26, no. 1 (1940): 16–50.

Zwilling, Anne-Laure (ed.). *Corps, religion et diversité*. Louvain-la-Neuve: Academia/ L'Harmattan, 2019.

Index

www.ingramcontent.com/pod-product-compliance
Lightning Source LLC
LaVergne TN
LVHW010624300926
849162LV00001B/58